Presidents, Vice Presidents, Cabinet Members,
Supreme Court Justices, 1789–2003

Presidents, Vice Presidents, Cabinet Members, Supreme Court Justices, 1789–2003

Vital and Official Data

COMPILED BY
KEITH L. JUSTICE

McFarland & Company, Inc., Publishers
Jefferson, North Carolina, and London

For my parents, Everett and Frances

Library of Congress Cataloguing-in-Publication Data

Presidents, vice presidents, cabinet members, Supreme Court justices,
1789–2003 : vital and official data /
compiled by Keith L. Justice.
p.   cm.
Includes bibliographical references and index.

ISBN 0-7864-1044-2 (illustrated case binding : 50# alkaline paper) ∞

1. United States— Officials and employees— History— Directories.
2. United States— Politics and government — Directories.
I. Justice, Keith L.
JK6.P74   2003   351.73'092'2 — dc21   2003004184

British Library cataloguing data are available

On the cover: President Lincoln with his cabinet *(Library of Congress);*
The Supreme Court in 1864 *(Art Today)*

Manufactured in the United States of America

McFarland & Company, Inc., Publishers
Box 611, Jefferson, North Carolina 28640
www.mcfarlandpub.com

Contents

Preface

This book is a complete revision and updating of my 1985 volume titled *Public Office Index; Vol. 1, U.S. Presidents, Vice Presidents, Cabinet Members, Supreme Court Justices*. Much has happened since that first edition was published — Reagan completed his administration, George Herbert Bush was president for four years, William Jefferson Clinton was president for eight years, and George Bush's son, George Walker Bush, was elected president. A new department was created in 1988 — the Department of Veterans Affairs — and in the wake of the September 11 terrorist attacks on the United States in 2001, President Bush and Congress have created a new Cabinet level office called the Department of Homeland Security. Former Pennsylvania governor Tom Ridge has been appointed and confirmed as Secretary of this newest Cabinet position.

As of February 2003 all of the younger Bush's 2001 Cabinet appointments are still serving except for Secretary of the Treasury Paul Henry O'Neill, who was replaced in early 2003 by John William Snow. Bush has made no Supreme Court appointments.

Most of the listings in this volume are either chronological or alphabetical; a few, such as the appendix for time served in office, are arranged by the amount of time each person spent in office with those serving the longest amount of time listed first.

One appendix lists the number of former presidents living at any one time.

The format of some of the listings has been changed from the 1985 volume. For example, a Cabinet member's service to more than one president has been listed separately, and those who served a few extra days until the next appointee could be sworn in are given separate credit for the additional days. There is sufficient cross-referencing so that almost any information covered by this book can be found fairly quickly if it is not provided in one particular entry.

Exact dates for some of the offices, particularly Cabinet positions, can be difficult to locate. There are a number of different dates, such as the date of appointment, the date of confirmation, the day sworn in and the first day of service, which might be used to delineate a Cabinet member's service, but in many cases some of these dates are not available. An attempt has been made to clarify which dates are being used in a given entry — the date of appointment, the date of confirmation by the Senate, or the date a Cabinet member assumed office.

Another new feature is the numerical indicators which provide information on the number of days an electee or appointee held office (and thus one can rank office-holders by the time spent in office). These numbers made the assembly of some of the appendices easier, and it is simpler by far to find an average using a number representing days rather than a group of numbers representing years, months and days, so once the numbers were calculated it seemed appropriate to include them in the main entries alongside the years-months-days calculation, despite their modest utility.

The years-months-days date comparisons used throughout the index were not calculated using calendars, but because all dates were calculated the same way, any comparison of days is accurate for ranking purposes. As an example of the method used, if an officeholder was confirmed on March 28, 1885, and he resigned effective September 29, 1891, his time in office would be figured as six years (1885 to 1891), six months (March 28 to September 28), and one day (Sept. 28 to Sept. 29), with one day added because if he was in office over six years, there was a leap year during his tenure. His time in office would be calculated as "6y 6m 2d." When converting the time in office to days in office for easier ranking in some of the appendices, the method was to multiply six years by 365 days (2,190), add six months times 30 days per month (180), plus two days (2), plus one day for a "leap year," for a total of 2,373 days. As noted, this is not an exact method of figuring the number of days in office, but because the method was applied exactly the same in all cases, the index comparisons and rankings are valid.

In a few cases (as, for example, with Benjamin Stoddert) the exact date of birth is unknown. The year of birth, at least, was available for every officeholder listed in this work, so when the exact date of birth was unavailable, the officeholder's age at appointment, confirmation, resignation, and death were calculated as if he had been born on the last day of his birth month or year.

Abbreviations were deleted in the first line of each biographical listing and the name of the office spelled out to make the entries easier to interpret, but the abbreviations were retained for the sake of brevity in the "Other offices held" line of some entries and in the index. The "other offices held" line is not provided for every entry because it is not applicable to every person; rather, it indicates other offices an individual held that are listed in other sections of the book. For example, if an officeholder held two Cabinet positions and also was a Supreme Court Justice, his service dates are listed in the Cabinet biographical entries and the last of the Cabinet entries will include an "Other offices held" line to remind the reader that this person was also a Supreme Court Justice and is included in one of the other listings.

The numbers shown as part of the office title entries (e.g., Herbert Hoover, President 31 or Aaron Burr, Vice President 3) do not necessarily represent the "official" government number designations used by the various government offices. The numbers are for cross-reference purposes in this volume only. Specific circumstances play a role in assignment of numbers; for example, Edwin M. Stanton is listed in this index as Associate Justice 36 because he was the 36th Associate Justice nominated by a president and confirmed by the Senate to the Supreme Court. But Stanton died four days after his confirmation, so he did not hear any cases presented to the Supreme Court. In some official listings, he is not considered to have served as a justice of the U.S. Supreme Court at all. He is included here because he was nominated and confirmed, however brief his tenure. Throughout the history of the Supreme Court, seven nominees were confirmed but declined to serve. They have been excluded from this listing.

There are dozens, even hundreds, of

books about many of the presidents. However, information on some of the people who were an integral part of a president's administration can be very difficult to find. This volume serves as a convenient reference source to the many men and women who have served their country in these important offices, providing basic biographical information that places them in the context of service to the U.S. government at a particular point in American history. Few of the officeholders represented here, with the exception of the presidents and a few of the vice presidents and Supreme Court justices, are household names. But these elected officials and the Cabinet members and Supreme Court justices appointed by the presidents, represent a chain of service first forged shortly after Washington's inauguration and which continues unbroken to the present day. Each of the 42 men who have served as president, the 46 who have served as vice president, the 539 men and women who have held Cabinet positions and the 109 who have served as Supreme Court justices have played a role in shaping the offices they held and therefore our government.

Abbreviations

AG . . . . . . Secretary of Agriculture
AT . . . . . . Attorney General
AJ . . . . Associate Justice
CJ . . . . Chief Justice
CL . . . . . . Secretary of Commerce and Labor
CM . . . . . . Secretary of Commerce
DF . . . . . . Secretary of Defense
ED . . . . . . Secretary of Education
EN . . . . . . Secretary of Energy
HD . . . . . . Secretary of Housing and Urban Development
HH . . . . . . Secretary of Health and Human Services
HS . . . . . . Secretary of Homeland Security
HW . . . . . Secretary of Health, Education and Welfare
IN . . . . Secretary of the Interior
LB . . . . Secretary of Labor
NV . . . . . . Secretary of the Navy
PG . . . . . . Postmaster General
PR . . . . . . President
ST . . . . Secretary of State
TR . . . . . . Secretary of Transportation
TY . . . . . . Secretary of the Treasury
VP . . . . . . Vice President
WR . . . . . . Secretary of War
VA . . . . . . Secretary of Veterans Affairs

Administration and Cabinet Summaries

George Washington 1789–1797

Vice President
John Adams 1789–1797

Secretary of State
Thomas Jefferson 1789–1794
Edmund Randolph 1794–1795
Timothy Pickering 1795–1797

Secretary of the Treasury
Alexander Hamilton 1789–1795
Oliver Wolcott 1795–1797

Secretary of War
Henry Knox 1789–1795
Timothy Pickering 1795
James McHenry 1795–1797

Attorney General
Edmund Randolph 1789–1794
William Bradford 1794–1795
Charles Lee 1795–1797

Postmaster General
Samuel Osgood 1789–1791
Timothy Pickering 1791–1795
Joseph Habersham 1795–1797

John Adams 1797–1801

Vice President
Thomas Jefferson 1797–1801
Secretary of State
Timothy Pickering 1797–1800
John Marshall 1800–1801

Secretary of the Treasury
Oliver Wolcott 1797–1800
Samuel Dexter 1801

Secretary of War
James McHenry 1797–1800
Samuel Dexter 1800

Attorney General
Charles Lee 1797–1801

Postmaster General
Joseph Habersham 1797–1801

Secretary of the Navy
Benjamin Stoddert 1798–1801

Thomas Jefferson 1801–1809

Vice President
Aaron Burr 1801–1805
George Clinton 1805–1809

Secretary of State
James Madison 1801–1809

Secretary of the Treasury
Samuel Dexter 1801
Albert Gallatin 1801–1809

Secretary of War
Henry Dearborn 1801–1809

Attorney General
Levi Lincoln 1801–1804
John Breckenridge 1805–1806
Caesar A. Rodney 1807

Postmaster General
Joseph Habersham 1801
Gideon Granger 1801–1809

Secretary of the Navy
Benjamin Stoddert 1801
Robert Smith 1801–1809

James Madison 1809–1817

Vice President
George Clinton 1809–1812
Elbridge Gerry 1813–1814

Secretary of State
Robert Smith 1809–1811
James Monroe 1811–1814, 1815–1817

Secretary of the Treasury
Albert Gallatin 1809–1814
George W. Campbell 1814
Alexander J. Dallas 1814–1816
William H. Crawford 1816–1817

Secretary of War
William Eustis 1809–1812
John Armstrong 1813–1814
James Monroe 1814–1815
William H. Crawford 1815–1816

Attorney General
Caesar A. Rodney 1809–1811
William Pinkney 1811–1814
Richard Rush 1814–1817

Postmaster General
Gideon Granger 1809–1814
Return J. Meigs, Jr. 1814–1817

Secretary of the Navy
Paul Hamilton 1809–1812
William Jones 1813–1814
Benjamin W. Crowninshield 1814–1817

James Monroe 1817–1825

Vice President
Daniel D. Tompkins 1817–1825

Secretary of State
John Q. Adams 1817–1825

Secretary of the Treasury
William H. Crawford 1817–1825

Secretary of War
John C. Calhoun 1817–1825

Attorney General
Richard Rush 1817
William Wirt 1817–1825

Postmaster General
Return J. Meigs, Jr. 1817–1823
John McLean 1823–1825

Secretary of the Navy
Benjamin W. Crowninshield 1817–1818
Smith Thompson 1818–1823
Samuel L. Southard 1823–1825

John Quincy Adams 1825–1829

Vice President
John C. Calhoun 1825–1829

Secretary of State
Henry Clay 1825–1829

Secretary of the Treasury
Richard Rush 1825–1829

Secretary of War
James Barbour 1825–1828
Peter B. Porter 1828–1829

Attorney General
William Wirt 1825–1829

Postmaster General
John McLean 1825–1829

Secretary of the Navy
Samuel L. Southard 1825–1829

Andrew Jackson 1829–1837

Vice President
John C. Calhoun 1829–1832
Martin Van Buren 1833–1837

Secretary of State
Martin Van Buren 1829–1831
Edward Livingston 1831–1833
Louis McLane 1833–1834
John Forsyth 1834–1837

Secretary of the Treasury
Samuel D. Ingham 1829–1831
Louis McLane 1831–1833
William J. Duane 1833
Roger B. Taney 1833–1834
Levi Woodbury 1834–1837

Secretary of War
John H. Eaton 1829–1831
Lewis Cass 1831–1836

Attorney General
John M. Berrien 1829–1831
Roger B. Taney 1831–1833
Benjamin F. Butler 1833–1837

Postmaster General
William T. Barry 1829–1835
Amos Kendall 1835–1837

Secretary of the Navy
John Branch 1829–1831
Levi Woodbury 1831–1834
Mahlon Dickerson 1834–1837

Martin Van Buren 1837–1841

Vice President
  Richard M. Johnson 1837–1841
Secretary of State
  John Forsyth 1837–1841
Secretary of the Treasury
  Levi Woodbury 1837–1841
Secretary of War
  Joel R. Poinsett 1837–1841
Attorney General
  Benjamin F. Butler 1837–1838
  Felix Grundy 1838–1840
  Henry Dilworth 1840–1841
Postmaster General
  Amos Kendall 1837–1840
  John M. Niles 1840–1841
Secretary of the Navy
  Mahlon Dickerson 1837–1838
  James K. Paulding 1838–1841

William Henry Harrison 1841

Vice President
  John Tyler 1841
Secretary of State
  Daniel Webster 1841
Secretary of the Treasury
  Thomas Ewing 1841
Secretary of War
  John Bell 1841
Attorney General
  John J. Crittenden 1841
Postmaster General
  Francis Granger 1841
Secretary of the Navy
  George E. Badger 1841

John Tyler 1841–1845

Secretary of State
  Daniel Webster 1841–1843
  Abel P. Upshur 1843–1844
  John C. Calhoun 1844–1845
Secretary of the Treasury
  Thomas Ewing 1841
  Walter Forward 1841–1843
  John C. Spencer 1843–1844
  George M. Bibb 1844–1845
Secretary of War
  John Bell 1841

John C. Spencer 1841–1843
James M. Porter 1843–1844
William Wilkins 1844–1845
Attorney General
  John C. Crittenden 1841
  Hugh S. Legare 1841–1843
  John Nelson 1843–1845
Postmaster General
  Francis Granger 1841
  Charles A. Wickliffe 1841–1845
Secretary of the Navy
  George E. Badger 1841
  Abel P. Upshur 1841–1843
  David Henshaw 1843–1844
  Thomas W. Gilmer 1844
  John Y. Mason 1844–1845

James K. Polk 1845–1849

Vice President
  George M. Dallas 1845–1849
Secretary of State
  James Buchanan 1845–1849
Secretary of the Treasury
  Robert J. Walker 1845–1849
Secretary of War
  William L. Marcy 1845–1849
Attorney General
  John Y. Mason 1845–1846
  Nathan Clifford 1846–1848
  Isaac Toucey 1848–1849
Postmaster General
  Cave Johnson 1845–1849
Secretary of the Navy
  George Bancroft 1845–1846
  John Y. Mason 1846–1849

Zachary Taylor 1849–1850

Vice President
  Millard Fillmore 1849–1850
Secretary of State
  John M. Clayton 1849–1850
Secretary of the Treasury
  William A. Meredith 1849–1850
Secretary of War
  George W. Crawford 1849–1850
Attorney General
  Reverdy Johnson 1849–1850
Postmaster General
  Jacob Collamer 1849–1850

Secretary of the Navy
William B. Preston 1849–1850
Secretary of the Interior
Thomas Ewing 1849–1850

Millard Fillmore 1850–1853

Secretary of State
Daniel Webster 1850–1852
Edward Everett 1852–1853
Secretary of the Treasury
Thomas Corwin 1850–1853
Secretary of War
Charles M. Conrad 1850–1853
Attorney General
John J. Crittenden 1850–1853
Postmaster General
Nathan K. Hall 1850–1852
Samuel D. Hubbard 1852–1853
Secretary of the Navy
William A. Graham 1850–1852
John P. Kennedy 1852–1853
Secretary of the Interior
Thomas M.T. McKennan 1850
Alexander H. Holmes 1850–1853

Franklin Pierce 1853–1857

Vice President
William R. King 1853
Secretary of State
William L. Marcy 1853–1857
Secretary of the Treasury
James Guthrie 1853–1857
Secretary of War
Jefferson Davis 1853–1857
Attorney General
Caleb Cushing 1853–1857
Postmaster General
James Campbell 1853–1857
Secretary of the Navy
James C. Dobbin 1853–1857
Secretary of the Interior
Robert McClelland 1853–1857

James Buchanan 1857–1861

Vice President
John C. Breckenridge 1857–1861

Secretary of State
Lewis Cass 1857–1860
Jeremiah S. Black 1860–1861
Secretary of the Treasury
Howell Cobb 1857–1860
Phillip F. Thomas 1860–1861
John A. Dix 1861
Secretary of War
John B. Floyd 1857–1861
Attorney General
Jeremiah S. Black 1857–1860
Edwin M. Stanton 1860–1861
Postmaster General
Aaron V. Brown 1857–1859
Joseph Holt 1859–1861
Horatio King 1861
Secretary of the Navy
Isaac Toucey 1857–1861
Secretary of the Interior
Jacob Thompson 1857–1861

Abraham Lincoln 1861–1865

Vice President
Hannibal Hamlin 1861–1865
Andrew Johnson 1865
Secretary of State
William H. Seward 1861–1865
Secretary of the Treasury
Salmon P. Chase 1861–1865
William P. Fessenden 1864–1865
Hugh McCulloch 1865
Secretary of War
Simon Cameron 1861–1862
Edwin M. Stanton 1862–1865
Attorney General
Edward Bates 1861–1864
James Speed 1864–1865
Postmaster General
Montgomery Blair 1861–1864
William Dennison 1864–1865
Secretary of the Navy
Gideon Welles 1861–1863
Secretary of the Interior
Caleb B. Smith 1861–1863
John P. Usher 1863–1865

Andrew Johnson 1865–1869

Secretary of State
William H. Seward 1865–1869

Secretary of the Treasury
Hugh McCulloch 1865–1869

Secretary of War
Edwin M. Stanton 1865–1867
Edwin M. Stanton 1868
John M. Schofield 1868–1869

Attorney General
James Speed 1865–1866
Henry Stanbery 1866–1868
William A. Evarts 1868–1869

Postmaster General
William Dennison 1865–1866
Alexander W. Randall 1866–1869

Secretary of the Navy
Gideon Welles 1865–1869

Secretary of the Interior
John P. Usher 1865
James Harlan 1865–1866
Orville H. Browning 1866–1869

Ulysses S. Grant 1869–1877

Vice President
Schuyler Colfax 1869–1873
Henry Wilson 1873–1877

Secretary of State
Elihu B. Washburne 1869
Hamilton Fish 1869–1877

Secretary of the Treasury
George S. Boutwell 1869–1873
William A. Richardson 1873–1874
Benjamin H. Bristow 1874–1876
Lot M. Morrill 1876–1877

Secretary of War
John A. Rawlins 1869
William T. Sherman 1869
William W. Belknap 1869–1876
Alphonso Taft 1876
James D. Cameron 1876–1877

Attorney General
Ebenezer R. Hoar 1869–1870
Amos T. Akerman 1870–1872
George H. Williams 1872–1875
Edward Pierrepont 1875–1876
Alphonso Taft 1876–1877

Postmaster General
John A.J. Creswell 1869–1874
James W. Marshall 1874
Marshall Jewell 1874–1876
James N. Tyner 1876–1877

Secretary of the Navy
Adolph E. Borie 1869
George M. Robeson 1869–1877

Secretary of the Interior
Jacob D. Cox 1869–1870
Columbus O. Deachariah Chandler
1875–1877

Rutherford B. Hayes 1877–1881

Vice President
William A. Wheeler 1877–1881

Secretary of State
William A. Evarts 1877–1881

Secretary of the Treasury
John Sherman 1877–1881

Secretary of War
George W. McCrary 1877–1879
Alexander Ramsey 1879–1881

Attorney General
Charles Devens 1877–1881

Postmaster General
David M. Key 1877–1880
Horace Maynard 1880–1881

Secretary of the Navy
Richard W. Thompson 1877–1880
Nathan Goff, Jr. 1881

Secretary of the Interior
Carl Schurz 1877–1881

James A. Garfield 1881

Vice President
Chester A. Arthur 1881

Secretary of State
James G. Blaine 1881

Secretary of the Treasury
William Windom 1881

Secretary of War
Robert T. Lincoln 1881

Attorney General
Wayne McVeagh 1881

Postmaster General
Thomas L. James 1881

Secretary of the Navy
William H. Hunt 1881

Secretary of the Interior
Samuel J. Kirkwood 1881

Chester A. Arthur 1881–1885

Secretary of State
  James G. Blaine 1881
  Frederick T. Frelinghuysen 1881–1885
Secretary of the Treasury
  William Windom 1881
  Charles J. Folger 1881–1884
  Walter Q. Gresham 1884
  Hugh McCulloch 1884–1885
Secretary of War
  Robert T. Lincoln 1881–1885
Attorney General
  Wayne McVeagh 1881
  Benjamin H. Brewster 1881–1885
Postmaster General
  Thomas L. James 1881
  Timothy O. Howe 1882–1883
  Walter Q. Gresham 1883–1884
  Frank Hatton 1884–1885
Secretary of the Navy
  William H. Hunt 1881–1882
  William E. Chandler 1882–1885
Secretary of the Interior
  Samuel J. Kirkwood 1881–1882
  Henry M. Teller 1882–1885

Grover Cleveland 1885–1889

Vice President
  Thomas A. Hendricks 1885–1889
Secretary of State
  Thomas F. Bayard 1885–1889
Secretary of the Treasury
  Daniel Manning 1885–1887
  Charles S. Fairchild 1887–1889
Secretary of War
  William C. Endicott 1885–1889
Attorney General
  Augustus H. Garland 1885–1889
Postmaster General
  William F. Vilas 1885–1888
  Donald M. Dickinson 1888–1889
Secretary of the Navy
  William C. Whitney 1885–1889
Secretary of the Interior
  Lucius Q. C. Lamar 1885–1888
  William F. Vilas 1888–1889
Secretary of Agriculture
  Norman J. Colman 1889

Benjamin Harrison 1889–1893

Vice President
  Levi P. Morton 1889–1893
Secretary of State
  James G. Blaine 1889–1892
  John W. Foster 1892–1893
Secretary of the Treasury
  William Windom 1889–1891
  Charles Foster 1891–1893
Secretary of War
  Redfield Proctor 1889–1891
  Stephen B. Elkins 1891–1893
Attorney General
  William H.H. Miller 1889–1893
Postmaster General
  John Wanamaker 1889–1893
Secretary of the Navy
  Benjamin F. Tracy 1889–1893
Secretary of the Interior
  Johan W. Noble 1889–1893
Secretary of Agriculture
  Jeremiah M. Rusk 1889–1893

Grover Cleveland 1893–1897

Vice President
  Adlai E. Stevenson 1893–1897
Secretary of State
  Walter Q. Gresham 1893–1895
  Richard Olney 1895–1897
Secretary of the Treasury
  John G. Carlisle 1893–1897
Secretary of War
  Daniel S. Lamont 1893–1897
Attorney General
  Richard Olney 1893–1895
  Judson Harmon 1895–1897
Postmaster General
  Wilson S. Bissell 1893–1895
  William L. Wilson 1895–1897
Secretary of the Navy
  Hilary A. Herbert 1893–1897
Secretary of the Interior
  Hoke Smith 1893–1896
  David R. Francis 1896–1897
Secretary of Agriculture
  Julius S. Morton 1893–1897

William McKinley 1897–1901

Vice President
Garret A. Hobart 1897–1899
Theodore Roosevelt 1901
Secretary of State
John Sherman 1897–1898
William R. Day 1898
John Hay 1898–1901
Secretary of the Treasury
Lyman J. Gage 1897–1901
Secretary of War
Russell A. Alger 1897–1899
Elihu Root 1899–1901
Attorney General
Joseph McKenna 1897–1898
John W. Griggs 1898–1901
Philander C. Knox 1901
Postmaster General
James A. Gary 1897–1898
Charles E. Smith 1898–1901
Secretary of the Navy
John D. Long 1897–1901
Secretary of the Interior
Cornelius N. Bliss 1897–1899
Ethan A. Hitchcock 1899–1901
Secretary of Agriculture
James Wilson 1897–1901

Theodore Roosevelt 1901–1909

Vice President
Charles W. Fairbanks 1905–1909
Secretary of State
John Hay 1901–1905
Elihu Root 1905–1909
Robert Bacon 1909
Secretary of the Treasury
Lyman J. Gage 1901–1902
Leslie M. Shaw 1902–1907
George B. Cortelyou 1907–1909
Secretary of War
Elihu Root 1901–1904
William H. Taft 1904–1908
Luke E. Wright 1908–1909
Attorney General
Philander C. Knox 1901–1904
William H. Moody 1904–1906
Charles J. Bonaparte 1906–1909
Postmaster General
Charles E. Smith 1901–1902

Henry C. Payne 1902–1904
Robert J. Wynne 1904–1905
George B. Cortelyou 1905–1907
George Meyer 1907–1909
Secretary of the Navy
John D. Long 1901–1902
William H. Moody 1902–1904
Paul Morton 1904–1905
Charles J. Bonaparte 1905–1906
Victor H. Metcalf 1906–1908
Truman H. Newberry 1908–1909
Secretary of the Interior
Ethan A. Hitchcock 1901–1907
James R. Garfield 1907–1909
Secretary of Agriculture
James Wilson 1901–1909
Secretary of Commerce and Labor
George B. Cortelyou 1903–1904
Victor H. Metcalf 1904–1906
Oscar S. Straus 1906–1909

William H. Taft 1909–1913

Vice President
James S. Sherman 1909–1912
Secretary of State
Philander C. Knox 1909–1913
Secretary of the Treasury
Franklin MacVeagh 1909–1913
Secretary of War
Jacob M. Dickinson 1909–1911
Henry L. Stimson 1911–1913
Attorney General
George W. Wickersham 1909–1913
Postmaster General
Frank H. Hitchcock 1909–1913
Secretary of the Navy
George Meyer 1909–1913
Secretary of the Interior
Richard A. Ballinger 1909–1911
Walter W. Fisher 1911–1913
Secretary of Agriculture
James Wilson 1909–1913
Secretary of Commerce and Labor
Charles Nagel 1909–1913

Woodrow Wilson 1913–1921

Vice President
Thomas R. Marshall 1913–1921

Secretary of State
William J. Bryan 1913–1915
Robert Lansing 1915–1920
Bainbridge Colby 1920–1921

Secretary of the Treasury
William G. McAdoo 1913–1918
Carter Glass 1918–1920
David F. Houston 1920–1921

Secretary of War
Lindley M. Garrison 1913–1916
Newton D. Baker 1916–1921

Attorney General
James C. McReynolds 1913–1914
Thomas W. Gregory 1914–1919
Alexander M. Palmer 1919–1921

Postmaster General
Albert S. Burleson 1913–1921

Secretary of the Navy
Josephus Daniels 1913–1921

Secretary of the Interior
Franklin K. Lane 1913–1920
John B. Payne 1920–1921

Secretary of Agriculture
David F. Houston 1913–1920
Edwin T. Meredith 1919–1921

Secretary of Commerce
William C. Redfield 1913–1919
Joshua W. Alexander 1919–1920

Secretary of Labor
William B. Wilson 1913–1921

Warren G. Harding 1921–1923

Vice President
Calvin Coolidge 1921–1923

Secretary of State
Charles E. Hughes 1921–1923

Secretary of the Treasury
Andrew W. Mellon 1921–1923

Secretary of War
John W. Weeks 1921–1923

Attorney General
Harry M. Daugherty 1921–1923

Postmaster General
William H. Hays 1921–1922
Hubert Work 1922–1923
Harry S. New 1923

Secretary of the Navy
Edwin Denby 1921–1923

Secretary of the Interior

Albert B. Fall 1921–1923
Hubert Work 1923

Secretary of Agriculture
Henry C. Wallace 1921–1923

Secretary of Commerce
Herbert C. Hoover 1921–1923

Secretary of Labor
James J. Davis 1921–1923

Calvin Coolidge 1923–1929

Vice President
Charles G. Dawes 1925–1929

Secretary of State
Charles E. Hughes 1923–1925
Frank B. Kellogg 1925–1929

Secretary of the Treasury
Andrew W. Mellon 1923–1929

Secretary of War
John W. Weeks 1923–1925
Dwight F. Davis 1925–1929

Attorney General
Harry M. Daugherty 1923–1924
Harlan F. Stone 1924–1925
John G. Sargent 1925–1929

Postmaster General
Harry S. New 1923–1929

Secretary of the Navy
Edwin Denby 1923–1924
Curtis D. Wilbur 1924–1929

Secretary of the Interior
Hubert Work 1923–1928
Roy O. West 1929

Secretary of Agriculture
Henry C. Wallace 1923–1924
Howard M. Gore 1924–1925
William M. Jardine 1925–1929

Secretary of Commerce
Herbert Hoover 1923–1928
William F. Whiting 1928–1929

Secretary of Labor
James J. Davis 1923–1929

Herbert Hoover 1929–1933

Vice President
Charles Curtis 1929–1933

Secretary of State
Henry L. Stimson 1929–1933

Secretary of the Treasury

Andrew W. Mellon 1929–1932
Ogden L. Mills 1932–1933

Secretary of War
James W. Good 1929
Patrick J. Hurley 1929–1933

Attorney General
William D. Mitchell 1929–1933

Postmaster General
Walter F. Brown 1929–1933

Secretary of the Navy
Charles F. Adams 1929–1933

Secretary of the Interior
Ray L. Wilbur 1929–1933

Secretary of Agriculture
Arthur M. Hyde 1929–1933

Secretary of Commerce
Robert P. Lamont 1929–1932
Roy D. Chapin 1932–1933

Secretary of Labor
James J. Davis 1929–1930
William N. Doak 1930–1933

Franklin D. Roosevelt 1933–1945

Vice President
John N. Garner 1933–1941
Henry A. Wallace 1941–1945
Harry S Truman 1945

Secretary of State
Cordell Hull 1933–1944
E.R. Stettinius, Jr. 1944–1945

Secretary of the Treasury
William H. Woodin 1933–1934
Henry Morgenthau, Jr. 1934–1945

Secretary of War
George H. Dern 1933–1936
Harry H. Woodring 1937–1940
Henry L. Stimson 1940–1945

Attorney General
Homer S. Cummings 1933–1939
Frank Murphy 1939–1940
Robert H. Jackson 1940–1941
Francis Biddle 1941–1945

Postmaster General
James A. Farley 1933–1940
Frank C. Walker 1940–1945

Secretary of the Navy
Claude A. Swanson 1933–1939
Charles Edison 1940
Frank Knox 1940–1944
James V. Forrestal 1944–1945

Secretary of the Interior
Harold L. Ickes 1933–1945

Secretary of Agriculture
Henry A. Wallace 1933–1940
Claude R. Wickard 1940–1945

Secretary of Commerce
Daniel C. Roper 1933–1938
Harry L. Hopkins 1939–1940
Jesse H. Jones 1940–1945
Henry A. Wallace 1945

Secretary of Labor
Frances Perkins 1933–1945

Harry S Truman 1945–1953

Vice President
Alben W. Barkley 1949–1953

Secretary of State
E.R. Stettinius, Jr. 1945
James F. Byrnes 1945–1947
George C. Marshall 1947–1949
Dean G. Acheson 1949–1953

Secretary of the Treasury
Henry Morgenthau, Jr. 1945
Fred M. Vinson 1945–1946
John W. Snyder 1946–1953

Secretary of War
Henry L. Stimson 1945
Robert P. Patterson 1945–1947
Kenneth C. Royall 1947

Secretary of Defense
James V. Forrestal 1947–1949
Louis A. Johnson 1949–1950
George C. Marshall 1950–1951
Robert A. Lovett 1951–1953

Attorney General
Francis Biddle 1945
Thomas C. Clark 1945–1949
James H. McGrath 1949–1953

Postmaster General
Frank C. Walker 1945
Robert E. Hannegan 1945–1947
Jesse M. Donaldson 1947–1953

Secretary of the Navy
James V. Forrestal 1945–1947

Secretary of the Interior
Harold L. Ickes 1945–1946
Julius A. Krug 1946–1949
Oscar L. Chapman 1950–1953

Secretary of Agriculture
Claude R. Wickard 1945

Clinton P. Anderson 1945–1948
Charles F. Brannan 1948–1953

Secretary of Commerce
Henry A. Wallace 1945–1946
William A. Harriman 1947–1948
Charles Sawyer 1948–1953

Secretary of Labor
Frances Perkins 1945
Lewis B. Schwellenbach 1945–1948

Dwight D. Eisenhower 1953–1961

Vice President
Richard M. Nixon 1953–1961

Secretary of State
John Foster Dulles 1953–1959
Christian A. Herter 1959–1961

Secretary of the Treasury
George M. Humphrey 1953–1957
Robert B. Anderson 1957–1959

Secretary of Defense
Charles E. Wilson 1953–1957
Neil H. McElroy 1957–1959
Thomas S. Gates, Jr. 1959–1961

Attorney General
Herbert Brownell, Jr. 1953–1958
William P. Rogers 1958–1961

Postmaster General
Arthur E. Summerfield 1953–1961

Secretary of the Interior
Douglas McKay 1953–1956
Frederick A. Seaton 1956–1961

Secretary of Agriculture
Ezra T. Benton 1953–1961

Secretary of Commerce
Sinclair Weeks 1953–1958
Lewis L. Strauss 1958–1959
Frederick H. Mueller 1959–1961

Secretary of Labor
Martin P. Durkin 1953
James P. Mitchell 1953–1961

*Secretary of Health, Education
and Welfare*
Oveta C. Lobby 1953–1955
Marion B. Folsom 1955–1958
Arthur S. Flemming 1958–1961

John F. Kennedy 1961–1963

Vice President
Lyndon B. Johnson 1961–1963

Secretary of State
Dean Rusk 1961–1963

Secretary of the Treasury
C. Douglas Dillon 1961–1963

Secretary of Defense
Robert S. McNamara 1961–1963

Attorney General
Robert F. Kennedy 1961–1963

Postmaster General
J. Edward Day 1961–1963
John A. Gronouski 1963

Secretary of the Interior
Stewart L. Udall 1961–1963

Secretary of Agriculture
Orville L. Freeman 1961–1963

Secretary of Commerce
Luther H. Hodges 1961–1963

Secretary of Labor
Arthur J. Goldberg 1961–1962
W. Willard Wirtz 1962–1963

*Secretary of Health, Education
and Welfare*
Abraham A. Ribicoff 1961–1962
Anthony J. Celebrezze 1962–1963

Lyndon B. Johnson 1963–1969

Vice President
Hubert H. Humphrey 1965–1969

Secretary of State
Dean Rusk 1963–1969

Secretary of the Treasury
C. Douglas Dillon 1963–1965
Henry H. Fowler 1965–1968
Joseph W. Barr 1968–1969

Secretary of Defense
Robert S. McNamara 1963–1968
Clark M. Clifford 1968–1969

Attorney General
Robert F. Kennedy 1963–1965
Nicholas D. Katzenbach 1965–1967
William R. Clark 1967–1969

Postmaster General
John A. Gronouski 1963–1965
Lawrence F. O'Brien 1965–1968
W. Marvin Watson 1968–1969

Secretary of the Interior
Stewart L. Udall 1963–1969

Secretary of Agriculture
Orville L. Freeman 1963–1969

Secretary of Commerce
Luther H. Hodges 1963–1965
John T. Connor 1965–1967
Alexander B. Trowbridge 1967–1968
Cyrus R. Smith 1968–1969

Secretary of Labor
W. Willard Wirtz 1963–1969

Secretary of Health, Education and Welfare
Anthony J. Celebrezze 1963–1965
John W. Gardner 1965–1968
Wilbur J. Cohen 1968–1969

Secretary of Housing and Urban Development
Robert R. Weaver 1966–1969
Robert C. Wood 1969

Secretary of Transportation
Alan S. Boyd 1967–1969

Richard M. Nixon 1969–1974

Vice President
Spiro T. Agnew 1969–1973
Gerald R. Ford 1973–1974

Secretary of State
William P. Rogers 1969–1973
Henry A. Kissinger 1973–1974

Secretary of the Treasury
David M. Kennedy 1969–1971
John B. Connolly 1971–1972
George P. Shultz 1972–1974
William E. Simon 1974

Secretary of Defense
Melvin R. Laird 1969–1973
Elliot L. Richardson 1973
James R. Schlesinger 1973–1974

Attorney General
John N. Mitchell 1969–1972
Richard G. Kleindienst 1972–1973
Elliot L. Richardson 1973
William B. Saxbe 1974

Postmaster General
Winton M. Blount 1969–1970

Secretary of the Interior
Walter J. Hickel 1969–1971
Rogers C.B. Morton 1971–1974

Secretary of Agriculture
Clifford M. Hardin 1969–1971
Earl L. Butz 1971–1974

Secretary of Commerce
Maurice H. Stans 1969–1972

Peter G. Peterson 1972–1973
Frederick B. Dent 1973–1974

Secretary of Labor
George P. Shultz 1969–1970
James D. Hodgson 1970–1973
Peter J. Brennan 1973–1974

Secretary of Health, Education and Welfare
Robert H. Finch 1969–1970
Elliot L. Richardson 1970–1973
Caspar W. Weinberger 1973–1974

Secretary of Housing and Urban Development
George W. Romney 1969–1973
James T. Lynn 1973–1974

Secretary of Transportation
John A. Volpe 1969–1974
Claude S. Brinegar 1974

Gerald R. Ford 1974–1977

Vice President
Nelson A. Rockefeller 1974–1977

Secretary of State
Henry A. Kissinger 1974–1977

Secretary of the Treasury
William E. Simon 1974–1977

Secretary of Defense
James R. Schlesinger 1974–1975
Donald R. Rumsfeld 1975–1977

Attorney General
William B. Saxbe 1974–1975
Edward H. Levi 1975–1977

Secretary of the Interior
Rogers C.B. Morton 1974–1975
Stanley K. Hathaway 1975
Thomas S. Kleppe 1975–1977

Secretary of Agriculture
Earl L. Butz 1974–1976
John A. Knebel 1976–1977

Secretary of Commerce
Frederick B. Dent 1974–1975
Rogers C.B. Morton 1975
Elliott L. Richardson 1975–1977

Secretary of Labor
Peter J. Brennan 1974–1975
John T. Dunlop 1975–1976
W.J. Usery, Jr. 1976–1977

Secretary of Health, Education and Welfare
Caspar W. Weinberger 1974–1975

Forrest D. Mathews 1975–1977

Secretary of Housing and Urban Development
James T. Lynn 1974–1975
Carla A. Hills 1975–1977

Secretary of Transportation
Claude S. Brinegar 1974–1975
William T. Coleman, Jr. 1975–1977

Jimmy [James Earl] Carter 1977–1981

Vice President
Walter F. Mondale 1977–1981

Secretary of State
Cyrus R. Vance 1977–1980
Edmund S. Muskie 1980–1981

Secretary of the Treasury
W. Michael Blumenthal 1977–1979
G. William Miller 1979–1981

Secretary of Defense
Harold Brown 1977–1981

Attorney General
Griffin B. Bell 1977–1979
Benjamin R. Civiletti 1979–1981

Secretary of the Interior
Cecil D. Andrus 1977–1981

Secretary of Agriculture
Bob Bergland 1977–1981

Secretary of Commerce
Juanita M. Kreps 1977–1979
Philip M. Klutznik 1979–1981

Secretary of Labor
F. Ray Marshall 1977–1981

Secretary of Health, Education and Welfare
Joseph A. Califano, Jr. 1977–1979
Patricia R. Harris 1979

Secretary of Health and Human Services
Patricia R. Harris 1979–1981

Secretary of Education
Shirley Hufstedler 1979–1981

Secretary of Housing and Urban Development
Patricia R. Harris 1977–1979
Moon Landrieu 1979–1981

Secretary of Transportation
Brock Adams 1977–1979
Neil E. Goldschmidt 1979–1981

Secretary of Energy
James R. Schlesinger 1977–1979
Robert W. Duncan, Jr. 1979–1981

Ronald Reagan 1981–1989

Vice President
George F. Bush 1981–1989

Secretary of State
Alexander M. Haig, Jr. 1981–1982
George P. Schultz 1982–1989

Secretary of the Treasury
Donald T. Regan 1981–1985
James A. Baker III 1985–1988
Nicholas F. Brady 1988

Secretary of Defense
Caspar W. Weinberger 1981–1987
Frank C. Carlucci 1987–1989

Attorney General
William F. Smith 1981–1985
Edwin Meese III 1985–1988
Richard Thornburgh 1988–1989

Secretary of the Interior
James G. Watt 1981–1983
William P. Clark 1983–1985
Donald P. Hodel 1985–1989

Secretary of Agriculture
John R. Block 1981–1986
Richard E. Lyng 1986–1989

Secretary of Commerce
Malcolm Baldridge 1981–1987
C. William Verity, Jr. 1987–1989

Secretary of Labor
Raymond J. Donovan 1981–1985
William E. Brock 1985–1987
Ann D. McLaughlin 1987–1989

Secretary of Health and Human Services
Richard S. Schweiker 1981–1983
Margaret H. Heckler 1983–1985
Otis R. Bowen 1985–1989

Secretary of Education
Terrel Bell 1981–1985
William J. Bennett 1985–1988
Lauro F. Cavasos 1988–1989

Secretary of Housing and Urban Development
Samuel R. Pierce, Jr. 1981–1989

Secretary of Transportation
Andrew L. Lewis, Jr. 1981–1983
Elizabeth H. Dole 1983–1987
James H. Burnley 1987–1989

Secretary of Energy
  James B. Edwards 1981–1982
  Donald P. Hodel 1982–1985
  John S. Herrington 1985–1989

George Bush 1989–1993

Vice President
  Dan Quayle 1989–1993
Secretary of State
  James A. Baker III 1989–1992
  Lawrence S. Eagleburger 1992–1993
Secretary of the Treasury
  Nicholas F. Brady 1989–1993
Secretary of Defense
  Richard B. Cheney 1989–1993
Attorney General
  Richard Thornburgh 1989–1991
  William P. Barr 1991–1993
Secretary of the Interior
  Manuel Lujan 1989–1993
Secretary of Agriculture
  Clayton K. Yeutter 1989–1991
  Edward Madigan 1991–1993
Secretary of Commerce
  Robert A. Mosbacher 1989–1992
  Barbara H. Franklin 1992–1993
Secretary of Labor
  Elizabeth Hanford Dole 1989–1991
  Lynn Martin 1991–1993
Secretary of Health and Human Services
  Louis W. Sullivan 1989–1993
Secretary of Education
  Lauro F. Cavazos 1989–1991
  Lamar Alexander 1991–1993
*Secretary of Housing and Urban
Development*
  Jack F. Kemp 1989–1993
Secretary of Transportation
  Samuel K. Skinner 1989–1992
  Andrew H. Card, Jr. 1992–1993
Secretary of Energy
  James D. Watkins 1989–1993
Secretary of Veterans Affairs
  Edward J. Derwinski 1989–1993

Bill [William Jefferson] Clinton 1993–2001

Vice President
  Al Gore 1993–2001

Secretary of State
  Warren M. Christopher 1993–1997
  Madeleine K. Albright 1997–2001
Secretary of the Treasury
  Lloyd Bentsen 1993–1995
  Robert E. Rubin 1995–1999
  Lawrence 1999–2001
Secretary of Defense
  Les Aspin 1993–1994
  William J. Perry 1994–1997
  William S. Cohen 1997–2001
Attorney General
  Janet Reno 1993–2001
Secretary of the Interior
  Bruce Babbitt 1993–2001
Secretary of Agriculture
  Mike Espy 1993–1995
  Dan Glickman 1995–2001
Secretary of Commerce
  Ronald H. Brown 1993–1996
  Mickey Kantor 1996–1997
  William M. Daley 1997–2000
  Norman Y. Mineta 2000–2001
Secretary of Labor
  Robert B. Reich 1993–1997
  Alexis M. Herman 1997–2001
Secretary of Health and Human Services
  Donna E. Shalala 1993–2001
Secretary of Education
  Richard W. Riley 1993–2001
*Secretary of Housing and Urban
Development*
  Henry G. Cisneros 1993–1997
  Andrew M. Cuomo 1997–2001
Secretary of Transportation
  Federico F. Pena 1993–1997
  Rodney E. Slater 1997–2001
Secretary of Energy
  Hazel R. O'Leary 1993–1997
  Federico F. Pena 1997–1998
  Bill Richardson 1998–2001
Secretary of Veterans Affairs
  Jesse Brown 1993–1998
  Hershel W. Gober (acting) 2000–2001

George Walker Bush 2001–

Vice President
  Dick [Richard Bruce] Cheney 2001–
Secretary of State
  Colin Luther Powell 2001–

Secretary of the Treasury
   Paul Henry O'Neill 2001–2003
   John William Snow 2003–
Secretary of Defense
   Donald Henry Rumsfeld 2001–
Attorney General
   John Ashcroft 2001–
Secretary of the Interior
   Gale Ann Norton 2001–
Secretary of Agriculture
   Ann Margaret Veneman 2001–
Secretary of Commerce
   Donald Louis Evans 2001–
Secretary of Labor
   Elaine Lan Chao 2001–

Secretary of Health and Human Services
   Tommy G. Thompson 2001–
Secretary of Education
   Roderick R. Paige 2001–
Secretary of Housing and Urban Development
   Melquiades Rafael Martinez 2001–
Secretary of Transportation
   Norman Y. Mineta 2001–
Secretary of Energy
   Spencer Abraham 2001–
Secretary of Veterans Affairs
   Anthony Joseph Principi 2001–
Secretary of Homeland Security
   Tom Ridge 2003–

Presidential Succession

George Washington 1789–1797
John Adams 1797–1801
Thomas Jefferson 1801–1809
James Madison 1809–1817
James Monroe 1817–1825
John Quincy Adams 1825–1829
Andrew Jackson 1829–1837
Martin Van Buren 1837–1841
William Henry Harrison 1841
John Tyler 1841–1845
James K. Polk 1845–1849
Zachary Taylor 1849–1850
Millard Fillmore 1850–1853
Franklin Pierce 1853–1857
James Buchanan 1857–1861
Abraham Lincoln 1861–1865
Andrew Johnson 1865–1869
Ulysses S. Grant 1869–1877
Rutherford B. Hayes 1877–1881
James A. Garfield 1881
Chester A. Arthur 1881–1885
Grover Cleveland 1885–1889

Benjamin Harrison 1889–1893
Grover Cleveland 1893–1897
William McKinley 1897–1901
Theodore Roosevelt 1901–1909
William H. Taft 1909–1913
Woodrow Wilson 1913–1921
Warren G. Harding 1921–1923
Calvin Coolidge 1923–1929
Herbert Hoover 1929–1933
Franklin D. Roosevelt 1933–1945
Harry S Truman 1945–1953
Dwight D. Eisenhower 1953–1961
John F. Kennedy 1961–1963
Lyndon B. Johnson 1963–1969
Richard M. Nixon 1969–1974
Gerald R. Ford 1974–1977
Jimmy Carter 1977–1981
Ronald Reagan 1981–1989
George Herbert Walker Bush 1989–1993
Bill Clinton 1993–2001
George Walker Bush 2001–

Biographical Data — Presidents

Adams, John — President 2

Date of birth	Oct 30, 1735
State of birth/residence	Massachusetts
Inauguration/age	Mar 4, 1797, at age 61
Left office/age	Mar 3, 1801, at age 65
Reason for leaving office	Term completed
Term of service	4y (1,461 days)
Date of death/age	Jul 4, 1826, at age 96
Term of retirement	25y 4m 1d (9,252 days)
Other offices held	VP-1

Adams, John Quincy — President 6

Date of birth	Jul 11, 1767
State of birth/residence	Massachusetts
Inauguration/age	Mar 4, 1825, at age 57
Left office/age	Mar 3, 1829, at age 61
Reason for leaving office	Term completed
Term of service	4y (1,461 days)
Date of death/age	Feb 23, 1848, at age 80
Term of retirement	18y 11m 20d (6,924 days)
Other offices held	ST-8

Arthur, Chester A. — President 21

Date of birth	Oct 5, 1830
State of birth	Vermont
State of residence	New York
Inauguration/age	Sep 20, 1881, at age 50
Left office/age	Mar 3, 1885, at age 53
Reason for leaving office	Term completed
Term of service	3y 5m 11d (1,256 days)
Date of death/age	Nov 18, 1886, at age 56
Term of retirement	1y 8m 15d (620 days)
Other offices held	VP-20

Buchanan, James   President 15

Date of birth . . . . Apr 23, 1791
State of birth/residence . . . . Pennsylvania
Inauguration/age . . . . Mar 4, 1857, at age 65
Left office/age . . . . Mar 3, 1861, at age 69
Reason for leaving office . . . . Term completed
Term of service . . . . 4y (1,461 days)
Date of death/age . . . . Jun 1, 1868, at age 77
Term of retirement . . . . 7y 2m 28d (2,644 days)
Other offices held ST-17

Bush, George Herbert Walker   President 41

Date of birth . . . . Jun 12, 1924
State of birth . . . . Massachusetts
State of residence . . . . Texas
Inauguration/age . . . . Jan 20, 1989, at age 64
Left office/age . . . . Jan 20, 1993, at age 68
Reason for leaving office . . . . Term completed
Term of service . . . . 4y (1,461 days)
Date of death/age . . . . — — — — —
Term of retirement . . . . — — — — —
Other offices held VP-43

Bush, George Walker   President 43

Date of birth . . . . Jul 6, 1946
State of birth/residence . . . . Texas
Inauguration/age . . . . Jan 20, 2001, at age 54
Left office/age . . . . — — — — —
Reason for leaving office . . . . — — — — —
Term of service . . . . — — — — —
Date of death/age . . . . — — — — —
Term of retirement . . . . — — — — —

Carter, Jimmy [James Earl]   President 39

Date of birth . . . . Oct 1, 1924
State of birth/residence . . . . Georgia
Inauguration/age . . . . Jan 20, 1977, at age 52
Left office/age . . . . Jan 20, 1981, at age 56
Reason for leaving office . . . . Term completed
Term of service . . . . 4y (1,461 days)
Date of death/age . . . . — — — — —
Term of retirement . . . . — — — — —

Cleveland, Grover   President 22

Date of birth . . . . Mar 18, 1837
State of birth . . . . New Jersey
State of residence . . . . New York
Inauguration/age . . . . Mar 4, 1885, at age 47
Left office/age . . . . Mar 3, 1889, at age 51
Reason for leaving office . . . . Term completed
Term of service . . . . 4y (1,461 days)
Time between offices 4y
Other offices held PR-24

Cleveland, Grover   President 24

Inauguration/age .... Mar 4, 1893, at age 55
Left office/age .... Mar 3, 1897, at age 59
Reason for leaving office .... Term completed
Term of service .... 4y (1,461 days)
Date of death/age .... Jun 24, 1908, at age 71
Total service .... 8y (2,922 days)
Term of retirement .... 11y 3m 21d (4,128 days)
Other offices held PR-22

Clinton, Bill [William Jefferson]   President 42

Date of birth .... Aug 19, 1946
State of birth/residence .... Arkansas
Inauguration/age .... Jan 20, 1993, at age 46
Left office/age .... Jan 20, 2001, at age 54
Reason for leaving office .... Term completed
Term of service .... 8y (2,922 days)
Date of death/age .... — — — —
Term of retirement .... — — — —

Coolidge, Calvin   President 30

Date of birth .... Jul 4, 1872
State of birth .... Vermont
State of residence .... Massachusetts
Inauguration/age .... Aug 3, 1923, at age 51
Reason for leaving office .... Term completed
Left office/age .... Mar 3, 1929, at age 57
Term of service .... 5y 7m (2,036 days)
Date of death/age .... Jan 5, 1933, at age 60
Term of retirement .... 3y 10m 2d (1,397 days)
Other offices held VP-29

Eisenhower, Dwight D.   President 34

Date of birth .... Oct 14, 1890
State of birth .... Texas
State of residence .... Kansas
Inauguration/age .... Jan 20, 1953, at age 62
Left office/age .... Jan 20, 1961, at age 70
Reason for leaving office .... Term completed
Term of service .... 8y (2,922 days)
Date of death/age .... Mar 28, 1969, at age 78
Term of retirement .... 8y 2m 8d (2,990 days)

Fillmore, Millard   President 13

Date of birth .... Jan 7, 1800
State of birth/residence .... New York
Inauguration/age .... Jul 10, 1850, at age 50
Left office/age .... Mar 3, 1853, at age 53
Reason for leaving office .... Term completed
Term of service .... 2y 7m 21d (961 days)
Date of death/age .... Mar 8, 1874, at age 74
Term of retirement .... 21y 5m (7,820 days)
Other offices held VP-12

Ford, Gerald R.   President 38

Date of birth	Jul 14, 1913
State of birth	Nebraska
State of residence	Michigan
Inauguration/age	Aug 9, 1974, at age 61
Left office/age	Jan 20, 1977, at age 63
Reason for leaving office	Term completed
Term of service	2y 5m 11d (891 days)
Date of death/age	—————
Term of retirement	—————
Other offices held	VP-40

Garfield, James A.   President 20

Date of birth	Nov 19, 1831
State of birth/residence	Ohio
Inauguration/age	Mar 4, 1881, at age 49
Left office/age	Sep 19, 1881, at age 49
Reason for leaving office	Assassinated
Term of service	6m 15d (195 days)
Date of death/age	Sep 19, 1881, at age 49
Term of retirement	None

Grant, Ulysses S.   President 18

Date of birth	Apr 27, 1822
State of birth/residence	Ohio
Inauguration/age	Mar 4, 1869, at age 46
Left office/age	Mar 3, 1877, at age 54
Reason for leaving office	Term completed
Term of service	8y (2,922 days)
Date of death/age	Jul 23, 1885, at age 63
Term of retirement	8y 4m 20d (3,062 days)

Harding, Warren G.   President 29

Date of birth	Nov 2, 1865
State of birth/residence	Ohio
Inauguration/age	Mar 4, 1921, at age 55
Left office/age	Aug 2, 1923, at age 57
Reason for leaving office	Died in office
Term of service	2y 4m (850 days)
Date of death/age	Aug 2, 1923, at age 57
Term of retirement	None

Harrison, Benjamin   President 23

Date of birth	Aug 20, 1833
State of birth	Ohio
State of residence	Indiana
Inauguration/age	Mar 4, 1889, at age 55
Left office/age	Mar 3, 1893, at age 59
Reason for leaving office	Completed term
Term of service	4y (1,461 days)
Date of death/age	Mar 13, 1901, at age 67
Term of retirement	8y 10d (2,932 days)

Harrison, William Henry   President 9

Date of birth . . . . Feb 9, 1773
State of birth/residence . . . . Virginia
Inauguration/age . . . . Mar 4, 1841, at age 68
Left office/age . . . . Apr 4, 1841, at age 68
Reason for leaving office . . . . Died in office
Term of service . . . . 1m (30 days)
Date of death/age . . . . Apr 4, 1841, at age 68
Term of retirement . . . . None

Hayes, Rutherford B.   President 19

Date of birth . . . . Oct 2, 1822
State of birth/residence . . . . Ohio
Inauguration/age . . . . Mar 4, 1877, at age 54
Left office/age . . . . Mar 3, 1881, at age 58
Reason for leaving office . . . . Completed term
Term of service . . . . 4y (1,461 days)
Date of death/age . . . . Jan 17, 1893, at age 70
Term of retirement . . . . 11y 10m 14d (4,331 days)

Hoover, Herbert   President 31

Date of birth . . . . Aug 10, 1874
State of birth . . . . Iowa
State of residence . . . . Oklahoma
Inauguration/age . . . . Mar 4, 1929, at age 54
Left office/age . . . . Mar 3, 1933, at age 58
Reason for leaving office . . . . Completed term
Term of service . . . . 4y (1,461 days)
Date of death/age . . . . Oct 20, 1964, at age 90
Term of retirement . . . . 31y 7m 17d (11,549 days)
Other offices held CM-3

Jackson, Andrew   President 7

Date of birth . . . . Mar 15, 1767
State of birth . . . . South Carolina
State of residence . . . . Tennessee
Inauguration/age . . . . Mar 4, 1829, at age 61
Left office/age . . . . Mar 3, 1837, at age 69
Reason for leaving office . . . . Completed term
Term of service . . . . 8y (2,922 days)
Date of death/age . . . . Jun 8, 1845, at age 78
Term of retirement . . . . 8y 3m 5d (3,017 days)

Jefferson, Thomas   President 3

Date of birth . . . . Apr 13, 1743
State of birth/residence . . . . Virginia
Inauguration/age . . . . Mar 4, 1801, at age 57
Left office/age . . . . Mar 3, 1809, at age 65
Reason for leaving office . . . . Completed term
Term of service . . . . 8y (2,922 days)
Date of death/age . . . . July 4, 1826, at age 83
Term of retirement . . . . 17y 4m 1d (6,330 days)
Other offices held VP-2, ST-1

Johnson, Andrew   President 17

Date of birth . . . . Dec 29, 1808
State of birth . . . . North Carolina
State of residence . . . . Tennessee
Inauguration/age . . . . Apr 15, 1865, at age 56
Left office/age . . . . Mar 3, 1869, at age 60
Reason for leaving office . . . . Completed term
Term of service . . . . 3y 10m 16d (1,411 days)
Date of death/age . . . . Jul 31, 1875, at age 66
Term of retirement . . . . 6y 4m 28d (2,339 days)
Other offices held VP-16

Johnson, Lyndon B.   President 36

Date of birth . . . . Aug 27, 1908
State of birth/residence . . . . Texas
Inauguration/age . . . . Nov 22, 1963, at age 55
Left office/age . . . . Jan 20, 1969, at age 61
Reason for leaving office . . . . Completed term
Term of service . . . . 5y 1m 29d (1,885 days)
Date of death/age . . . . Jan 22, 1973, at age 65
Term of retirement . . . . 4y 2d (1,463 days)
Other offices held VP-37

Kennedy, John F.   President 35

Date of birth . . . . May 29, 1917
State of birth/residence . . . . Massachusetts
Inauguration/age . . . . Jan 20, 1961, at age 43
Left office/age . . . . Nov 22, 1963, at age 46
Reason for leaving office . . . . Assassinated
Term of service . . . . 2y 10m 2d (1,032 days)
Date of death/age . . . . Nov 22, 1963, at age 46
Term of retirement . . . . None

Lincoln, Abraham   President 16

Date of birth . . . . Feb 12, 1809
State of birth . . . . Kentucky
State of residence . . . . Illinois
Inauguration/age . . . . Mar 4, 1861, at age 52
Left office/age . . . . Apr 15, 1865, at age 56
Reason for leaving office . . . . Assassinated
Term of service . . . . 4y 1m 11d (1,502 days)
Date of death/age . . . . Apr 15, 1865, at age 56
Term of retirement . . . . None

McKinley, William   President 25

Date of birth . . . . Jan 29, 1843
State of birth/residence . . . . Ohio
Inauguration/age . . . . Mar 4, 1897, at age 54
Left office/age . . . . Sep 14, 1901, at age 58
Reason for leaving office . . . . Assassinated
Term of service . . . . 3y 6m 10d (1,285 days)
Date of death/age . . . . Sep 14, 1901, at age 58
Term of retirement . . . . None

Madison, James   President 4

Date of birth .... Mar 16, 1751
State of birth/residence .... Virginia
Inauguration/age .... Mar 4, 1809, at age 57
Left office/age .... Mar 3, 1817, at age 65
Reason for leaving office .... Completed term
Term of service .... 8y (2,922 days)
Date of death/age .... Jun 28, 1836, at age 85
Term of retirement .... 19y 3m 25d (7,054 days)
Other offices held ST-5

Monroe, James   President 5

Date of birth .... Apr 28, 1758
State of birth/residence .... Virginia
Inauguration/age .... Mar 4, 1817, at age 58
Left office/age .... Mar 3, 1825, at age 66
Reason for leaving office .... Completed term
Term of service .... 8y (2,922 days)
Date of death/age .... Jul 4, 1831, at age 73
Term of retirement .... 6y 4m 1d (2,312 days)
Other offices held .... ST-7, WR (interim)

Nixon, Richard M.   President 37

Date of birth .... Jan 9, 1913
State of birth/residence .... California
Inauguration/age .... Jan 20, 1969, at age 56
Left office/age .... Aug 9, 1974, at age 61
Reason for leaving office .... Resigned
Term of service .... 5y 6m 20d (2,026 days)
Date of death/age .... Apr 22, 1994, at age 81
Term of retirement .... 19y 8m 13d (7,192 days)
Other offices held VP-36

Pierce, Franklin   President 14

Date of birth .... Nov 23, 1804
State of birth/residence .... New Hampshire
Inauguration/age .... Mar 4, 1853, at age 48
Left office/age .... Mar 3, 1857, at age 52
Reason for leaving office .... Completed term
Term of service .... 4y (1,461 days)
Date of death/age .... Oct 8, 1869, at age 64
Term of retirement .... 12y 7m 5d (4,598 days)

Polk, James K.   President 11

Date of birth .... Nov 2, 1795
State of birth .... North Carolina
State of residence .... Tennessee
Inauguration/age .... Mar 4, 1845, at age 49
Left office/age .... Mar 3, 1849, at age 53
Reason for leaving office .... Completed term
Term of service .... 4y (1,461 days)
Date of death/age .... Jun 15, 1849, at age 53
Term of retirement .... 3m 12d (102 days)

Reagan, Ronald   President 40

Date of birth	Feb 6, 1911
State of birth	Illinois
State of residence	California
Inauguration/age	Jan 20, 1981, at age 69
Left office/age	Jan 20, 1989, at age 77
Reason for leaving office	Completed term
Term of service	8y (2,922 days)
Date of death/age	—————
Term of retirement	—————

Roosevelt, Franklin D.   President 32

Date of birth	Jan 30, 1882
State of birth/residence	New York
Inauguration/age	Mar 4, 1933, at age 51
Left office/age	Apr 12, 1945, at age 63
Reason for leaving office	Died in office
Term of service	12y 1m 8d (4,421 days)
Date of death/age	Apr 12, 1945, at age 63
Term of retirement	None

Roosevelt, Theodore   President 26

Date of birth	Oct 27, 1858
State of birth/residence	New York
Inauguration/age	Sep 14, 1901, at age 42
Left office/age	Mar 3, 1909, at age 52
Reason for leaving office	Completed term
Term of service	7y 5m 17d (2,723 days)
Date of death/age	Jan 6, 1919, at age 60
Term of retirement	9y 10m 3d (3,590 days)
Other offices held	VP-25

Taft, William H.   President 27

Date of birth	Sep 15, 1857
State of birth/residence	Ohio
Inauguration/age	Mar 4, 1909, at age 51
Left office/age	Mar 3, 1913, at age 55
Reason for leaving office	Completed term
Term of service	4y (1,461 days)
Date of death/age	Mar 8, 1930, at age 72
Term of retirement	17y 5d (6,214 days)
Other offices held	CJ-10, WR-44

Taylor, Zachary   President 12

Date of birth	Nov 24, 1784
State of birth	Virginia
State of residence	Kentucky
Inauguration/age	Mar 4, 1849, at age 64
Left office/age	Jul 9, 1850, at age 65
Reason for leaving office	Died in office
Term of service	1y 4m 5d (490 days)
Date of death/age	Jul 9, 1850, at age 65
Term of retirement	None

Truman, Harry S   President 33

Date of birth . . . . May 8, 1884
State of birth/residence . . . . Missouri
Inauguration/age . . . . Apr 12, 1945, at age 60
Left office/age . . . . Jan 20, 1953, at age 68
Reason for leaving office . . . . Completed term
Term of service . . . . 7y 9m 8d (2,834 days)
Date of death/age . . . . Dec 26, 1972, at age 88
Term of retirement . . . . 19y 11m 6d (7,275 days)
Other offices held VP-34

Tyler, John   President 10

Date of birth . . . . Mar 29, 1790
State of birth/residence . . . . Virginia
Inauguration/age . . . . Apr 6, 1841, at age 51
Left office/age . . . . Mar 3, 1845, at age 54
Reason for leaving office . . . . Completed term
Term of service . . . . 4y 10m 25d (1,786 days)
Date of death/age . . . . Jan 18, 1862, at age 71
Term of retirement . . . . 16y 10m 15d (6,159 days)
Other offices held VP-10

Van Buren, Martin   President 8

Date of birth . . . . Dec 5, 1782
State of birth/residence . . . . New York
Inauguration/age . . . . Mar 4, 1837, at age 54
Left office/age . . . . Mar 3, 1841, at age 58
Reason for leaving office . . . . Completed term
Term of service . . . . 4y (1,461 days)
Date of death/age . . . . Jul 24, 1862, at age 79
Term of retirement . . . . 21y 4m 21d (7,811 days)
Other offices held VP-8, ST-10

Washington, George   President 1

Date of birth . . . . Feb 22, 1732
State of birth/residence . . . . Virginia
Inauguration/age . . . . Apr 30, 1789, at age 57
Left office/age . . . . Mar 3, 1797, at age 65
Reason for leaving office . . . . Completed term
Term of service . . . . 7y 10m 3d (2,859 days)
Date of death/age . . . . Dec 14, 1799, at age 67
Term of retirement . . . . 2y 9m 11d (1,011 days)

Wilson, Woodrow   President 28

Date of birth . . . . Dec 28, 1856
State of birth . . . . Virginia
State of residence . . . . New Jersey
Inauguration/age . . . . Mar 4, 1913, at age 56
Left office/age . . . . Mar 3, 1921, at age 64
Reason for leaving office . . . . Completed term
Term of service . . . . 8y (2,922 days)
Date of death/age . . . . Feb 3, 1924, at age 67
Term of retirement . . . . 2y 11m (1,060 days)

Vice Presidential Succession

John Adams 1789–1797
Thomas Jefferson 1797–1801
Aaron Burr 1801–1805
George Clinton 1805–1812
Elbridge Gerry 1813–1814
Daniel D. Tompkins 1817–1825
John C. Calhoun 1825–1832
Martin Van Buren 1833–1837
Richard M. Johnson 1837–1841
John Tyler 1841
George M. Dallas 1845–1849
Millard Fillmore 1849–1850
William R. King 1853
John C. Breckenridge 1857–1861
Hannibal Hamlin 1861–1865
Andrew Johnson 1865
Schuyler Colfax 1869–1873
Henry Wilson 1873–1875
William A. Wheeler 1877–1881
Chester A. Arthur 1881
Thomas A. Hendricks 1885
Levi P. Morton 1889–1893
Adlai E. Stevenson 1893–1897

Garrett A. Hobart 1897–1899
Theodore Roosevelt 1901
Charles W. Fairbanks 1905–1909
James S. Sherman 1909–1912
Thomas R. Marshall 1913–1921
Calvin Coolidge 1921–1923
Charles G. Dawes 1925–1929
Charles Curtis 1929–1933
John N. Garner 1933–1941
Henry A. Wallace 1941–1945
Harry S Truman 1945
Alben W. Barkley 1949–1953
Richard M. Nixon 1953–1961
Lyndon B. Johnson 1961–1963
Hubert H. Humphrey 1965–1969
Spiro T. Agnew 1969–1973
Gerald R. Ford 1973–1974
Nelson A. Rockefeller 1974–1977
Walter F. Mondale 1977–1981
George Herbert Bush 1981–1989
Dan Quayle 1989–1993
Al Gore 1993–2001
Dick [Richard B.] Cheney 2001–

Biographical Data —
Vice Presidents

Adams, John   Vice President 1

Date of birth . . . . Oct 30, 1735
State of birth/residence . . . . Massachusetts
Inauguration/age . . . . Apr 21, 1789, at age 53
President served . . . . Washington
Left office . . . . Mar 3, 1797, at age 61
Reason for leaving office . . . . Completed term
Term of service . . . . 7y 10m 10d (2,866 days)
Date of death . . . . Jul 4, 1826, at age 90
Term of retirement . . . . 29y 4m 1d (10,713 days)
Other offices held PR-2

Agnew, Spiro Theodore   Vice President 39

Date of birth . . . . Nov 9, 1918
State of birth/residence . . . . Maryland
Inauguration/age . . . . Jan 20, 1969, at age 50
President served . . . . Nixon
Left office . . . . Oct 10, 1973, at age 54
Reason for leaving office . . . . Resigned
Term of service . . . . 4y 8m 20d (1,721 days)
Date of death . . . . Sep 17, 1996, at age 78
Term of retirement . . . . 22y 11m 7d (8,372 days)

Arthur, Chester A.   Vice President 20

Date of birth . . . . Oct 5, 1830
State of birth . . . . Vermont
State of residence . . . . New York
Inauguration/age . . . . Mar 4, 1881, at age 50
President served . . . . Garfield
Left office . . . . Sep 19, 1881, at age 50
Reason for leaving office . . . . Garfield assassinated
Term of service . . . . 6m 15d (195 days)
Date of death . . . . Nov 18, 1886, at age 56
Term of retirement . . . . 5y 1m 29d (1,885 days)
Other offices held PR-21

Barkley, Alben W.   Vice President 35

Date of birth	Nov 24, 1877
State of birth/residence	Kentucky
Inauguration/age	Jan 20, 1949, at age 71
President served	Truman
Left office	Jan 20, 1953, at age 75
Reason for leaving office	Completed term
Term of service	4y (1,461 days)
Date of death	Apr 30, 1956, at age 78
Term of retirement	3y 3m 10d (1,195 days)

Breckinridge, John C.   Vice President 14

Date of birth	Jan 21, 1821
State of birth/residence	Kentucky
Inauguration/age	Mar 4, 1857, at age 36
President served	Buchanan
Left office	Mar 3, 1861, at age 40
Reason for leaving office	Completed term
Term of service	4y (1,461 days)
Date of death	May 17, 1875, at age 54
Term of retirement	14y 2m 14d (5,187 days)

Burr, Aaron   Vice President 3

Date of birth	Feb 6, 1756
State of birth	New Jersey
State of residence	New York
Inauguration/age	Mar 4, 1801, at age 45
President served	Jefferson
Left office	Mar 3, 1805, at age 49
Reason for leaving office	Completed term
Term of service	4y (1,461 days)
Date of death	Sep 14, 1836, at age 80
Term of retirement	31y 6m 11d (11,513 days)

Bush, George Herbert   Vice President 43

Date of birth	Jun 12, 1924
State of birth	Massachusetts
State of residence	Texas
Inauguration/age	Jan 20, 1981, at age 56
President served	Reagan
Left office	Jan 20, 1989, at age 64
Reason for leaving office	Completed term
Term of service	8y (2,922 days)
Date of death	— — — — —
Term of retirement	— — — — —
Other offices held	PR-41

Calhoun, John C.   Vice President 7

Date of birth	Mar 18, 1782
State of birth/residence	South Carolina
Inauguration/age	Mar 4, 1825, at age 42

President served .... John Quincy Adams
Left office .... Mar 3, 1829, at age 46
Reason for leaving office .... Completed term
Term of service .... 4y (1,461 days)

Calhoun, John C.   Vice President 7

Inauguration/age .... Mar 4, 1829, at age 46
President served .... Jackson
Left office .... Dec 28, 1832, at age 50
Reason for leaving office .... Resigned
Term of service .... 3y 9m 24d (1,389 days)
Total term of service .... 7y 9m 24d (2,850 days)
Date of death .... Mar 31, 1850, at age 68
Term of retirement .... 17y 3m 3d (6,302 days)
Other offices held WR-10, ST-16

Cheney, Dick   Vice President 46

Date of birth .... Jan 30, 1941
State of birth/residence .... Wyoming
Inauguration/age .... Jan 21, 2001, at age 59
President served .... George Walker Bush
Left office .... — — — —
Reason for leaving office .... — — — —
Term of service .... — — — —
Date of death .... — — — —
Term of retirement .... — — — —
Other offices held DF-17

Clinton, George   Vice President 4

Date of birth .... Jul 26, 1739
State of birth/residence .... New York
Inauguration/age .... Mar 4, 1805, at age 65
President served .... Jefferson
Left office .... Mar 3, 1809, at age 69
Reason for leaving office .... Completed term
Term of service .... 4y (1,461 days)

Clinton, George   Vice President 4

Inauguration/age .... Mar 4, 1809, at age 69
President served .... Madison
Left office .... Apr 20, 1812 at 72
Reason for leaving office .... Died in office
Term of service .... 3y 1m 16d (1,141 days)
Total term of service .... 7y 1m 16d (2,602 days)
Date of death .... Apr 20, 1812, at age 72
Term of retirement .... None

Colfax, Schuyler   Vice President 17

Date of birth .... Mar 23, 1823
State of birth .... New York
State of residence .... Indiana

Inauguration/age .... Mar 4, 1869, at age 45
President served .... Grant
Left office .... Mar 3, 1873, at age 49
Reason for leaving office .... Completed term
Term of service .... 4y (1,461 days)
Date of death .... Jan 13, 1885, at age 61
Term of retirement .... 11y 10m 10d (4,327 days)

Coolidge, Calvin   Vice President 29

Date of birth .... Jul 4, 1872
State of birth .... Vermont
State of residence .... Massachusetts
Inauguration/age .... Mar 4, 1921, at age 48
President served .... Harding
Left office .... Aug 2, 1923, at age 51
Reason for leaving office .... President Harding died
       in office
Term of service .... 2y 5m (880 days)
Date of death .... Jan 5, 1933, at age 60
Term of retirement .... 9y 5m 2d (3,439 days)
Other offices held PR-30

Curtis, Charles   Vice President 31

Date of birth .... Jan 25, 1860
State of birth/residence .... Kansas
Inauguration/age .... Mar 4, 1929, at age 69
President served .... Hoover
Left office .... Mar 3, 1933, at age 73
Reason for leaving office .... Completed term
Term of service .... 4y (1,461 days)
Date of death .... Feb 8, 1936, at age 76
Term of retirement .... 2y 11m 5d (1,065 days)

Dallas, George M.   Vice President 11

Date of birth .... Jul 10, 1792
State of birth/residence .... Pennsylvania
Inauguration/age .... Mar 4, 1845, at age 52
President served .... Polk
Left office .... Mar 3, 1849, at age 56
Reason for leaving office .... Completed term
Term of service .... 4y (1,461 days)
Date of death .... Dec 31, 1864, at age 72
Term of retirement .... 15y 9m 28d (5,776 days)

Dawes, Charles G.   Vice President 30

Date of birth .... Aug 27, 1865
State of birth .... Ohio
State of residence .... Illinois
Inauguration/age .... Mar 4, 1925, at age 59
President served .... Coolidge
Left office .... Mar 3, 1929, at age 63
Reason for leaving office .... Completed term

Term of service .... 4y (1,461 days)
Date of death .... Apr 23, 1951, at age 86
Term of retirement .... 22y 1m 20d (8,085 days)

Fairbanks, Charles W.   Vice President 26

Date of birth .... May 11, 1852
State of birth .... Ohio
State of residence .... Indiana
Inauguration/age .... Mar 4, 1905, at age 52
President served .... Theodore Roosevelt
Left office .... Mar 3, 1909, at age 56
Reason for leaving office .... Completed term
Term of service .... 4y (1,461 days)
Date of death .... Jun 4, 1918, at age 66
Term of retirement .... 9y 3m 1d (3,378 days)

Fillmore, Millard   Vice President 12

Date of birth .... Jan 7, 1800
State of birth/residence .... New York
Inauguration/age .... Mar 4, 1849, at age 49
President served .... Taylor
Left office .... Jul 9, 1850, at age 50
Reason for leaving office .... President Taylor died in
                                              office
Term of service .... 1y 4m 5d (490 days)
Date of death .... Mar 8, 1874, at age 74
Term of retirement .... 23y 7m 27d (8,637 days)
Other offices held PR-13

Ford, Gerald R.   Vice President 40

Date of birth .... Jul 14, 1913
State of birth .... Nebraska
State of residence .... Michigan
Inauguration/age .... Dec 6, 1973, at age 60
President served .... Nixon
Left office .... Aug 9, 1974, at age 61
Reason for leaving office .... President Nixon resigned
Term of service .... 8m 3d (243 days)
Date of death .... — — — — —
Term of retirement .... — — — — —
Other offices held PR-38

Garner, John N.   Vice President 32

Date of birth .... Nov 22, 1868
State of birth/residence .... Texas
Inauguration/age .... Mar 4, 1933, at age 64
President served .... Franklin D. Roosevelt
Left office .... Jan 19, 1941, at age 72
Reason for leaving office .... Completed term
Term of service .... 7y 10m 15d (2,871 days)
Date of death .... Nov 7, 1967, at age 98
Term of retirement .... 26y 9m 19d (9,785 days)

Gerry, Elbridge   Vice President 5

Date of birth . . . . Jul 17, 1744
State of birth/residence . . . . Massachusetts
Inauguration/age . . . . Mar 4, 1813, at age 68
President served . . . . Madison
Left office . . . . Nov 23, 1814, at age 70
Reason for leaving office . . . . Died in office
Term of service . . . . 1y 8m 19d (624 days)
Date of death . . . . Nov 23, 1814, at age 70
Term of retirement . . . . None

Gore, Al   Vice President 45

Date of birth . . . . Mar 31, 1948
State of birth . . . . Washington, D.C.
State of residence . . . . Tennessee
Inauguration/age . . . . Jan 20, 1993, at age 44
President served . . . . Clinton
Left office . . . . Jan 20, 2001, at age 52
Reason for leaving office . . . . Completed term
Term of service . . . . 8y (2,922 days)
Date of death . . . . — — — — —
Term of retirement . . . . — — — — —

Hamlin, Hannibal   Vice President 15

Date of birth . . . . Aug 27, 1809
State of birth/residence . . . . Maine
Inauguration/age . . . . Mar 4, 1861, at age 51
President served . . . . Lincoln
Left office . . . . Mar 3, 1865, at age 55
Reason for leaving office . . . . Completed term
Term of service . . . . 4y (1,461 days)
Date of death . . . . Jul 4, 1891, at age 81
Term of retirement . . . . 26y 4m 1d (9,617 days)

Hendricks, Thomas A.   Vice President 21

Date of birth . . . . Sep 7, 1819
State of birth . . . . Ohio
State of residence . . . . Indiana
Inauguration/age . . . . Mar 4, 1885, at age 65
President served . . . . Cleveland
Left office . . . . Nov 25, 1885, at age 66
Reason for leaving office . . . . Died in office
Term of service . . . . 8m 21d (261 days)
Date of death . . . . Nov 25, 1885, at age 66
Term of retirement . . . . None

Hobart, Garrett A.   Vice President 24

Date of birth . . . . Jun 3, 1844
State of birth/residence . . . . New Jersey
Inauguration/age . . . . Mar 4, 1897, at age 52
President served . . . . McKinley

Left office .... Nov 21, 1899, at age 55
Reason for leaving office .... Died in office
Term of service .... 2y 8m 17d (987 days)
Date of death .... Nov 21, 1899, at age 55
Term of retirement .... None

Humphrey, Hubert A.   Vice President 38

Date of birth .... May 27, 1911
State of birth .... South Dakota
State of residence .... Minnesota
Inauguration/age .... Jan 20, 1965, at age 53
President served .... Lyndon B. Johnson
Left office .... Jan 20, 1969, at age 57
Reason for leaving office .... Completed term
Term of service .... 4y (1,461 days)
Date of death .... Jan 13, 1978, at age 66
Term of retirement .... 8y 11m 24d (3,276 days)

Jefferson, Thomas   Vice President 2

Date of birth .... Apr 13, 1743
State of birth/residence .... Virginia
Inauguration/age .... Mar 4, 1797, at age 53
President served .... John Adams
Left office .... Mar 3, 1801, at age 57
Reason for leaving office .... Completed term
Term of service .... 4y (1,461 days)
Date of death .... Jul 4, 1826, at age 83
Term of retirement .... 25y 4m 1d (9,252 days)
Other offices held PR-3, ST-1

Johnson, Andrew   Vice President 16

Date of birth .... Dec 29, 1808
State of birth .... North Carolina
State of residence .... Tennessee
Inauguration/age .... Mar 4, 1865, at age 56
President served .... Lincoln
Left office .... Apr 15, 1865, at age 56
Reason for leaving office .... President Lincoln
                                              assassinated
Term of service .... 1m 11d (41 days)
Date of death .... Jul 31, 1875, at age 66
Term of retirement .... 10y 3m 16d (3,758 days)
Other offices held PR-17

Johnson, Lyndon B.   Vice President 37

Date of birth .... Aug 27, 1908
State of birth/residence .... Texas
Inauguration/age .... Jan 20, 1961, at age 52
President served .... Kennedy
Left office .... Nov 22, 1963, at age 55
Reason for leaving office .... President Kennedy as-
                                              sassinated

Term of service .... 2y 10m 2d (1,032 days)
Date of death .... Jan 22, 1973, at age 64
Term of retirement .... 9y 2m (3,347 days)
Other offices held PR-36

Johnson, Richard M.   Vice President 9

Date of birth .... Oct 17, 1780
State of birth/residence .... Kentucky
Inauguration/age .... Mar 4, 1837, at age 56
President served .... Van Buren
Left office .... Mar 3, 1841, at age 60
Reason for leaving office .... Completed term
Term of service .... 4y (1,461 days)
Date of death .... Nov 19, 1850, at age 70
Term of retirement .... 9y 8m 16d (3,543 days)

King, William R.   Vice President 13

Date of birth .... Apr 7, 1786
State of birth .... North Carolina
State of residence .... Alabama
Inauguration/age .... Mar 4, 1853, at age 66
President served .... Pierce
Left office .... Apr 18, 1853, at age 67
Reason for leaving office .... Died in office
Term of service .... 1m 14d (44 days)
Date of death .... Apr 18, 1853, at age 67
Term of retirement .... None

Marshall, Thomas R.   Vice President 28

Date of birth .... Mar 14, 1854
State of birth/residence .... Indiana
Inauguration/age .... Mar 4, 1913, at age 58
President served .... Wilson
Left office .... Mar 3, 1921, at age 66
Reason for leaving office .... Completed term
Term of service .... 8y (2,922 days)
Date of death .... Jun 1, 1925, at age 71
Term of retirement .... 4y 2m 28d (1,549 days)

Mondale, Walter Frederick   Vice President 42

Date of birth .... Jan 5, 1928
State of birth/residence .... Minnesota
Inauguration/age .... Jan 20, 1977, at age 49
President served .... Carter
Left office .... Jan 20, 1981, at age 53
Reason for leaving office .... Completed term
Term of service .... 4y (1,461 days)
Date of death .... —————
Term of retirement .... —————

Morton, Levi P.   Vice President 22

Date of birth .... May 16, 1824
State of birth .... Vermont

State of residence . . . . New York
Inauguration/age . . . . Mar 4, 1889, at age 64
President served . . . . Benjamin Harrison
Left office . . . . Mar 3, 1893, at age 68
Reason for leaving office . . . . Completed term
Term of service . . . . 4y (1,461 days)
Date of death . . . . May 16, 1920, at age 96
Term of retirement . . . . 27y 2m 13d (9,934 days)

Nixon, Richard M.   Vice President 36

Date of birth . . . . Jan 9, 1913
State of birth/residence . . . . California
Inauguration/age . . . . Jan 20, 1953, at age 40
President served . . . . Eisenhower
Left office . . . . Jan 20, 1961, at age 48
Reason for leaving office . . . . Completed term
Term of service . . . . 8y (2,922 days)
Date of death . . . . Apr 22, 1994, at age 81
Term of retirement . . . . 33y 3m 2d (12,115 days)
Other offices held PR-37

Quayle, Dan   Vice President 44

Date of birth . . . . Feb 4, 1947
State of birth/residence . . . . Indiana
Inauguration/age . . . . Jan 20, 1989, at age 41
President served . . . . George Herbert Bush
Left office . . . . Jan 20, 1993, at age 45
Reason for leaving office . . . . Completed term
Term of service . . . . 4y (1,461 days)
Date of death . . . . — — — —
Term of retirement . . . . — — — —

Rockefeller, Nelson A.   Vice President 41

Date of birth . . . . Jul 8, 1908
State of birth . . . . Maine
State of residence . . . . New York
Inauguration/age . . . . Dec 19, 1974, at age 66
President served . . . . Ford
Left office . . . . Jan 20, 1977, at age 68
Reason for leaving office . . . . Completed term
Term of service . . . . 2y 1m 1d (761 days)
Date of death . . . . Jan 26, 1979, at age 70
Term of retirement . . . . 2y 6d (736 days)

Roosevelt, Theodore   Vice President 25

Date of birth . . . . Oct 27, 1858
State of birth/residence . . . . New York
Inauguration/age . . . . Mar 4, 1901, at age 42
President served . . . . McKinley
Left office . . . . Sep 14, 1901, at age 42
Reason for leaving office . . . . President McKinley
                                                              assassinated

Term of service . . . . 6m 10d (190 days)
Date of death . . . . Jan 6, 1919, at age 60
Term of retirement . . . . 17y 3m 23d (6,322 days)
Other offices held PR-26

Sherman, James S.   Vice President 27

Date of birth . . . . Oct 24, 1855
State of birth/residence . . . . New York
Inauguration/age . . . . Mar 4, 1909, at age 53
President served . . . . Taft
Left office . . . . Oct 30, 1912, at age 57
Reason for leaving office . . . . Died in office
Term of service . . . . 3y 7m 26d (1,331 days)
Date of death . . . . Oct 30, 1912, at age 57
Term of retirement . . . . None

Stevenson, Adlai E.   Vice President 23

Date of birth . . . . Oct 23, 1835
State of birth . . . . Kentucky
State of residence . . . . Illinois
Inauguration/age . . . . Mar 4, 1893, at age 57
President served . . . . Cleveland
Left office . . . . Mar 3, 1897, at age 61
Reason for leaving office . . . . Completed term
Term of service . . . . 4y (1,461 days)
Date of death . . . . Jun 14, 1914, at age 78
Term of retirement . . . . 17y 3m 11d (6,310 days)

Tompkins, Daniel D.   Vice President 6

Date of birth . . . . Jun 21, 1774
State of birth/residence . . . . New York
Inauguration/age . . . . Mar 4, 1817, at age 42
President served . . . . Monroe
Left office . . . . Mar 3, 1825, at age 50
Reason for leaving office . . . . Completed term
Term of service . . . . 8y (2,922 days)
Date of death . . . . Jun 11, 1825, at age 50
Term of retirement . . . . 3m 8d (98 days)

Truman, Harry S   Vice President 34

Date of birth . . . . May 8, 1884
State of birth/residence . . . . Missouri
Inauguration/age . . . . Jan 20, 1945, at age 60
President served . . . . Franklin D. Roosevelt
Left office . . . . Apr 12, 1945, at age 60
Reason for leaving office . . . . President Roosevelt
                                                               died in office
Term of service . . . . 2m 23d (83 days)
Date of death . . . . Dec 26, 1972, at age 88
Term of retirement . . . . 27y 8m 14d (10,115 days)
Other offices held PR-33

Tyler, John   Vice President 10

Date of birth	Mar 29, 1790
State of birth/residence	Virginia
Inauguration/age	Mar 4, 1841, at age 50
President served	William Henry Harrison
Left office	Apr 6, 1841, at age 51
Reason for leaving office	President Harrison died in office
Term of service	1m 2d (32 days)
Date of death	Jan 18, 1862, at age 71
Term of retirement	20y 9m 12d (7,587 days)
Other offices held	PR-10

Van Buren, Martin   Vice President 8

Date of birth	Dec 5, 1782
State of birth/residence	New York
Inauguration/age	Mar 4, 1833, at age 50
President served	Jackson
Left office	Mar 3, 1837, at age 54
Reason for leaving office	Completed term
Term of service	4y (1,461 days)
Date of death	Jul 24, 1862, at age 79
Term of retirement	20y 9m 12d (7,587 days)
Other offices held	PR-8, ST-10

Wallace, Henry A.   Vice President 33

Date of birth	Oct 7, 1888
State of birth/residence	Iowa
Inauguration/age	Jan 20, 1941, at age 52
President served	Franklin D. Roosevelt
Left office	Jan 20, 1945, at age 56
Reason for leaving office	Completed term
Term of service	4y (1,461 days)
Date of death	Nov 18, 1965, at age 77
Term of retirement	20y 10m (7,605 days)
Other offices held	AG-11, CM-10

Wheeler, William A.   Vice President 19

Date of birth	Jun 30, 1819
State of birth/residence	New York
Inauguration/age	Mar 4, 1877, at age 57
President served	Hayes
Left office	Mar 3, 1881, at age 61
Reason for leaving office	Completed term
Term of service	4y (1,461 days)
Date of death	Jun 4, 1887, at age 67
Term of retirement	6y 3m 1d (2,282 days)

Wilson, Henry   Vice President 18

Date of birth	Feb 16, 1812
State of birth	New Hampshire

State of residence .... Massachusetts
Inauguration/age .... Mar 4, 1873, at age 61
President served .... Grant
Left office .... Nov 22, 1875, at age 63
Reason for leaving office .... Died in office
Term of service .... 2y 3m 18d (838 days)
Date of death .... Nov 22, 1875, at age 63
Term of retirement .... None

Cabinet Succession

Secretary of State (1789–)

Thomas Jefferson 1789–1794 (Washington)
Edmund Randolph 1794–1795 (Washington)
Timothy Pickering 1795–1797 (Washington)
Timothy Pickering 1797–1800 (Adams)
John Marshall 1800–1801 (Adams)
James Madison 1801–1809 (Jefferson)
Robert Smith 1809–1811 (Madison)
James Monroe 1811–1814, 1815–1817 (Madison)
John Q. Adams 1817–1825 (Monroe)
Henry Clay 1825–1829 (Adams)
Martin Van Buren 1829–1831 (Jackson)
Edward Livingston 1831–1833 (Jackson)
Louis McLane 1833–1834 (Jackson)
John Forsyth 1834–1837 (Jackson)
John Forsyth 1837–1841 (Van Buren)
Daniel Webster 1841 (Harrison)
Daniel Webster 1841–1843 (Tyler)
Abel P. Upshur 1843–1844 (Tyler)
John C. Calhoun 1844–1845 (Tyler)
James Buchanan 1845–1849 (Polk)
John M. Clayton 1849–1850 (Taylor)
Daniel Webster 1850–1852 (Fillmore)
Edward Everett 1852–1853 (Fillmore)
William L. Marcy 1853–1857 (Pierce)
Lewis Cass 1857–1860 (Buchanan)
Jeremiah S. Black 1860–1861 (Buchanan)
William H. Seward 1861–1865 (Lincoln)
William H. Seward 1865–1869 (Johnson)
Elihu B. Washburne 1869 (Grant)
Hamilton Fish 1869–1877 (Grant)
William A. Evarts 1877–1881 (Hayes)

James G. Blaine 1881(Garfield)
James G. Blaine 1881 (Arthur)
Frederick T. Frelinghuysen 1881–1885 (Arthur)
Thomas F. Bayard 1885–1889 (Cleveland)
James G. Blaine 1889–1892 (Harrison)
John W. Foster 1892–1893 (Harrison)
Walter Q. Gresham 1893–1895 (Cleveland)
Richard Olney 1895–1897 (Cleveland)
John Sherman 1897–1898 (McKinley)
William R. Day 1898 (McKinley)
John Hay 1898–1901 (McKinley)
John Hay 1901–1905 (Roosevelt)
Elihu Root 1905–1909 (Roosevelt)
Robert Bacon 1909 (Roosevelt)
Philander C. Knox 1909–1913 (Taft)
William J. Bryan 1913–1915 (Wilson)
Robert Lansing 1915–1920 (Wilson)
Bainbridge Colby 1920–1921 (Wilson)
Charles E. Hughes 1921–1923 (Harding)
Charles E. Hughes 1923–1925 (Coolidge)
Frank B. Kellogg 1925–1929 (Coolidge)
Henry L. Stimson 1929–1933 (Hoover)
Cordell Hull 1933–1944 (Roosevelt)
E.R. Stettinius, Jr. 1944–1945 (Roosevelt)
E.R. Stettinius, Jr. 1945 (Truman)
James F. Byrnes 1945–1947 (Truman)
George C. Marshall 1947–1949 (Truman)
Dean G. Acheson 1949–1953 (Truman)
John Foster Dulles 1953–1959 (Eisenhower)
Christian A. Herter 1959–1961 (Eisenhower)
Dean Rusk 1961–1963 (Kennedy)

Dean Rusk 1963–1969 (Johnson)
William P. Rogers 1969–1973 (Nixon)
Henry A. Kissinger 1973–1974 (Nixon)
Henry A. Kissinger 1974–1977 (Ford)
Cyrus R. Vance 1977–1980 (Carter)
Edmund S. Muskie 1980–1981 (Carter)
Alexander M. Haig, Jr. 1981–1982 (Reagan)
George P. Schultz 1982–1989 (Reagan)
James A. Baker III (TX) 1989–1992
(George Herbert Bush)

Lawrence S. Eagleburger (MI) 1992–1993
(George Herbert Bush)
Warren M. Christopher (CA) 1993–1997
(Clinton)
Madeleine K. Albright (DC) 1997–2001
(Clinton)
Colin Luther Powell (VA) 2001– (George
Walker Bush)

Secretary of War (1789–1947)

Henry Knox (MA) 1789–1795 (Washington)
Timothy Pickering (PA) 1795 (Washington)
James McHenry (MD) 1796–1797
(Washington)
James McHenry (MD) 1797–1800 (Adams)
Samuel Dexter (MA) 1800 (Adams)
Henry Dearborn (MA) 1801–1809 (Jefferson)
William Eustis (MA) 1809–1812 (Madison)
John Armstrong (NY) 1813–1814 (Madison)
James Monroe (VA) 1814–1815 (Madison)
William H. Crawford (GA) 1815–1816
(Madison)
John C. Calhoun (SC) 1817–1825 (Monroe)
James Barbour (VA) 1825–1828 (Adams)
Peter B. Porter (NY) 1828–1829 (Adams)
John H. Eaton (TN) 1829–1831 (Jackson)
Lewis Cass (MI) 1831–1836 (Jackson)
Benjamin F. Butler (NY) 1837 (Jackson)
Joel R. Poinsett (SC) 1837–1841 (Van Buren)
John Bell (TN) 1841 (Harrison)
John Bell (TN) 1841 (Tyler)
John C. Spencer (NY) 1841–1843 (Tyler)
James M. Porter (PA) 1843–1844 (Tyler)
William Wilkins (PA) 1844–1845 (Tyler)
William L. Marcy (NY) 1845–1849 (Polk)
George W. Crawford (GA) 1849–1850
(Taylor)
Charles M. Conrad (LA) 1850–1853 (Fillmore)
Jefferson Davis (MS) 1853–1857 (Pierce)
John B. Floyd (VA) 1857–1861 (Buchanan)
Joseph Holt (KY) 1861 (Buchanan)
Simon Cameron (PA) 1861–1862 (Lincoln)
Edwin M. Stanton (PA) 1862–1865 (Lincoln)
Edwin M. Stanton (PA) 1865–1868 (Johnson)
John M. Schofield (IL) 1868–1869 (Johnson)

John A. Rawlins (IL) 1869 (Grant)
William T. Sherman (OH) 1869 (Grant)
William W. Belknap (IA) 1869–1876 (Grant)
Alphonso Taft (OH) 1876 (Grant)
James D. Cameron (PA) 1876–1877 (Grant)
George W. McCrary (IA) 1877–1879 (Hayes)
Alexander Ramsey (MN) 1879–1881 (Hayes)
Robert T. Lincoln (IL) 1881 (Garfield)
Robert T. Lincoln (IL) 1881–1885 (Arthur)
William C. Endicott (MA) 1885–1889
(Cleveland)
Redfield Proctor (VT) 1889–1891 (Harrison)
Stephen B. Elkins (WV) 1891–1893 (Harrison)
Daniel S. Lamont (NY) 1893–1897
(Cleveland)
Russell A. Alger (MI) 1897–1899 (McKinley)
Elihu Root (NY) 1899–1901 (McKinley)
Elihu Root (NY) 1901–1904 (Roosevelt)
William H. Taft (OH) 1904–1908 (Roosevelt)
Luke E. Wright (TN) 1908–1909 (Roosevelt)
Jacob M. Dickinson (TN) 1909–1911 (Taft)
Henry L. Stimson (NY) 1911–1913 (Taft)
Lindley M. Garrison (NJ) 1913–1916 (Wilson)
Newton D. Baker (OH) 1916–1921 (Wilson)
John W. Weeks (MA) 1921–1923 (Harding)
John W. Weeks (MA) 1923–1925 (Coolidge)
Dwight F. Davis (MO) 1925–1929 (Coolidge)
James W. Good (IL) 1929 (Hoover)
Patrick J. Hurley (OK) 1929–1933 (Hoover)
George H. Dern (UT) 1933–1936 (Roosevelt)
Harry H. Woodring (KS) 1937–1940
(Roosevelt)
Henry L. Stimson (NY) 1940–1945 (Roosevelt)
Robert B. Patterson (NY) 1945–1947 (Truman)
Kenneth C. Royall (NC) 1947 (Truman)

SECRETARY OF THE TREASURY (1789–)

Alexander Hamilton (NY) 1789–1795 (Washington)

Oliver Wolcott (CT) 1795–1797 (Washington)

Oliver Wolcott (CT) 1797–1801 (Adams)

Samuel Dexter (MA) 1801 (Adams)

Samuel Dexter (MA) 1801 (Jefferson)

Albert Gallatin (PA) 1801–1809 (Jefferson)

Albert Gallatin (PA) 1809–1814 (Madison)

George W. Campbell (TN) 1814 (Madison)

Alexander J. Dallas (PA) 1814–1816 (Madison)

William H. Crawford (GA) 1816–1817 (Madison)

William H. Crawford (GA) 1817–1825 (Monroe)

Richard Rush (PA) 1825–1829 (Adams)

Samuel D. Ingham (PA) 1829–1831 (Jackson)

Louis McLane (DE) 1831–1833 (Jackson)

William J. Duane (PA) 1833 (Jackson)

Roger B. Taney (MD) 1833–1834 (Jackson)

Levi Woodbury (NH) 1834–1837 (Jackson)

Levi Woodbury (NH) 1837–1841 (Van Buren)

Thomas Ewing (OH) 1841 (Harrison)

Thomas Ewing (OH) 1841 (Tyler)

Walter Forward (PA) 1841–1843 (Tyler)

John C. Spencer (NY) 1843–1844 (Tyler)

George M. Bibb (KY) 1844–1845 (Tyler)

Robert J. Walker (MS) 1845–1849 (Polk)

William M. Meredith (PA) 1849–1850 (Taylor)

Thomas Corwin (OH) 1850–1853 (Fillmore)

James Guthrie (KY) 1853–1857 (Pierce)

Howell Cobb (GA) 1857–1860 (Buchanan)

Phillip F. Thomas (MD) 1860–1861 (Buchanan)

John A. Dix (NY) 1861 (Buchanan)

Salmon P. Chase (OH) 1861–1864 (Lincoln)

William P. Fessenden (ME) 1864–1865 (Lincoln)

Hugh McCulloch (IN) 1865 (Lincoln)

Hugh McCulloch (IN) 1865–1869 (Johnson)

George S. Boutwell (MA) 1869–1873 (Grant)

William A. Richardson (MA) 1873–1874 (Grant)

Benjamin H. Bristow (KY) 1874–1876 (Grant)

Lot M. Morrill (ME) 1876–1877 (Grant)

John Sherman (OH) 1877–1881 (Hayes)

William Windom (MN) 1881 (Garfield)

Charles J. Folger (NY) 1881–1884 (Arthur)

Walter Q. Gresham (IN) 1884 (Arthur)

Hugh McCulloch (IN) 1884–1885 (Arthur)

Daniel Manning (NY) 1885–1887 (Cleveland)

Charles S. Fairchild (NY) 1887–1889 (Cleveland)

William Windom (MN) 1889–1891 (Harrison)

Charles Foster (OH) 1891–1893 (Harrison)

John G. Carlisle (KY) 1893–1897 (Cleveland)

Lyman G. Gage (IL) 1897–1901 (McKinley)

Lyman G. Gage (IL) 1901–1902 (Roosevelt)

Leslie M. Shaw (IA) 1902–1907 (Roosevelt)

George B. Cortelyou (NY) 1907–1909 (Roosevelt)

Franklin MacVeagh (IL) 1909–1913 (Taft)

William G. McAdoo (NY) 1913–1918 (Wilson)

Carter Glass (VA) 1918–1920 (Wilson)

David F. Houston (MO) 1920–1921 (Wilson)

Andrew W. Mellon (PA) 1921–1923 (Harding)

Andrew W. Mellon (PA) 1923–1929 (Coolidge)

Andrew W. Mellon (PA) 1929–1932 (Hoover)

Ogden L. Mills (NY) 1932–1933 (Hoover)

William H. Woodin (NY) 1933–1934 (Roosevelt)

Henry Morgenthau, Jr. (NY) 1934–1945 (Roosevelt)

Fred M. Vinson (KY) 1945–1946 (Truman)

John W. Snyder (MO) 1946–1953 (Truman)

George M. Humphrey (OH) 1953–1957 (Eisenhower)

Robert B. Anderson (CT) 1957–1961 (Eisenhower)

C. Douglas Dillon (NJ) 1961–1963 (Kennedy)

C. Douglas Dillon ((NJ) 1963–1965 (Johnson)

Henry H. Fowler (VA) 1965–1968 (Johnson)

Joseph W. Barr (IN) 1968–1969 (Johnson)

David M. Kennedy (IL) 1969–1971 (Nixon)

John B. Connally (TX) 1971–1972 (Nixon)

George P. Shultz (IL) 1972–1974 (Nixon)

William E. Simon (NJ) 1974 (Nixon)

William E. Simon (NJ) 1974–1977 (Ford)

W. Michael Blumenthal (MI) 1977–1979 (Carter)

G. William Miller (RI) 1979–1981 (Carter)

Donald T. Regan (NY) 1981–1985 (Reagan)

James A. Baker III (TX) 1985–1988 (Reagan)

Nicholas F. Brady (NJ) 1988–1989 (Reagan)

Nicholas F. Brady (NJ) 1989–1993 (George Herbert Bush)

Lloyd Bentsen (TX) 1993–1995 (Clinton)

Robert E. Rubin (NY) 1995–1999
  (Clinton)
Lawrence H. Summers (CT) 1999–2001 (Clinton)

Paul Henry O'Neill (PA) 2001–2003
  (George Walker Bush)
John William Snow (VA) 2003–
  (George Walker Bush)

ATTORNEY GENERAL (1789–)

Edmund Randolph (VA) 1789–1794 (Washington)
William Bradford (PA) 1794–1795 (Washington)
Charles Lee (VA) 1795–1797 (Washington)
Charles Lee (VA) 1797–1801 (Adams)
Levi Lincoln (MA) 1801–1804 (Jefferson)
John Breckenridge (KY) 1805–1806 (Jefferson)
Caesar A. Rodney (DE) 1807 (Jefferson)
Caesar A. Rodney (DE) 1807–1811 (Madison)
William Pinkney (MD) 1811–1814 (Madison)
Richard Rush (PA) 1814–1817 (Madison)
Richard Rush (PA) 1817 (Monroe)
William Wirt (VA) 1817–1825 (Monroe)
William Wirt (VA) 1825–1829 (Adams)
John M. Berrien (GA) 1829–1831 (Jackson)
Roger B. Taney (MD) 1831–1833 (Jackson)
Benjamin F. Butler (NY) 1833–1837 (Jackson)
Benjamin F. Butler (NY) 1837–1838 (Van Buren)
Felix Grundy (TN) 1838–1840 (Van Buren)
Henry D. Gilpin (PA) 1840–1841 (Van Buren)
John J. Crittenden (KY) 1841 (Harrison)
John J. Crittenden (KY) 1841 (Tyler)
Hugh S. Legare (SC) 1841–1843 (Tyler)
John Nelson (MD) 1843–1845 (Tyler)
John Y. Mason (VA) 1845–1846 (Polk)
Nathan Clifford (ME) 1846–1848 (Polk)
Isaac Toucey (CT) 1848–1849 (Polk)
Reverdy Johnson (MD) 1849–1850 (Taylor)
John J. Crittenden (KY) 1850–1853 (Filmore)
Caleb Cushing (MA) 1853–1857 (Pierce)
Jeremiah S. Black (PA) 1857–1860 (Buchanan)
Edwin M. Stanton (PA) 1860–1861 (Buchanan)
Edward Bates (MO) 1861–1864 (Lincoln)
James Speed (KY) 1864–1865 (Lincoln)
James Speed (KY) 1865–1866 (Johnson)
Henry Stanbery (OH) 1866–1868 (Johnson)
William M. Evarts (NY) 1868–1869 (Johnson)
Ebenezer R. Hoar (MA) 1869–1870 (Grant)
Amos T. Akerman (GA) 1870–1871 (Grant)

George H. Williams (OR) 1871–1875 (Grant)
Edwards Pierrepont (NY) 1875–1876 (Grant)
Alphonso Taft (OH) 1876–1877 (Grant)
Charles Devens (MA) 1877–1881 (Hayes)
Wayne MacVeagh (PA) 1881 (Garfield)
Benjamin H. Brewster (PA) 1882–1885 (Arthur)
Augustus Garland (AR) 1885–1889 (Cleveland)
William H.H. Miller (IN) 1889–1893 (Harrison)
Richard Olney (MA) 1893–1895 (Cleveland)
Judson Harmon (OH) 1895–1897 (Cleveland)
Joseph McKenna (CA) 1897–1898 (McKinley)
John W. Griggs (NJ) 1898–1901 (McKinley)
Philander C. Knox (PA) 1901 (McKinley)
Philander C. Knox (PA) 1901–1904 (Roosevelt)
William H. Moody (MA) 1904–1906 (Roosevelt)
Charles J. Bonaparte (MD) 1906–1909 (Roosevelt)
George W. Wickersham (NY) 1909–1913 (Taft)
J.C. McReynolds (TN) 1913–1914 (Wilson)
Thomas W. Gregory ((TX) 1914–1919 (Wilson)
A. Mitchell Palmer (PA) 1919–1921 (Wilson)
Harry M. Daugherty (OH) 1921–1923 (Harding)
Harry M. Daugherty (OH) 1923–1924 (Coolidge)
Harlan F. Stone (NY) 1924–1925 (Coolidge)
John G. Sargent (VT) 1925–1929 (Coolidge)
William D. Mitchell (MN) 1929–1933 (Hoover)
Homer S. Cummings (CT) 1933–1939 (Roosevelt)
Frank Murphy (MI) 1939–1940 (Roosevelt)
Robert H. Jackson (NY) 1940–1941 (Roosevelt)
Francis Biddle (PA) 1941–1945 (Roosevelt)
Thomas C. Clark (TX) 1945–1949 (Truman)
J. Howard McGrath (RI) 1949–1952 (Truman)
J.P. McGranery (PA) 1952–1953 (Truman)

Herbert Brownell, Jr. (NY) 1953–1958 (Eisenhower)

William P. Rogers (MD) 1958–1961 (Eisenhower)

Robert F. Kennedy (MA) 1961–1963 (Kennedy)

Robert F. Kennedy (MA) 1963–1965 (Johnson)

Nicholas Katzenbach (IL) 1965–1967 (Johnson)

Ramsey Clark (TX) 1967–1969 (Johnson)

John N. Mitchell (NY) 1969–1972 (Nixon)

Richard G. Kleindienst (AZ) 1972–1973 (Nixon)

Elliott L. Richardson (MA) 1973 (Nixon)

William B. Saxbe (OH) 1973–1974 (Nixon)

William B. Saxbe (OH) 1974–1975 (Ford)

Edward H. Levi (IL) 1975–1977 (Ford)

Griffin B. Bell (GA) 1977–1979 (Carter)

Benjamin R. Civiletti (MD) 1979–1981 (Carter)

William French Smith (CA) 1981–1985 (Reagan)

Edwin Meese III (CA) 1985–1988 (Reagan)

Richard Thornburgh (PA) 1988–1989 (Reagan)

Richard Thornburgh (PA) 1989–1991 (George Herbert Bush)

William P. Barr (NY) 1991–1993 (George Herbert Bush)

Janet Reno (FL) 1993–2001 (Clinton)

John Ashcroft (MO) 2001– (George Walker Bush)

Postmaster General (1789–1970)

Samuel Osgood 1789–1791 (Washington)

Timothy Pickering 1791–1795 (Washington)

Joseph Habersham 1795–1797 (Washington)

Joseph Habersham 1797–1801 (Adams)

Joseph Habersham 1801 (Jefferson)

Gideon Granger 1801–1809 (Jefferson)

Gideon Granger 1809–1814 (Madison)

Return J. Meigs, Jr. 1814–1817 (Madison)

Return J. Meigs, Jr. 1817–1823 (Monroe)

John McLean 1823–1825 (Monroe)

John McLean 1825–1829 (Adams)

William T. Barry 1829–1835 (Jackson)

Amos Kendall 1835–1837 (Jackson)

Amos Kendall 1837–1840 (Van Buren)

John M. Niles 1840–1841 (Van Buren)

Francis Granger 1841 (Harrison)

Francis Granger 1841 (Tyler)

Charles A. Wickliffe 1841–1845 (Tyler)

Cave Johnson 1845–1849 Polk)

Jacob Collamer 1849–1850 (Taylor)

Nathan K. Hall 1850–1852 (Fillmore)

Samuel D. Hubbard 1852–1853 (Fillmore)

James Campbell 1853–1857 (Pierce)

Aaron V. Brown 1857–1859 (Buchanan)

Joseph Holt 1859–1861 (Buchanan)

Horatio King 1861 (Buchanan)

Montgomery Blair 1861–1864 (Lincoln)

William Dennison 1864–1865 (Lincoln)

William Dennison 1865–1866 (Johnson)

Alexander W. Randall 1866–1869 (Johnson)

John A.J. Creswell 1869–1874 (Grant)

James W. Marshall 1874 (Grant)

Marshall Jewell 1874–1876 (Grant)

James N. Tyner 1876–1877 (Grant)

David M. Key 1877–1880 (Hayes)

Horace Maynard 1880–1881 (Hayes)

Thomas L. James 1881 (Garfield)

Thomas L. James 1881 (Arthur)

Timothy O. Howe 1882–1883 (Arthur)

Walter Q. Gresham 1883–1884 (Arthur)

Frank Hatton 1884–1885 (Arthur)

William F. Vilas 1885–1888 (Cleveland)

Donald M. Dickinson 1888–1889 (Cleveland)

John Wanamaker 1889–1893 (Harrison)

Wilson S. Bissell 1893–1895 (Cleveland)

William L. Wilson 1895–1897 (Cleveland)

James A. Gary 1897–1898 (McKinley)

Charles E. Smith 1898–1901 (McKinley)

Charles E. Smith 1901–1902 (Roosevelt)

Henry C. Payne 1902–1904 (Roosevelt)

Robert J. Wynne 1904–1905 (Roosevelt)

George B. Cortelyou 1905–1907 (Roosevelt)

George Meyer 1907–1909 (Roosevelt)

Frank H. Hitchcock 1909–1913 (Taft)

Albert S. Burleson 1913–1921 (Wilson)

William H. Hays 1921–1922 (Harding)

Hubert Work 1922–1923 (Harding)

Harry S. New 1923 (Harding)

Harry S. New 1923–1929 (Coolidge)

Walter F. Brown 1929–1933 (Hoover)

James A. Farley 1933–1940 (Roosevelt)

Frank C. Walker 1940–1945 (Roosevelt)

Frank C. Walker 1945 (Truman)
Robert E. Hannegan 1945–1947 (Truman)
Jesse M. Donaldson 1947–1953 (Truman)
Arthur E. Summerfield 1953–1961 (Eisenhower)
J. Edward Day 1961–1963 (Kennedy)

John A. Gronouski 1963 (Kennedy)
John A. Gronouski 1963–1965 (Johnson)
Lawrence F. O'Brien 1965–1968 (Johnson)
W. Marvin Watson 1968–1969 (Johnson)
Winton M. Blount 1969–1970 (Nixon)

SECRETARY OF THE NAVY (1798–1947)

Benjamin Stoddert (MD) 1798–1801 (Adams)
Benjamin Stoddert (MD) 1801 (Jefferson)
Robert Smith (MD) 1801–1809 (Jefferson)
Paul Hamilton (SC) 1809–1813 (Madison)
William Jones (PA) 1813–1814 (Madison)
Benjamin W. Crowninshield (MA) 1814–1817 (Madison)
Benjamin W. Crowninshield (MA) 1817–1818 (Monroe)
Smith Thompson (NY) 1818–1823 (Monroe)
Samuel L. Southard (NJ) 1823–1825 (Monroe)
Samuel L. Southard (NJ) 1825–1829 (Adams)
John Branch (NC) 1829–1831 (Jackson)
Levi Woodbury (NH) 1831–1834 (Jackson)
Mahlon Dickerson (NJ) 1834–1837 (Jackson)
Mahlon Dickerson (NJ) 1837–1838 (Van Buren)
James K. Paulding (NY) 1838–1841 (Van Buren)
George E. Badger (NC) 1841 (Harrison)
George E. Badger (NC) 1841 (Tyler)
Abel P. Upshur (VA) 1841–1843 (Tyler)
David Henshaw (MA) 1843–1844 (Tyler)
Thomas W. Gilmer (VA) 1844 (Tyler)
John Y. Mason (VA) 1844–1845 (Tyler)
George Bancroft (MA) 1845–1846 (Polk)
John Y. Mason (VA) 1846–1849 (Polk)
William B. Preston (VA) 1849–1850 (Taylor)
William A. Graham (NC) 1850–1852 (Fillmore)
John P. Kennedy (MD) 1852–1853 (Fillmore)
James C. Dobbin (NC) 1853–1857 (Pierce)
Isaac Toucey (CT) 1857–1861 (Buchanan)
Gideon Welles (CT) 1861–1865 (Lincoln)

Gideon Welles (CT) 1865–1869 (Johnson)
Adolph E. Borie (PA) 1869 (Grant)
George M. Robeson (NJ) 1869–1877 (Grant)
Richard W. Thompson (IN) 1877–1881 (Hayes)
Nathan Goff, Jr. (WV) 1881 (Hayes)
William H. Hunt (LA) 1881–1882 (Garfield)
William E. Chandler (NH) 1882–1885 (Arthur)
William C. Whitney (NY) 1885–1889 (Cleveland)
Benjamin F. Tracy (NY) 1889–1893 (Harrison)
Hilary A. Herbert (AL) 1893–1897 (Cleveland)
John D. Long (MA) 1897–1901 (McKinley)
John D. Long (MA) 1901–1902 (Roosevelt)
William H. Moody (MA) 1902–1904 (Roosevelt)
Paul Morton (IL) 1904–1905 (Roosevelt)
Charles J. Bonaparte (MD) 1905–1906 (Roosevelt)
Victor H. Metcalf (CA) 1906–1908 (Roosevelt)
Truman H. Newberry (MI) 1908–1909 (Roosevelt)
George von L. Meyer (MA) 1909–1913 (Taft)
Josephus Daniels (NC) 1913–1921 (Wilson)
Edwin Denby (MI) 1921–1923 (Harding)
Edwin Denby (MI) 1923–1924 (Coolidge)
Curtis D. Wilbur (CA) 1924–1929 (Coolidge)
Charles Francis Adams (MA) 1929–1933 (Hoover)
Claude A. Swanson (VA) 1933–1940 (Roosevelt)
Charles Edison (NJ) 1940 (Roosevelt)
Frank Knox (IL) 1940–1944 (Roosevelt)
James V. Forrestal (NY) 1944–1945 (Roosevelt)
James V. Forrestal (NY) 1945 (Truman)

SECRETARY OF THE INTERIOR (1849–)

Thomas Ewing (OH) 1849–1850 (Taylor)
Thomas M.T. McKennan (PA) 1850 (Fillmore)

Alex H.H. Stuart (VA) 1850–1853 (Fillmore)
Robert McClelland (MI) 1853–1857 (Pierce)

Jacob Thompson (MS) 1857–1861 (Buchanan)
Caleb B. Smith (IN) 1861–1863 (Lincoln)
John P. Usher (IN) 1863–1865 (Lincoln)
John P. Usher (IN) 1865 (Johnson)
James Harlan (IA) 1865–1866 (Johnson)
Orville H. Browning (IL) 1866–1869 (Johnson)
Jacob D. Cox (OH) 1869–1870 (Grant)
Columbus Delano (OH) 1870–1875 (Grant)
Zachariah Chandler ((MI) 1875–1877 (Grant)
Carl Schurz (MO) 1877–1881 (Hayes)
Samuel J. Kirkwood (IA) 1881–1882 (Garfield)
Henry M. Teller (CO) 1882–1885 (Arthur)
Lucius Q.C. Lamar (MS) 1885–1888 (Cleveland)
William F. Vilas (WI) 1888–1889 (Cleveland)
John W. Noble (MO) 1889–1893 (Harrison)
Hoke Smith (GA) 1893–1896 (Cleveland)
David R. Francis (MO) 1896–1897 (Cleveland)
Cornelius N. Bliss (NY) 1897–1898 (McKinley)
Ethan A. Hitchcock (MO) 1898–1901 (McKinley)
Ethan A. Hitchcock (MO) 1901–1907 (Roosevelt)
James R. Garfield (OH) 1907–1909 (Roosevelt)
Richard A. Ballinger (WA) 1909–1911 (Taft)
Walter L. Fisher (IL) 1911–1913 (Taft)
Franklin K. Lane (CA) 1913–1920 (Wilson)

John B. Payne (IL) 1920–1921 (Wilson)
Albert B. Fall (NM) 1921–1923 (Harding)
Hubert Work (CO) 1923 (Harding)
Hubert Work (CO) 1923–1929 (Coolidge)
Roy O. West (IL) 1929 (Coolidge)
Ray Lyman Wilbur (CA) 1929–1933 (Hoover)
Harold L. Ickes (IL) 1933–1945 (Roosevelt)
Harold L. Ickes (IL) 1945–1946 (Truman)
Julius A. Krug (WI) 1946–1949 (Truman)
Oscar L. Chapman (CO) 1949–1953 (Truman)
Douglas McKay (OR) 1953–1956 (Eisenhower)
Fred A. Seaton (NE) 1956–1961 (Eisenhower)
Stewart L. Udall (AZ) 1961–1963 (Kennedy)
Stewart L. Udall (AZ) 1963–1969 (Johnson)
Walter J. Hickel (AK) 1969–1971 (Nixon)
Rogers C.B. Morton (MD) 1971 (Nixon)
Rogers C.B. Morton (MD) 1971–1975 (Ford)
Stanley K. Hathaway (WY) 1975 (Ford)
Thomas S. Kleppe (ND) 1975–1977 (Ford)
Cecil D. Andrus (ID) 1977–1981 (Carter)
James G. Watt (CO) 1981–1983 (Reagan)
William P. Clark (CA) 1983–1985 (Reagan)
Donald P. Hodel (OR) 1985–1989 (Reagan)
Manuel Lujan (NM) 1989–1993 (George Herbert Bush)
Bruce Babbitt (AZ) 1993–2001 (Clinton)
Gale Ann Norton (CO) 2001– (George Walker Bush)

Secretary of Agriculture (1889–)

Norman J. Colman (MO) 1889 (Cleveland)
Jeremiah M. Rusk (WI) 1889–1893 (Benjamin Harrison)
J. Sterling Morton (NE) 1893–1897 (Cleveland)
James Wilson (IA) 1897–1901 (McKinley)
James Wilson (IA) 1901–1909 (Theodore Roosevelt)
James Wilson (IA) 1909–1913 (Taft)
David F. Houston (MO) 1913–1920 (Wilson)
Edwin T. Meredith (IA) 1920–1921 (Wilson)
Henry C. Wallace (IA) 1921–1923 (Harding)
Henry C. Wallace (IA) 1923–1924 (Coolidge)
Howard M. Gore (WV) 1924–1925 (Coolidge)
William M. Jardine (KS) 1925–1929 (Coolidge)
Arthur M. Hyde (MO) 1929–1933 (Hoover)
Henry A. Wallace (IA) 1933–1940 (Franklin D. Roosevelt)

Claude R. Wickard (IN) 1940–1945 (Franklin D. Roosevelt)
Clinton P. Anderson (NM) 1945–1948 (Truman)
Charles F. Brannan (CO) 1948–1953 (Truman)
Ezra Taft Benson (UT) 1953–1961 (Eisenhower)
Orville L. Freeman (MN) 1961–1963 (Kennedy)
Orville L. Freeman (MN) 1963–1969 (Lyndon B. Johnson)
Clifford M. Hardin (IN) 1969–1971 (Nixon)
Earl L. Butz (IN) 1971–1974 (Nixon)
Earl L. Butz (IN) 1974–1976 (Ford)
John A. Knebel (VA) 1976–1977 (Ford)
Bob Berglund (MN) 1977–1981 (Carter)
John R. Block (IL) 1981–1986 (Reagan)
Richard E. Lyng (CA) 1986–1989 (Reagan)

Clayton K. Yeutter (NE) 1989–1991 (George Herbert Bush)

Edward Madigan (IL) 1991–1993 (George Herbert Bush)

Mike Espy (MS) 1993–1995 (Clinton)

Dan Glickman (KS) 1995–2001 (Clinton)

Ann Margaret Veneman (CA) 2001– (George Walker Bush)

SECRETARY OF COMMERCE AND LABOR (1903–1913)

George B. Cortelyou (NY) 1903–1904 (Theodore Roosevelt)

Victor H. Metcalf (CA) 1904–1906 (Theodore Roosevelt)

Oscar S. Straus (NY) 1906–1909 (Theodore Roosevelt)

Charles Nagel (MO) 1909–1913 (Taft)

SECRETARY OF COMMERCE (1913–)

William C. Redfield (NY) 1913–1919 (Wilson)

Joshua W. Alexander (MO) 1919–1921 (Wilson)

Herbert C. Hoover (CA) 1921–1923 (Harding)

Herbert C. Hoover (CA) 1923–1928 (Coolidge)

William F. Whiting (MA) 1928–1929 (Coolidge)

Robert P. Lamont (IL) 1929–1932 (Hoover)

Roy D. Chapin (MI) 1932–1933 (Hoover)

Daniel C. Roper (SC) 1933–1938 (Franklin D. Roosevelt)

Harry L. Hopkins (NY) 1939–1940 (Franklin D. Roosevelt)

Jesse Jones (TX) 1940–1945 (Franklin D. Roosevelt)

Henry A. Wallace (IA) 1945 (Franklin D. Roosevelt)

Henry A. Wallace (IA) 1945–1947 (Truman)

W. Averell Harriman (NY) 1947–1948 (Truman)

Charles Sawyer (OH) 1948–1953 (Truman)

Sinclair Weeks (MA) 1953–1958 (Eisenhower)

Lewis L. Straus (NY) 1958–1959 (Eisenhower)

Frederick H. Mueller (MI) 1959–1961 (Eisenhower)

Luther H. Hodges (NC) 1961–1963 (Kennedy)

Luther H. Hodges (NC) 1963–1965 (Lyndon B. Johnson)

John T. Connor (NJ) 1965–1967 (Lyndon B. Johnson)

Alex B. Trowbridge (NJ) 1967–1968 (Lyndon B. Johnson)

Cyrus R. Smith (NY) 1968–1969 (Lyndon B. Johnson)

Maurice H. Stans (MN) 1969–1972 (Nixon)

Peter G. Peterson (IL) 1972–1973 (Nixon)

Frederick B. Dent (SC) 1973–1974 (Nixon)

Frederick B. Dent (SC) 1974–1975 (Ford)

Rogers C.B. Morton (MD) 1975 (Ford)

Elliott L. Richardson (MA) 1975–1977 (Ford)

Juanita M. Kreps (NC) 1977–1979 (Carter)

Philip M. Klutznick (IL) 1979–1981 (Carter)

Malcolm Baldrige (CT) 1981–1987 (Reagan)

C. William Verity, Jr. (OH) 1987–1989 (Reagan)

Robert A. Mosbacher (TX) 1989–1992 (George Herbert Bush)

Barbara H. Franklin (PA) 1992–1993 (George Herbert Bush)

Ronald H. Brown (DC) 1993–1996 (Clinton)

Mickey Kantor (CA) 1996–1997 (Clinton)

William M. Daley (IL) 1997–2000 (Clinton)

Norman Y. Mineta (CA) 2000–2001 (Clinton)

Donald Louis Evans (TX) 2001– (George Walker Bush)

SECRETARY OF LABOR (1913–)

William B. Wilson (PA) 1913–1921 (Wilson)
James J. Davis (PA) 1921–1923 (Harding)
James J. Davis (PA) 1923–1929 (Coolidge)
James J. Davis (PA) 1929–1930 (Hoover)
William N. Doak (VA) 1930–1933 (Hoover)
Frances Perkins (NY) 1933–1945 (Franklin D. Roosevelt)
L.B. Schwellenbach (WA) 1945–1949 (Truman)
Maurice J. Tobin (MA) 1949–1953 (Truman)
Martin P. Durkin (IL) 1953 (Eisenhower)
James P. Mitchell (NJ) 1953–1961 (Eisenhower)
Arthur J. Goldberg (IL) 1961–1962 (Kennedy)
W. Willard Wirtz (IL) 1962–1963 (Kennedy)
W. Willard Wirtz (IL) 1963–1969 (Lyndon B. Johnson)
George P. Shultz (IL) 1969–1970 (Nixon)

James D. Hodgson (CA) 1970–1973 (Nixon)
Peter J. Brennan (NY) 1973–1974 (Nixon)
Peter J. Brennan (NY) 1974–1975 (Ford)
John T. Dunlop (CA) 1975–1976 ((Ford)
W.J. Usery, Jr. (GA) 1976–1977 (Ford)
F. Ray Marshall (TX) 1977–1981 (Carter)
Raymond J. Donovan (NJ) 1981–1985 (Reagan)
William E. Brock (TN) 1985–1987 (Reagan)
Ann D. McLaughlin (DC) 1987–1989 (Reagan)
Elizabeth Hanford Dole (NC) 1989–1991 (George Herbert Bush)
Lynn Martin (IL) 1991–1993 (George Herbert Bush)
Robert B. Reich (MA) 1993–1997 (Clinton)
Alexis M. Herman (AL) 1997–2001 (Clinton)
Elaine Lan Chao (KY) 2001– (George Walker Bush)

SECRETARY OF DEFENSE (1947–)

James V. Forrestal (NY) 1947–1949 (Truman)
Louis A. Johnson (WV) 1949–1950 (Truman)
George C. Marshall (PA) 1950–1951 (Truman)
Robert A. Lovett (NY) 1951–1953 (Truman)
Charles E. Wilson (MI) 1953–1957 (Eisenhower)
Neil H. McElroy (OH) 1957–1959 (Eisenhower)
Thomas S. Gates, Jr. (PA) 1959–1961 (Eisenhower)
Robert S. McNamara (MI) 1961–1963 (Kennedy)
Robert S. McNamara (MI) 1963–1968 (Lyndon B. Johnson)
Clark M.Clifford (MD) 1968–1969 (Lyndon B. Johnson)
Melvin R. Laird (WI) 1969–1973 (Nixon)

Elliot L. Richardson (MA) 1973 (Nixon)
James R. Schlesinger (VA) 1973–1974 (Nixon)
James R. Schlesinger (VA) 1974–1975 (Ford)
Donald Henry Rumsfeld (IL) 1975–1977 (Ford)
Harold Brown (CA) 1977–1981 (Carter)
Caspar W. Weinberger (CA) 1981–1987 (Reagan)
Frank C. Carlucci (PA) 1987–1989 (Reagan)
Richard B. Cheney (WY) 1989–1993 (George Herbert Bush)
Les Aspin (WI) 1993–1994 (Clinton)
William J. Perry (CA) 1994–1997 (Clinton)
William S. Cohen (ME) 1997–2001 (Clinton)
Donald Henry Rumsfeld (IL) 2001– (George Walker Bush)

SECRETARY OF HEALTH, EDUCATION AND WELFARE (1953–1979)

Oveta Culp Hobby (TX) 1953–1955 (Eisenhower)

Marion B. Folsom (NY) 1955–1958 (Eisenhower)

Arthur S. Flemming (OH) 1958–1961 (Eisenhower)

Abraham A. Ribicoff (CT) 1961–1962 (Kennedy)

Anthony J. Celebrezze (OH) 1962–1963 (Kennedy)

Anthony J. Celebrezze (1963–1965 (Lyndon B. Johnson)

John W. Gardner (NY) 1965–1968 (Lyndon B. Johnson)

Wilbur J. Cohen (MI) 1968–1969 (Lyndon B. Johnson)

Robert H. Finch (CA) 1969–1970 (Nixon)

Elliot L. Richardson (MA) 1970–1973 (Nixon)

Caspar W. Weinberger (CA) 1973–1974 (Nixon)

Caspar Weinberger (CA) 1974–1975 (Ford)

Forrest D. Mathews (AL) 1975–1977 (Ford)

Joseph A. Califano, Jr. (DC) 1977–1979 (Carter)

Patricia Roberts Harris (DC) 1979 (Carter)

SECRETARY OF HOUSING AND URBAN DEVELOPMENT (1966–)

Robert C. Weaver (WA) 1966–1969 (Lyndon B. Johnson)

Robert C. Wood (MA) 1969 (Lyndon B. Johnson)

George W. Romney (MI) 1969–1973 (Nixon)

James T. Lynn (OH) 1973–1974 Nixon)

James T. Lynn (OH) 1974–1975 (Ford)

Carla Anderson Hills (CA) 1975–1977 (Ford)

Patricia Roberts Harris (DC) 1977–1979 (Carter)

Moon Landrieu (LA) 1979–1981 (Carter)

Samuel R. Pierce, Jr. (NY) 1981–1989 (Reagan)

Jack F. Kemp (NY) 1989–1993 (George Herbert Bush)

Henry G. Cisneros ((TX) 1993–1997 (Clinton)

Andrew M. Cuomo (NY) 1997–2001 (Clinton)

Melquiades Rafael Martinez (FL) 2001– (George Walker Bush)

SECRETARY OF TRANSPORTATION (1967–)

Alan S. Boyd (FL) 1967–1969 (Lyndon B. Johnson)

John A. Volpe (MA) 1969–1973 (Nixon)

Claude S. Brinegar (CA) 1973–1974 (Nixon)

Claude S. Brinegar (CA) 1974–1975 (Ford)

William T. Coleman, Jr. (PA) 1975–1977 (Ford)

Brock Adams (WA) 1977–1979 (Carter)

Neil E. Goldschmidt (1979–1981 (Carter)

Andrew L. Lewis, Jr. (PA) 1981–1983 (Reagan)

Elizabeth Hanford Dole (NC) 1983–1987 (Reagan)

James H. Burnley (NC) 1987–1989 (Reagan)

Samuel K. Skinner (IL) 1989–1992 (George Herbert Bush)

Andrew H. Card, Jr. (MA) 1992–1993 (George Herbert Bush)

Frederico F. Pena (CO) 1993–1997 (Clinton)

Rodney E. Slater (AR) 1997–2001 (Clinton)

Norman Y. Mineta (CA) 2001– (George Walker Bush)

SECRETARY OF ENERGY (1977–)

James R. Schlesinger (VA) 1977–1979 (Carter)

Charles Duncan, Jr. (WY) 1979–1981 (Carter)

James B. Edwards (SC) 1981–1982 (Reagan)

Donald P. Hodel (OR) 1982–1985 (Reagan)

John S. Herrington (CA) 1985–1989 (Reagan)
James D. Watkins (CA) 1989–1993 (George Herbert Bush)
Hazel R. O'Leary (MN) 1993–1997 (Clinton)

Frederico F. Pena (CO) 1997–1998 (Clinton)
Bill Richardson (NM) 1998–2001 (Clinton)
Spencer Abraham (MI) 2001– (George Walker Bush)

SECRETARY OF HEALTH AND HUMAN SERVICES (1979–)

Patricia Roberts Harris (DC) 1979–1981 (Carter)
Richard S. Schweiker (PA) 1981–1983 (Reagan)
Margaret M. Heckler (MA) 1983–1985 (Reagan)

Otis R. Bowen (IN) 1985–1989 (Reagan)
Louis W. Sullivan (GA) 1989–1993 (George Herbert Bush)
Donna E. Shalala (WI) 1993–2001 (Clinton)
Tommy G. Thompson (WI) 2001– (George Walker Bush)

SECRETARY OF EDUCATION (1979–)

Shirley Hufstedler (CA) 1979–1981 (Carter)
Terrel Bell (UT) 1981–1985 (Reagan)
William J. Bennett (NY) 1985–1988 (Reagan)
Lauro F. Cavazos (TX) 1988–1989 (Reagan)
Lauro F. Cavasos (TX) 1989–1991 (George Herbert Bush)

Lamar Alexander (TN) 1991–1993 (George Herbert Bush)
Richard W. Riley (SC) 1993–2001 (Clinton)
Roderick R. Paige (TX) 2001– (George Walker Bush)

SECRETARY OF VETERANS AFFAIRS (1989–)

Edward J. Derwinski (IL) 1989–1993 (George Herbert Bush)
Jesse Brown (IL) 1993–1998 (Clinton)
Togo D. West, Jr. (NC) 1998–2000 (Clinton)

Hershel W. Gober [acting] (AR) 2000–2001 (Clinton)
Anthony Joseph Principi (CA) 2001– (George Walker Bush)

SECRETARY OF HOMELAND SECURITY (2002–)

Thomas Ridge (PA) 2003–
(George Walker Bush)

Cabinet Office Summary

Department of State — Originally created by an act of Congress on July 27, 1789, as the Department of Foreign Affairs, the name of the department was changed to the Department of State on September 15, 1789.

Department of War — The War Department was created by Congress on August 7, 1789. On September 18, 1947, the War Department became the Department of the Army. The Department of the Army and the departments of the Army, Navy and Air Force became branches of the Department of Defense.

Department of the Treasury — The Treasury Department was created by Congress on September 2, 1789.

Post Office Department — The Post Office Department was originally established as a branch of the Treasury Department on September 22, 1789. The Postmaster General was made a member of the president's Cabinet on March 9, 1829. The Postal Reorganization Act of 1970 changed the name of the organization to the U.S. Postal Service, and beginning July 1, 1970, the Postmaster General was no longer a member of the president's Cabinet.

Office of Attorney General — The attorney general's office was organized on September 24, 1789. The Justice Department was created by Congress on June 22, 1870.

Navy Department — The Navy Department was created on April 30, 1798. The Navy Department became one of the branches of the Department of Defense on September 18, 1947. The Secretary of the Navy became a non–Cabinet official on that date, though all three military departments — Army, Navy and Air Force — are represented in the Cabinet by the Secretary of Defense.

Department of the Interior — The Interior Department was created by Congress on March 3, 1849.

Department of Agriculture — The Agriculture Department was created by Congress on May 15, 1862, but the department was not at first represented in the president's Cabinet. The Secretary of Agriculture became a member of the Cabinet on February 8, 1889.

Department of Commerce and Labor — The Commerce and Labor Department was created by Congress on February 14, 1903. The department was divided into separate departments of Commerce and Labor on March 4, 1913.

Department of Commerce — The Commerce Department was a subdivision of the Commerce and Labor Department from the creation of the latter in 1903 until March 4, 1913, when the departments were separated and the Secretary of Commerce was commissioned as a separate Cabinet post.

Department of Labor — The Labor Department was part of the Commerce and Labor Department until March 4, 1913, when the dual department was divided into two separate offices and the Secretary of Labor became an individual Cabinet officer.

Department of Defense — The Defense Department was created on September 18, 1947, to act as a unifying office to oversee the interests of the Army, Navy and Air Force. The War Department became the Department of the Army, and it and the Department of the Navy, along with the new Department of the Air Force, became branches of the Department of Defense.

Department of Health, Education and Welfare — The Department of Health, Education and Welfare was created on April 11, 1953. Twenty-six years later, on September 27, 1979, the bureau was divided into the departments of Education and Health and Human Services.

Department of Housing and Urban Development — HUD was created by Congress on September 9, 1965.

Department of Transportation — The Transportation Department was created by Congress on October 15, 1966.

Department of Energy — The Energy Department was created by Congress on August 4, 1977.

Department of Health and Human Services — The Health and Human Services Department was created by Congress on September 27, 1979, when the Department of Health, Education and Welfare was divided into the Department of Health and Human Services and the Department of Education.

Department of Education — The Education Department was created by Congress on September 27, 1979, when HEW was divided into two separate departments, each represented by a secretary in the president's Cabinet.

Department of Veterans Affairs — The Department of Veterans Affairs was created by an act of Congress on October 25, 1988. The department officially opened its doors on March 15, 1989. The first secretary of the department was confirmed March 2, only 13 days prior to the department's opening.

Department of Homeland Security — Less than two weeks after the September 11, 2001, terrorist attacks on the World Trade Center towers in New York and the Pentagon in Washington, D.C., President George Walker Bush appointed popular two-term Pennsylvania governor Tom Ridge director of a newly created Office of Homeland Security. Just over a year later, Bush signed legislation to elevate the Office of Homeland Security to a department to be represented at the Cabinet level. The legislation, signed by Bush on November 25, 2002, designated the new governmental consolidation as the Department of Homeland Security and its responsibilities are divided into four general areas: border and transportation security; emergency preparedness and response; chemical, biological, radiological and nuclear counter measures; and information analysis and infrastructure protection. This bold concept would consolidate what has been variously estimated in print to be between 22 and 40 existing agencies with total combined budgets in excess of $40 billion and employing more than 170,000 workers. The creation of this office is considered to be the largest federal government reorganization since the creation of the Department of Defense in 1947. Once the homeland security office was designated a department, Bush nominated Ridge for the position as Secretary to oversee and coordinate the creation of the new department, and on January 22, 2003, Ridge was confirmed by the Senate.

Biographical Data — Cabinet Members

Abraham, Spencer   **Secretary of Energy 10**

Date of birth .... Jun 12, 1952
Resident .... Michigan
Date of appointment/age .... Jan 2, 2000, at age 48
Confirmed/age .... Jan 20, 2001, at age 48
Left office/age .... — — — — —
President served .... George Walker Bush
Other offices held .... — — — — —
Date of death/age .... — — — — —
Cabinet service .... — — — — —

Acheson, Dean G.   **Secretary of State 51**

Date of birth .... Apr 11, 1893
Residence .... Connecticut
Date of appointment/age .... Jan 19, 1949, at age 55
Assumed office/age .... Jan 21, 1949, at age 55
Left office/age .... Jan 20, 1953, at age 59
President served .... Truman
Date of death/age .... Oct 12, 1971, at age 78
Cabinet service .... 4y (1,461 days)

Adams, Brockman   **Secretary of Transportation 5**

Date of birth .... Jan 13, 1927
Residence .... Washington
Date of appointment/age .... Dec 15, 1976, at age 49
Assumed office/age .... Jan 21, 1977, at age 50
Left office/age .... Jul 21, 1979, at age 52
Date of death/age .... — — — — —
Cabinet service .... 2y 6m (910 days)

Adams, Charles Francis   **Secretary of the Navy 44**

Date of birth .... Aug 2, 1866
Residence .... Massachusetts

Date of appointment/age . . . . Mar 5, 1929, at age 62
Assumed office/age . . . . Mar 5, 1929, at age 62
Left office/age . . . . Mar 3, 1933, at age 66
President served . . . . Hoover
Date of death/age . . . . Jun 11, 1954, at age 87
Cabinet service . . . . 3y 11m 28d (1,453 days)

Adams, John Quincy   Secretary of State 8

Date of birth . . . . Jul 11, 1767
Residence . . . . Massachusetts
Date of appointment/age . . . . Mar 5, 1817, at age 49
Assumed office/age . . . . Sep 22, 1817, at age 50
Left office/age . . . . Mar 3, 1825, at age 57
President served . . . . Monroe
Date of death/age . . . . Feb 23, 1848, at age 80
Cabinet service . . . . 7y 5m 9d (2,715 days)
Other offices held PR-6

Akerman, Amos T.   Attorney General 31

Date of birth . . . . Feb 23, 1821
Residence . . . . Georgia
Date of appointment/age . . . . Jun 23, 1870, at age 49
Assumed office/age . . . . Jul 8, 1870, at age 49
Left office/age . . . . Jan 9, 1872, at age 50
President served . . . . Grant
Date of death/age . . . . Dec 21, 1880, at age 59
Cabinet service . . . . 1y 6m 1d (546 days)

Albright, Madeleine K.   Secretary of State 64

Date of birth . . . . May 15, 1937
Residence . . . . Washington, D.C.
Date of appointment/age . . . . Dec 5, 1996, at age 59
Confirmed/age . . . . Jan 23, 1997, at age 59
Left office/age . . . . Jan 20, 2001, at age 64
President served . . . . Clinton
Date of death/age . . . . — — — —
Cabinet service . . . . 3y 11m 27d (1,452 days)

Alexander, Joshua W.   Secretary of Commerce 2

Date of birth . . . . Jan 22, 1852
Residence . . . . Missouri
Date of appointment/age . . . . Dec 11, 1919, at age 67
Assumed office/age . . . . Dec 16, 1919, at age 67
Left office/age . . . . Mar 4, 1921, at age 69
President served . . . . Wilson
Date of death/age . . . . Feb 27, 1936, at age 84
Cabinet service . . . . 1y 2m 16d (441 days)

Alexander, Lamar   Secretary of Education 5

Date of birth . . . . Jul 3, 1940
Residence . . . . Tennessee

Date of appointment/age . . . . Dec 17, 1990, at age 50
Confirmed/age . . . . Mar 14, 1991, at age 50
Left office/age . . . . Jan 20, 1993, at age 52
President served . . . . George Herbert Bush
Date of death/age . . . . — — — — —
Cabinet service . . . . 1y 10m 6d (671 days)

Alger, Russell A.   Secretary of War 42

Date of birth . . . . Feb 27, 1836
Residence . . . . Michigan
Date of appointment/age . . . . Mar 5, 1897, at age 61
Assumed office/age . . . . Mar 5, 1897, at age 61
Left office/age . . . . Jul 31, 1899, at age 63
President served . . . . McKinley
Date of death/age . . . . Jan 24, 1907, at age 70
Cabinet service . . . . 2y 4m 26d (876 days)

Anderson, Clinton P.   Secretary of Agriculture 13

Date of birth . . . . Oct 23, 1895
Residence . . . . New Mexico
Date of appointment/age . . . . Jun 2, 1945, at age 49
Assumed office/age . . . . Jun 30, 1945, at age 49
Left office/age . . . . Jun 1, 1948, at age 52
President served . . . . Truman
Date of death/age . . . . Nov 11, 1975, at age 80
Cabinet service . . . . 2y 11m 1d (1,061 days)

Anderson, Robert B.   Secretary of the Treasury 56

Date of birth . . . . Jun 4, 1910
Residence . . . . Connecticut
Date of appointment/age . . . . May 29, 1957, at age 46
Assumed office/age . . . . Jul 29, 1957, at age 47
Left office/age . . . . Jan 20, 1961, at age 50
President served . . . . Eisenhower
Date of death/age . . . . Aug 14, 1989, at age 79
Cabinet service . . . . 3y 5m 22d (1,267 days)

Andrus, Cecil D.   Secretary of the Interior 42

Date of birth . . . . Aug 25, 1931
Residence . . . . Idaho
Date of appointment/age . . . . Dec 19, 1976, at age 45
Assumed office/age . . . . Jan 21, 1977, at age 45
Left office/age . . . . Jan 20, 1981, at age 49
President served . . . . Carter
Date of death/age . . . . — — — — —
Cabinet service . . . . 4y (1,461 days)

Armstrong, John   Secretary of War 7

Date of birth . . . . Nov 25, 1758
Residence . . . . New York
Date of appointment/age . . . . Jan 13, 1813, at age 54

Assumed office/age .... Feb 5, 1813, at age 54
Left office/age .... Aug 29, 1814, at age 55
President served .... Madison
Date of death/age .... Apr 1, 1843, at age 84
Cabinet service .... 1y 6m 24d (569 days)

Ashcroft, John   Attorney General 79

Date of birth .... May 9, 1942
Residence .... Missouri
Date of appointment/age .... Dec 22, 2000, at age 58
Confirmed/age .... Feb 1, 2001, at age 58
Left office/age .... —————
President served .... George Walker Bush
Date of death/age .... —————
Cabinet service .... —————

Aspin, Leslie, Jr.   Secretary of Defense 18

Date of birth .... Jul 21, 1938
Residence .... Wisconsin
Date of appointment/age .... Jan 20, 1993, at age 54
Assumed office/age .... Jan 20, 1993, at age 54
Left office/age .... Feb 2, 1994, at age 55
President served .... Clinton
Date of death/age .... May 21, 1995, at age 56
Cabinet service .... 1y 12d (377 days)

Babbitt, Bruce   Secretary of the Interior 47

Date of birth .... Jun 27, 1938
Residence .... Arizona
Date of appointment/age .... Jan 20, 1993, at age 54
Assumed office/age .... Jan 20, 1993, at age 54
Left office/age .... Jan 20, 2001, at age 62
President served .... Clinton
Date of death/age .... —————
Cabinet service .... 8y (2,922 days)

Bacon, Robert   Secretary of State 39

Date of birth .... Jul 5, 1860
Residence .... New York
Date of appointment/age .... Jan 27, 1909, at age 48
Assumed office/age .... Jan 27, 1909, at age 48
Left office/age .... Mar 4, 1909, at age 48
President served .... Theodore Roosevelt
Cabinet service .... 1m 5d (35 days)

Bacon, Robert   Secretary of State 39

Date of appointment/age .... Mar 4, 1909, at age 48
Assumed office/age .... Mar 4, 1909, at age 48
Left office/age .... Mar 5, 1909, at age 48
President served .... Taft

Date of death/age .... May 29, 1919, at age 58
Cabinet service 1d
Total Cabinet service .... 1m 6d (36 days)

Badger, George E.   Secretary of the Navy 12

Date of birth .... Apr 17, 1795
Residence .... North Carolina
Date of appointment/age .... Mar 5, 1841, at age 45
Assumed office/age .... Mar 5, 1841, at age 45
Left office/age .... Apr 4, 1841, at age 45
President served .... William Henry Harrison
Cabinet service .... 1m (30 days)

Badger, George E.   Secretary of the Navy 12

Date of appointment/age .... Apr 4, 1841, at age 45
Assumed office/age .... Apr 4, 1841, at age 45
Left office/age .... Sep 10, 1841, at age 46
President served .... Tyler
Date of death/age .... May 11, 1866, at age 71
Cabinet service 5m 6d
Total Cabinet service .... 6m 6d (186 days)

Baker, James Addison, III   Secretary of the Treasury 67

Date of birth .... Apr 28, 1930
Residence .... Texas
Date of appointment/age .... Jan 10, 1985, at age 54
Assumed office/age .... Jan 29, 1985, at age 54
Left office/age .... Aug 18, 1988, at age 58
President served .... Reagan
Cabinet service 3y 6m 19d

Baker, James Addison, III   Secretary of State 61

Date of appointment/age .... Jan 25, 1989, at age 58
Assumed office/age .... Jan 25, 1989, at age 58
Left office/age .... Aug 23, 1992, at age 62
President served .... George Herbert Bush
Date of death/age .... — — — —
Cabinet service .... 3y 6m 29d (1,304 days)
Total Cabinet service .... 7y 1m 18d (2,604 days)

Baker, Newton D.   Secretary of War 49

Date of birth .... Dec 3, 1871
Residence .... Ohio
Date of appointment/age .... Mar 7, 1916, at age 44
Assumed office/age .... Mar 9, 1916, at age 44
Left office/age .... Mar 4, 1921, at age 49
President served .... Wilson
Date of death/age .... Dec 25, 1937, at age 66
Cabinet service .... 4y 11m 26d (1,817 days)

Baldridge, Howard Malcolm   Secretary of Commerce 27

Date of birth .... Oct 4, 1922
Residence .... Connecticut
Date of appointment/age .... Dec 12, 1980, at age 58
Assumed office/age .... Jan 22, 1981, at age 58
Left office/age .... Jul 25, 1987, at age 64
President served .... Reagan
Date of death/age .... Jul 25, 1987, at age 64
Cabinet service .... 6y 6m 3d (2,374 days)

Ballinger, Richard A.   Secretary of the Interior 24

Date of birth .... Jul 9, 1858
Residence .... Washington
Date of appointment/age .... Mar 5, 1909, at age 50
Assumed office/age .... Mar 5, 1909, at age 50
Left office/age .... Mar 6, 1911, at age 52
President served .... Taft
Date of death/age .... Jun 6, 1922, at age 63
Cabinet service .... 1y 5m 29d (544 days)

Bancroft, George   Secretary of the Navy 17

Date of birth .... Oct 3, 1800
Residence .... Massachusetts
Date of appointment/age .... Mar 10, 1845, at age 44
Assumed office/age .... Mar 10, 1845, at age 44
Left office/age .... Sep 8, 1846, at age 45
President served .... Polk
Date of death/age .... Jan 17, 1891, at age 90
Cabinet service .... 1y 5m 29d (544 days)

Barbour, James   Secretary of War 11

Date of birth .... Jun 10, 1775
Residence .... Virginia
Date of appointment/age .... Mar 7, 1825, at age 49
Assumed office/age .... Mar 7, 1825, at age 49
Left office/age .... May 25, 1828, at age 52
President served .... John Quincy Adams
Date of death/age .... Jun 7, 1842, at age 66
Cabinet service .... 3y 2m 18d (1,173 days)

Barr, Joseph W.   Secretary of the Treasury 59

Date of birth .... Jan 17, 1918
Residence .... Indiana
Date of appointment/age .... Dec 24, 1968, at age 50
Assumed office/age .... Dec 24, 1968, at age 50
Left office/age .... Jan 20, 1969, at age 50
President served .... Lyndon B. Johnson
Date of death/age .... Feb 23, 1996, at age 77
Cabinet service .... 26d (26 days)

Barr, William P.   Attorney General 77

Date of birth .... May 23, 1950
Residence .... New York

Date of appointment/age . . . . Oct 16, 1991, at age 41
Confirmed/age . . . . Nov 20, 1991, at age 41
Left office/age . . . . Jan 20, 1993, at age 42
President served . . . . George Herbert Bush
Date of death/age . . . . —————
Cabinet service . . . . 1y 2m (425 days)

Barry, William T.   Postmaster General 7

Date of birth . . . . Feb 5, 1785
Residence . . . . Kentucky
Date of appointment/age . . . . Mar 9, 1829, at age 44
Assumed office/age . . . . Apr 6, 1829, at age 44
Left office/age . . . . Apr 30, 1835, at age 50
President served . . . . Jackson
Date of death/age . . . . Aug 30, 1835, at age 50
Cabinet service . . . . 6y 24d (2,215 days)

Bates, Edward   Attorney General 26

Date of birth . . . . Sep 4, 1793
Residence . . . . Missouri
Date of appointment/age . . . . Mar 5, 1861, at age 67
Assumed office/age . . . . Mar 5, 1861, at age 67
Left office/age . . . . Dec 4, 1864, at age 71
President served . . . . Lincoln
Date of death/age . . . . Mar 25, 1869, at age 75
Cabinet service . . . . 3y 8m 29d (1,364 days)

Bayard, Thomas Francis   Secretary of State 30

Date of birth . . . . Oct 29, 1828
Residence . . . . Delaware
Date of appointment/age . . . . Mar 6, 1885, at age 56
Assumed office/age . . . . Mar 6, 1885, at age 56
Left office/age . . . . Mar 3, 1889, at age 60
President served . . . . Cleveland
Cabinet service 3y 11m 25d

Bayard, Thomas Francis   Secretary of State 30

Date of appointment/age . . . . Mar 4, 1889, at age 60
Assumed office/age . . . . Mar 4, 1889, at age 60
Left office/age . . . . Mar 6, 1889, at age 60
President served . . . . Benjamin Harrison
Date of death/age . . . . Sep 28, 1898, at age 69
Cabinet service 2d
Total Cabinet service . . . . Senate 3y 11m 27d (1,452 days)

Belknap, William W.   Secretary of War 32

Date of birth . . . . Sep 22, 1829
Residence . . . . Iowa
Date of appointment/age . . . . Oct 25, 1869, at age 40
Assumed office/age . . . . Nov 1, 1869, at age 40

Left office/age .... Mar 1, 1876, at age 46
President served .... Grant
Date of death/age .... Oct 13, 1890, at age 61
Cabinet service .... 6y 4m (2,311 days)

Bell, Griffin Boyette   Attorney General 72

Date of birth .... Oct 31, 1918
Residence .... Georgia
Date of appointment/age .... Dec 21, 1976, at age 58
Assumed office/age .... Jan 26, 1977, at age 58
Left office/age .... Jul 20, 1979, at age 60
President served .... Carter
Date of death/age .... — — — —
Cabinet service .... 2y 5m 24d (904 days)

Bell, John   Secretary of War 17

Date of birth .... Feb 15, 1797
Residence .... Tennessee
Date of appointment/age .... Mar 5, 1841, at age 44
Assumed office/age .... Mar 5, 1841, at age 44
Left office/age .... Apr 4, 1841, at age 44
President served .... William Henry Harrison
Cabinet service 1m

Bell, John   Secretary of War 17

Date of appointment/age .... Apr 4, 1841, at age 44
Assumed office/age .... Apr 4, 1841, at age 44
Left office/age .... Sep 11, 1841, at age 44
President served .... Tyler
Date of death/age .... Sep 10, 1869, at age 72
Cabinet service 5m 6d
Total Cabinet service .... 6m 6d (186 days)

Bell, Terrel Howard   Secretary of Education 2

Date of birth .... Nov 11, 1921
Residence .... Utah
Date of appointment/age .... Jan 8, 1981, at age 59
Assumed office/age .... Jan 23, 1981, at age 59
Left office/age .... Feb 7, 1985, at age 64
President served .... Reagan
Date of death/age .... June 22, 1996, at age 74
Cabinet service .... 4y 15d (1,476 days)

Bennett, William John   Secretary of Education 3

Date of birth .... Jul 31, 1943
Residence .... New York
Date of appointment/age .... Jan 10, 1985, at age 41
Confirmed/age .... Feb 6, 1985, at age 41
Left office/age .... Sep 20, 1988, at age 43
President served .... Reagan

Date of death/age .... — — — — —
Cabinet service .... 3y 7m 14d (1,319 days)

Benson, Ezra Taft   Secretary of Agriculture 15

Date of birth .... Aug 4, 1899
Residence .... Utah
Date of appointment/age .... Jun 21, 1953, at age 53
Assumed office/age .... Jun 21, 1953, at age 53
Left office/age .... Jan 20, 1961, at age 61
President served .... Eisenhower
Date of death/age .... May 30, 1994, at age 94
Cabinet service .... 7y 7m (2,766 days)

Bentsen, Lloyd Millard, Jr.   Secretary of the Treasury 69

Date of birth .... Feb 11, 1921
Date of appointment/age .... Dec 10, 1992, at age 71
Confirmed/age .... Jan 20, 1993, at age 71
Left office/age .... Dec 22, 1994, at age 72
President served .... Clinton
Date of death/age .... — — — — —
Cabinet service .... 1y 11m 2d (697 days)

Berglund, Robert S. (Bob)   Secretary of Agriculture 20

Date of birth .... Jul 22, 1928
Residence .... Minnesota
Date of appointment/age .... Dec 21, 1976, at age 48
Assumed office/age .... Jan 21, 1977, at age 48
Left office/age .... Jan 20, 1981, at age 52
President served .... Carter
Date of death/age .... — — — — —
Cabinet service .... 4y (1,461 days)

Berrien, John M.   Attorney General 10

Date of birth .... Aug 23, 1781
Residence .... Georgia
Date of appointment/age .... Mar 9, 1829, at age 47
Assumed office/age .... Mar 9, 1829, at age 47
Left office/age .... Jun 22, 1831, at age 49
President served .... Jackson
Date of death/age .... Jan 1, 1856, at age 74
Cabinet service .... 2y 3m 13d (833 days)

Bibb, George M.   Secretary of the Treasury 17

Date of birth .... Oct 30, 1776
Residence .... Kentucky
Date of appointment/age .... Jun 15, 1844, at age 67
Assumed office/age .... Jul 4, 1844, at age 67
Left office/age .... Mar 7, 1845, at age 68
President served .... Tyler
Date of death/age .... Apr 14, 1859, at age 82
Cabinet service .... 8m 3d (243 days)

Biddle, Francis   Attorney General 58

Date of birth .... May 9, 1886
Residence .... Pennsylvania
Date of appointment/age .... Sep 5, 1941, at age 55
Assumed office/age .... Sep 5, 1941, at age 55
Left office/age .... Jun 30, 1945, at age 59
President served .... Franklin D. Roosevelt
Date of death/age .... Oct 4, 1968, at age 82
Cabinet service .... 3y 9m 25d (1,390 days)

Bissell, Wilson Shannon   Postmaster General 36

Date of birth .... Dec 31, 1847
Residence .... New York
Date of appointment/age .... Mar 6, 1893, at age 45
Assumed office/age .... Mar 6, 1893, at age 45
Left office/age .... Apr 3, 1895, at age 47
President served .... Cleveland
Date of death/age .... Oct 6, 1903, at age 55
Cabinet service .... 2y 28d (758 days)

Black, Jeremiah S.   Attorney General 24

Date of birth .... Jan 10, 1810
Residence .... Pennsylvania
Date of appointment/age .... Mar 6, 1857, at age 47
Assumed office/age .... Mar 11, 1857, at age 47
Left office/age .... Dec 21, 1860, at age 50
President served .... Buchanan
Cabinet service 3y 9m 10d

Black, Jeremiah S.   Secretary of State 23

Date of appointment/age .... Dec 17, 1860, at age 50
Assumed office/age .... Dec 21, 1860, at age 50
Left office/age .... Mar 4, 1861, at age 51
President served .... Buchanan
Date of death/age .... Aug 19, 1883, at age 73
Cabinet service 2m 11d
Total Cabinet service .... 3y 11m 21d (1,446 days)

Blaine, James G.   Secretary of State 28

Date of birth .... Jan 31, 1830
Residence .... Maine
Date of appointment/age .... Mar 5, 1881, at age 51
Assumed office/age .... Mar 7, 1881, at age 51
Left office/age .... Sep 19, 1881, at age 51
President served .... Garfield
Cabinet service 6m 12d

Blaine, James G.   Secretary of State 28

Date of appointment/age .... Sep 20, 1881, at age 51
Assumed office/age .... Sep 20, 1881, at age 51

Left office/age .... Dec 19, 1881, at age 51
President served .... Arthur
Cabinet service 2m 29d

Blaine, James G.   Secretary of State 31

Date of appointment/age .... Mar 5, 1889, at age 59
Assumed office/age .... Mar 7, 1889, at age 59
Left office/age .... Jun 3, 1892, at age 62
President served .... Benjamin Harrison
Date of death/age .... Jan 27, 1893, at age 62
Cabinet service 3y 2m 26d
Total Cabinet service .... 4y 2m 29d (1,550 days)

Blair, Montgomery   Postmaster General 20

Date of birth .... May 10, 1813
Residence .... Washington, D.C.
Date of appointment/age .... Mar 5, 1861, at age 47
Assumed office/age .... Mar 9, 1861, at age 47
Left office/age .... Sep 30, 1864, at age 51
President served .... Lincoln
Date of death/age .... Jul 27, 1883
Cabinet service .... 3y 6m 21d (1,296 days)

Bliss, Cornelius N.   Secretary of the Interior 21

Date of birth .... Jan 26, 1833
Residence .... New York
Date of appointment/age .... Mar 5, 1897, at age 64
Assumed office/age .... Mar 5, 1897, at age 64
Left office/age .... Feb 19, 1899, at age 66
President served .... McKinley
Date of death/age .... Oct 9, 1911, at age 78
Cabinet service .... 1y 11m 14d (709 days)

Block, John Rusling, III   Secretary of Agriculture 21

Date of birth .... Feb 15, 1935
Residence .... Illinois
Date of appointment/age .... Dec 23, 1980, at age 45
Assumed office/age .... Jan 20, 1981, at age 45
Left office/age .... Feb 14, 1986, at age 51
President served .... Reagan
Date of death/age .... ————
Cabinet service .... 5y 25d (1,851 days)

Blount, Winton Malcolm   Postmaster General 59

Date of birth .... Feb 1, 1921
Residence .... Alabama
Date of appointment/age .... Jan 20, 1969, at age 47
Assumed office/age .... Jan 21, 1969, at age 47
Left office/age .... Jun 30, 1970, at age 50
President served .... Nixon

Date of death/age .... —————
Cabinet service .... 1y 5m 9d (524 days)

Blumenthal, Werner Michael   Secretary of the Treasury 64

Date of birth .... Jan 3, 1926
Residence .... Michigan
Date of appointment/age .... Dec 15, 1976, at age 50
Assumed office/age .... Jan 21, 1977, at age 51
Left office/age .... Jul 20, 1979, at age 53
President served .... Carter
Date of death/age .... —————
Cabinet service .... 2y 5m 29d (909 days)

Bonaparte, Charles J.   Secretary of the Navy 37

Date of birth .... Jun 9, 1851
Residence .... Maryland
Date of appointment/age .... Jul 1, 1905, at age 54
Assumed office/age .... Jul 1, 1905, at age 54
Left office/age .... Dec 16, 1906, at age 55
President served .... Theodore Roosevelt
Cabinet service 1y 5m 15d

Bonaparte, Charles J.   Attorney General 46

Date of appointment/age .... Dec 12, 1906, at age 55
Assumed office/age .... Dec 17, 1906, at age 55
Left office/age .... Mar 4, 1909, at age 57
President served .... Theodore Roosevelt
Date of death/age .... Jun 28, 1921, at age 70
Cabinet service 2y 2m 15d
Total Cabinet service .... 3y 8m (1,335 days)

Borie, Adolph E.   Secretary of the Navy 25

Date of birth .... Nov 25, 1809
Residence .... Pennsylvania
Date of appointment/age .... Mar 5, 1869, at age 59
Assumed office/age .... Mar 9, 1869, at age 59
Left office/age .... Jun 24, 1869, at age 59
President served .... Grant
Date of death/age .... Feb 5, 1880, at age 70
Cabinet service .... 3m 15d (105 days)

Boutwell, George S.   Secretary of the Treasury 28

Date of birth .... Jan 28, 1818
Residence .... Massachusetts
Date of appointment/age .... Mar 11, 1869, at age 51
Assumed office/age .... Mar 11, 1869, at age 51
Left office/age .... Mar 16, 1873, at age 55
President served .... Grant
Date of death/age .... Feb 27, 1905, at age 87
Cabinet service .... 4y 5d (1,466 days)

Bowen, Otis Ray

Secretary of Health and Human Services 4

Date of birth	Feb 26, 1918
Residence	Indiana
Date of appointment/age	Nov 7, 1985, at age 67
Confirmed/age	Dec 12, 1985, at age 67
Left office/age	Jan 20, 1989, at age 70
President served	Reagan
Date of death/age	—————
Cabinet service	3y 1m 18d (1,143 days)

Boyd, Alan S.

Secretary of Transportation 1

Date of birth	Jul 20, 1922
Residence	Florida
Date of appointment/age	Jan 10, 1967, at age 46
Assumed office/age	Jan 16, 1967, at age 46
Left office/age	Jan 20, 1969, at age 47
President served	Lyndon B. Johnson
Date of death/age	—————
Cabinet service	2y 4d (734 days)

Bradford, William

Attorney General 2

Date of birth	Sep 14, 1755
Residence	Pennsylvania
Date of appointment/age	Jan 28, 1794, at age 38
Assumed office/age	Jan 29, 1794, at age 38
Left office/age	Aug 23, 1795, at age 39
President served	Washington
Date of death/age	Aug 23, 1795, at age 39
Cabinet service	1y 6m 25d (570 days)

Brady, Nicholas Frederick

Secretary of the Treasury 68

Date of birth	Apr 11, 1930
Residence	New Jersey
Date of appointment/age	Aug 10, 1988, at age 58
Assumed office/age	Aug 18, 1988, at age 58
Left office/age	Jan 20, 1989, at age 58
President served	Reagan
Cabinet service	5m 2d

Brady, Nicholas Frederick

Secretary of the Treasury 68

Date of appointment/age	Jan 20, 1989, at age 58
Assumed office/age	Jan 20, 1989, at age 58
Left office/age	Jan 20, 1993, at age 62
President served	George Herbert Bush
Date of death/age	—————
Cabinet service	4y
Total Cabinet service	4y 5m 2d (1,613 days)

Branch, John

Secretary of the Navy 8

Date of birth	Nov 4, 1782
Residence	North Carolina

Date of appointment/age . . . . Mar 9, 1829, at age 46
Assumed office/age . . . . Mar 9, 1829, at age 46
Left office/age . . . . May 11, 1831, at age 48
President served . . . . Jackson
Date of death/age . . . . Jan 4, 1863, at age 80
Cabinet service . . . . 2y 2m 2d (792 days)

Brannan, Charles Franklin   Secretary of Agriculture 14

Date of birth . . . . Aug 23, 1903
Residence . . . . Colorado
Date of appointment/age . . . . May 29, 1948, at age 44
Assumed office/age . . . . Jun 2, 1948, at age 44
Left office/age . . . . Jan 20, 1953, at age 49
President served . . . . Truman
Date of death/age . . . . Jul 2, 1992, at age 88
Cabinet service . . . . 4y 7m 18d (1,689 days)

Breckenridge, John   Attorney General 5

Date of birth . . . . Dec 2, 1760
Residence . . . . Kentucky
Date of appointment/age . . . . Aug 7, 1805, at age 44
Assumed office/age . . . . Aug 7, 1805, at age 44
Left office/age . . . . Dec 14, 1806, at age 46
President served . . . . Jefferson
Date of death/age . . . . Dec 14, 1806, at age 46
Cabinet service . . . . 1y 4m 7d (492 days)

Brennan, Peter J.   Secretary of Labor 13

Date of birth . . . . May 24, 1918
Residence . . . . New York
Date of appointment/age . . . . Nov 29, 1972, at age 54
Confirmed/age . . . . Jan 31, 1973, at age 54
Left office/age . . . . Aug 9, 1974, at age 56
President served . . . . Nixon
Cabinet service 1y 6m 9d

Brennan, Peter J.   Secretary of Labor 13

Date of appointment/age . . . . Aug 9, 1974, at age 56
Assumed office/age . . . . Aug 9, 1974, at age 56
Left office/age . . . . Mar 1, 1975, at age 56
President served . . . . Ford
Date of death/age . . . . Oct 2, 1996, at age 78
Cabinet service 6m 20d
Total Cabinet service . . . . 2y 29d (759 days)

Brewster, Benjamin H.   Attorney General 37

Date of birth . . . . Oct 13, 1816
Residence . . . . Pennsylvania
Date of appointment/age . . . . Dec 19, 1881, at age 65

Assumed office/age .... Jan 3, 1882, at age 65
Left office/age .... Mar 8, 1885, at age 68
President served .... Arthur
Date of death/age .... Apr 4, 1888, at age 71
Cabinet service .... 3y 2m 5d (1,160 days)

Brinegar, Claude Stout   Secretary of Transportation 3

Date of birth .... Dec 16, 1926
Residence .... California
Date of appointment/age .... Dec 7, 1972, at age 45
Assumed office/age .... Jan 19, 1973, at age 46
Left office/age .... Aug 9, 1974, at age 47
President served .... Nixon
Cabinet service 1y 6m 21d

Brinegar, Claude Stout   Secretary of Transportation 3

Date of appointment/age .... Aug 9, 1974, at age 47
Assumed office/age .... Aug 9, 1974, at age 47
Left office/age .... Feb 1, 1975, at age 48
President served .... Ford
Date of death/age .... ————
Cabinet service 5m 23d
Total Cabinet service .... 2y 14d (744 days)

Bristow, Benjamin H.   Secretary of the Treasury 30

Date of birth .... Jun 20, 1832
Residence .... Kentucky
Date of appointment/age .... Jul 3, 1874, at age 42
Assumed office/age .... Jul 3, 1874, at age 42
Left office/age .... Jun 20, 1876, at age 44
President served .... Grant
Date of death/age .... Jun 22, 1890, at age 58
Cabinet service .... 1y 11m 17d (712 days)

Brock, William Emerson, III (Bill)   Secretary of Labor 18

Date of birth .... Nov 23, 1930
Residence .... Tennessee
Date of appointment/age .... Apr 29, 1985, at age 54
Assumed office/age .... Apr 29, 1985, at age 54
Left office/age .... Dec 17, 1987, at age 57
President served .... Reagan
Date of death/age .... ————
Cabinet service .... 2y 7m 18d (958 days)

Brown, Aaron Venable   Postmaster General 17

Date of birth .... Aug 15, 1795
Residence .... Tennessee
Date of appointment/age .... Mar 6, 1857, at age 61
Assumed office/age .... Mar 6, 1857, at age 61
Left office/age .... Mar 8, 1859, at age 63
President served .... Buchanan

Date of death/age .... Mar 8, 1859, at age 63
Cabinet service .... 2y 2d (732 days)

Brown, Harold   Secretary of Defense 14

Date of birth .... Sep 19, 1927
Residence .... California
Date of appointment/age .... Dec 22, 1976, at age 49
Assumed office/age .... Jan 21, 1977, at age 49
Left office/age .... Jan 20, 1981, at age 53
President served .... Carter
Date of death/age .... — — — —
Cabinet service .... 4y (1,461 days)

Brown, Jesse   Secretary of Veterans Affairs 2

Date of birth .... Mar 27, 1944
Residence .... Illinois
Date of appointment/age .... Dec 17, 1992, at age 48
Confirmed/age .... Jan 21, 1993, at age 48
Left office/age .... Jan 2, 1998, at age 53
President served .... Clinton
Date of death/age .... — — — —
Cabinet service .... 4y 11m 11d (1,802 days)

Brown, Ronald Harmon   Secretary of Commerce 31

Date of birth .... Aug 1, 1941
Residence .... Washington, D.C.
Date of appointment/age .... Jan 21, 1993, at age 51
Assumed office/age .... Jan 21, 1993, at age 51
Left office/age .... Apr 3, 1996, at age 54
President served .... Clinton
Date of death/age .... Apr 3, 1996, at age 54
Cabinet service .... 3y 2m 12d (1,167 days)

Brown, Walter Folger   Postmaster General 49

Date of birth .... May 31, 1869
Residence .... Ohio
Date of appointment/age .... Mar 5, 1929, at age 59
Assumed office/age .... Mar 6, 1929, at age 59
Left office/age .... Mar 3, 1933, at age 63
President served .... Hoover
Date of death/age .... Jan 26, 1961, at age 91
Cabinet service .... 3y 11m 27d (1,452 days)

Brownell, Herbert, Jr.   Attorney General 62

Date of birth .... Feb 20, 1904
Residence .... New York
Date of appointment/age .... Jan 21, 1953, at age 48
Assumed office/age .... Jan 21, 1953, at age 48
Left office/age .... Jan 26, 1958, at age 53
President served .... Eisenhower
Date of death/age .... May 1, 1996, at age 92
Cabinet service .... 3y 11m 27d (1,452 days)

Browning, Orville H. 　　Secretary of the Interior 9

Date of birth .... Feb 10, 1806
Residence .... Illinois
Date of appointment/age .... Jul 27, 1866, at age 60
Assumed office/age .... Sep 1, 1866, at age 60
Left office/age .... Mar 3, 1869, at age 63
President served .... Andrew Johnson
Date of death/age .... Aug 10, 1881, at age 75
Cabinet service .... 2y 6m 2d (912 days)

Bryan, William J. 　　Secretary of State 41

Date of birth .... Mar 18, 1860
Residence .... Nebraska
Date of appointment/age .... Mar 5, 1913, at age 52
Assumed office/age .... Mar 5, 1913, at age 52
Left office/age .... Jun 8, 1915, at age 55
President served .... Wilson
Date of death/age .... Jul 26, 1925, at age 65
Cabinet service .... 2y 3m 3d (823 days)

Buchanan, James 　　Secretary of State 17

Date of birth .... Apr 23, 1791
Residence .... Pennsylvsania
Date of appointment/age .... Mar 6, 1845, at age 53
Assumed office/age .... Mar 10, 1845, at age 53
Left office/age .... Mar 3, 1849, at age 57
President served .... Polk
Cabinet service 3y 11m 23d

Buchanan, James 　　Secretary of State 17

Date of appointment/age .... Mar 4, 1849, at age 57
Assumed office/age .... Mar 4, 1849, at age 57
Left office/age .... Mar 7, 1849, at age 57
President served .... Taylor
Date of death/age .... Jun 1, 1868, at age 77
Cabinet service 3d
Total Cabinet service .... 3y 11m 23d (1,448 days)
Other offices held PR-15

Burleson, Albert Sidney 　　Postmaster General 45

Date of birth .... Jun 7, 1863
Residence .... Texas
Date of appointment/age .... Mar 5, 1913, at age 49
Assumed office/age .... Mar 5, 1913, at age 49
Left office/age .... Mar 4, 1921, at age 57
President served .... Wilson
Date of death/age .... Nov 24, 1937, at age 74
Cabinet service .... 8y (2,922 days)

Burnley, James Horace, IV 　　Secretary of Transportation 9

Date of birth .... Jul 30, 1948
Residence .... North Carolina

Date of appointment/age . . . . Dec 3, 1987, at age 39
Assumed office/age . . . . Dec 3, 1987, at age 39
Left office/age . . . . Jan 20, 1989, at age 40
President served . . . . Reagan
Date of death/age . . . . — — — — —
Cabinet service . . . . 1y 1m 17d (412 days)

Butler, Benjamin Franklin　　　　Attorney General 12

Date of birth . . . . Dec 14, 1795
Residence . . . . New York
Date of appointment/age . . . . Nov 15, 1833, at age 37
Assumed office/age . . . . Nov 18, 1833, at age 37
Left office/age . . . . Mar 3, 1837, at age 41
President served . . . . Jackson
Cabinet service 3y 3m 15d

Butler, Benjamin Franklin　　　　Attorney General 12

Date of appointment/age . . . . Mar 4, 1837, at age 41
Assumed office/age . . . . Mar 4, 1837, at age 41
Left office/age . . . . Sep 1, 1838, at age 41
President served . . . . Van Buren
Cabinet service 1y 5m 27d

Butler, Benjamin Franklin　　　　Secretary of War (interim)

Date of appointment/age . . . . Mar 3, 1837, at age 41
Assumed office/age . . . . Mar 3, 1837, at age 41
Left office/age . . . . Mar 4, 1837, at age 41
President served . . . . Jackson
Cabinet service 1d

Butler, Benjamin Franklin　　　　Secretary of War (interim)

Date of appointment/age . . . . Mar 4, 1837, at age 41
Assumed office/age . . . . Mar 4, 1837, at age 41
Left office/age . . . . Mar 14, 1837, at age 41
President served . . . . Van Buren
Date of death/age . . . . Nov 8, 1858, at age 62
Cabinet service 10d
Total Cabinet service . . . . 4y 9y 23d (1,754 days)

Butz, Earl Laver　　　　Secretary of Agriculture 18

Date of birth . . . . Jul 3, 1909
Residence . . . . Indiana
Date of appointment/age . . . . Nov 11, 1971, at age 62
Assumed office/age . . . . Dec 2, 1971, at age 62
Left office/age . . . . Aug 9, 1974, at age 65
President served . . . . Nixon
Cabinet service 2y 8m 7d

Butz, Earl Laver　　　　Secretary of Agriculture 18

Date of appointment/age . . . . Aug 9, 1974, at age 65
Assumed office/age . . . . Aug 9, 1974, at age 65

Left office/age .... Oct 5, 1976, at age 67
President served .... Ford
Date of death/age .... ————
Cabinet service 2y 1m 26d
Total Cabinet service .... 4y 10m 3d (1,764 days)

Byrnes, James Francis — Secretary of State 49

Date of birth .... May 2, 1879
Residence .... South Carolina
Date of appointment/age .... Jul 2, 1945, at age 66
Assumed office/age .... Jul 3, 1945, at age 66
Left office/age .... Jan 20, 1947, at age 67
President served .... Truman
Date of death/age .... Apr 9, 1972, at age 92
Cabinet service 1y 6m 17d (562)
Other offices held AJ-76

Calhoun, John Caldwell — Secretary of War 10

Date of birth .... Mar 18, 1782
Residence .... South Carolina
Date of appointment/age .... Oct 8, 1817, at age 35
Assumed office/age .... Dec 10, 1817, at age 35
Left office/age .... Mar 3, 1825, at age 42
President served .... Monroe
Cabinet service 7y 2m 17d

Calhoun, John Caldwell — Secretary of State 16

Date of appointment/age .... Mar 6, 1844, at age 61
Assumed office/age .... Apr 1, 1844, at age 62
Left office/age .... Mar 3, 1845, at age 62
President served .... Tyler
Cabinet service 11m 2d

Calhoun, John Caldwell — Secretary of State 16

Date of appointment/age .... Mar 4, 1845, at age 62
Assumed office/age .... Mar 4, 1845, at age 62
Left office/age .... Mar 5, 1845, at age 62
President served .... Polk
Date of death/age .... Mar 31, 1850, at age 68
Cabinet service 1d
Total Cabinet service .... 8y 1m 20d (2,967 days)
Other offices held VP-7

Califano, Joseph A., Jr. — Secretary of Health Education and Welfare 12

Date of birth .... May 15, 1931
Residence .... Washington, D.C.
Date of appointment/age .... Dec 24, 1976, at age 45
Assumed office/age .... Jan 25, 1977, at age 45
Left office/age .... Aug 4, 1979, at age 48
President served .... Carter

Date of death/age .... — — — — —
Cabinet service .... 2y 6m 10d (920 days)

Cameron, James D.   Secretary of War 34

Date of birth .... May 14, 1833
Residence .... Pennsylvania
Date of appointment/age .... May 22, 1876, at age 43
Assumed office/age .... Jun 1, 1876, at age 43
Left office/age .... Mar 11, 1877, at age 43
President served .... Grant
Date of death/age .... Aug 30, 1918, at age 85
Cabinet service .... 9m 10d (280 days)

Cameron, Simon   Secretary of War 27

Date of birth .... Mar 8, 1799
Residence .... Pennsylvania
Date of appointment/age .... Mar 5, 1861, at age 61
Assumed office/age .... Mar 11, 1861, at age 62
Left office/age .... Jan 19, 1862, at age 62
President served .... Lincoln
Date of death/age .... Jun 26, 1889, at age 90
Cabinet service .... 10m 8d (308 days)

Campbell, George W.   Secretary of the Treasury 5

Date of birth .... Feb 8, 1769
Residence .... Tennessee
Date of appointment/age .... Feb 9, 1814, at age 45
Assumed office/age .... Feb 9, 1814, at age 45
Left office/age .... Oct 13, 1814, at age 45
President served .... Madison
Date of death/age .... Feb 17, 1848, at age 79
Cabinet service .... 8m 4d (244 days)

Campbell, James   Postmaster General 16

Date of birth .... Sep 1, 1812
Residence .... Pennsylvania
Date of appointment/age .... Mar 7, 1853, at age 40
Assumed office/age .... Mar 7, 1853, at age 40
Left office/age .... Mar 5, 1857, at age 44
President served .... Pierce
Date of death/age .... Jan 27, 1893, at age 80
Cabinet service .... 3y 11m 29d (1,454 days)

Card, Andrew H., Jr.   Secretary of Transportation 11

Date of birth .... May 10, 1947
Residence .... Massachusetts
Date of appointment/age .... Jan 22, 1992, at age 44
Assumed office/age .... Jan 22, 1992, at age 44
Left office/age .... Jan 20, 1993, at age 45
President served .... George Herbert Bush
Date of death//age .... — — — — —
Cabinet service .... 11m 29d (359 days)

Carlisle, John G.   Secretary of the Treasury 41

Date of birth	Sep 5, 1835
Residence	Kentucky
Date of appointment/age	Mar 6, 1893, at age 57
Assumed office/age	Mar 6, 1893, at age 57
Left office/age	Mar 4, 1897, at age 61
President served	Cleveland
Date of death/age	Jul 31, 1910, at age 74
Cabinet service	3y 11m 28d (1,453 days)

Carlucci, Frank Charles, III   Secretary of Defense 16

Date of birth	Oct 18, 1930
Residence	Pennsylvania
Date of appointment/age	Nov 21, 1987, at age 57
Assumed office/age	Nov 21, 1987, at age 57
Left office/age	Jan 20, 1989, at age 58
President served	Reagan
Date of death/age	————
Cabinet service	1y 2m (425 days)

Cass, Lewis   Secretary of War 14

Date of birth	Oct 9, 1782
Residence	Michigan
Date of appointment/age	Aug 1, 1831, at age 48
Assumed office/age	Aug 8, 1831, at age 48
Left office/age	Oct 4, 1836, at age 53
President served	Jackson
Cabinet service	5y 1m 26d

Cass, Lewis   Secretary of State 22

Date of appointment/age	Mar 6, 1857, at age 74
Assumed office/age	Mar 6, 1857, at age 74
Left office/age	Dec 14, 1860, at age 78
President served	Buchanan
Date of death/age	Jun 17, 1866, at age 83
Cabinet service	3y 9m 8d
Total Cabinet service	8y 11m 4d (3,256 days)

Cavazos, Lauro Fred, Jr.   Secretary of Education 4

Date of birth	Jan 4, 1927
Residence	Texas
Date of appointment/age	Sep 20, 1988, at age 61
Confirmed/age	Sep 20, 1988, at age 61
Left office/age	Jan 20, 1989, at age 62
President served	Reagan
Cabinet service	4m

Cavazos, Lauro Fred, Jr.   Secretary of Education 4

Date of appointment/age	Jan 20, 1989, at age 62
Assumed office/age	Jan 20, 1989, at age 62

Left office/age .... Mar 14, 1991, at age 64
President served .... George Herbert Bush
Date of death/age .... — — — — —
Cabinet service 2y 1m 22d
Total cabinet service .... 2y 5m 22d (902 days)

Celebrezze, Anthony J.

Secretary of Health, Education and Welfare 5

Date of birth .... Sep 4, 1910
Residence .... Ohio
Date of appointment/age .... Jul 31, 1962, at age 51
Assumed office/age .... Jul 31, 1962, at age 51
Left office/age .... Nov 22, 1963, at age 53
President served .... Kennedy
Cabinet service 1y 3m 22d

Celebrezze, Anthony J.

Secretary of Health, Education and Welfare 5

Date of appointment/age .... Nov 22, 1963, at age 53
Assumed office/age .... Nov 22, 1963, at age 53
Left office/age .... Aug 17, 1965, at age 54
President served .... Lyndon B. Johnson
Date of death/age .... Oct 30, 1998, at age 88
Cabinet service 1y 8m 25d
Total Cabinet service .... 3y 17d (1,112 days)

Chandler, William E.

Secretary of the Navy 30

Date of birth .... Dec 28, 1835
Residence .... New Hampshire
Date of appointment/age .... Apr 12, 1882, at age 46
Assumed office/age .... Apr 17, 1882, at age 46
Left office/age .... Mar 5, 1885, at age 49
President served .... Arthur
Date of death/age .... Nov 30, 1917, at age 81
Cabinet service .... 2y 10m 16d (1,046 days)

Chandler, Zachariah

Secretary of the Interior 12

Date of birth .... Dec 10, 1813
Residence .... Michigan
Date of appointment/age .... Oct 19, 1875, at age 61
Assumed office/age .... Oct 19, 1875, at age 61
Left office/age .... Mar 11, 1877, at age 63
President served .... Grant
Date of death/age .... Nov 1, 1879, at age 65
Cabinet service .... 1y 4m 20d (505 days)

Chao, Elaine Lan

Secretary of Labor 24

Date of birth .... Mar 26, 1953
Residence .... Kentucky
Date of appointment/age .... Jan 11, 2001, at age 47

Confirmed/age . . . . Jan 29, 2001, at age 47
Left office/age . . . . — — — — —
President served . . . . George Walker Bush
Date of death/age . . . . — — — — —
Cabinet service . . . . — — — — —

Chapin, Roy D.   Secretary of Commerce 6

Date of birth . . . . Feb 23, 1880
Residence . . . . Michigan
Date of appointment/age . . . . Dec 14, 1932, at age 52
Assumed office/age . . . . Dec 14, 1932, at age 52
Left office/age . . . . Mar 3, 1933, at age 53
President served . . . . Hoover
Date of death/age . . . . Feb 16, 1936, at age 55
Cabinet service . . . . 2m 17d (77 days)

Chapman, Oscar L.   Secretary of the Interior 34

Date of birth . . . . Oct 22, 1896
Residence . . . . Colorado
Date of appointment/age . . . . Nov 11, 1949, at age 53
Assumed office/age . . . . Dec 1, 1949, at age 53
Left office/age . . . . Jan 20, 1953, at age 56
President served . . . . Truman
Date of death/age . . . . Feb 8, 1978, at age 81
Cabinet service . . . . 3y 2d (1,097 days)

Chase, Salmon Portland   Secretary of the Treasury 25

Date of birth . . . . Jan 13, 1808
Residence . . . . Ohio
Date of appointment/age . . . . Mar 5, 1861, at age 63
Assumed office/age . . . . Mar 7, 1861, at age 63
Left office/age . . . . Jul 4, 1864, at age 56
President served . . . . Lincoln
Date of death/age . . . . May 7, 1873, at age 65
Cabinet service . . . . 3y 2m 27d (1,182 days)
Other offices held CJ-6

Cheney, Richard B. (Dick)   Secretary of Defense 17

Date of birth . . . . Jan 30, 1941
Residence . . . . Wyoming
Date of appointment/age . . . . Mar 10, 1989, at age 58
Confirmed/age . . . . Mar 17, 1989, at age 58
Left office/age . . . . Jan 20, 1993, at age 62
President served . . . . George Herbert Bush
Date of death/age . . . . — — — — —
Cabinet service . . . . 3y 10m 3d (1,398 days)
Other offices held VP-46

Christopher, Warren Minor   Secretary of State 63

Date of birth . . . . Oct 27, 1925
Residence . . . . California

Date of appointment/age . . . . Dec 22, 1992, at age 67
Assumed office/age . . . . Jan 20, 1993, at age 67
Left office/age . . . . Jan 23, 1997, at age 71
President served . . . . Clinton
Date of death/age . . . . — — — —
Cabinet service . . . . 4y 3d (1,464 days)

Cisneros, Henry Gabriel

Secretary of Housing and Urban Development 10

Date of birth . . . . Jun 11, 1947
Residence . . . . Texas
Date of appointment/age . . . . Jan 21, 1993, at age 45
Assumed office/age . . . . Jan 21, 1993, at age 45
Left office/age . . . . Jan 29, 1997, at age 49
President served . . . . Clinton
Date of death/age . . . . — — — —
Cabinet service . . . . 4y 8d (1,469 days)

Civiletti, Benjamin R.

Attorney General 73

Date of birth . . . . Jul 17, 1935
Residence . . . . Maryland
Date of appointment/age . . . . Jul 20, 1979, at age 44
Assumed office/age . . . . Aug 2, 1979, at age 44
Left office/age . . . . Jan 20, 1981, at age 45
President served . . . . Carter
Date of death/age . . . . — — — —
Cabinet service . . . . 1y 5m 18d (533 days)

Clark, Thomas C.

Attorney General 59

Date of birth . . . . Sep 23, 1899
Residence . . . . Texas
Date of appointment/age . . . . Jun 15, 1945, at age 45
Assumed office/age . . . . Jul 1, 1945, at age 45
Left office/age . . . . Aug 23, 1949, at age 49
President served . . . . Truman
Date of death/age . . . . Jun 13, 1977, at age 78
Cabinet service . . . . 4y 1m 22d (1,513 days)
Other offices held AJ-80

Clark, William Patrick

Secretary of the Interior 44

Date of birth . . . . Oct 23, 1931
Residence . . . . California
Date of appointment/age . . . . Oct 13, 1983, at age 51
Assumed office/age . . . . Nov 21, 1983, at age 52
Left office/age . . . . Feb 7, 1985, at age 53
President served . . . . Reagan
Date of death/age . . . . — — — —
Cabinet service . . . . 1y 2m 17d (442 days)

Clark, William Ramsey

Attorney General 66

Date of birth . . . . Dec 18, 1927
Residence . . . . Texas

Date of appointment/age . . . . Feb 28, 1967, at age 39
Assumed office/age . . . . Mar 2, 1967, at age 39
Left office/age . . . . Jan 20, 1969, at age 41
President served . . . . Lyndon B. Johnson
Date of death/age . . . . ————
Cabinet service . . . . 1y 10m 2d (667 days)

Clay, Henry   Secretary of State 9

Date of birth . . . . Apr 12, 1777
Residence . . . . Kentucky
Date of appointment/age . . . . Mar 7, 1825, at age 47
Assumed office/age . . . . Mar 7, 1825, at age 47
Left office/age . . . . Mar 3, 1829, at age 51
President served . . . . John Q. Adams
Date of death/age . . . . Jun 29, 1852, at age 75
Cabinet service . . . . 3y 11m 24d (1,449 days)

Clayton, John Middleton   Secretary of State 18

Date of birth . . . . Jul 24, 1796
Residence . . . . Delaware
Date of appointment/age . . . . Mar 7, 1849, at age 52
Assumed office/age . . . . Mar 7, 1849, at age 52
Left office/age . . . . Jul 9, 1850, at age 53
President served . . . . Taylor
Cabinet service 1y 4m 2d

Clayton, John Middleton   Secretary of State 18

Date of appointment/age . . . . Jul 9, 1850, at age 53
Assumed office/age . . . . Jul 9, 1850, at age 53
Left office/age . . . . July 22, 1850, at age 53
President served . . . . Fillmore
Date of death/age . . . . Nov 9, 1856, at age 60
Cabinet service 13d
Total Cabinet service . . . . 1y 4m 15d (500 days)

Clifford, Clark McAdams   Secretary of Defense 9

Date of birth . . . . Dec 25, 1906
Residence . . . . Maryland
Date of appointment/age . . . . Jan 19, 1968, at age 61
Assumed office/age . . . . Mar 1, 1968, at age 61
Left office/age . . . . Jan 20, 1969, at age 62
President served . . . . Lyndon B. Johnson
Date of death/age . . . . Oct 10, 1998, at age 91
Cabinet service . . . . 10m 19d (319 days)

Clifford, Nathan   Attorney General 19

Date of birth . . . . Aug 18, 1803
Residence . . . . Maine
Date of appointment/age . . . . Oct 17, 1846, at age 43
Assumed office/age . . . . Oct 17, 1846, at age 43
Left office/age . . . . Mar 18, 1848, at age 44

President served . . . . Polk
Date of death/age . . . . Jul 25, 1881, at age 77
Cabinet service . . . . ly 5m 1d (516 days)
Other offices held AJ-31

Cobb, Howell   Secretary of the Treasury 22

Date of birth . . . . Sep 7, 1815
Residence . . . . Georgia
Date of appointment/age . . . . Mar 6, 1857, at age 41
Assumed office/age . . . . Mar 6, 1857, at age 41
Left office/age . . . . Dec 9, 1860, at age 45
President served . . . . Buchanan
Date of death/age . . . . Oct 9, 1868, at age 53
Cabinet service . . . . 3y 9m 3d (1,368 days)

Cohen, Wilbur Joseph   Secretary of Health,
                                         Education and Welfare 7

Date of birth . . . . Jun 10, 1913
Residence . . . . Michigan
Date of appointment/age . . . . Mar 23, 1968, at age 55
Assumed office/age . . . . May 4, 1968, at age 55
Left office/age . . . . Jan 20, 1969, at age 55
President served . . . . Lyndon B. Johnson
Date of death/age . . . . May 18, 1987, at age 73
Cabinet service . . . . 9m 28d (298 days)

Cohen, William Sebastian   Secretary of Defense 20

Date of birth . . . . Aug 28, 1940
Residence . . . . Maine
Date of appointment/age . . . . Jan 24, 1997, at age 56
Confirmed/age . . . . Jan 24, 1997, at age 56
Left office/age . . . . Jan 20, 2001, at age 60
President served . . . . Clinton
Date of death/age . . . . — — — —
Cabinet service . . . . 3y 11m 27d (1,452 days)

Colby, Bainbridge   Secretary of State 43

Date of birth . . . . Dec 22, 1869
Residence . . . . New York
Date of appointment/age . . . . Mar 22, 1920, at age 50
Assumed office/age . . . . Mar 23, 1920, at age 50
Left office/age . . . . Mar 3, 1921, at age 51
President served . . . . Wilson
Date of death/age . . . . Apr 11, 1950, at age 80
Cabinet service . . . . 11m 20d (350 days)

Coleman, William Thaddeus, Jr.   Secretary of Transportation 4

Date of birth . . . . Jul 7, 1920
Residence . . . . Pennsylvania
Date of appointment/age . . . . Jan 15, 1975, at age 54
Sworn in/age . . . . Mar 7, 1975, at age 54
Left office/age . . . . Jan 20, 1977, at age 56

President served . . . . Ford
Date of death/age . . . . — — — — —
Cabinet service . . . . 1y 10m 16d (681 days)

Collamer, Jacob   Postmaster General 13

Date of birth . . . . Jan 8, 1791
Residence . . . . Vermont
Date of appointment/age . . . . Mar 8, 1849, at age 58
Assumed office/age . . . . Mar 8, 1849, at age 58
Left office/age . . . . Jul 22, 1850, at age 59
President served . . . . Taylor
Date of death/age . . . . Nov 9, 1865, at age 74
Cabinet service . . . . 1y 4m 14d (499 days)

Colman, Norman J.   Secretary of Agriculture 1

Date of birth . . . . May 16, 1827
Residence . . . . Missouri
Date of appointment/age . . . . Feb 13, 1889, at age 61
Assumed office/age . . . . Feb 13, 1889, at age 61
Left office/age . . . . Mar 6, 1889, at age 61
President served . . . . Cleveland
Date of death/age . . . . Nov 3, 1911, at age 84
Cabinet service . . . . 21d (21 days)

Connally, John Bowden, Jr.   Secretary of the Treasury 61

Date of birth . . . . Feb 27, 1917
Residence . . . . Texas
Date of appointment/age . . . . Dec 14, 1970, at age 53
Assumed office/age . . . . Feb 11, 1971, at age 53
Left office/age . . . . May 16, 1972, at age 54
President served . . . . Nixon
Date of death/age . . . . Jun 15, 1993, at age 76
Cabinet service . . . . 1y 3m 5d (460 days)

Connor, John T.   Secretary of Commerce 17

Date of birth . . . . Nov 3, 1914
Residence . . . . New Jersey
Date of appointment/age . . . . Jan 18, 1965, at age 50
Assumed office/age . . . . Jan 18, 1965, at age 50
Left office/age . . . . May 22, 1967, at age 52
President served . . . . Lyndon B. Johnson
Date of death/age . . . . Oct 6, 2000, at age 85
Cabinet service . . . . 2y 4m 4d (854 days)

Conrad, Charles M.   Secretary of War 23

Date of birth . . . . Dec 24, 1804
Residence . . . . Louisiana
Date of appointment/age . . . . Aug 15, 1850, at age 45
Assumed office/age . . . . Aug 15, 1850, at age 45
Left office/age . . . . Mar 6, 1853, at age 48
President served . . . . Fillmore

Date of death/age .... Feb 11, 1878, at age 73
Cabinet service .... 2y 6m 19d (929 days)

Cortelyou, George B.

Secretary of Commerce and Labor 1

Date of birth .... Jul 26, 1862
Residence .... New York
Date of appointment/age .... Feb 16, 1903, at age 40
Assumed office/age .... Feb 16, 1903, at age 40
Left office/age .... Jun 30, 1904, at age 41
President served .... Theodore Roosevelt
Cabinet service 1y 4m 14d

Cortelyou, George B.

Postmaster General 42

Date of appointment/age .... Mar 6, 1905, at age 42
Assumed office/age .... Mar 6, 1905, at age 42
Left office/age .... Mar 3, 1907, at age 44
President served .... Theodore Roosevelt
Cabinet service 1y 11m 27d

Cortelyou, George B.

Secretary of the Treasury 44

Date of appointment/age .... Jan 15, 1907, at age 44
Assumed office/age .... Mar 4, 1907, at age 44
Left office/age .... Mar 7, 1909, at age 46
President served .... Theodore Roosevelt
Date of death/age .... Oct 23, 1940, at age 78
Cabinet service 2y 3d
Total Cabinet service .... 5y 4m 14d (1,960 days)

Corwin, Thomas

Secretary of the Treasury 20

Date of birth .... Jul 29, 1794
Residence .... Ohio
Date of appointment/age .... Jul 23, 1850, at age 55
Assumed office/age .... Jul 23, 1850, at age 55
Left office/age .... Mar 6, 1853, at age 58
President served .... Fillmore
Date of death/age .... Dec 18, 1865, at age 71
Cabinet service .... 2y 7m 11d (951 days)

Cox, Jacob D.

Secretary of the Interior 10

Date of birth .... Oct 27, 1828
Residence .... Ohio
Date of appointment/age .... Mar 1869, at age 40
Assumed office/age .... Mar 9, 1869, at age 40
Left office/age .... Oct 31, 1870, at age 42
President served .... Grant
Date of death/age .... Aug 8, 1900, at age 71
Cabinet service .... 1y 7m 22d (597 days)

Crawford, George W.   Secretary of War 22

Date of birth . . . . Dec 22, 1798
Residence . . . . Georgia
Date of appointment/age . . . . Mar 8, 1849, at age 50
Assumed office/age . . . . Mar 14, 1849, at age 50
Left office/age . . . . Jul 22, 1850, at age 51
President served . . . . Taylor
Date of death/age . . . . Jul 22, 1872, at age 73
Cabinet service . . . . 1y 4m 8d (493 days)

Crawford, William Harris   Secretary of War 9

Date of birth . . . . Feb 24, 1772
Residence . . . . Georgia
Date of appointment/age . . . . Aug 1, 1815, at age 43
Assumed office/age . . . . Aug 8, 1815, at age 43
Left office/age . . . . Oct 21, 1816, at age 44
President served . . . . Madison
Cabinet service 1y 2m 13d

Crawford, William Harris   Secretary of the Treasury 7

Date of appointment/age . . . . Oct 22, 1816, at age 44
Assumed office/age . . . . Oct 22, 1816, at age 44
Left office/age . . . . Mar 3, 1817, at age 45
President served . . . . Madison
Cabinet service 4m 9d

Crawford, William Harris   Secretary of the Treasury 7

Date of appointment/age . . . . Mar 5, 1817, at age 45
Assumed office/age . . . . Mar 5, 1817, at age 45
Left office/age . . . . Mar 3, 1825, at age 53
President served . . . . Monroe
Date of death/age . . . . Sep 15, 1834, at age 62
Cabinet service 7y 11m 28d
Total Cabinet service . . . . 10y 10m 28d (3,980 days)

Creswell, John A.J.   Postmaster General 23

Date of birth . . . . Nov 18, 1828
Residence . . . . Maryland
Date of appointment/age . . . . Mar 5, 1869, at age 40
Assumed office/age . . . . Mar 5, 1869, at age 40
Left office/age . . . . Jul 6, 1874, at age 45
President served . . . . Grant
Date of death/age . . . . Dec 23, 1891, at age 63
Cabinet service . . . . 5y 4m 1d (1,947 days)

Crittenden, John J.   Attorney General 15

Date of birth . . . . Sep 10, 1787
Residence . . . . Kentucky
Date of appointment/age . . . . Mar 5, 1841, at age 53
Assumed office/age . . . . Mar 5, 1841, at age 53
Left office/age . . . . Apr 4, 1841, at age 53

President served . . . . William H. Harrison
Cabinet service 1m

Crittenden, John J.   Attorney General 15

Date of appointment/age . . . . Apr 4, 1841, at age 53
Assumed office/age . . . . Apr 4, 1841, at age 53
Left office/age . . . . Sep 11, 1841, at age 54
President served . . . . Tyler
Cabinet service 5m 7d

Crittenden, John J.   Attorney General 22

Date of appointment/age . . . . Jul 22, 1850, at age 62
Assumed office/age . . . . Aug 14, 1850, at age 62
Left office/age . . . . Mar 6, 1853, at age 65
President served . . . . Fillmore
Date of death/age . . . . Jul 26, 1863, at age 75
Cabinet service 2y 6m 20d
Total cabinet service . . . . 3y 27d (1,122 days)

Crowninshield, Benjamin W.   Secretary of the Navy 5

Date of birth . . . . Dec 27, 1772
Residence . . . . Massachusetts
Date of appointment/age . . . . Dec 19, 1814, at age 41
Assumed office/age . . . . Jan 16, 1815, at age 42
Left office/age . . . . Mar 3, 1817, at age 44
President served . . . . Madison
Cabinet service 2y 1m 15d

Crowninshield, Benjamin W.   Secretary of the Navy 5

Date of appointment/age . . . . Mar 4, 1817, at age 44
Assumed office/age . . . . Mar 4, 1817, at age 44
Left office/age . . . . Sep 30, 1818, at age 45
President served . . . . Monroe
Date of death/age . . . . Feb 3, 1851, at age 78
Cabinet service 1y 6m 26d
Total Cabinet service . . . . 3y 8m 11d (1,346 days)

Cummings, Homer S.   Attorney General 55

Date of birth . . . . Apr 30, 1870
Residence . . . . Connecticut
Date of appointment/age . . . . Mar 4, 1933, at age 62
Assumed office/age . . . . Mar 4, 1933, at age 62
Left office/age . . . . Jan 1, 1939, at age 68
President served . . . . Franklin D. Roosevelt
Date of death/age . . . . Sep 10, 1956, at age 86
Cabinet service . . . . 5y 9m 28d (2,124 days)

Cuomo, Andrew M.

Secretary of Housing and Urban Development 11

Date of birth .... Dec 6, 1957
Residence .... New York
Date of appointment/age .... Jan 29, 1997, at age 39
Confirmed/age .... Jan 29, 1997, at age 39
Left office/age .... Jan 20, 2001, at age 43
President served .... Clinton
Date of death/age .... — — — —
Cabinet service .... 3y 11m 22d (1,447 days)

Cushing, Caleb

Attorney General 23

Date of birth .... Jan 17, 1800
Residence .... Massachusetts
Date of appointment/age .... Mar 7, 1853, at age 53
Assumed office/age .... Mar 7, 1853, at age 53
Left office/age .... Mar 10, 1857, at age 57
President served .... Pierce
Date of death/age .... Jan 2, 1879, at age 78
Cabinet service .... 4y 3d (1,464 days)

Daley, William M.

Secretary of Commerce 33

Date of birth .... Aug 9, 1948
Date of appointment/age .... Jan 30, 1997, at age 48
Assumed office/age .... Jan 30, 1997, at age 48
Left office/age .... Jun 15, 2000, at age 52
President served .... Clinton
Date of death/age .... — — — —
Cabinet service .... 3y 4m 16d (1,231 days)

Dallas, Alexander J.

Secretary of the Treasury 6

Date of birth .... Jun 21, 1759
Residence .... Pennsylvania
Date of appointment/age .... Oct 6, 1814, at age 55
Assumed office/age .... Oct 14, 1814, at age 55
Left office/age .... Oct 21, 1816, at age 57
President served .... Madison
Date of death/age .... Jan 16, 1817, at age 57
Cabinet service .... 2y 7d (737 days)

Daniels, Josephus

Secretary of the Navy 41

Date of birth .... May 18, 1862
Residence .... North Carolina
Date of appointment/age .... Mar 5, 1913, at age 50
Assumed office/age .... Mar 5, 1913, at age 50
Left office/age .... Mar 4, 1921, at age 58
President served .... Wilson
Date of death/age .... Jan 15, 1948, at age 85
Cabinet service .... 8y (2,922 days)

Daugherty, Harry M.

Attorney General 51

Date of birth .... Jan 26, 1860
Residence .... Ohio

Date of appointment/age . . . . Mar 5, 1921, at age 61
Assumed office/age . . . . Mar 5, 1921, at age 61
Left office/age . . . . Aug 2, 1923, at age 63
President served . . . . Harding
Date of death/age . . . . Oct 12, 1941, at age 81
Cabinet service 2y 4m 28d

Daugherty, Harry M.   Attorney General 51

Date of birth . . . . Jan 26, 1860
Date of appointment/age . . . . Aug 2, 1923, at age 63
Assumed office/age . . . . Aug 2, 1923, at age 63
Left office/age . . . . Apr 8, 1924, at age 64
President served . . . . Coolidge
Date of death . . . . Oct 12, 1941, at age 81
Cabinet service 8m 6d
Total Cabinet service . . . . 3y 1m 4d (1,129 days)

Davis, Dwight F.   Secretary of War 51

Date of birth . . . . Jul 5, 1879
Residence . . . . Missouri
Date of appointment/age . . . . Oct 13, 1925, at age 46
Assumed office/age . . . . Oct 14, 1925, at age 46
Left office/age . . . . Mar 5, 1929, at age 49
President served . . . . Coolidge
Date of death/age . . . . Nov 28, 1945, at age 66
Cabinet service . . . . 3y 4m 19d (1,234 days)

Davis, James J.   Secretary of Labor 2

Date of birth . . . . Oct 27, 1873
Residence . . . . Pennsylvania
Date of appointment/age . . . . Mar 5, 1921, at age 47
Assumed office/age . . . . Mar 5, 1921, at age 47
Left office/age . . . . Aug 2, 1923, at age 49
President served . . . . Harding
Cabinet service 2y 4m 28d

Davis, James J.   Secretary of Labor 2

Date of appointment/age . . . . Aug 2, 1923, at age 49
Assumed office/age . . . . Aug 2, 1923, at age 49
Left office/age . . . . Mar 3, 1929, at age 55
President served . . . . Coolidge
Cabinet service 5y 7m 1d

Davis, James J.   Secretary of Labor 2

Date of appointment/age . . . . Mar 3, 1929, at age 55
Assumed office/age . . . . Mar 3, 1929, at age 55
Left office/age . . . . Dec 8, 1930, at age 57
President served . . . . Hoover
Date of death/age . . . . Nov 22, 1947, at age 74
Cabinet service 1y 9m 5d
Total Cabinet service . . . . 9y 9m 4d (3,561 days)

Davis, Jefferson   Secretary of War 24

Date of birth .... Jun 3, 1808
Residence .... Mississippi
Date of appointment/age .... Mar 7, 1853, at age 44
Assumed office/age .... Mar 7, 1853, at age 44
Left office/age .... Mar 2, 1857, at age 48
President served .... Pierce
Date of death/age .... Dec 6, 1889, at age 81
Cabinet service .... 3y 11m 25d (1,450 days)

Day, James Edward   Postmaster General 55

Date of birth .... Oct 11, 1914
Residence .... California
Date of appointment/age .... Jan 21, 1961, at age 46
Assumed office/age .... Jan 21, 1961, at age 46
Left office/age .... Sep 29, 1963, at age 48
President served .... Kennedy
Date of death/age .... Oct 29, 1996, at age 75
Cabinet service .... 2y 8m 8d (978 days)

Day, William Rufus   Secretary of State 36

Date of birth .... Apr 17, 1849
Residence .... Ohio
Date of appointment/age .... Apr 26, 1898, at age 49
Assumed office/age .... Apr 28, 1898, at age 49
Left office/age .... Sep 16, 1898, at age 49
President served .... McKinley
Date of death/age .... Jul 9, 1923, at age 74
Cabinet service .... 4m 19d (139 days)
Other offices held AJ-55

Dearborn, Henry   Secretary of War 5

Date of birth .... Feb 23, 1751
Residence .... Massachusetts
Date of appointment/age .... Mar 5, 1801, at age 50
Assumed office/age .... Mar 5, 1801, at age 50
Left office/age .... Feb 16, 1809, at age 57
President served .... Jefferson
Date of death/age .... Jun 6, 1829, at age 78
Cabinet service .... 7y 11m 11d (2,897 days)

Delano, Columbus O.   Secretary of the Interior 11

Date of birth .... Jun 5, 1809
Residence .... Ohio
Date of appointment/age .... Nov 1, 1870, at age 61
Assumed office/age .... Nov 1, 1870, at age 61
Left office/age .... Sep 30, 1875, at age 65
President served .... Grant
Date of death/age .... Oct 23, 1896, at age 87
Cabinet service .... 4y 10m 29d (1,790 days)

Denby, Edwin — Secretary of the Navy 42

Date of birth	Feb 18, 1870
Residence	Michigan
Date of appointment/age	Mar 5, 1921, at age 51
Assumed office/age	Mar 5, 1921, at age 51
Left office/age	Aug 2, 1923, at age 53
President served	Harding
Cabinet service	2y 4m 28d

Denby, Edwin — Secretary of the Navy 42

Date of appointment/age	Aug 2, 1923, at age 53
Assumed office/age	Aug 2, 1923, at age 53
Left office/age	Mar 17, 1924, at age 54
President served	Coolidge
Date of death	Feb 8, 1929, at age 58
Cabinet service	7m 15d
Total Cabinet service	3y 13d (1,108 days)

Dennison, William — Postmaster General 21

Date of birth	Nov 23, 1815
Residence	Ohio
Date of appointment/age	Sep 24, 1864, at age 48
Assumed office/age	Oct 1, 1864, at age 48
Left office/age	Jul 16, 1866, at age 50
President served	Lincoln
Date of death/age	Jun 15, 1882, at age 66
Cabinet service	1y 9m 15d (650 days)

Dent, Frederick Bailey — Secretary of Commerce 22

Date of birth	Aug 17, 1922
Residence	South Carolina
Date of appointment/age	Jan 18, 1973, at age 50
Assumed office/age	Feb 2, 1973, at age 50
Left office/age	Aug 9, 1974, at age 51
President served	Nixon
Cabinet service	1y 6m 7d

Dent, Frederick Bailey — Secretary of Commerce 22

Date of appointment/age	Aug 9, 1974, at age 51
Assumed office/age	Aug 9, 1974, at age 51
Left office/age	Mar 26, 1975, at age 52
President served	Ford
Date of death/age	— — — —
Cabinet service	7m 17d
Total Cabinet service	2y 2m 19d (809 days)

Dern, George H. — Secretary of War 54

Date of birth	Sep 8, 1872
Residence	Utah

Date of appointment/age . . . . Mar 4, 1933, at age 60
Assumed office/age . . . . Mar 4, 1933, at age 60
Left office/age . . . . Aug 27, 1936, at age 63
President served . . . . Franklin D. Roosevelt
Date of death/age . . . . Aug 27, 1936, at age 63
Cabinet service . . . . 3y 5m 23d (1,268 days)

Derwinski, Edward J.   Secretary of Veterans Affairs 1

Date of birth . . . . Sep 15, 1926
Residence . . . . Illinois
Date of appointment/age . . . . Mar 2, 1989, at age 62
Confirmed/age . . . . Mar 15, 1989, at age 62
Left office/age . . . . Oct 26, 1992, at age 66
President served . . . . George Herbert Bush
Date of death/age . . . . —————
Cabinet service . . . . 3y 7m 11d (1,316 days)

Devens, Charles   Attorney General 35

Date of birth . . . . Apr 4, 1820
Residence . . . . Massachusetts
Date of appointment/age . . . . Mar 10, 1877, at age 56
Assumed office/age . . . . Mar 12, 1877, at age 56
President served . . . . Hayes
Left office/age . . . . Mar 6, 1881, at age 60
Date of death/age . . . . Jan 7, 1891, at age 70
Cabinet service . . . . 3y 11m 24d (1,449 days)

Dexter, Samuel   Secretary of War 4

Date of birth . . . . May 14, 1761
Residence . . . . Massachusetts
Date of appointment/age . . . . May 13, 1800, at age 38
Assumed office/age . . . . Jun 12, 1800, at age 39
Left office/age . . . . Dec 31, 1800, at age 39
President served . . . . John Adams
Cabinet service 6m 19d

Dexter, Samuel   Secretary of the Treasury 3

Date of appointment/age . . . . Jan 1, 1801, at age 39
Assumed office/age . . . . Jan 1, 1801, at age 39
Left office/age . . . . Mar 4, 1801, at age 39
President served . . . . John Adams
Cabinet service 2m 3d

Dexter, Samuel   Secretary of the Treasury 3

Date of appointment/age . . . . Mar 4, 1801, at age 39
Assumed office/age . . . . Mar 4, 1801, at age 39

Left office/age .... May 6, 1801, at age 39
President served .... Jefferson
Date of death/age .... May 4, 1816, at age 54
Cabinet service 2m 2d
Total Cabinet service .... 10m 24d (324 days)

Dickerson, Mahlon   Secretary of the Navy 10

Date of birth .... April 17, 1770
Residence .... New Jersey
Date of appointment/age .... Jun 30, 1834, at age 64
Assumed office/age .... Jun 30, 1834, at age 64
Left office/age .... Mar 4, 1837, at age 66
President served .... Jackson
Cabinet service 2y 6m 4d

Dickerson, Mahlon   Secretary of the Navy 10

Date of appointment/age .... Mar 4, 1837, at age 66
Assumed office/age .... Mar 4, 1837, at age 66
Left office/age .... Jun 30, 1838, at age 68
President served .... Van Buren
Date of death/age .... Oct 5, 1853, at age 83
Cabinet service 1y 3m 26d
Total Cabinet service .... 3y 10m (1,395 days)

Dickinson, Donald M.   Postmaster General 34

Date of birth .... Jan 17, 1846
Residence .... Michigan
Date of appointment/age .... Jan 16, 1888, at age 41
Assumed office/age .... Jan 16, 1888, at age 41
Left office/age .... Mar 4, 1889, at age 43
President served .... Cleveland
Date of death/age .... Oct 15, 1917, at age 71
Cabinet service .... 1y 1m 16d (411 days)

Dickinson, Jacob M.   Secretary of War 46

Date of birth .... Jan 30, 1851
Residence .... Tennessee
Date of appointment/age .... Mar 5, 1909, at age 58
Assumed office/age .... Mar 5, 1909, at age 58
Left office/age .... May 21, 1911, at age 60
President served .... Taft
Date of death/age .... Dec 13, 1928, at age 77
Cabinet service .... 2y 2m 9d (799 days)

Dillon, Clarence Douglas   Secretary of the Treasury 57

Date of birth .... Aug 21, 1909
Residence .... New Jersey
Date of appointment/age .... Jan 21, 1961, at age 51
Assumed office/age .... Jan 21, 1961, at age 51
Left office/age .... Nov 22, 1963, at age 54

President served .... Kennedy
Cabinet service 2y 10m 1d

Dillon, Clarence Douglas   Secretary of the Treasury 57

Date of appointment/age .... Nov 22, 1963, at age 54
Assumed office/age .... Nov 22, 1963, at age 54
Left office/age .... Mar 31, 1965, at age 55
President served .... Lyndon B. Johnson
Date of death/age .... — — — —
Cabinet service 1y 4m 9d
Total Cabinet service .... 4y 2m 10d (1,531 days)

Dix, John A.   Secretary of the Treasury 24

Date of birth .... Jul 24, 1798
Residence .... New York
Date of appointment/age .... Jan 11, 1861, at age 62
Assumed office/age .... Jan 15, 1861, at age 62
Left office/age .... Mar 4, 1861, at age 62
President served .... Buchanan
Date of death/age .... Apr 21, 1879, at age 80
Cabinet service .... 1m 17d (47 days)

Doak, William N.   Secretary of Labor 3

Date of birth .... Dec 12, 1882
Residence .... Virginia
Date of appointment/age .... Dec 8, 1930, at age 47
Assumed office/age .... Dec 9, 1930, at age 47
Left office/age .... Mar 3, 1933, at age 50
President served .... Hoover
Date of death/age .... Oct 23, 1933, at age 50
Cabinet service .... 2y 2m 22d (812 days)

Dobbin, James C.   Secretary of the Navy 22

Date of birth .... Jan 17, 1814
Residence .... North Carolina
Date of appointment/age .... Mar 7, 1853, at age 39
Assumed office/age .... Mar 7, 1853, at age 39
Left office/age .... Mar 5, 1857, at age 43
President served .... Pierce
Date of death/age .... Aug 4, 1857, at age 43
Cabinet service .... 3y 11m 28d (1,453 days)

Dole, Elizabeth Hanford   Secretary of Transportation 8

Date of birth .... Jul 29, 1936
Residence .... North Carolina
Date of appointment/age .... Jan 6, 1983, at age 46
Confirmed/age .... Feb 7, 1983, at age 46
Left office/age .... Dec 3, 1987, at age 51
President served .... Reagan
Cabinet service 4y 9m 26d

Dole, Elizabeth Hanford   Secretary of Labor 20

Date of appointment/age . . . . Jan 25, 1989, at age 52
Assumed office/age . . . . Jan 25, 1989, at age 52
Left office/age . . . . Nov 23, 1990, at age 54
President served . . . . George Herbert Bush
Date of death/age . . . . — — — —
Cabinet service 1y 9m 28d
Total Cabinet service . . . . 6y 7m 24d (2,425 days)

Donaldson, Jesse Monroe   Postmaster General 53

Date of birth . . . . Aug 17, 1885
Residence . . . . Missouri
Date of appointment/age . . . . Dec 16, 1947, at age 62
Assumed office/age . . . . Dec 16, 1947, at age 62
Left office/age . . . . Jan 20, 1953, at age 67
President served . . . . Truman
Date of death/age . . . . Mar 25, 1970, at age 84
Cabinet service . . . . 5y 1m 4d (1,860 days)

Donovan, Raymond James   Secretary of Labor 17

Date of birth . . . . Aug 31, 1930
Residence . . . . New Jersey
Date of appointment/age . . . . Dec 16, 1980, at age 50
Confirmed/age . . . . Feb 3, 1981, at age 50
Left office/age . . . . Apr 29, 1985, at age 54
President served . . . . Reagan
Date of death/age . . . . — — — —
Cabinet service . . . . 4y 2m 26d (1,547 days)

Duane, William J.   Secretary of the Treasury 11

Date of birth . . . . May 9, 1780
Residence . . . . Pennsylvania
Date of appointment/age . . . . May 29, 1833, at age 53
Assumed office/age . . . . Jun 1, 1833, at age 53
Left office/age . . . . Sep 22, 1833, at age 53
President served . . . . Jackson
Date of death/age . . . . Sep 26, 1865, at age 85
Cabinet service . . . . 3m 21d (111 days)

Dulles, John Foster   Secretary of State 52

Date of birth . . . . Feb 25, 1888
Residence . . . . New York
Date of appointment/age . . . . Jan 21, 1953, at age 64
Assumed office/age . . . . Jan 21, 1953, at age 64
Left office/age . . . . Apr 21, 1959, at age 71
President served . . . . Eisenhower
Date of death/age . . . . May 24, 1959, at age 71
Cabinet service . . . . 6y 3m (2,281 days)

Duncan, Charles William, Jr.   Secretary of Energy 2

Date of birth . . . . Sep 9, 1926
Residence . . . . Wyoming

Date of appointment/age . . . . Jul 21, 1979, at age 52
Assumed office/age . . . . Jul 31, 1979, at age 52
Left office/age . . . . Jan 20, 1981, at age 54
President served . . . . Carter
Date of death/age . . . . — — — — —
Cabinet service . . . . 1y 5m 20d (535 days)

Dunlop, John Thomas   Secretary of Labor 14

Date of birth . . . . Jul 5, 1914
Residence . . . . California
Date of appointment/age . . . . Feb 9, 1975, at age 60
Assumed office/age . . . . Mar 18, 1975, at age 60
Left office/age . . . . Jan 31, 1976, at age 61
President served . . . . Ford
Date of death/age . . . . — — — — —
Cabinet service . . . . 10m 13d (313 days)

Durkin, Martin P.   Secretary of Labor 7

Date of birth . . . . Mar 18, 1894
Residence . . . . Illinois
Date of appointment/age . . . . Jan 21, 1953, at age 58
Assumed office/age . . . . Jan 21, 1953, at age 58
Left office/age . . . . Oct 8, 1953, at age 59
President served . . . . Eisenhower
Date of death/age . . . . Nov 13, 1955, at age 61
Cabinet service . . . . 8m 17d (257 days)

Eagleburger, Lawrence Sidney   Secretary of State (acting)

Date of birth . . . . Aug 1, 1930
Residence . . . . Florida
Date of appointment/age . . . . Aug 23, 1992, at age 62
Assumed office/age . . . . Aug 23, 1992, at age 62
Left office/age . . . . Dec 8, 1992, at age 62
President served . . . . George Herbert Bush
Cabinet service 3m 15d

Eagleburger, Lawrence Sidney   Secretary of State 62

Date of appointment/age . . . . Dec 8, 1992, at age 62
Assumed office/age . . . . Dec 8, 1992, at age 62
Left office/age . . . . Jan 19, 1993, at age 62
President served . . . . George Herbert Bush
Date of death/age . . . . — — — — —
Cabinet service 1m 11d
Total Cabinet service . . . . 4m 26d (146 days)

Eaton, John H.   Secretary of War 13

Date of birth . . . . Jun 18, 1790
Residence . . . . Tennessee
Date of appointment/age . . . . Mar 9, 1829, at age 38
Assumed office/age . . . . Mar 9, 1829, at age 38
Left office/age . . . . Jun 19, 1831, at age 41
President served . . . . Jackson

Date of death/age .... Nov 17, 1856, at age 66
Cabinet service .... 2y 3m 10d (830 days)

Edison, Charles   Secretary of the Navy 46

Date of birth .... Aug 3, 1890
Residence .... New Jersey
Date of appointment/age .... Jan 11, 1940, at age 49
Assumed office/age .... Jan 11, 1940, at age 49
Left office/age .... Jul 9, 1940, at age 49
President served .... Franklin D. Roosevelt
Date of death/age .... Jul 31, 1969, at age 78
Cabinet service .... 5m 28d (178 days)

Edwards, James Burrows   Secretary of Energy 3

Date of birth .... Jun 24, 1927
Residence .... South Carolina
Date of appointment/age .... Dec 23, 1980, at age 53
Assumed office/age .... Jan 21, 1981, at age 53
Left office/age .... Nov 5, 1982, at age 55
President served .... Reagan
Date of death/age .... — — — —
Cabinet service .... 1y 9m 13d (648 days)

Elkins, Stephen B.   Secretary of War 40

Date of birth .... Sep 26, 1841
Residence .... West Virginia
Date of appointment/age .... Dec 22, 1891, at age 50
Assumed office/age .... Dec 24, 1891, at age 50
Left office/age .... Mar 5, 1893, at age 51
President served .... Benjamin Harrison
Date of death/age .... Jan 4, 1911, at age 69
Cabinet service .... 1y 2m 9d (434 days)

Endicott, William C.   Secretary of War 38

Date of birth .... Nov 19, 1826
Residence .... Massachusetts
Date of appointment/age .... Mar 6, 1885, at age 58
Assumed office/age .... Mar 6, 1885, at age 58
Left office/age .... Mar 4, 1889, at age 62
President served .... Cleveland
Date of death/age .... May 6, 1900, at age 73
Cabinet service .... 3y 11m 28d (1,453 days)

Espy, Mike   Secretary of Agriculture 25

Date of birth .... Nov 30, 1953
Residence .... Mississippi
Date of appointment/age .... Jan 21, 1993, at age 39
Assumed office/age .... Jan 21, 1993, at age 39
Left office/age .... Dec 31, 1994, at age 41
President served .... Clinton
Date of death/age .... — — — —
Cabinet service .... 1y 11m 10d (705 days)

Eustis, William   Secretary of War 6

Date of birth .... Jun 10, 1753
Residence .... Massachusetts
Date of appointment/age .... Mar 7, 1809, at age 55
Assumed office/age .... Apr 8, 1809, at age 55
Left office/age .... Dec 31, 1812, at age 59
President served .... Madison
Date of death/age .... Feb 6, 1825, at age 71
Cabinet service .... 3y 8m 23d (1,358 days)

Evans, Donald Louis   Secretary of Commerce 35

Date of birth .... Jul 27, 1946
Residence .... Texas
Date of appointment/age .... Dec 20, 2000, at age 54
Assumed office/age .... Jan 20, 2001, at age 54
Left office/age .... — — — — —
President served .... George Walker Bush
Date of death/age .... — — — — —
Cabinet service .... — — — — —

Evarts, William M.   Attorney General 29

Date of birth .... Feb 6, 1818
Residence .... New York
Date of appointment/age .... Jul 15, 1868, at age 50
Assumed office/age .... Jul 20, 1868, at age 50
Left office/age .... Mar 4, 1869, at age 51
President served .... Andrew Johnson
Cabinet service 7m 12d

Evarts, William M.   Secretary of State 27

Date of appointment/age .... Mar 12, 1877, at age 59
Assumed office/age .... Mar 12, 1877, at age 59
Left office/age .... Mar 3, 1881, at age 63
President served .... Hayes
Cabinet service 3y 11m 24d

Evarts, William M.   Secretary of State 27

Date of appointment/age .... Mar 4, 1881, at age 63
Assumed office/age .... Mar 4, 1881, at age 63
Left office/age .... Mar 5, 1881, at age 63
President served .... Garfield
Date of death/age .... Feb 28, 1901, at age 83
Cabinet service 1d
Total Cabinet service .... 4y 7m 7d (1,678 days)

Everett, Edward   Secretary of State 20

Date of birth .... Apr 11, 1794
Residence .... Massachusetts
Date of appointment/age .... Nov 6, 1852, at age 58
Assumed office/age .... Nov 6, 1852, at age 58
Left office/age .... Mar 3, 1853, at age 58

President served .... Fillmore
Date of death/age .... Jan 15, 1865, at age 70
Cabinet service .... 3m 25d (115 days)

Ewing, Thomas   Secretary of the Treasury 14

Date of birth .... Dec 28, 1789
Residence .... Ohio
Date of appointment/age .... Mar 5, 1841, at age 51
Assumed office/age .... Mar 5, 1841, at age 51
Left office/age .... Apr 4, 1841, at age 51
President served .... William Henry Harrison
Cabinet service 1m

Ewing, Thomas   Secretary of the Treasury 14

Date of appointment/age .... Apr 4, 1841, at age 51
Assumed office/age .... Apr 4, 1841, at age 51
Left office/age .... Sep 13, 1841, at age 51
President served .... Tyler
Cabinet service 1m 13d

Ewing, Thomas   Secretary of the Interior 1

Date of appointment/age .... Mar 8, 1849, at age 59
Assumed office/age .... Mar 8, 1849, at age 59
Left office/age .... Jul 22, 1850, at age 60
President served .... Taylor
Date of death/age .... Oct 26, 1871, at age 81
Cabinet service 1y 4m 14d
Total Cabinet service .... 1y 6m 27d (572 days)

Fairchild, Charles S.   Secretary of the Treasury 38

Date of birth .... Apr 30, 1842
Residence .... New York
Date of appointment/age .... Apr 1, 1887, at age 44
Assumed office/age .... Apr 1, 1887, at age 44
Left office/age .... Mar 6, 1889, at age 46
President served .... Cleveland
Date of death/age .... Nov 24, 1924, at age 82
Cabinet service .... 1y 11m 5d (700 days)

Fall, Albert B.   Secretary of the Interior 28

Date of birth .... Nov 26, 1861
Residence .... New Mexico
Date of appointment/age .... Mar 5, 1921, at age 59
Assumed office/age .... Mar 5, 1921, at age 59
Left office/age .... Mar 4, 1923, at age 61
President served .... Harding
Date of death/age .... Nov 30, 1944, at age 83
Cabinet service .... 2y (730 days)

Farley, James A.   Postmaster General 50

Date of birth .... May 30, 1888
Residence .... New York

Date of appointment/age . . . . Mar 4, 1933, at age 44
Assumed office/age . . . . Mar 4, 1933, at age 44
Left office/age . . . . Sep 9, 1940, at age 52
President served . . . . Franklin D. Roosevelt
Date of death/age . . . . Jun 9, 1976, at age 88
Cabinet service . . . . 7y 6m 5d (2,741 days)

Fessenden, William P.   Secretary of the Treasury 26

Date of birth . . . . Oct 16, 1806
Residence . . . . Maine
Date of appointment/age . . . . Jul 1, 1864, at age 57
Assumed office/age . . . . Jul 5, 1864, at age 57
Left office/age . . . . Mar 3, 1865, at age 58
President served . . . . Lincoln
Date of death/age . . . . Sep 8, 1869, at age 62
Cabinet service . . . . 7m 26d (236 days)

Finch, Robert Hutchinson   Secretary of Health, Education and Welfare 8

Date of birth . . . . Oct 9, 1925
Residence . . . . California
Date of appointment/age . . . . Jan 20, 1969, at age 43
Assumed office/age . . . . Jan 29, 1969, at age 43
Left office/age . . . . Jun 6, 1970, at age 44
President served . . . . Nixon
Date of death/age . . . . Oct 10, 1995, at age 70
Cabinet service . . . . 1y 4m 15d (500 days)

Fish, Hamilton   Secretary of State 26

Date of birth . . . . Aug 3, 1808
Residence . . . . New York
Date of appointment/age . . . . Mar 11, 1869, at age 60
Assumed office/age . . . . Mar 17, 1869, at age 60
Left office/age . . . . Mar 3, 1877, at age 68
President served . . . . Grant
Cabinet service 7y 11m 14d

Fish, Hamilton   Secretary of State 26

Date of appointment/age . . . . Mar 4, 1877, at age 68
Assumed office/age . . . . Mar 4, 1877, at age 68
Left office/age . . . . Mar 11, 1877, at age 68
President served . . . . Hayes
Date of death/age . . . . Sep 6, 1893, at age 85
Cabinet service 7d
Total Cabinet service . . . . 7y 11m 21d (2,907 days)

Fisher, Walter L.   Secretary of the Interior 25

Date of birth . . . . Jul 4, 1862
Residence . . . . Illinois
Date of appointment/age . . . . Mar 7, 1911, at age 48

Assumed office/age .... Mar 7, 1911, at age 48
Left office/age .... Mar 4, 1913, at age 50
President served .... Taft
Date of death/age .... Nov 9, 1939, at age 73
Cabinet service .... 1y 11m 25d (720 days)

Flemming, Arthur Sherwood

Secretary of Health, Education and Welfare 3

Date of birth .... Jun 12, 1905
Residence .... Ohio
Date of appointment/age .... Aug 1, 1958, at age 53
Assumed office/age .... Aug 1, 1958, at age 53
Left office/age .... Jan 20, 1961, at age 55
President served .... Eisenhower
Date of death/age .... Sep 7, 1996, at age 90
Cabinet service .... 2y 5m 19d (899 days)

Floyd, John B.

Secretary of War 25

Date of birth .... Jun 1, 1806
Residence .... Virginia
Date of appointment/age .... Mar 6, 1857, at age 50
Assumed office/age .... Mar 6, 1857, at age 50
Left office/age .... Jan 17, 1861, at age 54
President served .... Buchanan
Date of death/age .... Aug 26, 1863, at age 57
Cabinet service .... 3y 10m 11d (1,406 days)

Folger, Charles J.

Secretary of the Treasury 34

Date of birth .... Apr 16, 1818
Residence .... New York
Date of appointment/age .... Oct 27, 1881, at age 63
Assumed office/age .... Nov 14, 1881, at age 63
Left office/age .... Sep 4, 1884, at age 66
President served .... Arthur
Date of death/age .... Sep 4, 1884, at age 66
Cabinet service .... 2y 9m 21d (1,021 days)

Folsom, Marion B.

Secretary of Health, Education and Welfare 2

Date of birth .... Nov 23, 1893
Residence .... New York
Date of appointment/age .... Aug 1, 1955, at age 61
Assumed office/age .... Aug 1, 1955, at age 61
Left office/age .... Jul 31, 1958, at age 64
President served .... Eisenhower
Date of death/age .... Sep 28, 1976, at age 82
Cabinet service .... 3y (1,095 days)

Forrestal, James V.

Secretary of the Navy 48

Date of birth .... Feb 15, 1892
Residence .... New York

Date of appointment/age . . . . May 18, 1944, at age 52
Assumed office/age . . . . May 18, 1944, at age 52
Left office/age . . . . Apr 12, 1945, at age 53
President served . . . . Franklin D. Roosevelt
Cabinet service 10m 25d

Forrestal, James V.   Secretary of the Navy 48

Date of appointment/age . . . . Apr 12, 1945, at age 53
Assumed office/age . . . . Apr 12, 1945, at age 53
Left office/age . . . . Sep 17, 1947, at age 55
President served . . . . Truman
Cabinet service 2y 5m 5d

Forrestal, James V.   Secretary of Defense 1

Date of appointment/age . . . . Aug 21, 1947, at age 55
Assumed office/age . . . . Sep 17, 1947, at age 55
Left office/age . . . . Mar 22, 1949, at age 57
President served . . . . Truman
Date of death/age . . . . May 22, 1949, at age 57
Cabinet service 1y 6m 5d
Total Cabinet service . . . . 4y 10m 5d (1,766 days)

Forsyth, John   Secretary of State 13

Date of birth . . . . Oct 22, 1780
Residence . . . . Georgia
Date of appointment/age . . . . Jun 27, 1834, at age 53
Assumed office/age . . . . Jul 31, 1834, at age 53
Left office/age . . . . Mar 4, 1837, at age 56
President served . . . . Jackson
Cabinet service 2y 8m 4d

Forsyth, John   Secretary of State 13

Date of appointment/age . . . . Mar 4, 1837, at age 56
Assumed office/age . . . . Mar 4, 1837, at age 56
Left office/age . . . . Mar 4, 1841, at age 60
President served . . . . Van Buren
Date of death/age . . . . Oct 21, 1841, at age 60
Cabinet service 4y
Total Cabinet service . . . . 6y 8m 4d (2,435 days)

Forward, Walter   Secretary of the Treasury 15

Date of birth . . . . Jan 24, 1786
Residence . . . . Pennsylvania
Date of appointment/age . . . . Sep 13, 1841, at age 55
Assumed office/age . . . . Sep 13, 1841, at age 55
Left office/age . . . . Feb 28, 1843, at age 57
President served . . . . Tyler
Date of death/age . . . . Nov 24, 1852, at age 66
Cabinet service . . . . 1y 5m 15d (530 days)

Foster, Charles   Secretary of the Treasury 40

Date of birth .... Apr 12, 1828
Residence .... Ohio
Date of appointment/age .... Feb 24, 1891, at age 62
Assumed office/age .... Feb 24, 1891, at age 62
Left office/age .... Mar 5, 1893, at age 64
President served .... Benjamin Harrison
Date of death/age .... Jan 9, 1904, at age 75
Cabinet service .... 2y 9d (739 days)

Foster, John W.   Secretary of State 32

Date of birth .... Mar 2, 1836
Residence .... Indiana
Date of appointment/age .... Jun 29, 1892, at age 56
Assumed office/age .... Jun 29, 1892, at age 56
Left office/age .... Feb 22, 1896, at age 59
President served .... Benjamin Harrison
Date of death/age .... Nov 15, 1917, at age 81
Cabinet service .... 7m 24d (234 days)

Fowler, Henry Hamill   Secretary of the Treasury 58

Date of birth .... Sep 5, 1908
Residence .... Virginia
Date of appointment/age .... Apr 1, 1965, at age 56
Assumed office/age .... Apr 1, 1965, at age 56
Left office/age .... Dec 20, 1968, at age 60
President served .... Lyndon B. Johnson
Date of death/age .... Jan 3, 2000, at age 91
Cabinet service .... 3y 8m 19d (1,354 days)

Francis, David R.   Secretary of the Interior 20

Date of birth .... Oct 1, 1850
Residence .... Missouri
Date of appointment/age .... Sep 1, 1896, at age 45
Assumed office/age .... Sep 4, 1896, at age 45
Left office/age .... Mar 4, 1897, at age 46
President served .... Cleveland
Date of death/age .... Jan 15, 1927, at age 76
Cabinet service .... 6m (180 days)

Franklin, Barbara Hackman   Secretary of Commerce 30

Date of birth .... Mar 19, 1940
Residence .... Pennsylvania
Appointed/age .... Feb 27, 1992, at age 51
Assumed office/age .... Feb 27, 1992, at age 51
Left office/age .... Jan 20, 1993, at age 52
President served .... George Herbert Bush
Date of death/age .... — — — —
Cabinet service .... 10m 24d (324 days)

Freeman, Orville Lothrop   Secretary of Agriculture 16

Date of birth .... May 9, 1918
Residence .... Minnesota

Date of appointment/age . . . . Jan 21, 1961, at age 42
Assumed office/age . . . . Jan 21, 1961, at age 42
Left office/age . . . . Nov 22, 1963, at age 45
President served . . . . Kennedy
Cabinet service 2y 10m 1d

Freeman, Orville Lothrop   Secretary of Agriculture 16

Date of appointment/age . . . . Nov 22, 1963, at age 45
Assumed office/age . . . . Nov 22, 1963, at age 45
Left office/age . . . . Jan 20, 1969, at age 50
President served . . . . Lyndon B. Jonson
Date of death/age . . . . — — — —
Cabinet service 5y 5y 1m 29d
Total Cabinet service . . . . 8y (2,922 days)

Frelinghuysen, Frederick T.   Secretary of State 29

Date of birth . . . . Aug 4, 1817
Residence . . . . New Jersey
Date of appointment/age . . . . Dec 12, 1881, at age 64
Assumed office/age . . . . Dec 19, 1881, at age 64
Left office/age . . . . Mar 5, 1885, at age 67
President served . . . . Arthur
Cabinet service 3y 2m 14d

Frelinghuysen, Frederick T.   Secretary of State 29

Date of appointment/age . . . . Mar 4, 1885, at age 67
Assumed office/age . . . . Mar 4, 1885, at age 67
Left office/age . . . . May 20, 1885, at age 67
President served . . . . Cleveland
Date of death/age . . . . May 20, 1885, at age 67
Cabinet service 2m 16d
Total Cabinet service . . . . 3y 5m (1,245 days)

Gage, Lyman J.   Secretary of the Treasury 42

Date of birth . . . . Jun 28, 1836
Residence . . . . Illinois
Date of appointment/age . . . . Mar 5, 1897, at age 60
Assumed office/age . . . . Mar 5, 1897, at age 60
Left office/age . . . . Sep 14, 1901, at age 65
President served . . . . McKinley
Cabinet service 4y 6m 9d

Gage, Lyman J.   Secretary of the Treasury 42

Date of appointment/age . . . . Sep 14, 1901, at age 65
Assumed office/age . . . . Sep 14, 1901, at age 65
Left office/age . . . . Jan 30, 1902, at age 65
President served . . . . Theodore Roosevelt
Date of death/age . . . . Jan 26, 1927, at age 90

Cabinet service 4m 26d
Total Cabinet service .... 4y 11m 5d (1,796 days)

Gallatin, Albert   Secretary of the Treasury 4

Date of birth .... Jan 29, 1761
Residence .... Pennsylvania
Date of appointment/age .... May 14, 1801, at age 40
Assumed office/age .... May 15, 1801, at age 40
Left office/age .... Mar 4, 1809, at age 48
President served .... Jefferson
Cabinet service 7y 9m 17d

Gallatin, Albert   Secretary of the Treasury 4

Date of appointment/age .... Mar 4, 1809, at age 48
Assumed office/age .... Mar 4, 1809, at age 48
Left office/age .... Feb 8, 1814, at age 53
President served .... Madison
Date of death/age .... Aug 12, 1849, at age 88
Cabinet service 4y 11m 4d
Total Cabinet service .... 12y 8m 21d (4,644 days)

Gardner, John W.   Secretary of Health, Education and Welfare 6

Date of birth .... Oct 8, 1912
Residence .... New York
Date of appointment/age .... Jul 27, 1965, at age 52
Assumed office/age .... Aug 18, 1965, at age 52
Left office/age .... Mar 1, 1968, at age 55
President served .... Lyndon B. Johnson
Date of death/age .... — — — —
Cabinet service .... 2y 6m 11d (921 days)

Garfield, James R.   Secretary of the Interior 23

Date of birth .... Oct 17, 1865
Residence .... Ohio
Date of appointment/age .... Jan 15, 1907, at age 41
Assumed office/age .... Mar 4, 1907, at age 41
Left office/age .... Mar 5, 1909, at age 43
President served .... Theodore Roosevelt
Date of death/age .... Mar 24, 1950, at age 84
Cabinet service .... 2y 1d (731 days)

Garland, Augustus H.   Attorney General 38

Date of birth .... Jun 11, 1832
Residence .... Arkansas
Date of appointment/age .... Mar 6, 1885, at age 52
Assumed office/age .... Mar 9, 1885, at age 52
Left office/age .... Mar 4, 1889, at age 56
President served .... Cleveland

Date of death/age .... Jan 26, 1899, at age 66
Cabinet service .... 3y 11m 26d (1,451 days)

Garrison, Lindley M.   Secretary of War 48

Date of birth .... Nov 28, 1864
Residence .... New Jersey
Date of appointment/age .... Mar 5, 1913, at age 48
Assumed office/age .... Mar 5, 1913, at age 48
Left office/age .... Feb 11, 1916, at age 51
President served .... Wilson
Date of death/age .... Oct 19, 1932, at age 67
Cabinet service .... 2y 11m 6d (1,066 days)

Gary, James Albert   Postmaster General 38

Date of birth .... Oct 22, 1833
State of birth .... Connecticut
State of residence .... Maryland
Date of appointment/age .... Mar 5, 1897, at age 63
Assumed office/age .... Mar 5, 1897, at age 63
Left office/age .... Apr 20, 1898, at age 64
President served .... McKinley
Date of death/age .... Oct 31, 1920, at age 87
Cabinet service .... 1y 1m 15d (410 days)

Gates, Thomas Sovereign, Jr.   Secretary of Defense 7

Date of birth .... Apr 10, 1906
Residence .... Pennsylvania
Date of appointment/age .... Dec. 2, 1959, at age 53
Assumed office/age .... Dec. 2, 1959, at age 53
Left office/age .... Jan. 20, 1961, at age 54
President served .... Eisenhower
Date of death/age .... Mar 25, 1983, at age 76
Cabinet service .... 1y 1m 18d (413 days)

Gilmer, Thomas W.   Secretary of the Navy 15

Date of birth .... Apr 6, 1802
Residence .... Virginia
Date of appointment/age .... Feb 15, 1844, at age 41
Assumed office/age .... Feb 19, 1844, at age 41
Left office/age .... Feb 28, 1844, at age 41
President served .... Tyler
Date of death/age .... Feb 28, 1844, at age 41
Cabinet service .... 9d (9 days)

Gilpin, Henry D.   Attorney General 14

Date of birth .... Apr 14, 1801
Residence .... Pennsylvania
Date of appointment/age .... Jan 11, 1840, at age 38
Assumed office/age .... Jan 11, 1840, at age 38
Left office/age .... Mar 3, 1841, at age 39
President served .... Van Buren

Date of death/age .... Jan 29, 1860, at age 58
Cabinet service .... 1y 1m 20d (415 days)

Glass, Carter   Secretary of the Treasury 47

Date of birth .... Jan 4, 1858
Residence .... Virginia
Date of appointment/age .... Dec 6, 1918, at age 60
Assumed office/age .... Dec 16, 1918, at age 60
Left office/age .... Feb 1, 1920, at age 62
President served .... Wilson
Date of death/age .... May 28, 1946, at age 88
Cabinet service .... 1y 1m 16d (411 days)

Glickman, Daniel Robert   Secretary of Agriculture 26

Date of birth .... Nov 24, 1944
Residence .... Kansas
Date of appointment/age .... Mar 31, 1995, at age 50
Assumed office/age .... Mar 31, 1995, at age 50
Left office/age .... Jan 20, 2001, at age 56
President served .... Clinton
Date of death/age .... — — — —
Cabinet service .... 4y 9m 20d (1,751 days)

Gober, Hershel W.   Secretary of Veterans Affairs (acting)

Date of birth .... Dec 21, 1936
Residence .... Arkansas
Date of appointment/age .... July 25, 2000, at age 63
Assumed office/age .... July 25, 2000, at age 63
Left office/age .... Jan 20, 2001, at age 64
President served .... Clinton
Date of death/age .... — — — —
Cabinet service .... 5m 26d (176 days)

Goff, Nathan, Jr.   Secretary of the Navy 28

Date of birth .... Feb 9, 1843
Residence .... West Virginia
Date of appointment/age .... Jan 6, 1881, at age 37
Assumed office/age .... Jan 6, 1881, at age 37
Left office/age .... Mar 6, 1881, at age 38
President served .... Hayes
Date of death/age .... Apr 24, 1920, at age 77
Cabinet service .... 2m (60 days)

Goldberg, Arthur Joseph   Secretary of Labor 9

Date of birth .... Aug 8, 1908
Residence .... Illinois
Date of appointment/age .... Jan 21, 1961, at age 52
Assumed office/age .... Jan 21, 1961, at age 52
Left office/age .... Sep 24, 1962, at age 54
President served .... Kennedy

Date of death/age .... Jan 19, 1990, at age 81
Cabinet service .... 1y 8m 3d (608 days)
Other offices held AJ-87

Goldschmidt, Neil E.   Secretary of Transportation 6

Date of birth .... Jun 16, 1940
Residence .... Oregon
Date of appointment/age .... Jul 28, 1979, at age 39
Assumed office/age .... Sep 22, 1979, at age 39
Left office/age .... Jan 20, 1981, at age 40
President served .... Carter
Date of death/age .... — — — — —
Cabinet service .... 1y 3m 28d (483 days)

Good, James W.   Secretary of War 52

Date of birth .... Sep 24, 1866
Residence .... Illinois
Date of appointment/age .... Mar 5, 1929, at age 62
Assumed office/age .... Mar 6, 1929, at age 62
Left office/age .... Nov 11, 1929, at age 63
President served .... Hoover
Date of death/age .... Nov 11, 1929, at age 63
Cabinet service .... 8m 3d (243 days)

Gore, Howard M.   Secretary of Agriculture 8

Date of birth .... Oct 12, 1887
Residence .... West Virginia
Date of appointment/age .... Nov 21, 1924, at age 37
Assumed office/age .... Nov 22, 1924, at age 37
Left office/age .... Mar 4, 1925, at age 37
President served .... Coolidge
Date of death/age .... Jun 20, 1947, at age 60
Cabinet service .... 3m 10d (100 days)

Graham, William A.   Secretary of the Navy 20

Date of birth .... Sep 5, 1804
Residence .... North Carolina
Date of appointment/age .... Jul 22, 1850, at age 45
Assumed office/age .... Aug 2, 1850, at age 45
Left office/age .... Jul 25, 1852, at age 47
President served .... Fillmore
Date of death/age .... Aug 11, 1875, at age 70
Cabinet service .... 1y 11m 23d (718 days)

Granger, Francis   Postmaster General 10

Date of birth .... Dec 1, 1792
State of birth .... Connecticut
State of residence .... New York
Date of appointment/age .... Mar 6, 1841, at age 48
Assumed office/age .... Mar 8, 1841, at age 48
Left office/age .... Sep 13, 1841, at age 48
President served .... Tyler

Date of death/age .... Aug 28, 1868, at age 75
Cabinet service .... 6m 5d (185 days)

Granger, Gideon   Postmaster General 4

Date of birth .... Jul 19, 1767
Residence .... New York
Date of appointment/age .... Nov 28, 1801, at age 34
Assumed office/age .... Nov 28, 1801, at age 34
Left office/age .... Mar 4, 1809, at age 41
President served .... Jefferson
Cabinet service 7y 3m 4d

Granger, Gideon   Postmaster General 4

Date of appointment/age .... Mar 4, 1809, at age 41
Assumed office/age .... Mar 4, 1809, at age 41
Left office/age .... Apr 10, 1814, at age 46
President served .... Madison
Date of death/age .... Dec 31, 1822, at age 55
Cabinet service 5y 1m 6d
Total Cabinet service .... 12y 4m 10d (4,513 days)

Gregory, Thomas W.   Attorney General 49

Date of birth .... Nov 6, 1861
Residence .... Texas
Date of appointment/age .... Aug 29, 1914, at age 52
Assumed office/age .... Sep 3, 1914, at age 52
Left office/age .... Mar 4, 1919, at age 57
President served .... Wilson
Date of death/age .... Feb 26, 1933, at age 71
Cabinet service .... 4y 6m 1d (1,642 days)

Gresham, Walter Q.   Postmaster General 31

Date of birth .... Mar 17, 1832
Residence .... Indiana
Date of appointment/age .... Apr 3, 1883, at age 51
Assumed office/age .... Apr 11, 1883, at age 51
Left office/age .... Sep 24, 1884, at age 52
President served .... Arthur
Cabinet service 1y 5m 13d

Gresham, Walter Q.   Secretary of the Treasury 35

Date of appointment/age .... Sep 24, 1884, at age 52
Assumed office/age .... Oct 28, 1884, at age 52
Left office/age .... Oct 28, 1884, at age 52
President served .... Arthur
Cabinet service 1m 3d

Gresham, Walter Q.   Secretary of State 33

Date of appointment/age .... Mar 6, 1893, at age 60
Assumed office/age .... Mar 6, 1893, at age 60

Left office/age .... May 28, 1895, at age 63
President served .... Cleveland
Date of death/age .... May 28, 1895, at age 63
Cabinet service 2y 2m 22d
Total Cabinet service .... 3y 9m 8d (1,373 days)
Offices held .... PG (31), TY (35), ST (33)

Griggs, John W.   Attorney General 43

Date of birth .... Jul 10, 1849
Residence .... New Jersey
Date of appointment/age .... Jan 25, 1898, at age 48
Assumed office/age .... Feb 1, 1898, at age 48
Left office/age .... Mar 31, 1901, at age 51
President served .... McKinley
Date of death/age .... Nov 28, 1927, at age 78
Cabinet service .... 3y 2m (1,155 days)

Gronouski, John Austin   Postmaster General 56

Date of birth .... Oct 26, 1919
Residence .... Wisconsin
Date of appointment/age .... Sep 30, 1963, at age 43
Assumed office/age .... Sep 30, 1963, at age 43
Left office/age .... Nov 2, 1965, at age 46
President served .... Lyndon B. Johnson
Date of death/age .... Jan 7, 1996, at age 76
Cabinet service .... 2y 1m 3d (763 days)

Grundy, Felix   Attorney General 13

Date of birth .... Sep 11, 1777
Residence .... Tennessee
Date of appointment/age .... Jul 5, 1838, at age 60
Assumed office/age .... Sep 1, 1838, at age 60
Left office/age .... Jan 10, 1840, at age 62
President served .... Van Buren
Date of death/age .... Dec 19, 1840, at age 63
Cabinet service .... 1y 4m 9d (494 days)

Guthrie, James   Secretary of the Treasury 21

Date of birth .... Dec 5, 1792
Residence .... Kentucky
Date of appointment/age .... Mar 7, 1853, at age 60
Assumed office/age .... Mar 7, 1853, at age 60
Left office/age .... Mar 5, 1857, at age 64
President served .... Pierce
Date of death/age .... Mar 13, 1869, at age 76
Cabinet service .... 3y 11m 28d (1,453 days)

Habersham, Joseph   Postmaster General 3

Date of birth .... Jul 28, 1751
Residence .... Georgia
Date of appointment/age .... Feb 25, 1795, at age 43

Assumed office/age .... Feb 25, 1795, at age 43
Left office/age .... Mar 3, 1797, at age 45
President served .... Washington
Cabinet service .... 2y 6d (736 days)

Habersham, Joseph   Postmaster General 3

Date of appointment/age .... Mar 4, 1797, at age 45
Assumed office/age .... Mar 4, 1797, at age 45
Left office/age .... Mar 3, 1801, at age 49
President served .... John Adams
Cabinet service .... 4y (1, 461 days)

Habersham, Joseph   Postmaster General 3

Date of appointment/age .... Mar 4, 1801, at age 49
Assumed office/age .... Mar 4, 1801, at age 49
Left office/age .... Nov 27, 1801, at age 50
President served .... Jefferson
Date of death/age .... Nov 17, 1815, at age 64
Cabinet service .... 8m 23d (263 days)
Total Cabinet service .... 6y 8m 29d (2,460 days)

Haig, Alexander Meigs, Jr.   Secretary of State 59

Date of birth .... Dec 2, 1924
Residence .... Connecticut
Date of appointment/age .... Dec 17, 1980, at age 56
Assumed office/age .... Jan 22, 1981, at age 56
Left office/age .... Jun 26, 1982, at age 57
President served .... Reagan
Date of death/age .... — — — —
Cabinet service .... 1y 5m 4d (519 days)

Hall, Nathan Kelsey   Postmaster General 14

Date of birth .... Mar 28, 1810
Residence .... New York
Date of appointment/age .... Jul 23, 1850, at age 40
Assumed office/age .... Jul 23, 1850, at age 40
Left office/age .... Aug 31, 1852, at age 42
President served .... Fillmore
Date of death/age .... Mar 2, 1874, at age 63
Cabinet service .... 2y 1m 21d (781 days)

Hamilton, Alexander   Secretary of the Treasury 1

Date of birth .... Jan 11, 1757
Residence .... New York
Date of appointment/age .... Sep 11, 1789, at age 32
Assumed office/age .... Sep 11, 1789, at age 32
Left office/age .... Feb 1, 1795, at age 38
President served .... Washington
Date of death/age .... Jul 12, 1804, at age 47
Cabinet service .... 5y 4m 21d (1,967 days)

Hamilton, Paul — Secretary of the Navy 3

Date of birth	Oct 16, 1762
Residence	South Carolina
Date of appointment/age	Mar 7, 1809, at age 46
Assumed office/age	May 15, 1809, at age 46
Left office/age	Dec 31, 1812, at age 50
President served	Madison
Date of death/age	Jun 30, 1816, at age 53
Cabinet service	3y 7m 16d (1,321 days)

Hannegan, Robert Emmet — Postmaster General 52

Date of birth	Jun 30, 1903
Residence	Missouri
Date of appointment/age	May 8, 1945, at age 41
Assumed office/age	Jul 1, 1945, at age 42
Left office/age	Dec 15, 1947, at age 44
President served	Truman
Date of death/age	Oct 6, 1949 at ag e46
Cabinet service	2y 5m 14d (894 days)

Hardin, Clifford — Secretary of Agriculture 17

Date of birth	Oct 9, 1915
Residence	Indiana
Date of appointment/age	Jan 20, 1969, at age 53
Assumed office/age	Jan 22, 1969, at age 53
Left office/age	Nov 11, 1971, at age 56
President served	Nixon
Date of death/age	— — — —
Cabinet service	2y 9m 19d (1,019 days)

Harlan, James — Secretary of the Interior 8

Date of birth	Aug 26, 1820
Residence	Iowa
Date of appointment/age	May 15, 1865, at age 44
Assumed office/age	May 15, 1865, at age 44
Left office/age	Aug 31, 1866, at age 46
President served	Andrew Johnson
Date of death/age	Oct 5, 1899, at age 75
Cabinet service	1y 3m 16d (471 days)

Harmon, Judson — Attorney General 41

Date of birth	Feb 3, 1846
Residence	Ohio
Date of appointment/age	Jun 8, 1895, at age 49
Assumed office/age	Jun 11, 1895, at age 49
Left office/age	Mar 6, 1897, at age 51
President served	Cleveland
Date of death/age	Feb 22, 1927, at age 81
Cabinet service	1y 8m 23d (628 days)

Harriman, William Averell — Secretary of Commerce 11

Date of birth	Nov 15, 1891
Residence	New York

Date of appointment/age . . . . Jan 28, 1947, at age 55
Assumed office/age . . . . Jan 28, 1947, at age 55
Left office/age . . . . May 5, 1948, at age 56
President served . . . . Truman
Date of death/age . . . . Jul 26, 1986, at age 94
Cabinet service . . . . 1y 3m 7d (462 days)

Harris, Patricia Roberts   Secretary of Housing and
                                                 Urban Development 6

Date of birth . . . . May 31, 1924
State of birth . . . . Illinois
Residence . . . . Washington, D.C.
Date of appointment/age . . . . Dec 22, 1976, at age 52
Assumed office/age . . . . Jan 21, 1977, at age 52
Left office/age . . . . Aug 4, 1979, at age 55
President served . . . . Carter
Cabinet service 2y 6m 14d

Harris, Patricia Roberts   Secretary of Health,
                                                 Education and Welfare 13

Date of appointment/age . . . . Jul 20, 1979, at age 55
Assumed office/age . . . . Aug 4, 1979, at age 55
Left office/age . . . . Oct 18, 1979, at age 55
President served . . . . Carter
Cabinet service 2m 14d

Harris, Patricia Roberts   Secretary of Health and
                                                 Human Services 1

Date of appointment/age . . . . Oct 18, 1979, at age 55
Assumed office/age . . . . Oct 18, 1979, at age 55
Left office/age . . . . Jan 20, 1981, at age 56
President served . . . . Carter
Date of death/age . . . . Mar 23, 1985, at age 60
Cabinet service 1y 3m 2d
Total Cabinet service . . . . 4y (1,461 days)
Offices held . . . . HD (6), HW (13), HH (1)

Hathaway, Stanley Knapp   Secretary of the Interior 40

Date of birth . . . . Jul 19, 1924
Residence . . . . Wyoming
Date of appointment/age . . . . Apr 4, 1975, at age 50
Assumed office/age . . . . Jun 12, 1975, at age 50
Left office/age . . . . Jul 25, 1975, at age 51
President served . . . . Ford
Date of death/age . . . . — — — —
Cabinet service . . . . 1m 13d (43 days)

Hatton, Frank   Postmaster General (interim)

Date of birth . . . . Apr 28, 1846
Residence . . . . Iowa
Date of appointment/age . . . . Mar 26, 1883, at age 36
Assumed office/age . . . . Mar 26, 1883, at age 36
Left office/age . . . . Apr 10, 1883, at age 36

President served . . . . Arthur
Cabinet service 15d

Hatton, Frank   Postmaster General (interim)

Date of appointment/age . . . . Sep 25, 1884, at age 38
Assumed office /age . . . . Sep 25, 1884, at age 38
Left office/age . . . . Oct 13, 1884, at age 38
President served . . . . Arthur
Cabinet service 18d

Hatton, Frank   Postmaster General 32

Date of appointment/age . . . . Oct 14, 1884, at age 38
Assumed office/age . . . . Oct 14, 1884, at age 38
Left office/age . . . . Mar 3, 1885, at age 38
President served . . . . Arthur
Cabinet service 4m 19d

Hatton, Frank   Postmaster General 32

Date of appointment/age . . . . Mar 4, 1884, at age 38
Assumed office/age . . . . Mar 4, 1884, at age 38
Left office/age . . . . Mar 5, 1884, at age 38
President served . . . . Cleveland
Date of death/age . . . . Apr 30, 1894, at age 48
Cabinet service 1d
Total Cabinet service . . . . 5m 23d (173 days)

Hay, John   Secretary of State 37

Date of birth . . . . Oct 8, 1838
Residence . . . . Washington, D.C.
Date of appointment/age . . . . Sep 20, 1898, at age 59
Assumed office/age . . . . Sep 30, 1898, at age 59
Left office/age . . . . Sep 14, 1901, at age 63
President served . . . . McKinley
Cabinet service 2y 11m 14d

Hay, John   Secretary of State 37

Date of appointment/age . . . . Sep 14, 1901, at age 63
Assumed office/age . . . . Sep 14, 1901, at age 63
Left office/age . . . . Jul 1, 1905, at age 66
President served . . . . Theodore Roosevelt
Date of death/age . . . . Jul 1, 1905, at age 66
Cabinet service 3y 9m 17d
Total Cabinet service . . . . 6y 9m 1d (2,462 days)

Hays, William Harrison   Postmaster General 46

Date of birth . . . . Nov 5, 1879
Residence . . . . Indiana
Date of appointment/age . . . . Mar 5, 1921, at age 41
Assumed office/age . . . . Mar 5, 1921, at age 41
Left office/age . . . . Mar 3, 1922, at age 42
President served . . . . Harding
Date of death/age . . . . Mar 7, 1954, at age 74
Cabinet service . . . . 11m 28d (358 days)

Heckler, Margaret Mary

Secretary of Health and Human Services 3

Date of birth	Jun 21, 1931
Residence	Massachusetts
Date of appointment/age	Jan 12, 1983, at age 51
Assumed office/age	Mar 4, 1983, at age 51
Left office/age	Dec 12, 1985, at age 54
President served	Reagan
Date of death/age	— — — —
Cabinet service	2y 9m 8d (1,008 days)

Henshaw, David

Secretary of the Navy 14

Date of birth	Apr 2, 1791
Residence	Massachusetts
Date of appointment/age	Jul 24, 1843, at age 52
Assumed office/age	Jul 24, 1843, at age 52
Left office/age	Feb 18, 1844, at age 52
President served	Tyler
Date of death/age	Nov 11, 1852, at age 61
Cabinet service	6m 25d (205 days)

Herbert, Hilary A.

Secretary of the Navy 33

Date of birth	Mar 12, 1834
Residence	Alabama
Date of appointment/age	Mar 6, 1893, at age 58
Assumed office/age	Mar 6, 1893, at age 58
Left office/age	Mar 4, 1897, at age 62
President served	Cleveland
Date of death/age	Mar 6, 1919, at age 94
Cabinet service	3y 11m 28d (1,453 days)

Herman, Alexis M.

Secretary of Labor 23

Date of birth	Jul 16, 1947
Place of birth	Alabama
Residence	Washington, D.C.
Date of appointment/age	May 9, 1997, at age 49
Assumed office/age	May 9, 1997, at age 49
Left office/age	Jan 20, 2001, at age 53
President served	Clinton
Date of death/age	— — — —
Cabinet service	2y 8m 11d (981 days)

Herrington, John Stewart

Secretary of Energy 5

Date of birth	May 31, 1939
Residence	California
Date of appointment/age	Jan 10, 1985at age 45
Assumed office/age	Feb 7, 1985, at age 45
Left office/age	Jan 20, 1989, at age 48
President served	Reagan
Date of death/age	— — — —
Cabinet service	3y 11m 13d (1,438 days)

Herter, Christian A.

Secretary of State 53

Date of birth	Mar 28, 1895
Residence	Massachusetts
Date of appointment/age	Apr 22, 1959, at age 64
Assumed office/age	Apr 22, 1959, at age 64
Left office/age	Jan 20, 1961, at age 65
President served	Eisenhower
Date of death/age	Dec 30, 1967, at age 72
Cabinet service	1y 8m 29d (634 days)

Hickel, Walter Joseph

Secretary of the Interior 38

Date of birth	Aug 18, 1919
Residence	Alaska
Date of appointment/age	Jan 20, 1969, at age 49
Assumed office/age	Jan 24, 1969, at age 49
Left office/age	Nov 25, 1970, at age 51
President served	Nixon
Date of death/age	— — — —
Cabinet service	1y 10m 1d (666 days)

Hills, Carla Anderson

Secretary of Housing and Urban Development 5

Date of birth	Jan 3, 1934
Residence	California
Date of appointment/age	Feb 14, 1975, at age 41
Assumed office/age	Mar 6, 1975, at age 41
Left office/age	Jan 20, 1977, at age 43
President served	Ford
Date of death/age	— — — —
Cabinet service	1y 10m 14d (679 days)

Hitchcock, Ethan A.

Secretary of the Interior 22

Date of birth	Sep 19, 1835
Residence	Missouri
Date of appointment/age	Dec 21, 1898, at age 63
Assumed office/age	Feb 20, 1899, at age 63
Left office/age	Sep 14, 1901, at age 65
President served	McKinley
Cabinet service	2y 6m 25d

Hitchcock, Ethan A.

Secretary of the Interior 22

Date of appointment/age	Sep 14, 1901, at age 65
Assumed office/age	Sep 14, 1901, at age 65
Left office/age	Mar 3, 1903, at age 67
President served	Theodore Roosevelt
Date of death/age	Apr 9, 1909, at age 73
Cabinet service	1y 5m 17d
Total Cabinet service	4y 12d (1,473 days)

Hitchcock, Frank Harris

Postmaster General 44

Date of birth	Oct 5, 1869
Residence	Massachusetts

Date of appointment/age . . . . Mar 5, 1909, at age 39
Assumed office/age . . . . Mar 5, 1909, at age 39
Left office/age . . . . Mar 4, 1913, at age 43
President served . . . . Taft
Date of death/age . . . . Aug 5, 1935, at age 65
Cabinet service . . . . 4y (1,461 days)

Hoar, Ebenezer   Attorney General 30

Date of birth . . . . Feb 21, 1816
Residence . . . . Massachusetts
Date of appointment/age . . . . Mar 5, 1869, at age 53
Assumed office/age . . . . Mar 11, 1869, at age 53
Left office/age . . . . Jul 7, 1870, at age 54
President served . . . . Grant
Date of death/age . . . . Jan 31, 1895, at age 79
Cabinet service . . . . 1y 3m 26d (481 days)

Hobby, Oveta Culp   Secretary of Health, Education and Welfare 1

Date of birth . . . . Jan 19, 1905
Residence . . . . Texas
Date of appointment/age . . . . Apr 11, 1953, at age 48
Assumed office/age . . . . Apr 11, 1953, at age 48
Left office/age . . . . Jul 31, 1955, at age 50
President served . . . . Eisenhower
Date of death/age . . . . Aug 16, 1995, at age 90
Cabinet service . . . . 2y 3m 20d (840 days)

Hodel, Donald Paul   Secretary of Energy 4

Date of birth . . . . May 23, 1935
Residence . . . . Oregon
Date of appointment/age . . . . Nov 6, 1982, at age 47
Assumed office/age . . . . Dec 8, 1982, at age 47
Left office/age . . . . Feb 7, 1985, at age 49
President served . . . . Reagan
Cabinet service 2y 2m

Hodel, Donald Paul   Secretary of the Interior 45

Date of appointment/age . . . . Jan 10, 1985, at age 49
Assumed office/age . . . . Feb 7, 1985, at age 49
Left office/age . . . . Jan 20, 1989, at age, at age 53
President served . . . . Reagan
Date of death/age . . . . — — — —
Cabinet service 3y 11m 13d
Total Cabinet service . . . . Gy 1m 13d (2,234 days)

Hodges, Luther H.   Secretary of Commerce 16

Date of birth . . . . Mar 9, 1898
Residence . . . . North Carolina
Date of appointment/age . . . . Jan 21, 1961, at age 62
Assumed office/age . . . . Jan 21, 1961, at age 62
Left office/age . . . . Jan 17, 1965, at age 66
President served . . . . Kennedy

Date of death/age .... Oct 6, 1974, at age 76
Cabinet service .... 3y 11m 27d (1,452 days)

Hodgson, James Day   Secretary of Labor 12

Date of birth .... Dec 3, 1913
Residence .... California
Date of appointment/age .... Jun 10, 1970, at age 56
Assumed office/age .... Jul 2, 1970, at age 56
Left office/age .... Jan 31, 1973, at age 59
President served .... Nixon
Date of death/age .... —————
Cabinet service .... 2y 6m 29d (939 days)

Holt, Joseph   Postmaster General 18

Date of birth .... Jan 6, 1807
Residence .... Kentucky
Date of appointment/age .... Mar 14, 1859, at age 52
Assumed office/age .... Mar 14, 1859, at age 52
Left office/age .... Dec 31, 1860, at age 53
President served .... Buchanan
Cabinet service .... 1y 9m 17d (652 days)

Holt, Joseph   Secretary of War 26 (Interim)

Date of appointment/age .... Jan 18, 1861, at age 54
Assumed office/age .... Jan 18, 1861, at age 54
Left office/age .... Mar 3, 1861, at age 54
President served .... Buchanan
Date of death/age .... Aug 1, 1894, at age 87
Cabinet service .... 1m 13d (43 days)
Total cabinet service .... 1y 11m (695 days)

Hoover, Herbert C.   Secretary of Commerce 3

Date of birth .... Aug 10, 1874
Residence .... California
Date of appointment/age .... Mar 5, 1921, at age 46
Assumed office/age .... Mar 5, 1921, at age 46
Left office/age .... Aug 2, 1923, at age 48
President served .... Harding
Cabinet service 2y 4m 28d

Hoover, Herbert C.   Secretary of Commerce 3

Date of appointment/age .... Aug 2, 1923, at age 48
Assumed office/age .... Aug 2, 1923, at age 48
Left office/age .... Aug 20, 1928, at age 54
President served .... Coolidge
Date of death/age .... Oct 20, 1964, at age 90
Cabinet service 5y 18d
Total Cabinet service .... 7y 5m 16d (2,722 days)
Other offices held PR-31

Hopkins, Harry L.   Secretary of Commerce 8

Date of birth .... Aug 17, 1890
Residence .... New York

Date of appointment/age . . . . Jan 23, 1939, at age 48
Assumed office/age . . . . Jan 23, 1939, at age 48
Left office/age . . . . Sep 18, 1940, at age 50
President served . . . . Franklin D. Roosevelt
Date of death/age . . . . Jan 29, 1946, at age 55
Cabinet service . . . . 1y 7m 26d (601 days)

Houston, David F.   Secretary of Agriculture 5
Date of birth . . . . Feb 17, 1866
Residence . . . . Missouri
Date of appointment/age . . . . Mar 5, 1913, at age 47
Assumed office/age . . . . Mar 6, 1913, at age 47
Left office/age . . . . Feb 1, 1920, at age 53
President served . . . . Wilson
Cabinet service 6y 10m 26d

Houston, David F.   Secretary of the Treasury 48
Date of appointment/age . . . . Jan 31, 1920, at age 53
Assumed office/age . . . . Feb 2, 1920, at age 53
Left office/age . . . . Mar 3, 1921, at age 55
President served . . . . Wilson
Date of death/age . . . . Sep 2, 1940, at age 74
Cabinet service 1y 1m 1d
Total Cabinet service . . . . 7y 11m 27d (2,913 days)

Howe, Timothy Otis   Postmaster General 30
Date of birth . . . . Feb 24, 1816
State of birth . . . . Maine
State of residence . . . . Wisconsin
Date of appointment/age . . . . Dec 20, 1881, at age 65
Assumed office/age . . . . Jan 5, 1882, at age 65
Left office/age . . . . Mar 25, 1883, at age 67
President served . . . . Arthur
Date of death/age . . . . Mar 25, 1883, at age 67
Cabinet service . . . . 1y 2m 20d (445 days)

Hubbard, Samuel Dickinson   Postmaster General 15
Date of birth . . . . Aug 10, 1799
Residence . . . . Connecticut
Date of appointment/age . . . . Aug 31, 1852, at age 53
Assumed office/age . . . . Sep 14, 1852, at age 53
Left office/age . . . . Mar 6, 1853, at age 53
President served . . . . Fillmore
Date of death/age . . . . Oct 8, 1855, at age 56
Cabinet service . . . . 5m 20d (170 days)

Hufstedler, Shirley Mount   Secretary of Education 1
Date of birth . . . . Aug 24, 1925
Residence . . . . California
Date of appointment/age . . . . Oct 30, 1979, at age 54
Assumed office/age . . . . Dec 1, 1979, at age 54
Left office/age . . . . Jan 20, 1981, at age 55
President served . . . . Carter

Date of death/age .... — — — — —
Cabinet service .... 1y 1m 19d (414 days)

Hughes, Charles Evans   Secretary of State 44

Date of birth .... Apr 11, 1862
Residence .... New York
Date of appointment/age .... Mar 4, 1921, at age 58
Assumed office/age .... Mar 5, 1921, at age 58
Left office/age .... Aug 2, 1923, at age 61
President served .... Harding
Cabinet service 2y 4m 28d

Hughes, Charles Evans   Secretary of State 44

Date of appointment/age .... Aug 2, 1923, at age 61
Assumed office/age .... Aug 2, 1923, at age 61
Left office/age .... Mar 4, 1925, at age 62
President served .... Coolidge
Date of death/age .... Aug 27, 1948, at age 86
Cabinet service 1y 7m 2d
Total Cabinet service .... 4y (1,461 days)
Other offices held CJ-11

Hull, Cordell   Secretary of State 47

Date of birth .... Oct 2, 1871
Residence .... Tennessee
Date of appointment/age .... Mar 4, 1933, at age 61
Assumed office/age .... Mar 4, 1933, at age 61
Left office/age .... Nov 30, 1944, at age 73
President served .... Franklin D. Roosevelt
Date of death/age .... Jul 23, 1955, at age 83
Cabinet service .... 11y 8m 26d (4,283 days)

Humphrey, George M.   Secretary of the Treasury 55

Date of birth .... Mar 8, 1890
Residence .... Ohio
Date of appointment/age .... Jan 21, 1953, at age 62
Assumed office/age .... Jan 21, 1953, at age 62
Left office/age .... Jul 28, 1957, at age 67
President served .... Eisenhower
Date of death/age .... Jan 20, 1970, at age 79
Cabinet service .... 4y 6m 7d (1,648 days)

Hunt, William H.   Secretary of the Navy 29

Date of birth .... Jun 12, 1823
Residence .... Louisiana
Date of appointment/age .... Mar 5, 1881, at age 57
Assumed office/age .... Mar 7, 1881, at age 57
Left office/age .... Apr 16, 1882, at age 58
President served .... Hayes
Date of death/age .... Feb 27, 1884, at age 60
Cabinet service .... 1y 1m 9d (404 days)

Hurley, Patrick J.   Secretary of War 53

Date of birth .... Jan 8, 1883
Residence .... Oklahoma
Date of appointment/age .... Dec 9, 1929, at age 46
Assumed office/age .... Dec 9, 1929, at age 46
Left office/age .... Mar 3, 1933, at age 50
President served .... Hoover
Date of death/age .... Jul 30, 1963, at age 80
Cabinet service .... 3y 2m 22d (1,177 days)

Hyde, Arthur M.   Secretary of Agriculture 10

Date of birth .... Jul 12, 1877
Residence .... Missouri
Date of appointment/age .... Mar 5, 1929, at age 51
Assumed office/age .... Mar 6, 1929, at age 51
Left office/age .... Mar 3, 1933, at age 55
President served .... Hoover
Date of death/age .... Oct 17, 1947, at age 70
Cabinet service .... 3y 11m 11d (1,436 days)

Ickes, Harold L.   Secretary of the Interior 32

Date of birth .... Mar 15, 1874
Residence .... Illinois
Date of appointment/age .... Mar 3, 1933, at age 58
Assumed office/age .... Mar 4, 1933, at age 58
Left office/age .... Apr 12, 1945, at age 71
President served .... Roosevelt
Cabinet service 12y 1m 8d

Ickes, Harold L.   Secretary of the Interior 32

Date of appointment/age .... Apr 12, 1945, at age 71
Assumed office/age .... Apr 12, 1945, at age 71
Left office/age .... Feb 15, 1946, at age 71
President served .... Truman
Date of death/age .... Feb 3, 1952, at age 77
Cabinet service 10m 3d
Total Cabinet service .... 12y 11m 11d (4,724 days)

Ingham, Samuel D.   Secretary of the Treasury 9

Date of birth .... Sep 16, 1779
Residence .... Pennsylvania
Date of appointment/age .... Mar 6, 1829, at age 49
Assumed office/age .... Mar 6, 1829, at age 49
Left office/age .... Jun 20, 1831, at age 51
President served .... Jackson
Date of death/age .... Jun 5, 1860, at age 80
Cabinet service .... 2y 3m 14d (834 days)

Jackson, Robert H.   Attorney General 57

Date of birth .... Feb 13, 1892
Residence .... New York
Date of appointment/age .... Jan 18, 1940, at age 47
Assumed office/age .... Jan 18, 1940, at age 47

Left office/age .... Sep 4, 1941, at age 49
President served .... Franklin D. Roosevelt
Date of death/age .... Oct 9, 1954, at age 62
Cabinet service .... 1y 7m 17d (592 days)
Other offices held AJ-77

James, Thomas Lemuel — Postmaster General 29

Date of birth .... Mar 29, 1831
Residence .... New York
Date of appointment/age .... Mar 5, 1881, at age 49
Assumed office/age .... Mar 8, 1881, at age 49
Left office/age .... Jan 4, 1882, at age 50
President served .... Arthur
Date of death/age .... Sep 11, 1916, at age 85
Cabinet service .... 9m 27d (297 days)

Jardine, William M. — Secretary of Agriculture 9

Date of birth .... Jan 16, 1879
Residence .... Kansas
Date of appointment/age .... Feb 18, 1925, at age 46
Assumed office/age .... Mar 5, 1925, at age 46
Left office/age .... Mar 5, 1929, at age 50
President served .... Coolidge
Date of death/age .... Jan 17, 1955, at age 76
Cabinet service .... 4y (1,461 days)

Jefferson, Thomas — Secretary of State 1

Date of birth .... Apr 13, 1743
Residence .... Virginia
Date of appointment/age .... Sep 26, 1789, at age 46
Assumed office/age .... Mar 22, 1790, at age 46
Left office/age .... Jan 2, 1794, at age 50
President served .... Washington
Date of death/age .... Jul 4, 1826, at age 83
Cabinet service .... 3y 9m 11d (1,376 days)
Other offices held PR-3, VP-2

Jewell, Marshall — Postmaster General 25

Date of birth .... Oct 20, 1825
State of birth .... New Hampshire
State of residence .... Connecticut
Date of appointment/age .... Aug 24, 1874, at age 48
Assumed office/age .... Sep 1, 1874, at age 48
Left office/age .... Jul 11, 1876, at age 50
President served .... Grant
Date of death/age .... Feb 10, 1883, at age 57
Cabinet service .... 1y 10m 10d (675 days)

Johnson, Cave — Postmaster General 12

Date of birth .... Jan 11, 1793
Residence .... Tennessee
Date of appointment/age .... Mar 6, 1845, at age 62
Assumed office/age .... Mar 6, 1845, at age 62

Left office/age .... Mar 5, 1849, at age 56
President served .... Polk
Date of death/age .... Nov 23, 1866, at age 73
Cabinet service .... 4y (1,461 days)

Johnson, Louis A.   Secretary of Defense 2

Date of birth .... Jan 10, 1891
Residence .... West Virginia
Date of appointment/age .... Mar 23, 1949, at age 58
Assumed office/age .... Mar 28, 1949, at age 58
Left office/age .... Sep 20, 1950, at age 59
President served .... Truman
Date of death/age .... Apr 24, 1966, at age 75
Cabinet service .... 1y 5m 23d (538 days)

Johnson, Reverdy   Attorney General 21

Date of birth .... May 21, 1796
Residence .... Maryland
Date of appointment/age .... Mar 8, 1849, at age 52
Assumed office/age .... Mar 8, 1849, at age 52
Left office/age .... Jul 22, 1850, at age 54
President served .... Taylor
Date of death/age .... Feb 10, 1876, at age 79
Cabinet service .... 1y 4m 14d (499 days)

Jones, Jesse   Secretary of Commerce 9

Date of birth .... Apr 5, 1874
Residence .... Texas
Date of appointment/age .... Sep 16, 1940, at age 66
Assumed office/age .... Sep 19, 1940, at age 66
Left office/age .... Mar 1, 1945, at age 70
President served .... Franklin D. Roosevelt
Date of death/age .... Jun 1, 1956, at age 82
Cabinet service .... 4y 5m 10d (1,621 days)

Jones, William   Secretary of the Navy 4

Date of birth 1760
Residence .... Pennsylvania
Date of appointment/age .... Jan 12, 1813, at age 52
Assumed office/age .... Jan 19, 1813, at age 52
Left office/age .... Dec 1, 1814, at age 53
President served .... Madison
Date of death/age .... Sep 6, 1831, at age 70
Cabinet service .... 1y 10m 12d (677 days)

Kantor, Michael (Mickey)   Secretary of Commerce 32

Date of birth .... Aug 7, 1939
Residence .... California
Date of appointment/age .... Apr 12, 1996, at age 56
Assumed office/age .... Apr 12, 1996, at age 56
Left office/age .... Jan 20, 1997, at age 57
President served .... Clinton

Date of death/age .... —————
Cabinet service .... 9m 17d (287 days)

Katzenbach, Nicholas de Belleville   Attorney General 65

Date of birth .... Jan 17, 1922
Residence .... Illinois
Date of appointment/age .... Feb 13, 1965, at age 43
Assumed office/age .... Feb 13, 1965, at age 43
Left office/age .... Mar 9, 1967, at age 45
President served .... Lyndon B. Johnson
Date of death/age .... —————
Cabinet service .... 1y 7m 19d (594 days)

Kellog, Frank Billings   Secretary of State 45

Date of birth .... Dec 22, 1856
Residence .... Minnesota
Date of appointment/age .... Feb 16, 1925, at age 68
Assumed office/age .... Mar 5, 1925, at age 68
Left office/age .... Mar 3, 1929, at age 72
President served .... Coolidge
Cabinet service 3y 11m 28d

Kellog, Frank Billings   Secretary of State 45

Date of appointment/age .... Mar 4, 1929, at age 72
Assumed office/age .... Mar 4, 1929, at age 72
Left office/age .... Mar 29, 1929, at age 72
President served .... Hoover
Date of death/age .... Dec 21, 1937, at age 80
Cabinet service 25d
Total Cabinet service .... 4y 23d (1,484 days)

Kemp, Jack F.   Secretary of Housing and Urban Development 9

Date of birth .... Jul 13, 1935
Residence .... New York
Date of appointment/age .... Feb 6, 1989, at age 53
Assumed office/age .... Feb 6, 1989, at age 53
Left office/age .... Jan 20, 1993, at age 57
President served .... George Herbert Bush
Date of death/age .... —————
Cabinet service .... 3y 11m 14d (1,439 days)

Kendall, Amos   Postmaster General 8

Date of birth .... Aug 16, 1789
Residence .... Kentucky
Date of appointment/age .... May 1, 1835, at age 45
Assumed office/age .... May 1, 1835, at age 45
Left office/age .... Mar 4, 1837, at age 47
President served .... Jackson
Cabinet service 1y 10m 3d

Kendall, Amos   Postmaster General 8

Date of appointment/age . . . . Mar 4, 1837, at age 47
Assumed office/age . . . . Mar 4, 1837, at age 47
Left office/age . . . . May 24, 1840, at age 50
President served . . . . Van Buren
Date of death/age . . . . Nov 12, 1869, at age 80
Cabinet service 3y 2m 20d
Total Cabinet service . . . . 5y 23d (1,849 days)

Kennedy, David M.   Secretary of the Treasury 60

Date of birth . . . . Jul 21, 1905
Residence . . . . Illinois
Date of appointment/age . . . . Jan 20, 1969, at age 63
Assumed office/age . . . . Jan 22, 1969, at age 63
Left office/age . . . . Feb 1, 1971, at age 65
President served . . . . Nixon
Date of death/age . . . . May 1, 1996, at age 90
Cabinet service . . . . 2y 10d (740 days)

Kennedy, John P.   Secretary of the Navy 21

Date of birth . . . . Oct 25, 1795
Residence . . . . Maryland
Date of appointment/age . . . . Jul 22, 1852, at age 56
Assumed office/age . . . . Jul 26, 1852, at age 56
Left office/age . . . . Mar 6, 1853, at age 57
President served . . . . Fillmore
Date of death/age . . . . Aug 18, 1870, at age 74
Cabinet service . . . . 7m 8d (218 days)

Kennedy, Robert F.   Attorney General 64

Date of birth . . . . Nov 20, 1925
Residence . . . . Massachusetts
Date of appointment/age . . . . Jan 21, 1961, at age 35
Assumed office/age . . . . Jan 21, 1961, at age 35
Left office/age . . . . Nov 22, 1963, at age 38
President served . . . . Kennedy
Cabinet service 2y 10m 1d

Kennedy, Robert F.   Attorney General 64

Date of appointment/age . . . . Nov 22, 1963, at age 38
Assumed office/age . . . . Nov 22, 1963, at age 38
Left office/age . . . . Feb 12, 1965, at age 39
President served . . . . Lyndon B. Johnson
Date of death/age . . . . Jun 6, 1968, at age 42
Cabinet service 1y 2m 21d
Total Cabinet service . . . . 4y 22d (1,483 days)

Key, David McKendree   Postmaster General 27

Date of birth . . . . Jan 27, 1824
Residence . . . . Tennessee

Date of appointment/age . . . . Mar 12, 1877, at age 53
Assumed office/age . . . . Mar 12, 1877, at age 53
Left office/age . . . . Aug 24, 1880, at age 56
President served . . . . Hayes
Date of death/age . . . . Feb 3, 1900, at age 76
Cabinet service . . . . 3y 5m 12d (1,257 days)

King, Horatio   Postmaster General 19

Date of birth . . . . Jun 21, 1811
Residence . . . . Maine
Date of appointment/age . . . . Feb 12, 1861, at age 49
Assumed office/age . . . . Feb 12, 1861, at age 49
Left office/age . . . . Mar 8, 1861, at age 49
President served . . . . Buchanan
Date of death/age . . . . May 20, 1897, at age 85
Cabinet service . . . . 24d (24 days)

Kirkwood, Samuel J.   Secretary of the Interior 14

Date of birth . . . . Dec 20, 1813
Residence . . . . Iowa
Date of appointment/age . . . . Mar 5, 1881, at age 67
Assumed office/age . . . . Mar 8, 1881, at age 67
Left office/age . . . . Apr 16, 1882, at age 68
President served . . . . Garfield
Date of death/age . . . . Sep 1, 1894, at age 80
Cabinet service . . . . 1y 1m 8d (403 days)

Kissinger, Henry A.   Secretary of State 56

Date of birth . . . . May 27, 1923
Residence . . . . Washington, D.C.
Date of appointment/age . . . . Aug 22, 1973, at age 50
Assumed office/age . . . . Sep 21, 1973, at age 50
Left office/age . . . . Aug 9, 1974, at age 51
President served . . . . Nixon
Cabinet service 10m 19d

Kissinger, Henry A.   Secretary of State 56

Date of appointment/age . . . . Aug 9, 1974, at age 51
Assumed office/age . . . . Aug 9, 1974, at age 51
Left office/age . . . . Jan 21, 1977, at age 53
President served . . . . Ford
Date of death/age . . . . — — — —
Cabinet service 2y 5m 12d
Total Cabinet service . . . . 3y 4m 1d (1,216 days)

Kleindienst, Richard Gordon   Attorney General 68

Date of birth . . . . Aug 5, 1923
Residence . . . . Arizona
Date of appointment/age . . . . Jun 12, 1972, at age 48
Assumed office/age . . . . Jun 12, 1972, at age 48
Left office/age . . . . Apr 30, 1973, at age 49

President served .... Nixon
Date of death/age .... Feb 3, 2000, at age 76
Cabinet service .... 10m 18d (318 days)

Kleppe, Thomas Savig   Secretary of the Interior 41

Date of birth .... Jul 1, 1919
Residence .... North Dakota
Date of appointment/age .... Sep 5, 1975, at age 56
Assumed office/age .... Oct 10, 1975, at age 56
Left office/age .... Jan 20, 1977, at age 57
President served .... Ford
Date of death/age .... — — — —
Cabinet service .... 1y 3m 10d (465 days)

Klutznik, Philip M.   Secretary of Commerce 26

Date of birth .... Jul 9, 1907
Residence .... Illinois
Date of appointment/age .... Nov 17, 1979, at age 72
Assumed office/age .... Dec 21, 1979, at age 72
Left office/age .... Jan 20, 1981, at age 73
President served .... Carter
Date of death/age .... — — — —
Cabinet service .... 1y 1m (395 days)

Knebel, John A.   Secretary of Agriculture 19

Date of birth .... Oct 4, 1936
Residence .... Virginia
Date of appointment/age .... Oct 5, 1976, at age 40
Assumed office/age .... Oct 5, 1976, at age 40
Left office/age .... Jan 24, 1977, at age 40
President served .... Ford
Date of death/age .... — — — —
Cabinet service .... 3m 19d (109 days)

Knox, Henry   Secretary of War 1

Date of birth .... Jul 25, 1750
Residence .... Massachusetts
Date of appointment/age .... Sep 12, 1789, at age 39
Assumed office/age .... Sep 12, 1789, at age 39
Left office/age .... Jan 1, 1795, at age 44
President served .... Washington
Date of death/age .... Oct 25, 1806, at age 56
Cabinet service .... 5y 3m 20d (1,936 days)

Knox, Philander Chase   Attorney General 44

Date of birth .... May 6, 1853
Residence .... Pennsylvania
Date of appointment/age .... Apr 5, 1901, at age 47
Assumed office/age .... Apr 9, 1901, at age 47
Left office/age .... Sep 14, 1901, at age 48
President served .... McKinley
Cabinet service 5m 5d

Knox, Philander Chase   Attorney General 44

Date of appointment/age . . . .   Sep 14, 1901, at age 48
Assumed office/age . . . .   Sep 14, 1901, at age 48
Left office/age . . . .   Jun 30, 1904, at age 51
President served . . . .   Theodore Roosevelt
Cabinet service 2y 9m 16d

Knox, Philander Chase   Secretary of State 40

Date of appointment/age . . . .   Mar 5, 1909, at age 55
Assumed office/age . . . .   Mar 5, 1909, at age 55
Left office/age . . . .   Mar 3, 1913, at age 59
President served . . . .   Taft
Cabinet service 3y 11m 28d

Knox, Philander Chase   Secretary of State 40

Date of appointment/age . . . .   Mar 4, 1913, at age 59
Assumed office/age . . . .   Mar 4, 1913, at age 59
Left office/age . . . .   Mar 5, 1913, at age 59
President served . . . .   Wilson
Date of death/age . . . .   Oct 12, 1921, at age 68
Cabinet service 1d
Total Cabinet service . . . .   7y 2m 22d (2,638 days)

Knox, William Franklin   Secretary of the Navy 47

Date of birth . . . .   Jan 1, 1874
Residence . . . .   Illinois
Date of appointment/age . . . .   Jul 10, 1940, at age 66
Assumed office/age . . . .   Jul 10, 1940, at age 66
Left office/age . . . .   Apr 28, 1944, at age 70
President served . . . .   Franklin D. Roosevelt
Date of death/age . . . .   Apr 28, 1944, at age 70
Cabinet service . . . .   3y 9m 18d (1,383 days)

Kreps, Juanita M.   Secretary of Commerce 25

Date of birth . . . .   Jan 11, 1921
Residence . . . .   North Carolina
Date of appointment/age . . . .   Dec 21, 1976, at age 55
Assumed office/age . . . .   Jan 21, 1977, at age 56
Left office/age . . . .   Oct 31, 1979, at age 58
President served . . . .   Carter
Date of death/age . . . .   — — — —
Cabinet service . . . .   2y 9m 10d (1,010 days)

Krug, Julius A.   Secretary of the Interior 33

Date of birth . . . .   Nov 23, 1907
Residence . . . .   Wisconsin
Date of appointment/age . . . .   Mar 6, 1946, at age 38
Assumed office/age . . . .   Mar 18, 1946, at age 38
Left office/age . . . .   Nov 30, 1949, at age 42
President served . . . .   Truman
Date of death/age . . . .   Mar 26, 1970, at age 62
Cabinet service . . . .   3y 8m 12d (1,347 days)

Laird, Melvin B.   Secretary of Defense 10

Date of birth .... Sep 1, 1922
Residence .... Wisconsin
Date of appointment/age .... Jan 20, 1969, at age 46
Assumed office/age .... Jan 22, 1969, at age 46
Left office/age .... Jan 20, 1973, at age 50
President served .... Nixon
Date of death/age .... — — — —
Cabinet service .... 3y 11y 26d (1,451 days)

Lamar, Lucius Q.C.   Secretary of the Interior 16

Date of birth .... Sep 17, 1825
Residence .... Mississippi
Date of appointment/age .... Mar 6, 1885, at age 59
Assumed office/age .... Mar 6, 1885, at age 59
Left office/age .... Jan 10, 1888, at age 62
President served .... Cleveland
Date of death/age .... Jan 23, 1893, at age 67
Cabinet service .... 2y 10m 4d (1,034 days)
Other offices held AJ-45

Lamont, Daniel S.   Secretary of War 41

Date of birth .... Feb 9, 1851
Residence .... New York
Date of appointment/age .... Mar 6, 1893, at age 42
Assumed office/age .... Mar 6, 1893, at age 42
Left office/age .... Mar 4, 1897, at age 46
President served .... Cleveland
Date of death/age .... Jul 23, 1905, at age 54
Cabinet service .... 3y 11m 28d (1,453 days)

Lamont, Robert P.   Secretary of Commerce 5

Date of birth .... Dec 1, 1867
Residence .... Illinois
Date of appointment/age .... Mar 5, 1929, at age 61
Assumed office/age .... Mar 5, 1929, at age 61
Left office/age .... Aug 7, 1932, at age 64
President served .... Hoover
Date of death/age .... Feb 19, 1948, at age 80
Cabinet service .... 3y 5m 2d (1,247 days)

Landrieu, Maurice Edwin (Moon)   Secretary of Housing and Urban Development 7

Date of birth .... Jul 23, 1930
Residence .... Louisiana
Date of appointment/age .... Jul 28, 1979, at age 49
Assumed office/age .... Sep 25, 1979, at age 49
Left office/age .... Jan 20, 1981, at age 50
President served .... Carter
Date of death/age .... — — — —
Cabinet service .... 1y 3m 26d (481 days)

Lane, Franklin K.   Secretary of the Interior 26

Date of birth .... Jul 15, 1864
Residence .... California
Date of appointment/age .... Mar 5, 1913, at age 48
Assumed office/age .... Mar 5, 1913, at age 48
Left office/age .... Mar 12, 1920, at age 55
President served .... Wilson
Date of death/age .... May 18, 1921, at age 56
Cabinet service .... 8y 2m 13d (2,995 days)

Lansing, Robert   Secretary of State 42

Date of birth .... Oct 17, 1864
Residence .... New York
Date of appointment/age .... Jun 23, 1915, at age 50
Assumed office/age .... Jun 23, 1915, at age 50
Left office/age .... Feb 13, 1920, at age 55
President served .... Wilson
Date of death/age .... Oct 30, 1928, at age 64
Cabinet service .... 4y 7m 21d (1,692 days)

Lee, Charles   Attorney General 3

Date of birth 1758
Residence .... Virginia
Date of appointment/age .... Nov 30, 1795, at age 36
Assumed office/age .... Dec 10, 1795, at age 36
Left office/age .... Mar 3, 1797, at age 39
President served .... Washington
Cabinet service 1y 2m 21d

Lee, Charles   Attorney General 3

Date of appointment/age .... Mar 4, 1797, at age 39
Assumed office/age .... Mar 4, 1797, at age 39
Left office/age .... Mar 3, 1801, at age 43
President served .... John Adams
Date of death/age .... Jun 24, 1815, at age 56
Cabinet service 4y
Total Cabinet service .... 5y 2m 21d (1,907 days)

Legare, Hugh S.   Attorney General 16

Date of birth .... Jan 2, 1797
Residence .... South Carolina
Date of appointment/age .... Sep 20, 1841, at age 44
Assumed office/age .... Sep 20, 1841, at age 44
Left office/age .... Jun 20, 1843, at age 56
President served .... Tyler
Date of death/age .... Jun 20, 1843, at age 56
Cabinet service .... 1y 9m (635 days)

Levi, Edward Hirsh   Attorney General 71

Date of birth .... Jun 26, 1911
Residence .... Illinois

Date of appointment/age . . . . Jan 15, 1975, at age 63
Assumed office/age . . . . Feb 6, 1975, at age 63
Left office/age . . . . Jan 20, 1977, at age 65
President served . . . . Ford
Date of death/age . . . . Mar 7, 2000, at age 88
Cabinet service . . . . 1y 11m 14d (709 days)

Lewis, Andrew Lindsay, Jr.   Secretary of Transportation 7

Date of birth . . . . Nov 3, 1931
Residence . . . . Pennsylvania
Date of appointment/age . . . . Dec 12, 1980, at age 49
Assumed office/age . . . . Jan 23, 1981, at age 49
Left office/age . . . . Feb 1, 1983, at age 51
President served . . . . Reagan
Date of death/age . . . . —————
Cabinet service . . . . 2y 9d (739 days)

Lincoln, Levi   Attorney General 4

Date of birth . . . . May 15, 1749
Residence . . . . Massachusetts
Date of appointment/age . . . . Mar 5, 1801, at age 51
Assumed office/age . . . . Mar 5, 1801, at age 51
Left office/age . . . . Dec 31, 1804, at age 55
President served . . . . Jefferson
Date of death/age . . . . Apr 14, 1820, at age 70
Cabinet service . . . . 3y 9m 26d (1,391 days)

Lincoln, Robert T.   Secretary of War 37

Date of birth . . . . Aug 1, 1843
Residence . . . . Illinois
Date of appointment/age . . . . Mar 5, 1881, at age 37
Assumed office/age . . . . Mar 11, 1881, at age 37
Left office/age . . . . Sep 19, 1881, at age 38
President served . . . . Garfield
Cabinet service 6m 8d

Lincoln, Robert T.   Secretary of War 37

Date of appointment/age . . . . Sep 19, 1881, at age 38
Assumed office/age . . . . Sep 19, 1881, at age 38
Left office/age . . . . Mar 5, 1885, at age 41
President served . . . . Arthur
Date of death/age . . . . Jul 26, 1926, at age 82
Cabinet service 3y 5m 14d
Total Cabinet service . . . . 3y 11m 22d (1,447 days)

Livingston, Edward   Secretary of State 11

Date of birth . . . . May 28, 1764
Residence . . . . Louisiana
Date of appointment/age . . . . May 24, 1831, at age 66
Assumed office/age . . . . May 24, 1831, at age 66
Left office/age . . . . May 28, 1833, at age 69
President served . . . . Jackson

Date of death/age .... May 23, 1836, at age 71
Cabinet service .... 2y 4d (734 days)

Long, John D.   Secretary of the Navy 34

Date of birth .... Oct 27, 1838
Residence .... Massachusetts
Date of appointment/age .... Mar 5, 1897, at age 58
Assumed office/age .... Mar 5, 1897, at age 58
Left office/age .... Sep 14, 1901, at age 62
President served .... McKinley
Cabinet service 4y 6m 9d

Long, John D.   Secretary of the Navy 34

Date of appointment/age .... Sep 14, 1901, at age 62
Assumed office/age .... Sep 14, 1901, at age 62
Left office/age .... Apr 30, 1902, at age 63
President served .... McKinley
Date of death/age .... Aug 28, 1915, at age 76
Cabinet service 7m 16d
Total Cabinet service .... 5y 1m 25d (1,881 days)

Lovett, Robert Abercrombie   Secretary of Defense 4

Date of birth .... Sep 14, 1895
Residence .... New York
Date of appointment/age .... Sep 14, 1951, at age 56
Assumed office/age .... Sep 17, 1951, at age 56
Left office/age .... Jan 20, 1953, at age 57
President served .... Truman
Date of death/age .... May 7, 1986, at age 90
Cabinet service .... 1y 4m 10d (495 days)

Lujan, Manuel   Secretary of the Interior 46

Date of birth .... May 12, 1928
Residence .... New Mexico
Date of appointment/age .... Feb 3, 1989, at age 60
Assumed office/age .... Feb 3, 1989, at age 60
Left office/age .... Jan 20, 1993, at age 64
President served .... George Herbert Bush
Date of death/age .... — — — —
Cabinet service .... 3y 11m 17d (1,442 days)

Lyng, Richard Edmund   Secretary of Agriculture 22

Date of birth .... Jun 29, 1918
Residence .... California
Confirmed/age .... Mar 7, 1986, at age 67
Left office/age .... Jan 20, 1989, at age 70
President served .... Reagan
Date of death/age .... — — — —
Cabinet service .... 2y 10m 13d (1,043 days)

Lynn, James Thomas

Secretary of Housing and Urban Development 4

Date of birth .... Feb 27, 1927
Residence .... Ohio
Date of appointment/age .... Dec 6, 1972, at age 45
Assumed office/age .... Jan 31, 1973, at age 45
Left office/age .... Aug 9, 1974, at age 47
President served .... Nixon
Cabinet service 1y 6m 9d

Lynn, James Thomas

Secretary of Housing and Urban Development 4

Date of appointment/age .... Aug 9, 1974, at age 47
Assumed office/age .... Aug 9, 1974, at age 47
Left office/age .... Jan 1, 1975, at age 47
President served .... Ford
Date of death/age .... — — — —
Cabinet service 4m 23d
Total Cabinet service .... 1y 11m 2d (697 days)

McAdoo, William G.

Secretary of the Treasury 46

Date of birth .... Oct 31, 1863
Residence .... New York
Date of appointment/age .... Mar 5, 1913, at age 49
Assumed office/age .... Mar 6, 1913, at age 49
Left office/age .... Dec 15, 1918, at age 55
President served .... Wilson
Date of death/age .... Feb 1, 1941, at age 77
Cabinet service .... 5y 9m 9d (2,105 days)

McClelland, Robert

Secretary of the Interior 4

Date of birth .... Aug 1, 1807
Residence .... Michigan
Date of appointment/age .... Mar 7, 1853, at age 45
Assumed office/age .... Mar 7, 1853, at age 45
Left office/age .... Mar 9, 1857, at age 49
President served .... Pierce
Date of death/age .... Aug 30, 1880, at age 73
Cabinet service .... 4y 2d (1,463 days)

McCrary, George W.

Secretary of War 35

Date of birth .... Aug 29, 1835
Residence .... Iowa
Date of appointment/age .... Mar 12, 1877, at age 41
Assumed office/age .... Mar 12, 1877, at age 41
Left office/age .... Dec 11, 1879, at age 44
President served .... Hayes
Date of death/age .... Jun 23, 1890, at age 54
Cabinet service .... 2y 8m 29d (999 days)

McCulloch, Hugh

Secretary of the Treasury 27

Date of birth .... Dec 7, 1808
Residence .... Indiana

Date of appointment/age . . . . Mar 7, 1865, at age 56
Assumed office/age . . . . Mar 9, 1865, at age 56
Left office/age . . . . Apr 15, 1865, at age 56
President served . . . . Lincoln
Cabinet service 1m 6d

McCulloch, Hugh   Secretary of the Treasury 27

Date of appointment/age . . . . Apr 15, 1865, at age 56
Assumed office/age . . . . Apr 15, 1865, at age 56
Left office/age . . . . Mar 4, 1869, at age 60
President served . . . . Andrew Johnson
Cabinet service 3y 10m 18d

McCulloch, Hugh   Secretary of the Treasury 36

Date of appointment/age . . . . Oct 28, 1884, at age 75
Assumed office/age . . . . Oct 31, 1884, at age 75
Left office/age . . . . Mar 7, 1885, at age 76
President served . . . . Arthur
Date of death/age . . . . May 24, 1895, at age 86
Cabinet service 4m 7d
Total Cabinet service . . . . 4y 4m 1d (1,582 days)

McElroy, Neil H.   Secretary of Defense 6

Date of birth . . . . Oct 30, 1904
Residence . . . . Ohio
Date of appointment/age . . . . Aug 19, 1957, at age 52
Assumed office/age . . . . Oct 9, 1957, at age 52
Left office/age . . . . Dec 1, 1960, at age 56
President served . . . . Eisenhower
Date of death/age . . . . Nov 30, 1972, at age 68
Cabinet service . . . . 3y 3m 11d (1,196 days)

McGranery, James Patrick   Attorney General 61

Date of birth . . . . Jul 8, 1895
Residence . . . . Pennsylvania
Date of appointment/age . . . . May 27, 1952, at age 56
Assumed office/age . . . . May 27, 1952, at age 56
Left office/age . . . . Jan 20, 1953, at age 57
President served . . . . Truman
Date of death/age . . . . Dec 23, 1962, at age 66
Cabinet service . . . . 7m 24d (234 days)

McGrath, J. Howard   Attorney General 60

Date of birth . . . . Nov 28, 1903
Residence . . . . Rhode Island
Date of appointment/age . . . . Aug 19, 1949, at age 45
Assumed office/age . . . . Aug 19, 1949, at age 45
Left office/age . . . . May 26, 1952, at age 48
President served . . . . Truman
Date of death/age . . . . Sep 2, 1966, at age 62
Cabinet service . . . . 2y 9m 7d (1,007 days)

McHenry, James　　　Secretary of War 3

Date of birth .... Nov 16, 1753
Residence .... Maryland
Date of appointment/age .... Jan 27, 1796, at age 42
Assumed office/age .... Feb 6, 1796, at age 42
Left office/age .... Mar 4, 1797, at age 43
President served .... Washington
Cabinet service 1y 26d

McHenry, James　　　Secretary of War 3

Date of appointment/age .... Mar 4, 1797, at age 43
Assumed office/age .... Mar 4, 1797, at age 43
Left office/age .... May 31, 1800, at age 46
President served .... John Adams
Date of death/age .... May 3, 1816, at age 62
Cabinet service 3y 2m 27d
Total Cabinet service .... 4y 3m 23d (1,574 days)

McKay, Douglas　　　Secretary of the Interior 35

Date of birth .... Jun 24, 1893
Residence .... Oregon
Date of appointment/age .... Jan 21, 1953, at age 59
Assumed office/age .... Jan 21, 1953, at age 59
Left office/age .... Jun 7, 1956, at age 61
President served .... Eisenhower
Date of death/age .... Jul 22, 1959, at age 66
Cabinet service .... 3y 4m 17d (1,232 days)

McKenna, Joseph　　　Attorney General 42

Date of birth .... Aug 10, 1843
Residence .... California
Date of appointment/age .... Mar 5, 1897, at age 53
Assumed office/age .... Mar 7, 1897, at age 53
Left office/age .... Jan 25, 1898, at age 54
President served .... McKinley
Date of death/age .... Nov 21, 1926, at age 83
Cabinet service .... 10m 18d (318 days)
Other offices held AJ-53

McKennan, Thomas M.T.　　　Secretary of the Interior 2

Date of birth .... Mar 31, 1794
Residence .... Pennsylvania
Date of appointment/age .... Aug 15, 1850, at age 56
Assumed office/age .... Aug 15, 1850, at age 56
Left office/age .... Aug 26, 1850, at age 56
President served .... Fillmore
Date of death/age .... Jul 9, 1852, at age 58
Cabinet service .... 11d (11 days)

McLane, Louis　　　Secretary of the Treasury 10

Date of birth .... May 28, 1786
Residence .... Delaware

Date of appointment/age . . . . Aug 8, 1831, at age 45
Assumed office/age . . . . Aug 8, 1831, at age 45
Left office/age . . . . May 31, 1833, at age 47
President served . . . . Jackson
Cabinet service 1y 9m 23d

McLane, Louis   Secretary of State 12

Date of appointment/age . . . . May 29, 1833, at age 47
Assumed office/age . . . . May 29, 1833, at age 47
Left office/age . . . . Jun 30, 1834, at age 48
President served . . . . Jackson
Date of death/age . . . . Oct 7, 1857, at age 71
Cabinet service 1y 1m 1d
Total Cabinet service . . . . 2y 10m 24d (1,054 days)

McLaughlin, Ann Dore   Secretary of Labor 19

Date of birth . . . . Nov 16, 1941
Residence . . . . Washington, D.C.
Date of appointment/age . . . . Dec 17, 1987, at age 46
Assumed office/age . . . . Dec 17, 1987, at age 46
Left office/age . . . . Jan 20, 1989, at age 47
President served . . . . Reagan
Date of death . . . . — — — — —
Cabinet service . . . . 1y 1m 3d (398 days)

McLean, John   Postmaster General 6

Date of birth . . . . Mar 11, 1785
Residence . . . . Ohio
Date of appointment/age . . . . Jun 26, 1823, at age 38
Assumed office/age . . . . Jul 1, 1823, at age 38
Left office/age . . . . Mar 4, 1825, at age 39
President served . . . . Monroe
Cabinet service 1y 8m 3d

McLean, John   Postmaster General 6

Date of appointment/age . . . . Mar 4, 1825, at age 39
Assumed office/age . . . . Mar 4, 1825, at age 39
Left office/age . . . . Mar 4, 1829, at age 43
President served . . . . John Quincy Adams
Date of death/age . . . . Apr 4, 1861, at age 76
Cabinet service 4y
Total Cabinet service . . . . 5y 8m 3d (2,069 days)
Other offices held AJ-18

McNamara, Robert Strange   Secretary of Defense 8

Date of birth . . . . Jun 9, 1916
Residence . . . . Michigan
Date of appointment/age . . . . Jan 21, 1961, at age 44
Assumed office/age . . . . Jan 21, 1961, at age 44
Left office/age . . . . Nov 22, 1963, at age 47
President served . . . . Kennedy
Cabinet service 2y 10m 1d

McNamara, Robert Strange   Secretary of Defense 8

Date of appointment/age . . . . Nov 22, 1963, at age 47
Assumed office/age . . . . Nov 22, 1963, at age 47
Left office/age . . . . Feb 29, 1968, at age 51
President served . . . . Lyndon B. Johnson
Date of death/age . . . . — — — —
Cabinet service 4y 3m 7d
Total Cabinet service . . . . 7y 1m 8d (2,594 days)

McReynolds, James C.   Attorney General 48

Date of birth . . . . Feb 3, 1862
Residence . . . . Tennessee
Date of appointment/age . . . . Mar 5, 1913, at age 51
Assumed office/age . . . . Mar 6, 1913, at age 51
Left office/age . . . . Sep 2, 1914, at age 52
President served . . . . Wilson
Date of death/age . . . . Aug 24, 1947, at age 84
Cabinet service . . . . 1y 5m 27d (542 days)
Other offices held AJ-62

MacVeagh, Franklin   Secretary of the Treasury 45

Date of birth . . . . Nov 22, 1837
Residence . . . . Illinois
Date of appointment/age . . . . Mar 5, 1909, at age 71
Assumed office/age . . . . Mar 8, 1909, at age 71
Left office/age . . . . Mar 5, 1913, at age 75
President served . . . . Taft
Date of death/age . . . . Jul 6, 1934, at age 96
Cabinet service . . . . 3y 11m 27d (1,452 days)

McVeagh, Isaac Wayne   Attorney General 36

Date of birth . . . . Apr 19, 1833
Residence . . . . Pennsylvania
Date of appointment/age . . . . Mar 5, 1881, at age 47
Assumed office/age . . . . Mar 7, 1881, at age 47
Left office/age . . . . Sep 19, 1881, at age 48
President served . . . . Garfield
Cabinet service 6m 12d

McVeagh, Isaac Wayne   Attorney General 36

Date of appointment/age . . . . Sep 19, 1881, at age 48
Assumed office/age . . . . Sep 19, 1881, at age 48
Left office/age . . . . Nov 13, 1881, at age 48
President served . . . . Arthur
Date of death/age . . . . Jan 11, 1917, at age 83
Cabinet service 1m 25d
Total Cabinet service . . . . 8m 7d (247 days)

Madigan, Edward   Secretary of Agriculture 24

Date of birth . . . . Jan 13, 1936
Residence . . . . Illinois

Date of appointment/age . . . . Mar 7, 1991, at age 55
Assumed office/age . . . . Mar 7, 1991, at age 55
Left office/age . . . . Jan 20, 1993, at age 57
President served . . . . George Herbert Bush
Date of death/age . . . . — — — —
Cabinet service . . . . 1y 10m 13d (678 days)

Madison, James   Secretary of State 5

Date of birth . . . . Mar 16, 1751
Residence . . . . Virginia
Date of appointment/age . . . . Mar 5, 1801, at age 49
Assumed office/age . . . . May 2, 1801, at age 50
Left office/age . . . . Mar 3, 1809, at age 57
President served . . . . Jefferson
Date of death/age . . . . Jun 28, 1836, at age 85
Cabinet service . . . . 7y 10m 1d (2,857 days)
Other offices held PR-4

Manning, Daniel   Secretary of the Treasury 37

Date of birth . . . . May 16, 1831
Residence . . . . New York
Date of appointment/age . . . . Mar 6, 1885, at age 53
Assumed office/age . . . . Mar 8, 1885, at age 53
Left office/age . . . . Mar 31, 1887, at age 55
President served . . . . Cleveland
Date of death/age . . . . Dec 24, 1887, at age 56
Cabinet service . . . . 2y 23d (753 days)

Marcy, William Learned   Secretary of War 21

Date of birth . . . . Dec 12, 1786
Residence . . . . New York
Date of appointment/age . . . . Mar 6, 1845, at age 58
Assumed office/age . . . . Mar 8, 1845, at age 58
Left office/age . . . . Mar 3, 1849, at age 62
President served . . . . Polk
Cabinet service 3y 11m 25d

Marcy, William Learned   Secretary of War 21

Date of appointment/age . . . . Mar 4, 1849, at age 62
Assumed office/age . . . . Mar 4, 1849, at age 62
Left office/age . . . . Mar 8, 1849, at age 62
President served . . . . Taylor
Cabinet service 4d

Marcy, William Learned   Secretary of State 21

Date of appointment/age . . . . Mar 7, 1853, at age 66
Assumed office/age . . . . Mar 7, 1853, at age 66
Left office/age . . . . Mar 3, 1857, at age 70
President served . . . . Pierce
Cabinet service 3y 11m 28d

Marcy, William Learned　　　Secretary of State 21

Date of appointment/age . . . . Mar 4, 1857, at age 70
Assumed office/age . . . . Mar 4, 1858, at age 70
Left office/age . . . . Mar 6, 1857, at age 70
President served . . . . Buchanan
Dates of death/age . . . . Jul 4, 1857, at age 70
Cabinet service 2d
Total Cabinet service . . . . 7y 11m 27d (2,913 days)

Marshall, Freddie Ray　　　Secretary of Labor 16

Date of birth . . . . Aug 22, 1928
Residence . . . . Texas
Date of appointment/age . . . . Dec 22, 1976, at age 48
Assumed office/age . . . . Jan 27, 1977, at age 48
Left office/age . . . . Jan 20, 1981, at age 22
President served . . . . Carter
Date of death/age . . . . — — — —
Cabinet service . . . . 3y 11m 24d (1,449 days)

Marshall, George C., Jr.　　　Secretary of State 50

Date of birth . . . . Dec 31, 1880
Residence . . . . Pennsylvania
Date of appointment/age . . . . Jan 8, 1947, at age 66
Assumed office/age . . . . Jan 21, 1947, at age 66
Left office/age . . . . Jan 20, 1949, at age 68
President served . . . . Truman
Cabinet service 2y

Marshall, George C., Jr.　　　Secretary of Defense 3

Date of appointment/age . . . . Sep 21, 1950, at age 69
Assumed office/age . . . . Sep 21, 1950, at age 69
Left office/age . . . . Sep 16, 1951, at age 70
President served . . . . Truman
Date of death/age . . . . Oct 15, 1959, at age 78
Cabinet service 11m 25d
Total Cabinet service . . . . 2y 11m 25d (1,085 days)

Marshall, James William　　　Postmaster General 24

Date of birth . . . . Aug 14, 1822
Residence . . . . Virginia
Date of appointment/age . . . . Jul 3, 1874, at age 51
Assumed office/age . . . . Jul 7, 1874, at age 51
Left office/age . . . . Aug 24, 1874, at age 52
President served . . . . Grant
Date of death/age . . . . Feb 5, 1910, at age 87
Cabinet service . . . . 1m 17d (47 days)

Marshall, John　　　Secretary of State 4

Date of birth . . . . Sep 24, 1755
Residence . . . . Virginia
Date of appointment/age . . . . May 13, 1800, at age 44
Assumed office/age . . . . Jun 6, 1800, at age 44

Left office/age	Feb 4, 1801, at age 45
President served	John Adams
Date of death/age	Jul 6, 1835, at age 79
Cabinet service	7m 29d (239 days)
Other offices held	CJ-4

Martin, Lynn M.   Secretary of Labor 21

Date of birth	Dec 26, 1939
Residence	Illinois
Date of appointment/age	Dec 14, 1990, at age 50
Confirmed/age	Feb 7, 1991, at age 51
Left office/age	Jan 20, 1993, at age 53
President served	George Herbert Bush
Date of death/age	— — — — —
Cabinet service	1y 11m 13d (708 days)

Martinez, Melquiades Rafael   Secretary of Housing and Urban Development 12

Date of birth	Oct 23, 1946
Residence	Florida
Date of appointment/age	Dec 20, 2000, at age 54
Confirmed/age	Jan 23, 2001, at age 54
Left office/age	— — -
President served	George Walker Bush
Date of death/age	— — — — —
Cabinet service	— — — — —
Offices held	— — — — —

Mason, John Young   Secretary of the Navy 16

Date of birth	Apr 18, 1799
Residence	Virginia
Date of appointment/age	Mar 14, 1844, at age 44
Assumed office/age	Mar 26, 1844, at age 44
Left office/age	Mar 3, 1845, at age 45
President served	Tyler
Cabinet service	11m 5d

Mason, John Young   Secretary of the Navy 16

Date of appointment/age	Mar 4, 1845, at age 45
Assumed office/age	Mar 4, 1845, at age 45
Left office/age	Mar 9, 1845, at age 45
President served	Polk
Cabinet service	5d

Mason, John Young   Attorney General 18

Date of appointment/age	Mar 6, 1845, at age 45
Assumed office/age	Mar 11, 1845, at age 45
Left office/age	Oct 16, 1846, at age 47
President served	Polk
Cabinet service	1y 7m 5d (580 days)

Mason, John Young   Secretary of the Navy 18

Date of appointment/age . . . . Sep 9, 1846, at age 47
Assumed office/age . . . . Sep 9, 1846, at age 47
Left office/age . . . . Mar 3, 1849, at age 49
President served . . . . Polk
Cabinet service 2y 5m 22d
Total Cabinet service . . . . 4y 11m 6d (1,797 days)

Mason, John Young   Secretary of the Navy 18

Date of appointment/age . . . . Mar 4, 1849, at age 49
Assumed office/age . . . . Mar 4, 1849, at age 49
Left office/age . . . . Mar 7, 1849, at age 49
President served . . . . Taylor
Date of death/age . . . . Oct 3, 1859, at age 60
Cabinet service 3d
Total Cabinet service . . . . 5y 10d (1,836 days)

Mathews, Forrest D.   Secretary of Health, Education and Welfare 11

Date of birth . . . . Dec 6, 1935
Residence . . . . Alabama
Date of appointment/age . . . . Jun 27, 1975, at age 39
Assumed office/age . . . . Jul 23, 1975, at age 39
Left office/age . . . . Jan 20, 1977, at age 41
President served . . . . Ford
Date of death/age . . . . — — — —
Cabinet service . . . . 1y 5m 28m (543 days)

Maynard, Horace   Postmaster General 28

Date of birth . . . . Aug 30, 1814
Residence . . . . Tennessee
Date of appointment/age . . . . Jun 2, 1880, at age 65
Assumed office/age . . . . Aug 25, 1880, at age 65
Left office/age . . . . Mar 7, 1881, at age 66
President served . . . . Hayes
Date of death/age . . . . May 3, 1882, at age 67
Cabinet service . . . . 6m 10d (190 days)

Meese, Edwin L., III   Attorney General 75

Date of birth . . . . Dec 2, 1931
Residence . . . . California
Date of appointment/age . . . . Feb 25, 1985, at age 54
Assumed office/age . . . . Feb 25, 1985, at age 54
Left office/age . . . . Aug 11, 1988, at age 56
President served . . . . Reagan
Date of death/age . . . . — — — —
Cabinet service . . . . 3y 5m 17d (1,262 days)

Meigs, Return Jonathan, Jr.   Postmaster General 5

Date of birth . . . . Nov 17, 1764
Residence . . . . Ohio

Date of appointment/age . . . . Mar 17, 1814, at age 49
Assumed office/age . . . . Apr 11, 1814, at age 49
Left office/age . . . . Mar 4, 1817, at age 52
President served . . . . Madison
Cabinet service 2y 10m 21d

Meigs, Return Jonathan, Jr.   Postmaster General 5

Date of appointment/age . . . . Mar 4, 1817, at age 52
Assumed office/age . . . . Mar 4, 1817, at age 52
Left office/age . . . . Jun 30, 1823, at age 58
President served . . . . Monroe
Date of death/age . . . . Mar 29, 1824, at age 59
Cabinet service 6y 3m 26d
Total Cabinet service . . . . 9y 2m 17d (3,364 days)

Mellon, Andrew W.   Secretary of the Treasury 49

Date of birth . . . . Mar 24, 1855
Residence . . . . Pennsylvania
Date of appointment/age . . . . Mar 4, 1921, at age 65
Assumed office/age . . . . Mar 5, 1921, at age 65
Left office/age . . . . Aug 2, 1923, at age 67
President served . . . . Harding
Cabinet service 2y 4m 28d

Mellon, Andrew W.   Secretary of the Treasury 49

Date of appointment/age . . . . Aug 2, 1923, at age 67
Assumed office/age . . . . Aug 2, 1923, at age 67
Left office/age . . . . Mar 4, 1929, at age 73
President served . . . . Coolidge
Cabinet service 5y 7m 2d

Mellon, Andrew W.   Secretary of the Treasury 49

Date of appointment/age . . . . Mar 4, 1929, at age 73
Assumed office/age . . . . Mar 4, 1929, at age 73
Left office/age . . . . Feb 12, 1932, at age 76
President served . . . . Hoover
Date of death/age . . . . Aug 26, 1937, at age 82
Cabinet service 2y 11m 8d
Total Cabinet service . . . . 10y 11m 8d (3,990 days)

Meredith, Edwin T.   Secretary of Agriculture 6

Date of birth . . . . Dec 23, 1876
Residence . . . . Iowa
Date of appointment/age . . . . Jan 31, 1920, at age 43
Assumed office/age . . . . Feb 2, 1920, at age 43
Left office/age . . . . Mar 4, 1921, at age 44
President served . . . . Wilson
Date of death/age . . . . Jun 17, 1928, at age 51
Cabinet service . . . . 1y 1m 2d (397 days)

Meredith, William M.   Secretary of the Treasury 19

Date of birth . . . . Jun 8, 1799
Residence . . . . Pennsylvania

Date of appointment/age . . . . Mar 8, 1849, at age 49
Assumed office/age . . . . Mar 8, 1849, at age 49
Left office . . . . Jul 22, 1850, at age 50
President served . . . . Taylor
Date of death/age . . . . Aug 17, 1873, at age 74
Cabinet service . . . . 1y 4m 14d (499 days)

Metcalf, Victor H.   Secretary of Commerce and Labor 2

Date of birth . . . . Oct 10, 1853
Residence . . . . California
Date of appointment/age . . . . Jul 1, 1904, at age 50
Assumed office/age . . . . Jul 1, 1904, at age 50
Left office/age . . . . Dec 16, 1906, at age 53
President served . . . . Theodore Roosevelt
Cabinet service 2y 5m 15d

Metcalf, Victor H.   Secretary of the Navy 38

Date of appointment/age . . . . Dec 12, 1906, at age 53
Assumed office/age . . . . Dec 17, 1906, at age 53
Left office/age . . . . Nov 30, 1908, at age 55
President served . . . . Theodore Roosevelt
Date of death/age . . . . Feb 20, 1936, at age 82
Cabinet service 1y 11m 13d
Total Cabinet service . . . . 4y 4m 28d (1,609 days)

Meyer, George von L.   Postmaster General 43

Date of birth . . . . Jun 24, 1858
Residence . . . . Massachusetts
Date of appointment/age . . . . Jan 15, 1907, at age 48
Assumed office/age . . . . Mar 4, 1907, at age 48
Left office/age . . . . Mar 4, 1909, at age 50
President served . . . . Theodore Roosevelt
Cabinet service 2y

Meyer, George von L.   Secretary of the Navy 40

Date of appointment/age . . . . Mar 5, 1909, at age 50
Assumed office/age . . . . Mar 5, 1909, at age 50
Left office/age . . . . Mar 4, 1913, at age 54
President served . . . . Taft
Date of death/age . . . . Mar 9, 1918, at age 59
Cabinet service 4y
Total Cabinet service . . . . 6y (2,191 days)

Miller, George William   Secretary of the Treasury 65

Date of birth . . . . Mar 9, 1925
Residence . . . . Rhode Island
Date of appointment/age . . . . Jul 20, 1979, at age 54
Assumed office/age . . . . Aug 3, 1979, at age 54
Left office/age . . . . Jan 20, 1981, at age 55
President served . . . . Carter

Date of death/age .... — — — — —
Cabinet service .... 1y 5m 17d (532 days)

Miller, William H.H.   Attorney General 39

Date of birth .... Sep 6, 1840
Residence .... Indiana
Date of appointment/age .... Mar 5, 1889, at age 48
Assumed office/age .... Mar 5, 1889, at age 48
Left office/age .... Mar 4, 1893, at age 52
President served .... Benjamin Harrison
Date of death/age .... May 25, 1917, at age 76
Cabinet service .... 4y (1,461 days)

Mills, Ogden L.   Secretary of the Treasury 50

Date of birth .... Aug 23, 1884
Residence .... New York
Date of appointment/age .... Feb 10, 1932, at age 47
Assumed office/age .... Feb 13, 1932, at age 47
Left office/age .... Mar 4, 1933, at age 38
President served .... Hoover
Date of death/age .... Oct 11, 1937, at age 53
Cabinet service .... 1y 20d (385 days)

Mineta, Norman Yoshio   Secretary of Commerce 34

Date of birth .... Nov 12, 1931
Residence .... California
Date of appointment/age .... Jul 20, 2000, at age 68
Confirmed/age .... Jul 20, 2000, at age 68
Left office/age .... Jan 20, 2001, at age 69
President served .... Clinton
Cabinet service 6m

Mineta, Norman Yoshio   Secretary of Transportation 14

Date of appointment/age .... Jan 2, 2001, at age 69
Confirmed/age .... Jan 24, 2001, at age 69
Left office/age .... — — — — —
President served .... George Walker Bush
Date of death/age .... — — — — —
Cabinet service .... — — — — —
Total Cabinet service .... — — — — —
Offices held .... CM (14), TR (14)

Mitchell, James P.   Secretary of Labor 8

Date of birth .... Nov 12, 1900
Residence .... New Jersey
Date of appointment/age .... Oct 9, 1953, at age 52
Assumed office/age .... Oct 9, 1953, at age 52
Left office/age .... Jan 20, 1961, at age 60
President served .... Eisenhower
Date of death/age .... Oct 19, 1964, at age 63
Cabinet service .... 7y 3m 11d (2,657 days)

Mitchell, John Newton   Attorney General 67

Date of birth .... Sep 15, 1913
Residence .... New York
Date of appointment/age .... Jan 20, 1969, at age 55
Assumed office/age .... Jan 22, 1969, at age 55
Left office/age .... Feb 16, 1972, at age 58
President served .... Nixon
Date of death/age .... Nov 9, 1988, at age 75
Cabinet service .... 3y 25d (1,120 days)

Mitchell, William D.   Attorney General 54

Date of birth .... Sep 9, 1874
Residence .... Minnesota
Date of appointment/age .... Mar 5, 1929, at age 54
Assumed office/age .... Mar 6, 1929, at age 54
Left office/age .... Mar 3, 1933, at age 58
President served .... Hoover
Date of death/age .... Aug 24, 1955, at age 80
Cabinet service .... 3y 11m 27d (1,452 days)

Monroe, James   Secretary of State 7

Date of birth .... Apr 28, 1758
Residence .... Virginia
Date of appointment/age .... Apr 2, 1811, at age 52
Assumed office/age .... Apr 6, 1811, at age 52
Left office/age .... Mar 4, 1817, at age 58
President served .... Madison
Cabinet service 5y 10m 26d

Monroe, James   Secretary of War 8 (Interim)

Date of appointment/age .... Jan 1, 1813, at age 54
Assumed office/age .... Jan 1, 1813, at age 54
Left office/age .... Feb 5, 1813, at age 54
President served .... Madison
Date of death/age .... Jul 4, 1831, at age 73
Cabinet service 1m 4d
Total Cabinet service .... 6y (2,191 days)
Other offices held PR-5

Moody, William H.   Secretary of the Navy 35

Date of birth .... Dec 23, 1853
Residence .... Massachusetts
Date of appointment/age .... Apr 29, 1902, at age 48
Assumed office/age .... May 1, 1902, at age 48
Left office/age .... Jul 1, 1904, at age 50
President served .... Theodore Roosevelt
Cabinet service 2y

Moody, William H.   Attorney General 45

Date of appointment/age .... Jul 1, 1904, at age 50
Assumed office/age .... Jul 1, 1904, at age 50

Left office/age .... Dec 16, 1906, at age 52
President served .... Theodore Roosevelt
Date of death/age .... Jul 2, 1917, at age 63
Cabinet service 2y 5m 15d
Total Cabinet service .... 4y 5m 15d (1,626 days)
Other offices held AJ-56

Morgenthau, Henry, Jr.   Secretary of the Treasury 52

Date of birth .... May 11, 1891
Residence .... New York
Date of appointment/age .... Jan 8, 1934, at age 42
Assumed office/age .... Jan 8, 1934, at age 42
Left office/age .... Jul 22, 1945, at age 54
President served .... Franklin D. Roosevelt
Date of death/age .... Feb 6, 1967, at age 75
Cabinet service .... 11y 6m 14d (4,211 days)

Morrill, Lot M.   Secretary of the Treasury 31

Date of birth .... May 3, 1812
Residence .... Maine
Date of appointment/age .... Jun 21, 1876, at age 64
Assumed office/age .... Jul 7, 1876, at age 64
Left office/age .... Mar 9, 1877, at age 64
President served .... Grant
Date of death/age .... Jan 10, 1983, at age 70
Cabinet service .... 8m 2d (242 days)

Morton, J. Sterling   Secretary of Agriculture 3

Date of birth .... Apr 22, 1832
Residence .... Nebraska
Date of appointment/age .... Mar 6, 1893, at age 60
Assumed office/age .... Mar 6, 1893, at age 60
Left office/age .... Mar 4, 1897, at age 64
President served .... Cleveland
Date of death/age .... Apr 27, 1902, at age 70
Cabinet service .... 3y 11m 26d (1,451 days)

Morton, Paul   Secretary of the Navy 36

Date of birth .... May 22, 1857
Residence .... Illinois
Date of appointment/age .... Jul 1, 1904, at age 47
Assumed office/age .... Jul 1, 1904, at age 47
Left office/age .... Jun 30, 1905, at age 48
President served .... Theodore Roosevelt
Date of death/age .... Jan 20, 1911, at age 53
Cabinet service .... 1y (365 days)

Morton, Rogers C.B.   Secretary of the Interior 39

Date of birth .... Sep 19, 1914
Residence .... Maryland
Date of appointment/age .... Nov 25, 1970, at age 56
Assumed office/age .... Jan 29, 1971, at age 56

Left office/age .... Aug 9, 1974, at age 59
President served .... Nixon
Cabinet service 3y 6m 11d

Morton, Rogers C.B.   Secretary of the Interior 39

Date of appointment/age .... Aug 9, 1974, at age 59
Assumed office/age .... Aug 9, 1974, at age 59
Left office/age .... Apr 26, 1975, at age 60
President served .... Ford
Cabinet service 8m 17d

Morton, Rogers C.B.   Secretary of Commerce 23

Date of appointment/age .... Mar 28, 1975, at age 60
Assumed office/age .... Apr 26, 1975, at age 60
Left office/age .... Dec 11, 1975, at age 61
President served .... Ford
Date of death/age .... Apr 19, 1979, at age 64
Cabinet service 7m 15d
Total Cabinet service .... 4y 10m 13d (1,774 days)
Offices held .... IN (29), CM (23)

Mosbacher, Robert Adam   Secretary of Commerce 29

Date of birth .... Mar 11, 1927
Residence .... Texas
Date of appointment/age .... Feb 1, 1989, at age 61
Assumed office/age .... Feb 1, 1989, at age 61
Left office/age .... Jan 15, 1992, at age 64
President served .... George Herbert Bush
Date of death/age .... ————
Cabinet service .... 2y 11m 14d (1,074 days)

Mueller, Frederick H.   Secretary of Commerce 15

Date of birth .... Nov 22, 1893
Residence .... Michigan
Date of appointment/age .... Aug 10, 1959, at age 65
Assumed office/age .... Aug 10, 1959, at age 65
Left office/age .... Jan 20, 1961, at age 67
President served .... Eisenhower
Date of death/age .... Aug 31, 1976, at age 82
Cabinet service .... 1y 5m 10d (525 days)

Murphy, Frank W.   Attorney General 56

Date of birth .... Apr 13, 1890
Residence .... Michigan
Date of appointment/age .... Jan 17, 1939, at age 48
Assumed office/age .... Jan 17, 1939, at age 48
Left office/age .... Jan 17, 1940, at age 49
President served .... Franklin D. Roosevelt
Date of death/age .... Jul 19, 1949, at age 59
Cabinet service .... 1y (365 days)
Other offices held AJ-75

Muskie, Edmund Sixtus — Secretary of State 58

Date of birth .... Mar 28, 1914
Residence .... Maine
Date of appointment/age .... Apr 30, 1980, at age 66
Assumed office/age .... May 8, 1980, at age 66
Left office/age .... Jan 20, 1981, at age 66
President served .... Carter
Date of death/age .... Mar 26, 1996, at age 81
Cabinet service .... 8m 12d (252 days)

Nagel, Charles — Secretary of Commerce and Labor 4

Date of birth .... Aug 9, 1849
Residence .... Missouri
Date of appointment/age .... Mar 5, 1909, at age 59
Assumed office/age .... Mar 5, 1909, at age 59
Left office/age .... Mar 4, 1913, at age 63
President served .... Taft
Date of death/age .... Jan 5, 1940, at age 90
Cabinet service .... 4y (1,461 days)

Nelson, John — Attorney General 17

Date of birth .... Jun 1, 1794
Residence .... Maryland
Date of appointment/age .... Jul 1, 1843, at age 49
Assumed office/age .... Jul 1, 1843, at age 49
Left office/age .... Mar 10, 1845, at age 50
President served .... Tyler
Date of death/age .... Jan 8, 1860, at age 65
Cabinet service .... 1y 8m 9d (614 days)

New, Harry Stewart — Postmaster General 48

Date of birth .... Dec 31, 1858
Residence .... Indiana
Date of appointment/age .... Feb 27, 1923, at age 64
Assumed office/age .... Mar 5, 1923, at age 64
Left office/age .... Aug 2, 1923, at age 64
President served .... Harding
Cabinet service 4m 28d

New, Harry Stewart — Postmaster General 48

Date of appointment/age .... Aug 3, 1923, at age 64
Assumed office/age .... Aug 3, 1923, at age 64
Left office/age .... Mar 3, 1929, at age 70
President served .... Coolidge
Cabinet service 5y 7m

New, Harry Stewart — Postmaster General 48

Date of appointment/age .... Mar 4, 1929, at age 70
Assumed office/age .... Mar 4, 1929, at age 70
Left office/age .... Mar 5, 1929, at age 70

President served . . . . Hoover
Date of death/age . . . . May 9, 1939, at age 78
Cabinet service 1d
Total Cabinet service . . . . 5y 11m 29d (2,185 days)

Newberry, Truman H.   Secretary of the Navy 39

Date of birth . . . . Nov 5, 1864
Residence . . . . Michigan
Date of appointment/age . . . . Dec 1, 1908, at age 44
Assumed office/age . . . . Dec 1, 1908, at age 44
Left office/age . . . . Mar 4, 1909, at age 44
President served . . . . Theodore Roosevelt
Date of death/age . . . . Oct 3, 1945, at age 80
Cabinet service . . . . 3m 3d (93 days)

Niles, John Milton   Postmaster General 9

Date of birth . . . . Aug 20, 1787
Residence . . . . Connecticut
Date of appointment/age . . . . May 19, 1840, at age 52
Assumed office/age . . . . May 19, 1840, at age 52
Left office/age . . . . Mar 4, 1841, at age 53
President served . . . . Van Buren
Date of death/age . . . . May 31, 1856, at age 68
Cabinet service . . . . 9m 7d (277 days)

Noble, John W.   Secretary of the Interior 18

Date of birth . . . . Oct 26, 1831
Residence . . . . Missouri
Date of appointment/age . . . . Mar 5, 1889, at age 57
Assumed office/age . . . . Mar 7, 1889, at age 57
Left office/age . . . . Mar 4, 1893, at age 61
President served . . . . Benjamin Harrison
Date of death/age . . . . Mar 22, 1912, at age 80
Cabinet service . . . . 3y 11m 25d (1,450 days)

Norton, Gale Ann   Secretary of the Interior 48

Date of birth . . . . Mar 11, 1954
Residence . . . . Colorado
Date of appointment/age . . . . Dec 29, 2000, at age 46
Confirmed/age . . . . Jan 30, 2001, at age 46
Left office/age . . . . — — — —
President served . . . . George Walker Bush
Date of death/age . . . . — — — —
Cabinet service . . . . — — — —

O'Brien, Lawrence F.   Postmaster General 57

Date of birth . . . . Jul 7, 1917
Residence . . . . Massachusetts
Date of appointment/age . . . . Nov 3, 1965, at age 48
Assumed office/age . . . . Nov 3, 1965, at age 48
Left office/age . . . . Apr 10, 1968, at age 50
President served . . . . Lyndon B. Johnson

Date of death/age .... — — — — —
Cabinet service .... 2y 5m 7d (887 days)

O'Leary, Hazel Rollins   Secretary of Energy 7

Date of birth .... May 17, 1937
State of birth .... Virginia
State of residence .... Minnesota
Date of appointment/age .... Dec 21, 1992, at age 55
Confirmed/age .... Jan 21, 1993, at age 55
Left office/age .... Mar 12, 1997, at age 60
President served .... Clinton
Date of death .... — — — — —
Cabinet service .... 4y 1m 18d (1,509 days)

Olney, Richard   Attorney General 40

Date of birth .... Sep 15, 1835
Residence .... Massachusetts
Date of appointment/age .... Mar 6, 1893, at age 57
Assumed office/age .... Mar 6, 1893, at age 57
Left office/age .... Jun 10, 1895, at age 59
President served .... Cleveland
Cabinet service 2y 3m 4d

Olney, Richard   Secretary of State 34

Date of appointment/age .... Jun 8, 1895, at age 59
Assumed office/age .... Jun 10, 1895, at age 59
Left office/age .... Mar 3, 1897, at age 61
President served .... Cleveland
Cabinet service 1y 8m 21d

Olney, Richard   Secretary of State 34

Date of appointment/age .... Mar 4, 1897, at age 61
Assumed office/age .... Mar 4, 1897, at age 61
Left office/age .... Mar 5, 1897, at age 61
President served .... McKinley
Date of death/age .... Apr 1917, at age 81
Cabinet service 1d
Total Cabinet service .... 3y 11m 26d (1,451 days)
Offices held .... AT (40), ST (34)

O'Neill, Paul Henry   Secretary of the Treasury 72

Date of birth .... Dec 4, 1935
Residence .... Pennsylvania
Date of appointment/age .... Dec 20, 2000 at age 65
Confirmed/age .... Jan 20, 2001 at age 65
Left office/age .... Jan 29, 2003 at age 67
President served .... George Walker Bush
Date of death/age .... — — — — —
Cabinet service .... 739 days

Osgood, Samuel   Postmaster General 1

Date of birth .... Feb 3, 1747
Residence .... Massachusetts

Date of appointment/age . . . . Sep 26, 1789, at age 42
Assumed office/age . . . . Sep 26, 1789, at age 42
Left office/age . . . . Aug 18, 1791, at age 44
President served . . . . Washington
Date of death/age . . . . Aug 12, 1813, at age 66
Cabinet service . . . . 1y 10m 23d (688 days)

Paige, Roderick R.   Secretary of Education 7

Date of birth . . . . Jun 17, 1933
Residence . . . . Texas
Appointed/age . . . . Dec 29, 2000, at age 67
Confirmed/age . . . . Jan 20, 2001, at age 67
Left office/age . . . . — — — — —
President served . . . . George Walker Bush
Date of death/age . . . . — — — — —
Cabinet service . . . . — — — — —
Offices held . . . . — — — — —

Palmer, Alexander Mitchell   Attorney General 50

Date of birth . . . . May 4, 1872
Residence . . . . Pennsylvania
Date of appointment/age . . . . Mar 5, 1919, at age 46
Assumed office/age . . . . Mar 5, 1919, at age 46
Left office/age . . . . Mar 4, 1921, at age 48
President served . . . . Wilson
Date of death/age . . . . May 11, 1936, at age 64
Cabinet service . . . . 2y (730 days)

Patterson, Robert P.   Secretary of War 57

Date of birth . . . . Feb 12, 1891
Residence . . . . New York
Date of appointment/age . . . . Sep 26, 1945, at age 54
Assumed office/age . . . . Sep 27, 1945, at age 54
Left office/age . . . . Jul 24, 1947, at age 56
President served . . . . Truman
Date of death/age . . . . Jan 22, 1952, at age 60
Cabinet service . . . . 1y 9m 27d (662 days)

Paulding, James K.   Secretary of the Navy 11

Date of birth . . . . Aug 22, 1778
Residence . . . . New York
Date of appointment/age . . . . Jun 25, 1838, at age 59
Assumed office/age . . . . Jul 1, 1838, at age 59
Left office/age . . . . Mar 4, 1841, at age 62
President served . . . . Van Buren
Date of death/age . . . . Apr 6, 1860, at age 81
Cabinet service . . . . 2y 8m 3d (973 days)

Payne, Henry C.   Postmaster General 40

Date of birth . . . . Nov 23, 1843
Residence . . . . Wisconsin
Date of appointment/age . . . . Jan 9, 1902, at age 58

Assumed office/age .... Jan 9, 1902, at age 58
Left office/age .... Oct 4, 1904, at age 60
President served .... Theodore Roosevelt
Date of death/age .... Oct 4, 1904, at age 60
Cabinet service .... 2y 9m (1,000 days)

Payne, John B.   Secretary of the Interior 27

Date of birth .... Jan 26, 1855
Residence .... Illinois
Date of appointment/age .... Feb 28, 1920, at age 65
Assumed office/age .... Mar 13, 1920, at age 65
Left office/age .... Mar 4, 1921, at age 66
President served .... Wilson
Date of death/age .... Jan 24, 1934, at age 79
Cabinet service .... 11m 19d (349 days)

Pena, Frederico F.   Secretary of Transportation 12

Date of birth .... Mar 15, 1947
State of birth .... Texas
State of residence .... Colorado
Date of appointment/age .... Jan 21, 1993, at age 45
Confirmed/age .... Jan 21, 1993, at age 45
Left office/age .... Feb 14, 1997, at age 49
President served .... Clinton
Cabinet service 4y 24d

Pena, Frederico F.   Secretary of Energy 8

Date of appointment/age .... Mar 12, 1997, at age 49
Confirmed/age .... Mar 12, 1997, at age 49
Left office/age .... Apr 6, 1998, at age 51
President served .... Clinton
Date of death/age .... — — — —
Cabinet service 1y 25d
Total Cabinet service .... 5y 1m 19d (1,875 days)

Perkins, Frances   Secretary of Labor 4

Date of birth .... Apr 10, 1880
Residence .... New York
Date of appointment/age .... Mar 4, 1933, at age 52
Assumed office/age .... Mar 4, 1933, at age 52
Left office/age .... Jun 30, 1945, at age 65
President served .... Franklin D. Roosevelt
Date of death/age .... May 14, 1965, at age 85
Cabinet service .... 12y 3m 26d (4,499 days)

Perry, William James   Secretary of Defense 19

Date of birth .... Oct 11, 1927
Residence .... California
Confirmed/age .... Feb 3, 1994, at age 66
Sworn in/age .... Feb 3, 1994, at age 66
Left office/age .... Jan 20, 1997, at age 69
President served .... Clinton

Date of death/age .... — — — — —
Cabinet service .... 2y 11m 17d (1,077 days)

Peterson, Peter George   Secretary of Commerce 21

Date of birth .... Jun 5, 1926
Residence .... Illinois
Date of appointment/age .... Jan 28, 1972, at age 45
Assumed office/age .... Feb 22, 1972, at age 45
Left office/age .... Jan 18, 1973, at age 46
President served .... Nixon
Date of death/age .... — — — — —
Cabinet service .... 10m 27d (327 days)

Pickering, Timothy   Postmaster General 2

Date of birth .... Jul 17, 1745
Residence .... Pennsylvania
Date of appointment/age .... Aug 12, 1791, at age 46
Assumed office/age .... Aug 19, 1791, at age 46
Left office/age .... Feb 25, 1795, at age 49
President served .... Washington
Cabinet service 3y 6m 3d

Pickering, Timothy   Secretary of War 2

Date of appointment/age .... Jan 2, 1795, at age 49
Assumed office/age .... Jan 2, 1795, at age 49
Left office/age .... Dec 9, 1795, at age 50
President served .... Washington
Cabinet service 11m 7d

Pickering, Timothy   Secretary of War (interim)

Date of appointment/age .... Dec 10, 1795, at age 50
Assumed office/age .... Dec 10, 1795, at age 50
Left office/age .... Feb 5, 1796, at age 50
President served .... Washington
Cabinet service 1m 26d

Pickering, Timothy   Secretary of State (interim)

Date of appointment/age .... Aug 20, 1795, at age 50
Assumed office/age .... Aug 20, 1795, at age 50
Left office/age .... Dec 10, 1795, at age 50
President served .... Washington
Cabinet service 3m 20d

Pickering, Timothy   Secretary of State 3

Date of appointment/age .... Mar 4, 1797, at age 51
Assumed office/age .... Mar 4, 1797, at age 51
Left office/age .... May 12, 1800, at age 54
President served .... John Adams
Date of death/age .... Jan 29, 1829, at age 83
Cabinet service 3y 2m 8d
Total Cabinet service .... 8y 1m 5d (2,952 days)
Offices held .... PG (2), WR (2), ST (3)

Pierce, Samuel Riley, Jr.

Secretary of Housing and Urban Development 8

Date of birth . . . . Sep 8, 1922
Residence . . . . New York
Date of appointment/age . . . . Dec 23, 1980, at age 58
Assumed office/age . . . . Jan 22, 1981, at age 58
Left office/age . . . . Jan 20, 1989, at age 66
President served . . . . Reagan
Date of death/age . . . . Oct 31, 2000, at age 78
Cabinet service . . . . 7y 11m 28d (2,914 days)

Pierrepont, Edwards

Attorney General 33

Date of birth . . . . Mar 4, 1817
Residence . . . . New York
Date of appointment/age . . . . Apr 26, 1875, at age 58
Assumed office/age . . . . May 15, 1875, at age 58
Left office/age . . . . May 31, 1876, at age 59
President served . . . . Grant
Date of death/age . . . . Mar 6, 1892, at age 75
Cabinet service . . . . 1y 16d (381 days)

Pinkney, William

Attorney General 7

Date of birth . . . . Mar 17, 1764
Residence . . . . Maryland
Date of appointment/age . . . . Dec 11, 1811, at age 47
Assumed office/age . . . . Jan 6, 1812, at age 47
Left office/age . . . . Feb 10, 1814, at age 49
President served . . . . Madison
Date of death/age . . . . Feb 25, 1822, at age 57
Cabinet service . . . . 2y 1m 4d (764 days)

Poinsett, Joel R.

Secretary of War 16

Date of birth . . . . Mar 2, 1779
Residence . . . . South Carolina
Date of appointment/age . . . . Mar 7, 1837, at age 58
Assumed office/age . . . . Mar 14, 1837, at age 58
Left office/age . . . . Mar 4, 1841, at age 62
President served . . . . Van Buren
Date of death/age . . . . Dec 12, 1851, at age 72
Cabinet service . . . . 3y 11m 20d (1,445 days)

Porter, James M.

Secretary of War 19

Date of birth . . . . Jan 6, 1793
Residence . . . . Pennsylvania
Date of appointment/age . . . . Mar 8, 1843, at age 50
Assumed office/age . . . . Mar 8, 1843, at age 50
Left office/age . . . . Feb 19, 1844, at age 51
President served . . . . Tyler
Date of death/age . . . . Nov 11, 1862, at age 69
Cabinet service . . . . 11m 11d (341 days)

Porter, Peter B.   Secretary of War 12

Date of birth .... Aug 14, 1773
Residence .... New York
Date of appointment/age .... May 26, 1828, at age 54
Assumed office/age .... Jun 21, 1828, at age 54
Left office/age .... Mar 4, 1829, at age 55
President served .... John Quincy Adams
Date of death/age .... Mar 20, 1844, at age 70
Cabinet service .... 8m 11d (251 days)

Powell, Colin Luther   Secretary of State 65

Date of birth .... Apr 5, 1937
Residence .... Virginia
Date of appointment/age .... Dec 16, 2000, at age 63
Confirmed/age .... Jan 20, 2001, at age 63
Left office/age .... —————
President served .... George Walker Bush
Date of death/age .... —————
Cabinet service .... —————

Preston, William B.   Secretary of the Navy 19

Date of birth .... Nov 29, 1805
Residence .... Virginia
Date of appointment/age .... Mar 8, 1849, at age 43
Assumed office/age .... Mar 8, 1849, at age 43
Left office/age .... Jul 22, 1850, at age 44
President served .... Taylor
Date of death/age .... Nov 16, 1862, at age 56
Cabinet service .... 1y 4m 14d (499 days)

Principi, Anthony Joseph   Secretary of Veterans Affairs 4

Date of birth .... Apr 16, 1944
Residence .... California
Appointed/age .... Dec 29, 2000, at age 56
Confirmed/age .... Jan 23, 2001, at age 56
Left office/age .... —————
President served .... George Walker Bush
Date of death/age .... —————
Cabinet service .... —————

Proctor, Redfield   Secretary of War 39

Date of birth .... Jun 1, 1831
Residence .... Vermont
Date of appointment/age .... Mar 5, 1889, at age 57
Assumed office/age .... Mar 5, 1889, at age 57
Left office/age .... Dec 5, 1891, at age 60
President served .... Benjamin Harrison
Date of death/age .... Mar 4, 1908, at age 76
Cabinet service .... 2y 9m (1,000 days)

Ramsey, Alexander — Secretary of War 36

Date of birth .... Sep 8, 1815
Residence .... Minnesota
Date of appointment/age .... Dec 10, 1879, at age 64
Assumed office/age .... Dec 12, 1879, at age 64
Left office/age .... Mar 10, 1881, at age 65
President served .... Hayes
Date of death/age .... Apr 22, 1903, at age 87
Cabinet service .... 1y 2m 26d (451 days)

Randall, Alexander Williams — Postmaster General (Interim)

Date of birth .... Oct 31, 1819
Residence .... Wisconsin
Date of appointment/age .... Jul 17, 1866, at age 46
Assumed office/age .... Jul 17, 1866, at age 46
Left office/age .... Jul 25, 1866, at age 46
President served .... Andrew Johnson
Cabinet service 8d

Randall, Alexander Williams — Postmaster General 22

Date of appointment/age .... Jul 25, 1866, at age 46
Assumed office/age .... Jul 25, 1866, at age 46
Left office/age .... Mar 3, 1869, at age 49
President served .... Andrew Johnson
Cabinet service 2y 7m 6d
Total Cabinet service .... 2y 7m 14d (954 days)

Randolph, Edmund — Attorney General 1

Date of birth .... Aug 10, 1753
Residence .... Virginia
Date of appointment/age .... Sep 26, 1789, at age 36
Assumed office/age .... Feb 2, 1790, at age 36
Left office/age .... Jan 28, 1794, at age 40
President served .... Washington
Cabinet service 3y 11m 26d

Randolph, Edmund — Secretary of State 2

Date of appointment/age .... Jan 2, 1794, at age 40
Assumed office/age .... Jan 2, 1794, at age 40
Left office/age .... Aug 20, 1795, at age 42
President served .... Washington
Date of death/age .... Sep 12, 1813, at age 60
Cabinet service 1y 7m 18d
Total Cabinet service .... 5y 7m 14d (2,050 days)

Rawlins, John A. — Sectretary of War 30

Date of birth .... Feb 13, 1831
Residence .... Illinois
Date of appointment/age .... Mar 11, 1869, at age 38
Assumed office/age .... Mar 11, 1869, at age 38

Left office/age .... Sep 6, 1869, at age 38
President served .... Grant
Date of death/age .... Sep 6, 1869, at age 38
Cabinet service .... 5m 25d (175 days)

Redfield, William C.   Secretary of Commerce 1

Date of birth .... Jun 18, 1858
Residence .... New York
Date of appointment/age .... Mar 5, 1913, at age 54
Assumed office/age .... Mar 5, 1913, at age 54
Left office/age .... Dec 15, 1919, at age 61
President served .... Wilson
Date of death/age .... Jun 13, 1932, at age 73
Cabinet service .... 6y 9m 10d (2,471 days)

Regan, Donald Thomas   Secretary of the Treasury 66

Date of birth .... Dec 21, 1918
Residence .... New York
Date of appointment/age .... Dec 12, 1980, at age 61
Assumed office/age .... Jan 22, 1981, at age 62
Left office/age .... Jan 29, 1985, at age 66
President served .... Reagan
Date of death/age .... ————
Cabinet service .... 4y 7d (1,468 days)

Reich, Robert B.   Secretary of Labor 22

Date of birth .... Jun 24, 1946
Residence .... Massachusetts
Assumed office/age .... Jan 21, 1993, at age 46
Left office/age .... May 9, 1997, at age 50
President served .... Clinton
Date of death/age .... ————
Cabinet service .... 4y 3m 18d (1,569 days)

Reno, Janet   Attorney General 78

Date of birth .... Jul 21, 1938
Residence .... Florida
Nominated/age .... Feb 11, 1993, at age 54
Confirmed/age .... Mar 11, 1993, at age 54
Left office/age .... Jan 20, 2001, at age 62
President served .... Clinton
Date of death/age .... ————
Cabinet service .... 7y 10m 9d (2,865 days)

Ribicoff, Abraham Alexander   Secretary of Health,
                                          Education and Welfare 4

Date of birth .... Apr 9, 1910
Residence .... Connecticut
Date of appointment/age .... Jan 21, 1961, at age 50
Assumed office/age .... Jan 21, 1961, at age 50
Left office/age .... Jul 30, 1962, at age 52
President served .... Kennedy

Date of death/age .... Feb 22, 1998, at age 87
Cabinet service .... 1y 6m 9d (554 days)

Richardson, Elliot Lee

Secretary of Health, Education and Welfare 9

Date of birth .... Jul 20, 1920
Residence .... Massachusetts
Date of appointment/age .... Jun 7, 1970, at age 49
Assumed office/age .... Jun 16, 1970, at age 49
Left office/age .... Jan 20, 1973, at age 52
President served .... Nixon
Cabinet service 2y 7m 4d

Richardson, Elliot Lee

Secretary of Defense 11

Date of appointment/age .... Nov 28, 1972, at age 52
Assumed office/age .... Jan 29, 1973, at age 52
Left office/age .... Apr 30, 1973, at age 52
President served .... Nixon
Cabinet service 3m 1d

Richardson, Elliot Lee

Attorney General 69

Date of appointment/age .... Apr 30, 1973, at age 52
Assumed office/age .... May 23, 1973, at age 52
Left office/age .... Oct 20, 1973, at age 53
President served .... Nixon
Cabinet service 4m 27d

Richardson, Elliot Lee

Secretary of Commerce 24

Date of appointment/age .... Nov 4, 1975, at age 55
Assumed office/age .... Dec 11, 1975, at age 55
Left office/age .... Jan 20, 1977, at age 56
President served .... Ford
Date of death/age .... Dec 31, 1999, at age 79
Cabinet service 1y 1m 9d
Total Cabinet service .... 4y 4m 11d (1,592 days)

Richardson, William A.

Secretary of the Treasury 29

Date of birth .... Nov 2, 1821
Residence .... Massachusetts
Date of appointment/age .... Mar 17, 1873, at age 51
Assumed office/age .... Mar 17, 1873, at age 51
Left office/age .... Jun 3, 1874, at age 52
President served .... Grant
Date of death/age .... Oct 19, 1896, at age 74
Cabinet service .... 1y 2m 17d (442 days)

Richardson, William Blaine (Bill)

Secretary of Energy 9

Date of birth .... Nov 15, 1947
Residence .... New Mexico
Confirmed/age .... Aug 18, 1998, at age 50
Left office/age .... Jan 20, 2001, at age 53

President served . . . . Clinton
Date of death/age . . . . ————
Cabinet service . . . . 2y 5m 2d (882 days)

Ridge, Thomas   Secretary of Homeland Security 1

Date of birth . . . . Aug 26, 1945
Residence . . . . Pennsylvania
Nominated/age . . . . Nov 25, 2002 at age 57
Confirmed/age . . . . Jan 22, 2003 at age 57
Left office/age . . . . ————
President served . . . . George Walker Bush
Date of death/age . . . . ————
Cabinet service . . . . ————

Riley, Richard Wilson   Secretary of Education 6

Date of birth . . . . Jan 2, 1933
Residence . . . . South Carolina
Confirmed/age . . . . Jan 21, 1993, at age 60
Left office/age . . . . Jan 20, 2001, at age 68
President served . . . . Clinton
Date of death/age . . . . ————
Cabinet service . . . . 8y (2,922 days)

Robeson, George M.   Secretary of the Navy 26

Date of birth . . . . Mar 16, 1829
Residence . . . . New Jersey
Date of appointment/age . . . . Jun 25, 1869, at age 40
Assumed office/age . . . . Jun 25, 1869, at age 40
Left office/age . . . . Mar 11, 1877, at age 47
President served . . . . Grant
Date of death/age . . . . Sep 27, 1897, at age 68
Cabinet service . . . . 7y 8m 14d (2,810 days)

Rodney, Caesar Augustus   Attorney General 6

Date of birth . . . . Jan 4, 1772
Residence . . . . Delaware
Date of appointment/age . . . . Jan 20, 1807, at age 35
Assumed office/age . . . . Jan 20, 1807, at age 35
Left office/age . . . . Mar 3, 1809, at age 37
President served . . . . Jefferson
Cabinet service 2y 14d

Rodney, Caesar Augustus   Attorney General 6

Date of appointment/age . . . . Mar 4, 1809, at age 37
Assumed office/age . . . . Mar 4, 1809, at age 37
Left office/age . . . . Dec 5, 1811, at age 39
President served . . . . Madison
Date of death/age . . . . Jun 10, 1824, at age 52
Cabinet service 2y 9m 1d
Total Cabinet service . . . . 4y 9m 15d (1,746 days)

Rogers, William Pierce

Attorney General 63

Date of birth .... Jun 23, 1913
Residence .... Maryland
Date of appointment/age .... Jan 27, 1958, at age 44
Assumed office/age .... Jan 27, 1958, at age 44
Left office/age .... Jan 20, 1961, at age 47
President served .... Eisenhower
Cabinet service 2y 11m 23d

Rogers, William Pierce

Secretary of State 55

Date of appointment/age .... Jan 12, 1969, at age 55
Assumed office/age .... Jan 21, 1969, at age 55
Left office/age .... Sep 3, 1973, at age 60
President served .... Nixon
Date of death/age .... Jan 2, 2001, at age 87
Cabinet service 4y 7m 13d
Total Cabinet service .... 7y 7m 6d (2,772 days)

Romney, George Wilcken

Secretary of Housing and Urban Development 3

Date of birth .... Jul 8, 1907
Residence .... Michigan
Date of appointment/age .... Dec 12, 1968, at age 61
Assumed office/age .... Jan 21, 1969, at age 61
Left office/age .... Nov 28, 1973, at age 66
President served .... Nixon
Date of death/age .... Jul 26, 1995, at age 88
Cabinet service .... 4y 10m 7d (1,768 days)

Root, Elihu

Secretary of War 43

Date of birth .... Feb 15, 1845
Residence .... New York
Date of appointment/age .... Aug 1, 1899, at age 54
Assumed office/age .... Aug 1, 1899, at age 54
Left office/age .... Sep 14, 1901, at age 56
President served .... McKinley
Cabinet service 2y 1m 13d

Root, Elihu

Secretary of War 43

Date of appointment/age .... Sep 14, 1901, at age 56
Assumed office/age .... Sep 14, 1901, at age 56
Left office/age .... Jan 31, 1904, at age 58
President served .... Theodore Roosevelt
Cabinet service 2y 4m 17d

Root, Elihu

Secretary of State 38

Date of appointment/age .... Jul 7, 1905, at age 60
Assumed office/age .... Jul 19, 1905, at age 60
Left office/age .... Jan 26, 1909, at age 63
President served .... Theodore Roosevelt
Date of death/age .... Feb 7, 1937, at age 91

Cabinet service 3y 6m 7d
Total Cabinet service .... 8y 7d (2,929 days)

Roper, Daniel C. — Secretary of Commerce 7

Date of birth .... Apr 1, 1867
Residence .... South Carolina
Date of appointment/age .... Mar 4, 1933, at age 65
Assumed office/age .... Mar 4, 1933, at age 65
Left office/age .... Dec 23, 1938, at age 71
President served .... Franklin D. Roosevelt
Date of death/age .... Apr 11, 1943, at age 76
Cabinet service .... 5y 9m 19d (2,115 days)

Royall, Kenneth C. — Secretary of War 58

Date of birth .... Jul 24, 1894
Residence .... North Carolina
Date of appointment/age .... Jul 21, 1947, at age 52
Assumed office/age .... Jul 25, 1947, at age 53
Left office/age .... Sep 17, 1947, at age 53
President served .... Truman
Date of death/age .... May 27, 1971, at age 76
Cabinet service .... 1m 23d (53 days)

Rubin, Robert E. — Secretary of the Treasury 70

Date of birth .... Aug 29, 1938
Residence .... New York
Assumed office/age .... Jan 10, 1995, at age 56
Left office/age .... Jul 2, 1999, at age 60
President served .... Clinton
Date of death/age .... — — — —
Cabinet service .... 4y 5m 22d (1,633 days)

Rumsfeld, Donald H. — Secretary of Defense 13

Date of birth .... Jul 9, 1932
Residence .... Illinois
Date of appointment/age .... Nov 4, 1975, at age 43
Assumed office/age .... Nov 20, 1975, at age 43
Left office/age .... Jan 20, 1977, at age 44
President served .... Ford
Cabinet service 1y 2m

Rumsfeld, Donald H. — Secretary of Defense 21

Date of appointment/age .... Dec 28, 2000, at age 68
Confirmed/age .... Jan 20, 2001, at age 68
Left office/age .... — — — —
President served .... George Walker Bush
Date of death/age .... — — — —
Cabinet service .... — — — —
Total Cabinet service .... — — — —

Rush, Richard — Attorney General 8

Date of birth .... Aug 29, 1780
Residence .... Pennsylvania

Date of appointment/age .... Feb 10, 1814, at age 33
Assumed office/age .... Feb 11, 1814, at age 33
Left office/age .... Mar 3, 1817, at age 36
President served .... Madison
Cabinet service 3y 20d

Rush, Richard   Attorney General 8

Date of appointment/age .... Mar 4, 1817, at age 36
Assumed office/age .... Mar 4, 1817, at age 36
Left office/age .... Oct 30, 1817, at age 37
President served .... Monroe
Cabinet service 7m 26d

Rush, Richard   Secretary of the Treasury 8

Date of appointment/age .... Mar 7, 1825, at age 44
Assumed office/age .... Aug 1, 1825, at age 44
Left office/age .... Mar 3, 1829, at age 48
President served .... John Quincy Adams
Date of death/age .... Jul 30, 1859, at age 78
Cabinet service 3y 7m 2d
Total Cabinet service .... 7y 3m 18d (2,664 days)

Rusk, Dean   Secretary of State 54

Date of birth .... Feb 9, 1909
Residence .... New York
Date of appointment/age .... Jan 21, 1961, at age 51
Assumed office/age .... Jan 21, 1961, at age 51
Left office/age .... Nov 22, 1963, at age 54
President served .... Kennedy
Cabinet service 2y 10m 1d

Rusk, Dean   Secretary of State 54

Date of appointment/age .... Nov 22, 1963, at age 54
Assumed office/age .... Nov 22, 1963, at age 54
Left office/age .... Jan 20, 1969, at age 59
President served .... Lyndon B. Johnson
Date of death/age .... Dec 20, 1994, at age 85
Cabinet service 5y 1m 29d
Total Cabinet service .... 8y (2,922 days)

Rusk, Jeremiah M.   Secretary of Agriculture 2

Date of birth .... Jun 17, 1830
Residence .... Wisconsin
Date of appointment/age .... Mar 5, 1889, at age 58
Assumed office/age .... Mar 7, 1889, at age 58
Left office/age .... Mar 5, 1893, at age 62
President served .... Benjamin Harrison
Date of death/age .... Nov 21, 1893, at age 63
Cabinet service .... 3y 11m 26d (1,451 days)

Sargent, John G.   Attorney General 53

Date of birth .... Oct 13, 1860
Residence .... Vermont
Date of appointment/age .... Mar 17, 1925, at age 64
Assumed office/age .... Mar 18, 1925, at age 64
Left office/age .... Mar 5, 1929, at age 68
President served .... Coolidge
Date of death/age .... Mar 5, 1939, at age 78
Cabinet service .... 3y 11m 18d (1,443 days)

Sawyer, Charles   Secretary of Commerce 12

Date of birth .... Feb 10, 1887
Residence .... Ohio
Date of appointment/age .... May 6, 1948, at age 61
Assumed office/age .... May 6, 1948, at age 61
Left office/age .... Jan 20, 1953, at age 65
President served .... Truman
Date of death/age .... Apr 7, 1979, at age 92
Cabinet service .... 4y 8m 14d (1,715 days)

Saxbe, William B.   Attorney General 70

Date of birth .... Jun 24, 1916
Residence .... Ohio
Date of appointment/age .... Nov 1, 1973, at age 57
Assumed office/age .... Jan 4, 1974, at age 57
Left office/age .... Aug 9, 1974, at age 58
President served .... Nixon
Cabinet service 7m 5d

Saxbe, William B.   Attorney General 70

Date of appointment/age .... Aug 9, 1974, at age 58
Assumed office/age .... Aug 9, 1974, at age 58
Left office/age .... Dec 14, 1974, at age 58
President served .... Ford
Date of death/age .... —— —— —— ——
Cabinet service 4m 5d
Total Cabinet service .... 11m 10d (340 days)

Schlesinger, James Rodney   Secretary of Defense 12

Date of birth .... Feb 15, 1929
Residence .... Virginia
Date of appointment/age .... May 10, 1973, at age 44
Assumed office/age .... Jun 29, 1973, at age 44
Left office/age .... Aug 9, 1974, at age 45
President served .... Nixon
Cabinet service 1y 1m 11d

Schlesinger, James Rodney   Secretary of Defense 12

Date of appointment/age .... Aug 9, 1974, at age 45
Assumed office/age .... Aug 9, 1974, at age 45
Left office/age .... Nov 3, 1975, at age 46

President served . . . . Ford
Cabinet service 1y 2m 25d

Schlesinger, James Rodney   Secretary of Energy 1

Date of appointment/age . . . . Aug 5, 1977, at age 48
Assumed office/age . . . . Oct 1, 1977, at age 48
Left office/age . . . . Aug 25, 1979, at age 50
President served . . . . Carter
Date of death/age . . . . ————
Cabinet service 1y 10m 24d
Total Cabinet service . . . . 4y 3m (1,551 days)

Schofield, John M.   Secretary of War 29

Date of birth . . . . Sep 29, 1831
Residence . . . . Illinois
Date of appointment/age . . . . May 28, 1868, at age 36
Assumed office/age . . . . Jun 1, 1868, at age 36
Left office/age . . . . Mar 10, 1869, at age 37
President served . . . . Andrew Johnson
Date of death/age . . . . Mar 4, 1906, at age 74
Cabinet service . . . . 9m 9d (279 days)

Schurz, Carl   Secretary of the Interior 13

Date of birth . . . . Mar 2, 1829
Residence . . . . Missouri
Date of appointment/age . . . . Mar 12, 1877, at age 48
Assumed office/age . . . . Mar 12, 1877, at age 48
Left office/age . . . . Mar 3, 1881, at age 52
President served . . . . Hayes
Cabinet service . . . . 3y 11m 19d (1,444 days)

Schurz, Carl   Secretary of the Interior 13

Date of appointment/age . . . . Mar 4, 1881, at age 52
Assumed office/age . . . . Mar 4, 1881, at age 52
Left office/age . . . . Mar 7, 1881, at age 52
President served . . . . Garfield
Date of death/age . . . . Mar 4, 1906, at age 77
Cabinet service 3d
Total Cabinet service . . . . 3y 11m 22d (1,447 days)

Schweiker, Richard Schultz   Secretary of Health and Human Services 2

Date of birth . . . . Jun 1, 1926
Residence . . . . Pennsylvania
Date of appointment/age . . . . Dec 12, 1980, at age 54
Assumed office/age . . . . Jan 22, 1981, at age 54
Left office/age . . . . Jan 12, 1983, at age 56
President served . . . . Reagan
Date of death/age . . . . ————
Cabinet service . . . . 1y 11m 21d (716 days)

Schwellenbach, Lewis B.   Secretary of Labor 5

Date of birth .... Sep 20, 1894
Residence .... Washington
Date of appointment/age .... Jun 1, 1945, at age 50
Assumed office/age .... Jul 1, 1945, at age 50
Left office/age .... Jun 10, 1948, at age 53
President served .... Truman
Date of death/age .... Jun 10, 1948, at age 53
Cabinet service .... 2y 11m 9d (1,069 days)

Seaton, Fred A.   Secretary of the Interior 36

Date of birth .... Dec 11, 1909
Residence .... Nebraska
Date of appointment/age .... Jun 8, 1956, at age 46
Assumed office/age .... Jun 8, 1956, at age 46
Left office/age .... Jan 20, 1961, at age 51
President served .... Eisenhower
Date of death/age .... Jan 17, 1974, at age 64
Cabinet service .... 4y 7m 12d (1,683 days)

Seward, William H.   Secretary of State 24

Date of birth .... May 16, 1801
Residence .... New York
Date of appointment/age .... Mar 5, 1861, at age 59
Assumed office/age .... Mar 5, 1861, at age 59
Left office/age .... Apr 15, 1865, at age 63
President served .... Lincoln
Cabinet service 4y 1m 10d

Seward, William H.   Secretary of State 24

Date of appointment/age .... Apr 15, 1865, at age 63
Assumed office/age .... Apr 15, 1865, at age 63
Left office/age .... Mar 4, 1869, at age 67
President served .... Andrew Johnson
Date of death/age .... Oct 10, 1972, at age 71
Cabinet service 3y 10m 17d
Total Cabinet service .... 7y 11m 27d (2,913 days)

Shalala, Donna Edna   Secretary of Health and Human Services 6

Date of birth .... Feb 14, 1941
Residence .... Wisconsin
Nominated/age .... Dec 11, 1992, at age 51
Confirmed/age .... Jan 21, 1993, at age 51
Left office/age .... Jan 20, 2001, at age 59
President served .... Clinton
Date of death/age .... — — — —
Cabinet service .... 8y (2,922 days)

Shaw, Leslie M.   Secretary of the Treasury 43

Date of birth .... Nov 2, 1848
Residence .... Iowa

Date of appointment/age . . . . Jan 9, 1902, at age 53
Assumed office/age . . . . Feb 1, 1902, at age 53
Left office/age . . . . Mar 3, 1907, at age 58
President served . . . . Theodore Roosevelt
Date of death/age . . . . Mar 28, 1932, at age 83
Cabinet service . . . . 5y 1m 2d (1,858 days)

Sherman, John   Secretary of the Treasury 32

Date of birth . . . . May 10, 1823
Residence . . . . Ohio
Date of appointment/age . . . . Mar 8, 1877, at age 53
Assumed office/age . . . . Mar 10, 1877, at age 53
Left office/age . . . . Mar 3, 1881, at age 57
President served . . . . Hayes
Cabinet service 3y 11m 23d

Sherman, John   Secretary of State 35

Date of appointment/age . . . . Mar 5, 1897, at age 73
Assumed office/age . . . . Mar 5, 1897, at age 73
Left office/age . . . . Apr 27, 1898, at age 73
President served . . . . McKinley
Date of death/age . . . . Oct 22, 1900, at age 77
Cabinet service 1y 1m 22d
Total Cabinet service . . . . 5y 1m 15d (1,871 days)

Sherman, William T.   Secretary of War 31

Date of birth . . . . Feb 8, 1820
Residence . . . . Ohio
Date of appointment/age . . . . Sep 9, 1869, at age 49
Assumed office/age . . . . Sep 11, 1869, at age 49
Left office/age . . . . Oct 31, 1869, at age 49
President served . . . . Grant
Date of death/age . . . . Feb 14, 1891, at age 71
Cabinet service . . . . 1m 20d (50 days)

Shultz, George Pratt   Secretary of Labor 11

Date of birth . . . . Dec 13, 1920
Residence . . . . Illinois
Date of appointment/age . . . . Dec 12, 1968, at age 47
Assumed office/age . . . . Jan 22, 1969, at age 48
Left office/age . . . . Jul 1, 1970, at age 49
President served . . . . Nixon
Cabinet service 1y 5m 9d

Shultz, George Pratt   Secretary of the Treasury 62

Date of appointment/age . . . . May 16, 1972, at age 51
Assumed office/age . . . . Jun 12, 1972, at age 51
Left office/age . . . . May 8, 1974, at age 53
President served . . . . Nixon
Cabinet service 1y 10m 22d

Shultz, George Pratt   Secretary of State 60

Date of appointment/age . . . . Jul 16, 1982, at age 61
Assumed office/age . . . . Jul 16, 1982, at age 61
Left office/age . . . . Jan 20, 1989, at age 68
President served . . . . Reagan
Date of death/age . . . . — — — —
Cabinet service 6y 6m 5d
Total Cabinet service . . . . 9y 10m 6d (3,593 days)

Simon, William E.   Secretary of the Treasury 63

Date of birth . . . . Nov 27, 1927
Residence . . . . New Jersey
Date of appointment/age . . . . Apr 18, 1974, at age 46
Assumed office/age . . . . May 1, 1974, at age 46
Left office/age . . . . Aug 9, 1974, at age 46
President served . . . . Nixon
Cabinet service 3m 8d

Simon, William E.   Secretary of the Treasury 63

Date of appointment/age . . . . Aug 9, 1974, at age 46
Assumed office/age . . . . Aug 9, 1974, at age 46
Left office/age . . . . Jan 20, 1977, at age 49
President served . . . . Ford
Date of death/age . . . . Jun 3, 2000, at age 72
Cabinet service 2y 5m 11d
Total Cabinet service . . . . 2y 8m 19d (989 days)

Skinner, Samuel Knox   Secretary of Transportation 10

Date of birth . . . . Jun 10, 1938
Residence . . . . Illinois
Confirmed/age . . . . Feb 1, 1989, at age 50
Left office/age . . . . Jan 22, 1992, at age 53
President served . . . . George Herbert Walker Bush
Date of death/age . . . . — — — —
Cabinet service . . . . 2y 11m 21d (1,081 days)

Slater, Rodney E.   Secretary of Transportation 13

Date of birth . . . . Feb 23, 1955
Residence . . . . Arkansas
Confirmed/age . . . . Feb 14, 1997, at age 41
Left office/age . . . . Jan 20, 2001, at age 45
President served . . . . Clinton
Date of death/age . . . . — — — —
Cabinet service . . . . 3y 11m 6d (1,431 days)

Smith, Caleb B.   Secretary of the Interior 6

Date of birth . . . . Apr 16, 1808
Residence . . . . Indiana
Date of appointment/age . . . . Mar 5, 1861, at age 52
Assumed office/age . . . . Mar 5, 1861, at age 52
Left office/age . . . . Dec 31, 1862, at age 54

President served . . . . Lincoln
Date of death/age . . . . Jan 7, 1864, at age 55
Cabinet service . . . . 1y 9m 26d (661 days)

Smith, Charles Emory   Postmaster General 39

Date of birth . . . . Feb 18, 1842
Residence . . . . Pennsylvania
Date of appointment/age . . . . Apr 21, 1898, at age 56
Assumed office/age . . . . Apr 21, 1898, at age 56
Left office/age . . . . Sep 14, 1901, at age 59
President served . . . . McKinley
Cabinet service 3y 4m 24d

Smith, Charles Emory   Postmaster General 39

Date of appointment/age . . . . Sep 14, 1901, at age 59
Assumed office/age . . . . Sep 14, 1901, at age 59
Left office/age . . . . Jan 8, 1902, at age 59
President served . . . . Roosevelt
Date of death/age . . . . Jan 19, 1908, at age 65
Cabinet service 3m 25d
Total Cabinet service . . . . 3y 8m 19d (1,354 days)

Smith, Cyrus R.   Secretary of Commerce 19

Date of birth . . . . Sep 9, 1899
Residence . . . . New York
Date of appointment/age . . . . Feb 17, 1968, at age 68
Assumed office/age . . . . Mar 2, 1968, at age 68
Left office/age . . . . Jan 20, 1969, at age 69
President served . . . . Lyndon B. Johnson
Date of death/age . . . . Apr 4, 1990, at age 90
Cabinet service . . . . 10m 18d (318 days)

Smith, Hoke   Secretary of the Interior 19

Date of birth . . . . Sep 2, 1855
Residence . . . . Georgia
Date of appointment/age . . . . Mar 6, 1893, at age 37
Assumed office/age . . . . Mar 6, 1893, at age 37
Left office/age . . . . Aug 31, 1896, at age 40
President served . . . . Cleveland
Date of death/age . . . . Nov 27, 1931, at age 76
Cabinet service . . . . 3y 5m 25d (1,270 days)

Smith, Robert   Secretary of the Navy 2

Date of birth . . . . Nov 3, 1757
Residence . . . . Maryland
Date of appointment/age . . . . Jul 15, 1801, at age 43
Assumed office/age . . . . Jul 27, 1801, at age 43
Left office/age . . . . Mar 7, 1809, at age 51
President served . . . . Jefferson
Cabinet service 7y 7m 8d

Smith, Robert   Secretary of State 6

Date of appointment/age . . . . Mar 6, 1809, at age 51
Assumed office/age . . . . Mar 6, 1809, at age 51
Left office/age . . . . Apr 6, 1811, at age 53
President served . . . . Madison
Date of death/age . . . . Nov 26, 1842, at age 85
Cabinet service 2y 1m
Total Cabinet service . . . . 9y 8m 8d (3,535 days)

Smith, William French   Attorney General 74

Date of birth . . . . Aug 26, 1917
Residence . . . . California
Date of appointment/age . . . . Dec 12, 1980, at age 63
Assumed office/age . . . . Jan 23, 1981, at age 63
Left office/age . . . . Feb 22, 1985, at age 67
President served . . . . Reagan
Date of death/age . . . . Oct 29, 1990, at age 73
Cabinet service . . . . 4y 1m (1,491 days)

Snow, John William   Secretary of the Treasury 73

Date of birth . . . . Aug 2, 1939
State of birth . . . . Ohio
Residence . . . . Virginia
Nominated/age . . . . Dec 9, 2002 at age 63
Confirmed/age . . . . Jan 30, 2003 at age 63
Left office/age . . . . — — — —
President served . . . . George Walker Bush
Date of death/age . . . . — — — —
Cabinet service . . . . — — — —

Snyder, John Wesley   Secretary of the Treasury 54

Date of birth . . . . Jun 21, 1895
Residence . . . . Missouri
Date of appointment/age . . . . Jun 12, 1946, at age 50
Assumed office/age . . . . Jun 25, 1946, at age 51
Left office/age . . . . Jan 20, 1953, at age 57
President served . . . . Truman
Date of death/age . . . . Oct 8, 1985, at age 90
Cabinet service . . . . 6y 6m 26d (2,397 days)

Southard, Samuel L.   Secretary of the Navy 7

Date of birth . . . . Jun 9, 1787
Residence . . . . New Jersey
Date of appointment/age . . . . Sep 16, 1823, at age 36
Assumed office/age . . . . Sep 16, 1823, at age 36
Left office/age . . . . Mar 3, 1825, at age 37
President served . . . . Monroe
Cabinet service 1y 5m 15d

Southard, Samuel L.   Secretary of the Navy 7

Date of appointment/age . . . . Mar 4, 1825, at age 37
Assumed office/age . . . . Mar 4, 1825, at age 37

Left office/age .... Mar 3, 1829, at age 41
President served .... John Quincy Adams
Date of death/age .... Jun 26, 1842, at age 55
Cabinet service 4y
Total Cabinet service .... 5y 5m 15d (1,991 days)

Speed, James — Attorney General 27

Date of birth .... Mar 11, 1812
Residence .... Kentucky
Date of appointment/age .... Dec 2, 1864, at age 52
Assumed office/age .... Dec 5, 1864, at age 52
Left office/age .... Apr 15, 1865, at age 53
President served .... Lincoln
Cabinet service 4m 10d

Speed, James — Attorney General 27

Residence .... Kentucky
Date of appointment/age .... Apr 15, 1865, at age 53
Assumed office/age .... Apr 15, 1865, at age 53
Left office/age .... Jul 16, 1866, at age 54
President served .... Andrew Johnson
Date of death/age .... Jun 25, 1887, at age 75
Cabinet service 1y 3m 1d
Total Cabinet service .... 1y 7m 11d (586 days)

Spencer, John C. — Secretary of War 18

Date of birth .... Jan 8, 1788
Residence .... New York
Date of appointment/age .... Oct 12, 1841, at age 53
Assumed office/age .... Oct 12, 1841, at age 53
Left office/age .... Mar 7, 1843, at age 55
President served .... Tyler
Cabinet service 1y 4m 23d

Spencer, John C. — Secretary of the Treasury 16

Date of appointment/age .... Mar 3, 1843, at age 55
Assumed office/age .... Mar 8, 1843, at age 55
Left office/age .... May 1, 1844, at age 56
President served .... Tyler
Date of death/age .... May 17, 1855, at age 67
Cabinet service 1y 1m 24d
Total Cabinet service 2y 6m 17d (927days)

Stanbery, Henry — Attorney General 28

Date of birth .... Feb 20, 1803
Residence .... Ohio
Date of appointment/age .... Jul 23, 1866, at age 63
Assumed office/age .... Mar 12, 1868, at age 65
Left office/age .... Jul 20, 1868, at age 65
President served .... Andrew Johnson
Date of death/age .... Jun 26, 1881, at age 78
Cabinet service .... 4m 8d (128 days)

Stans, Maurice Hubert   Secretary of Commerce 20

Date of birth .... Mar 22, 1908
Residence .... New York
Date of appointment/age .... Dec 12, 1968, at age 60
Assumed office/age .... Jan 22, 1969, at age 60
Left office/age .... Feb 20, 1972, at age 63
President served .... Nixon
Date of death/age .... Apr 14, 1998, at age 90
Cabinet service .... 3y 28d (1,123 days)

Stanton, Edwin McMasters   Attorney General 25

Date of birth .... Dec 19, 1814
Residence .... Pennsylvania
Date of appointment/age .... Dec 20, 1860, at age 46
Assumed office/age .... Dec 22, 1860, at age 46
Left office/age .... Mar 3, 1861, at age 46
President served .... Buchanan
Cabinet service 2m 11d

Stanton, Edwin McMasters   Secretary of War 28

Date of appointment/age .... Jan 15, 1862, at age 47
Assumed office/age .... Jan 20, 1862, at age 47
Left office/age .... Apr 15, 1865, at age 50
President served .... Lincoln
Cabinet service 3y 2m 25d

Stanton, Edwin McMasters   Secretary of War 28

Date of appointment/age .... Apr 15, 1865, at age 50
Assumed office/age .... Apr 15, 1865, at age 50
Left office/age .... Aug 12, 1867, at age 53
President served .... Andrew Johnson
Date of death/age .... Dec 24, 1869, at age 55
Cabinet service 2y 3m 27d
Total Cabinet service .... 5y 9m 3d (2,099 days)
Other offices held AJ-36

Stettinius, Edward Reilly, Jr.   Secretary of State 48

Date of birth .... Oct 22, 1900
Residence .... Virginia
Date of appointment/age .... Nov 30, 1944, at age 44
Assumed office/age .... Dec 1, 1944, at age 44
Left office/age .... Apr 12, 1945, at age 44
President served .... Roosevelt
Cabinet service 4m 11d

Stettinius, Edward Reilly, Jr.   Secretary of State 48

Date of appointment/age .... Apr 12, 1945, at age 44
Assumed office/age .... Apr 12, 1945, at age 44
Left office/age .... Jul 2, 1945, at age 44
President served .... Truman

Date of death/age .... Oct 31, 1949, at age 49
Cabinet service 3m
Total Cabinet service .... 7m 11d (221 days)

Stimson, Henry Lewis   Secretary of War 47

Date of birth .... Sep 21, 1867
Residence .... New York
Date of appointment/age .... May 16, 1911, at age 43
Assumed office/age .... May 22, 1911, at age 43
Left office/age .... Mar 3, 1913, at age 45
President served .... Taft
Cabinet service 1y 9m 9d

Stimson, Henry Lewis   Secretary of State 46

Date of appointment/age .... Mar 4, 1929, at age 61
Assumed office/age .... Mar 29, 1929, at age 61
Left office/age .... Mar 3, 1933, at age 65
President served .... Hoover
Cabinet service 3y 11m 26d

Stimson, Henry Lewis   Secretary of War 56

Date of appointment/age .... Jul 10, 1940, at age 72
Assumed office/age .... Jul 10, 1940, at age 72
Left office/age .... Sep 26, 1945, at age 78
President served .... Franklin D. Roosevelt
Date of death/age .... Oct 20, 1950, at age 83
Cabinet service 4y 9m 2d
Total Cabinet service .... 10y 5m 15d (3,817 days)

Stoddert, Benjamin   Secretary of the Navy 1

Date of birth 1751
Residence .... Maryland
Date of appointment/age .... May 21, 1798, at age 46
Assumed office/age .... Jun 18, 1798, at age 46
Left office/age .... Mar 3, 1801, at age 49
President served .... John Adams
Cabinet service 2y 8m 13d

Stoddert, Benjamin   Secretary of the Navy 1

Date of appointment/age .... Mar 4, 1801, at age 49
Assumed office/age .... Mar 4, 1801, at age 49
Left office/age .... Apr 1, 1801, at age 49
President served .... Jefferson
Date of death/age .... Dec 17, 1813, at age 61
Cabinet service 28d
Total Cabinet service .... 2y 9m 11d (1,011 days)

Stone, Harlan Fiske   Attorney General 52

Date of birth .... Oct 11, 1872
Residence .... New York
Date of appointment/age .... Apr 7, 1924, at age 51
Assumed office/age .... Apr 9, 1924, at age 51

Left office/age .... Mar 3, 1925, at age 52
President served .... Coolidge
Date of death/age .... Apr 22, 1946, at age 73
Cabinet service .... 10m 22d (322 days)
Other offices held AJ-68, CJ-12

Straus, Oscar S.

Secretary of Commerce and Labor 3

Date of birth .... Dec 23, 1850
Residence .... New York
Date of appointment/age .... Dec 12, 1906, at age 55
Assumed office/age .... Dec 17, 1906, at age 55
Left office/age .... Mar 4, 1909, at age 58
President served .... Theodore Roosevelt
Date of death/age .... May 3, 1926, at age 75
Cabinet service .... 2y 2m 13d (803 days)

Strauss, Lewis L.

Secretary of Commerce 14

Date of birth .... Jan 31, 1896
Residence .... New York
Date of appointment/age .... Nov 13, 1958, at age 62
Assumed office/age .... Nov 13, 1958, at age 62
Left office/age .... Aug 9, 1959, at age 63
President served .... Eisenhower
Date of death/age .... Jan 21, 1974, at age 77
Cabinet service .... 8m 27d (267 days)

Stuart, Alex H.H.

Secretary of the Interior 3

Date of birth .... Apr 2, 1807
Residence .... Virginia
Date of appointment/age .... Sep 12, 1850, at age 43
Assumed office/age .... Sep 16, 1850, at age 43
Left office/age .... Mar 6, 1853, at age 45
President served .... Fillmore
Date of death/age .... Feb 13, 1891, at age 83
Cabinet service .... 2y 5m 18d (898 days)

Sullivan, Louis Wade

Secretary of Health and Human Services 5

Date of birth .... Nov 3, 1933
Residence .... Georgia
Confirmed/age .... Mar 1, 1989, at age 55
Left office/age .... Jan 20, 1993, at age 59
President served .... George Herbert Bush
Date of death/age .... — — — —
Cabinet service .... 3y 10m 19d (1,414 days)

Summerfield, Arthur Ellsworth

Postmaster General 54

Date of birth .... Mar 17, 1899
Residence .... Michigan
Date of appointment/age .... Jan 21, 1953, at age 53
Assumed office/age .... Jan 21, 1953, at age 53

Left office/age .... Jan 20, 1961, at age 61
President served .... Eisenhower
Date of death/age .... Apr 26, 1972, at age 73
Cabinet service .... 8y (2,922 days)

Summers, Lawrence H.　　　　Secretary of the Treasury 71

Date of birth .... Nov 30, 1954
Residence .... Connecticut
Assumed office/age .... Jul 2, 1999, at age 44
Left office/age .... Jan 20, 2001, at age 46
President served .... Clinton
Date of death/age .... ————
Cabinet service .... 1y 6m 18d (563 days)

Swanson, Claude A.　　　　Secretary of the Navy 45

Date of birth .... Mar 31, 1862
Residence .... Virginia
Date of appointment/age .... Mar 4, 1933, at age 70
Assumed office/age .... Mar 4, 1933, at age 70
Left office/age .... Jul 7, 1939, at age 77
President served .... Franklin D. Roosevelt
Date of death/age .... Jul 7, 1939, at age 77
Cabinet service .... 6y 4m 3d (2,314 days)

Taft, Alphonso　　　　Secretary of War 33

Date of birth .... Nov 5, 1810
Residence .... Ohio
Date of appointment/age .... Mar 8, 1876, at age 65
Assumed office/age .... Mar 8, 1876, at age 65
Left office/age .... May 31, 1876, at age 65
President served .... Grant
Cabinet service 2m 23d

Taft, Alphonso　　　　Attorney General 34

Date of appointment/age .... May 22, 1876, at age 65
Assumed office/age .... Jun 1, 1876, at age 65
Left office/age .... Mar 11, 1877, at age 66
President served .... Grant
Date of death/age .... May 21, 1891, at age 80
Cabinet service 9m 10d
Total Cabinet service .... 1y 3d (368 days)

Taft, William H.　　　　Secretary of War 44

Date of birth .... Sep 15, 1857
Residence .... Ohio
Date of appointment/age .... Jan 11, 1904, at age 46
Assumed office/age .... Feb 1, 1904, at age 46
Left office/age .... June 30, 1908, at age 50
President served .... Theodore Roosevelt
Date of death/age .... Mar 8, 1930, at age 72
Cabinet service .... 4y 4m 29d (1,610 days)
Other offices held PR-27, CJ-10

Taney, Roger Brooke   Attorney General 11

Date of birth .... Mar 17, 1777
Residence .... Maryland
Date of appointment/age .... Jul 20, 1831, at age 54
Assumed office/age .... Jul 20, 1831, at age 54
Left office/age .... Sep 23, 1833, at age 56
President served .... Jackson
Cabinet service 2y 2m 3d

Taney, Roger Brooke   Secretary of the Treasury 12

Date of appointment/age .... Sep 23, 1833, at age 56
Assumed office/age .... Sep 23, 1833, at age 56
Left office/age .... Jun 24, 1834, at age 57
President served .... Jackson
Date of death/age .... Oct 12, 1864, at age 87
Cabinet service 9m 1d
Total Cabinet service .... 2y 11m 4d (1,064 days)
Other offices held CJ-5

Teller, Henry M.   Secretary of the Interior 15

Date of birth .... May 23, 1830
Residence .... Colorado
Date of appointment/age .... Apr 6, 1882, at age 51
Assumed office/age .... Apr 17, 1882, at age 51
Left office/age .... Mar 3, 1885, at age 54
President served .... Arthur
Date of death/age .... Feb 23, 1914, at age 83
Cabinet service .... 2y 10m 14d (1,044 days)

Thomas, Phillip F.   Secretary of the Treasury 23

Date of birth .... Sep 12, 1810
Residence .... Maryland
Date of appointment/age .... Dec 12, 1860, at age 50
Assumed office/age .... Dec 12, 1860, at age 50
Left office/age .... Jan 14, 1861, at age 50
President served .... Buchanan
Date of death/age .... Oct 2, 1890, at age 80
Cabinet service .... 1m 2d (32 days)

Thompson, Jacob   Secretary of the Interior 5

Date of birth .... May 15, 1810
Residence .... Mississippi
Date of appointment/age .... Mar 6, 1857, at age 46
Assumed office/age .... Mar 10, 1857, at age 46
Left office/age .... Jan 9, 1861, at age 50
President served .... Buchanan
Date of death/age .... Mar 24, 1885, at age 74
Cabinet service .... 3y 10m (1,395 days)

Thompson, Richard W.   Secretary of the Navy 27

Date of birth .... Jun 9, 1809
Residence .... Indiana

Date of appointment/age	Mar 12, 1877, at age 67
Assumed office/age	Mar 12, 1877, at age 67
Left office/age	Dec 19, 1880, at age 71
President served	Hayes
Date of death/age	Feb 9, 1900, at age 90
Cabinet service	3y 9m 7d (1,372 days)

Thompson, Smith — Secretary of the Navy 6

Date of birth	Jan 17, 1768
Residence	New York
Date of appointment/age	Nov 9, 1818, at age 50
Assumed office/age	Jan 1, 1819, at age 50
Left office/age	Aug 31, 1823, at age 55
President served	Monroe
Date of death/age	Dec 18, 1843, at age 75
Cabinet service	4y 7m (1,671 days)
Other offices held	AJ-16

Thompson, Tommy G. — Secretary of Health and Human Services 7

Date of birth	Nov 19, 1941
Residence	Wisconsin
Appointed/age	Dec 20, 2000, at age 59
Confirmed/age	Jan 23, 2001, at age 59
Left office/age	—————
President served	George Walker Bush
Date of death/age	—————
Cabinet service	—————
Offices held	—————

Thornburgh, Richard — Attorney General 76

Date of birth	Jul 16, 1932
Residence	Pennsylvania
Confirmed/age	Aug 12, 1988, at age 56
Left office/age	Jan 20, 1989, at age 56
President served	Reagan
Cabinet service	5m 18d

Thornburgh, Richard — Attorney General 76

Confirmed/age	Jan 20, 1989, at age 56
Left office/age	Nov 20, 1991, at age 59
President served	George Herbert Bush
Date of death/age	—————
Cabinet service	2y 10m
Total Cabinet service	3y 3m 18d (1,203 days)

Tobin, Maurice J. — Secretary of Labor 6

Date of birth	May 22, 1901
Residence	Massachusetts
Date of appointment/age	Aug 13, 1948, at age 47
Assumed office/age	Aug 13, 1948, at age 47
Left office/age	Jan 20, 1953, at age 51

President served .... Truman
Date of death/age .... Jul 19, 1953, at age 52
Cabinet service .... 4y 5m 7d (1,618 days)

Toucey, Isaac   Attorney General 20

Date of birth .... Nov 15, 1792
Residence .... Connecticut
Date of appointment/age .... Jun 21, 1848, at age 55
Assumed office/age .... Jun 29, 1848, at age 55
Left office/age .... Mar 3, 1849, at age 56
President served .... Polk
Cabinet service 8m 3d

Toucey, Isaac   Attorney General 20

Date of appointment/age .... Mar 3, 1849, at age 56
Assumed office/age .... Mar 3, 1849, at age 56
Left office/age .... Mar 7, 1849, at age 56
President served .... Taylor
Cabinet service 4d

Toucey, Isaac   Secretary of the Navy 23

Date of appointment/age .... Mar 6, 1857, at age 64
Assumed office/age .... Mar 6, 1857, at age 64
Left office/age .... Mar 3, 1861, at age 68
President served .... Buchanan
Cabinet service 3y 11m 25d

Toucey, Isaac   Secretary of the Navy 23

Date of appointment/age .... Mar 4, 1861, at age 68
Assumed office/age .... Mar 4, 1861, at age 68
Left office/age .... Mar 5, 1861, at age 68
President served .... Lincoln
Date of death/age .... Jul 30, 1869, at age 76
Cabinet service 1d
Total Cabinet service .... 4y 8m 3d (1,704 days)

Tracy, Benjamin F.   Secretary of the Navy 32

Date of birth .... Apr 26, 1830
Residence .... New York
Date of appointment/age .... Mar 5, 1889, at age 58
Assumed office/age .... Mar 5, 1889, at age 58
Left office/age .... Mar 5, 1893, at age 62
President served .... Benjamin Harrison
Date of death/age .... Aug 6, 1915, at age 85
Cabinet service .... 4y (1,461 days)

Trowbridge, Alex Buel, Jr.   Secretary of Commerce 18

Date of birth .... Dec 12, 1929
Residence .... New Jersey
Date of appointment/age .... May 23, 1967, at age 37
Assumed office/age .... Jun 9, 1967, at age 37

Left office/age .... Feb 29, 1968, at age 38
President served .... Lyndon B. Johnson
Date of death/age .... —————
Cabinet service .... 8m 20d (260 days)

Tyner, James Noble   Postmaster General 26

Date of birth .... Jan 17, 1826
Residence .... Indiana
Date of appointment/age .... Jul 12, 1876, at age 50
Assumed office/age .... Jul 12, 1876, at age 50
Left office/age .... Mar 11, 1877, at age 51
President served .... Grant
Date of death/age .... Dec 6, 1904, at age 78
Cabinet service .... 7m 29d (239 days)

Udall, Stewart Lee   Secretary of the Interior 37

Date of birth .... Jan 31, 1920
Residence .... Arizona
Date of appointment/age .... Dec 8, 1960, at age 40
Assumed office/age .... Jan 22, 1961, at age 40
Left office/age .... Nov 22, 1963, at age 43
President served .... Kennedy
Cabinet service 2y 10m

Udall, Stewart Lee   Secretary of the Interior 37

Date of appointment/age .... Nov 22, 1963, at age 43
Assumed office/age .... Nov 22, 1963, at age 43
Left office/age .... Jan 20, 1969, at age, at age 48
President served .... Lyndon B. Johnson
Date of death/age .... —————
Cabinet service 5y 1m 29d
Total Cabinet service .... 7y 11m 29d (2,915 days)

Upshhur, Abel P.   Secretary of the Navy 13

Date of birth .... Jun 17, 1791
Residence .... Virginia
Date of appointment/age .... Sep 13, 1841, at age 50
Assumed office/age .... Oct 11, 1841, at age 50
Left office/age .... Jul 23, 1843, at age 52
President served .... Tyler
Cabinet service 1y 9m 12d

Upshur, Abel P.   Secretary of State 15

Date of appointment/age .... Jul 24, 1843, at age 52
Assumed office/age .... Jul 24, 1843, at age 52
Left office/age .... Feb 28, 1844, at age 52
President served .... Tyler
Date of death/age .... Feb 28, 1844, at age 52
Cabinet service 7m 4d
Total Cabinet service .... 2y 4m 16d (866 days)

Usery, William Julian, Jr. (Willie)   Secretary of Labor 15

Date of birth .... Dec 21, 1923
Residence .... Georgia
Date of appointment/age .... Jan 23, 1976, at age 52
Assumed office/age .... Feb 5, 1976, at age 52
Left office/age .... Jan 20, 1977, at age 53
President served .... Ford
Date of death/age .... —————
Cabinet service .... 11m 15d (345 days)

Usher, John P.   Secretary of the Interior 7

Date of birth .... Jan 9, 1816
Residence .... Indiana
Date of appointment/age .... Jan 8, 1863, at age 46
Assumed office/age .... Jan 8, 1863, at age 46
Left office/age .... Apr 15, 1865
President served .... Lincoln
Cabinet service 2y 3m 7d

Usher, John P.   Secretary of the Interior 7

Date of appointment/age .... Apr 15, 1865, at age 49
Assumed office/age .... Apr 15, 1865, at age 49
Left office/age .... May 14, 1865, at age 49
President served .... Andrew Johnson
Date of death/age .... Apr 13, 1889, at age 73
Cabinet service 29d
Total Cabinet service .... 2y 4m 6d (856 days)

Van Buren, Martin   Secretary of State 10

Date of birth .... Dec 5, 1782
Residence .... New York
Date of appointment/age .... Mar 6, 1829, at age 46
Assumed office/age .... Mar 28, 1829, at age 46
Left office/age .... May 23, 1831, at age 48
President served .... Jackson
Date of death/age .... Jul 24, 1862, at age 79
Cabinet service .... 2y 1m 25d (785 days)
Other offices held VP-8, PR-8

Vance, Cyrus Roberts   Secretary of State 57

Date of birth .... Mar 27, 1917
Residence .... New York
Date of appointment/age .... Dec 4, 1976, at age 59
Confirmed/age .... Jan 21, 1977, at age 59
Left office/age .... Apr 28, 1980, at age 63
President served .... Carter
Date of death/age .... Jan 12, 2002, at age 84
Cabinet service .... 3y 3m 9d (1,194 days)

Veneman, Ann Margaret   Secretary of Agriculture 27

Date of birth .... Jun 29, 1949
Residence .... California

Nominated/age .... Dec 20, 2000, at age 51
Confirmed/age .... Jan 20, 2001, at age 51
Left office/age .... — — — —
President served .... George Walker Bush
Date of death/age .... — — — —
Cabinet service .... — — — —

Verity, Calvin William, Jr.   Secretary of Commerce 28

Date of birth .... Jan 26, 1917
Residence .... Ohio
Appointed/age .... Oct 19, 1987, at age 70
Confirmed/age .... Oct 19, 1987, at age 70
Left office/age .... Jan 20, 1989, at age 71
President served .... Reagan
Date of death/age .... — — — —
Cabinet service .... 1y 3m 1d (456 days)

Vilas, William F.   Postmaster General 33

Date of birth .... Jul 9, 1840
Residence .... Wisconsin
Date of appointment/age .... Mar 6, 1885, at age 44
Assumed office/age .... Mar 6, 1885, at age 44
Left office/age .... Jan 15, 1888, at age 47
President served .... Cleveland
Cabinet service 2y 10m 9d

Vilas, William F.   Secretary of the Interior 17

Date of appointment/age .... Jan 16, 1888, at age 47
Assumed office/age .... Jan 16, 1888, at age 47
Left office/age .... Mar 6, 1889, at age 48
President served .... Cleveland
Date of death/age .... Aug 27, 1908, at age 68
Cabinet service 1y 1m 18d
Total Cabinet service .... 3y 11m 27d (1,452 days)

Vinson, Frederick Moore   Secretary of the Treasury 53

Date of birth .... Jan 22, 1890
Residence .... Kentucky
Date of appointment/age .... Jul 18, 1945, at age 55
Assumed office/age .... Jul 23, 1945, at age 55
Left office/age .... Jun 24, 1946, at age 56
President served .... Truman
Date of death/age .... Sep 8, 1953, at age 63
Cabinet service .... 11m 1d (331 days)
Other offices held CJ-13

Volpe, John Anthony   Secretary of Transportation 2

Date of birth .... Dec 8, 1908
Residence .... Massachusetts
Date of appointment/age .... Dec 12, 1968, at age 60
Assumed office/age .... Jan 21, 1969, at age 60
Left office/age .... Jan 20, 1973, at age 64

President served .... Nixon
Date of death/age .... Sep 11, 1994, at age 85
Cabinet service .... 4y (1,461 days)

Walker, Frank Comerford   Postmaster General 51

Date of birth .... May 30, 1886
Residence .... Pennsylvania
Date of appointment/age .... Sep 10, 1940, at age 54
Assumed office/age .... Sep 10, 1940, at age 54
Left office/age .... May 31, 1945, at age 59
President served .... Franklin D. Roosevelt
Date of death/age .... Sep 13, 1959, at age 73
Cabinet service .... 4y 8m 21d (1,722 days)

Walker, Robert J.   Secretary of the Treasury 18

Date of birth .... Jul 19, 1801
Residence .... Mississippi
Date of appointment/age .... Mar 6, 1845, at age 43
Assumed office/age .... Mar 8, 1845, at age 43
Left office/age .... Mar 5, 1849, at age 47
President served .... Polk
Date of death/age .... Nov 11, 1869, at age 68
Cabinet service .... 3y 11m 27d (1,452 days)

Wallace, Henry A.   Secretary of Agriculture 11

Date of birth .... Oct 7, 1888
Residence .... Iowa
Date of appointment/age .... Mar 4, 1933, at age 44
Assumed office/age .... Mar 4, 1933, at age 44
Left office/age .... Sep 4, 1940, at age 51
President served .... Franklin D. Roosevelt
Cabinet service 7y 6m

Wallace, Henry A.   Secretary of Commerce 10

Date of appointment/age .... Mar 1, 1945, at age 56
Assumed office/age .... Mar 2, 1945, at age 56
Left office/age .... Apr 12, 1945, at age 57
President served .... Franklin D. Roosevelt
Cabinet service 1m 10d

Wallace, Henry A.   Secretary of Commerce 10

Date of appointment/age .... April 12, 1945, at age 57
Assumed office/age .... Apr 12, 1945, at age 57
Left office/age .... Sep 27, 1946, at age 57
President served .... Truman
Date of death/age .... Nov 18, 1965, at age 77
Cabinet service 1y 5m 15d
Total Cabinet service .... 9y 25d (3,312 days)
Other offices held VP-33

Wallace, Henry Cantwell — Secretary of Agriculture 7

Date of birth .... May 11, 1866
Residence .... Iowa
Date of appointment/age .... Mar 5, 1921, at age 54
Assumed office/age .... Mar 5, 1921, at age 54
Left office/age .... Aug 2, 1923, at age 57
President served .... Harding
Cabinet service 2y 4m 28d

Wallace, Henry Cantwell — Secretary of Agriculture 7

Date of appointment/age .... Aug 2, 1923, at age 57
Assumed office/age .... Aug 2, 1923, at age 57
Left office/age .... Oct 25, 1924, at age 58
President served .... Coolidge
Date of death/age .... Oct 25, 1924, at age 58
Cabinet service 1y 2m 23d
Total Cabinet service .... 3y 7m 21d (1,326 days)

Wanamaker, John — Postmaster General 35

Date of birth .... Jul 11, 1838
Residence .... Pennsylvania
Date of appointment/age .... Mar 5, 1889, at age 50
Assumed office/age .... Mar 5, 1889, at age 50
Left office/age .... Mar 3, 1893, at age 54
President served .... Benjamin Harrison
Cabinet service 3y 11m 26d

Wanamaker, John — Postmaster General 35

Date of appointment/age .... Mar 4, 1893, at age 54
Assumed office/age .... Mar 4, 1893, at age 54
Left office/age .... Mar 5, 1893, at age 54
President served .... Cleveland
Date of death/age .... Dec 12, 1922, at age 84
Cabinet service 1d
Total Cabinet service .... 3y 11m 27d (1,452 days)

Washburne, Elihu B. — Secretary of State 25

Date of birth .... Sep 23, 1816
Residence .... Illinois
Date of appointment/age .... Mar 5, 1869, at age 52
Assumed office/age .... Mar 5, 1869, at age 52
Left office/age .... Mar 16, 1869, at age 52
President served .... Grant
Date of death/age .... Oct 23, 1887, at age 71
Cabinet service .... 11d (11 days)

Watkins, James David — Secretary of Energy 6

Date of birth .... Mar 7, 1927
Residence .... California
Confirmed/age .... Mar 1, 1989, at age 61

Left office/age . . . . Jan 20, 1993, at age 65
President served . . . . George Herbert Bush
Date of death/age . . . . — — — —
Cabinet service . . . . 3y 10m 19d (1,414 days)

Watson, William Marvin   Postmaster General 58

Date of birth . . . . Jun 6, 1924
Residence . . . . Texas
Date of appointment/age . . . . Apr 10, 1968, at age 43
Assumed office/age . . . . Apr 26, 1968, at age 43
Left office/age . . . . Jan 20, 1969, at age 44
President served . . . . Lyndon B. Johnson
Date of death/age . . . . — — — —
Cabinet service . . . . 8m 23d (263 days)

Watt, James Gaius   Secretary of the Interior 43

Date of birth . . . . Jan 31, 1938
Residence . . . . Colorado
Date of appointment/age . . . . Dec 23, 1980, at age 42
Assumed office/age . . . . Jan 21, 1981, at age 42
Left office/age . . . . Nov 21, 1983, at age 45
President served . . . . Reagan
Date of death/age . . . . — — — —
Cabinet service . . . . 2y 10m (1,030 days)

Weaver, Robert Clifton   Secretary of Housing and Urban Development 1

Date of birth . . . . Dec 29, 1907
Residence . . . . Washington
Date of appointment/age . . . . Jan 18, 1966, at age 58
Assumed office/age . . . . Jan 18, 1966, at age 58
Left office/age . . . . Jan 20, 1969, at age 21
President served . . . . Lyndon B. Johnson
Date of death/age . . . . Jul 17, 1997, at age 89
Cabinet service . . . . 3y 2d (1,097 days)

Webster, Daniel   Secretary of State 14

Date of birth . . . . Jan 18, 1782
Residence . . . . Massachusetts
Date of appointment/age . . . . Mar 5, 1841, at age 59
Assumed office/age . . . . Mar 5, 1841, at age 59
Left office/age . . . . Apr 4, 1841, at age 59
President served . . . . William H. Harrison
Cabinet service 1m

Webster, Daniel   Secretary of State 14

Date of appointment/age . . . . Apr 4, 1841, at age 59
Assumed office/age . . . . Apr 4, 1841, at age 59
Left office/age . . . . May 9, 1843, at age 61
President served . . . . Tyler
Cabinet service 2y 1m 5d

Webster, Daniel   Secretary of State 19

Date of appointment/age . . . . Jul 22, 1850, at age 67
Assumed office/age . . . . Jul 22, 1850, at age 68
Left office/age . . . . Oct 24, 1852, at age 70
President served . . . . Fillmore
Date of death/age . . . . Oct 24, 1852, at age 70
Cabinet service 2y 3m 2d
Total Cabinet service . . . . 5y 5m 7d (1,983 days)

Weeks, John W.   Secretary of War 50

Date of birth . . . . Apr 11, 1860
Residence . . . . Massachusetts
Date of appointment/age . . . . Mar 5, 1921, at age 60
Assumed office/age . . . . Mar 5, 1921, at age 60
Left office/age . . . . Aug 2, 1923, at age 63
President served . . . . Harding
Cabinet service 2y 4m 28d

Weeks, John W.   Secretary of War 50

Date of appointment/age . . . . Aug 2, 1923, at age 63
Assumed office/age . . . . Aug 2, 1923, at age 63
Left office/age . . . . Jul 12, 1926, at age 66
President served . . . . Coolidge
Date of death/age . . . . Jul 12, 1926, at age 66
Cabinet service 2y 11m 10d
Total Cabinet service . . . . 5y 4m 8d (1,954 days)

Weeks, Sinclair   Secretary of Commerce 13

Date of birth . . . . Jun 15, 1893
Residence . . . . Massachusetts
Date of appointment/age . . . . Jan 21, 1953, at age 59
Assumed office/age . . . . Jan 21, 1953, at age 59
Left office/age . . . . Nov 12, 1958, at age 65
President served . . . . Eisenhower
Date of death/age . . . . Jan 27, 1972, at age 78
Cabinet service . . . . 4y 9m 22d (1,753 days)

Weinberger, Caspar Willard   Secretary of Health, Education and Welfare 10

Date of birth . . . . Aug 18, 1917
Residence . . . . California
Date of appointment/age . . . . Nov 28, 1972, at age 55
Assumed office/age . . . . Feb 12, 1973, at age 55
Left office/age . . . . Aug 9, 1974, at age 56
President served . . . . Nixon
Cabinet service 1y 5m 28d

Weinberger, Caspar Willard   Secretary of Health, Education and Welfare 10

Date of appointment/age . . . . Aug 9, 1974, at age 56
Assumed office/age . . . . Aug 9, 1974, at age 56

Left office/age .... Aug 8, 1975, at age 57
President served .... Ford
Cabinet service 1y

Weinberger, Caspar Willard   Secretary of Defense 15

Date of appointment/age .... Dec 12, 1980, at age 63
Assumed office/age .... Jan 21, 1981, at age 63
Left office/age .... Nov 23, 1987, at age 69
President served .... Reagan
Date of death/age .... — — — —
Cabinet service 6y 10m 2d
Total Cabinet service .... 9y 4m (3,407 days)

Welles, Gideon   Secretary of the Navy 24

Date of birth .... Jul 1, 1802
Residence .... Connecticut
Date of appointment/age .... Mar 5, 1861, at age 58
Assumed office/age .... Mar 7, 1861, at age 58
Left office/age .... Apr 15, 1865, at age 62
President served .... Lincoln
Cabinet service 4y 1m 8d

Welles, Gideon   Secretary of the Navy 24

Date of appointment/age .... Apr 15, 1865, at age 62
Assumed office/age .... Apr 15, 1865, at age 62
Left office/age .... Mar 3, 1869, at age 66
President served .... Andrew Johnson
Date of death/age .... Feb 11, 1878, at age 75
Cabinet service 3y 10m 16d
Total Cabinet service .... 7y 11m 24d (2,910 days)

West, Roy Owen   Secretary of the Interior 30

Date of birth .... Oct 27, 1868
Residence .... Illinois
Date of appointment/age .... Jan 21, 1929, at age 60
Assumed office/age .... Jan 21, 1929, at age 60
Left office/age .... Mar 3, 1929, at age 60
President served .... Coolidge
Date of death/age .... Nov 29, 1958, at age 90
Cabinet service .... 1m 10d (40 days)

West, Togo Dennis, Jr.   Secretary of Veterans Affairs
                                             (interim)

Date of birth .... Jun 21, 1942
State of birth .... North Carolina
Residence .... Washington, D.C.
Appointed/age .... Jan 2, 1998, at age 55
Left office/age .... Apr 28, 1998, at age 55
President served .... Clinton
Cabinet service 4m 3d

West, Togo Dennis, Jr.   Secretary of Veterans Affairs 3

Appointed/age	Apr 28, 1998, at age 55
Confirmed/age	Apr 28, 1998, at age 55
Left office/age	Jan 20, 2001, at age 58
President served	Clinton
Date of death/age	——————
Cabinet service	2y 8m 15d
Total Cabinet service	3y 18d (1,113 days)

Whiting, William F.   Secretary of Commerce 4

Date of birth	Jul 20, 1864
Residence	Massachusetts
Date of appointment/age	Dec 11, 1928, at age 64
Assumed office/age	Dec 11, 1928, at age 64
Left office/age	Mar 4, 1929, at age 64
President served	Coolidge
Date of death/age	Aug 31, 1936, at age 72
Cabinet service	2m 21d (81 days)

Whitney, William C.   Secretary of the Navy 31

Date of birth	Jul 5, 1841
Residence	New York
Date of appointment/age	Mar 6, 1885, at age 43
Assumed office/age	Mar 6, 1885, at age 43
Left office/age	Mar 4, 1889, at age 47
President served	Cleveland
Date of death/age	Feb 2, 1904, at age 62
Cabinet service	3y 11m 28d (1,453 days)

Wickard, Claude R.   Secretary of Agriculture 12

Date of birth	Feb 28, 1893
Residence	Indiana
Date of appointment/age	Aug 27, 1940, at age 47
Assumed office/age	Sep 5, 1940, at age 47
Left office/age	Jun 29, 1945, at age 52
President served	Franklin D. Roosevelt
Date of death/age	Apr 29, 1967, at age 74
Cabinet service	4y 9m 24d (1,755 days)

Wickersham, George Woodward   Attorney General 47

Date of birth	Sep 19, 1858
Residence	New York
Date of appointment/age	Mar 5, 1909, at age 50
Assumed office/age	Mar 5, 1909, at age 50
Left office/age	Mar 3, 1913, at age 54
President served	Taft
Cabinet service	3y 11m 26d

Wickersham, George Woodward   Attorney General 47

Date of appointment/age	Mar 4, 1913, at age 54
Assumed office/age	Mar 4, 1913, at age 54

Left office/age .... Mar 5, 1913, at age 54
President served .... Wilson
Date of death/age .... Jan 25, 1936, at age 77
Cabinet service 1d
Total Cabinet service .... 3y 11m 27d (1,452 days)

Wickliffe, Charles Anderson   Postmaster General 11

Date of birth .... Jun 8, 1788
Residence .... Kentucky
Date of appointment/age .... Sep 13, 1841, at age 53
Assumed office/age .... Oct 13, 1841, at age 53
Left office/age .... Mar 5, 1945, at age 56
President served .... Tyler
Date of death/age .... Oct 31, 1869, at age 81
Cabinet service .... 3y 4m 20d (1,235 days)

Wilbur, Curtis D.   Secretary of the Navy 43

Date of birth .... May 10, 1867
Residence .... California
Date of appointment/age .... Mar 18, 1924, at age 56
Assumed office/age .... Mar 18, 1924, at age 56
Left office/age .... Mar 4, 1929, at age 61
President served .... Coolidge
Date of death/age .... Sep 8, 1954, at age 87
Cabinet service .... 4y 11m 14d (1,805 days)

Wilbur, Ray Lyman   Secretary of the Interior 31

Date of birth .... Apr 13, 1875
Residence .... California
Date of appointment/age .... Mar 5, 1929, at age 53
Assumed office/age .... Mar 5, 1929, at age 53
Left office/age .... Mar 3, 1933, at age 57
President served .... Hoover
Date of death/age .... Jun 26, 1949, at age 74
Cabinet service .... 3y 11m 28d (1,453 days)

Wilkins, William   Secretary of War 20

Date of birth .... Dec 20, 1779
Residence .... Pennsylvania
Date of appointment/age .... Feb 15, 1844, at age 64
Assumed office/age .... Feb 20, 1844, at age 64
Left office/age .... Mar 7, 1845, at age 65
President served .... Tyler
Date of death/age .... Jun 23, 1865, at age 85
Cabinet service .... 1y 15d (380 days)

Williams, George H.   Attorney General 32

Date of birth .... Mar 26, 1820
Residence .... Oregon
Date of appointment/age .... Dec 14, 1871, at age 51
Assumed office/age .... Jan 10, 1872, at age 51

Left office/age .... May 14, 1875, at age 55
President served .... Grant
Date of death/age .... Apr 4, 1910, at age 90
Cabinet service .... 3y 4m 4d (1,219 days)

Wilson, Charles E. — Secretary of Defense 5

Date of birth .... Jul 18, 1890
Residence .... Michigan
Date of appointment/age .... Jan 28, 1953, at age 62
Assumed office/age .... Jan 28, 1953, at age 62
Left office/age .... Oct 8, 1957, at age 67
President served .... Eisenhower
Date of death/age .... Sep 26, 1961, at age 71
Cabinet service .... 4y 8m 10d (1,711 days)

Wilson, James — Secretary of Agriculture 4

Date of birth .... Aug 16, 1836
Residence .... Iowa
Date of appointment/age .... Mar 5, 1897, at age 60
Assumed office/age .... Mar 5, 1897, at age 60
Left office/age .... Sep 14, 1901, at age 64
President served .... McKinley
Cabinet service 4y 6m 9d

Wilson, James — Secretary of Agriculture 4

Date of appointment/age .... Sep 14, 1901, at age 64
Assumed office/age .... Sep 14, 1901, at age 64
Left office/age .... Mar 3, 1909, at age 72
President served .... Theodore Roosevelt
Cabinet service 7y 5m 17d

Wilson, James — Secretary of Agriculture 4

Date of appointment/age .... Mar 4, 1909, at age 72
Assumed office/age .... Mar 4, 1909, at age 72
Left office/age .... Mar 3, 1913, at age 76
President served .... Taft
Date of death/age .... Aug 26, 1920, at age 84
Cabinet service 4y
Total Cabinet service .... 15y 11m 26d (5,834 days)

Wilson, William B. — Secretary of Labor 1

Date of birth .... Apr 2, 1862
Residence .... Pennsylvania
Date of appointment/age .... Mar 5, 1913, at age 50
Assumed office/age .... Mar 5, 1913, at age 50
Left office/age .... Mar 4, 1921, at age 58
President served .... Wilson
Date of death/age .... May 26, 1934, at age 72
Cabinet service .... 8y (2,922 days)

Wilson, William Lyne — Postmaster General 37

Date of birth .... May 3, 1843
Residence .... West Virginia

Date of appointment/age . . . . Mar 3, 1895, at age 51
Assumed office/age . . . . Apr 4, 1895, at age 51
Left office/age . . . . Mar 5, 1897, at age 53
President served . . . . Cleveland
Date of death/age . . . . Oct 17, 1900, at age 57
Cabinet service . . . . 1y 11m 1d (696 days)

Windom, William   Secretary of the Treasury 33

Date of birth . . . . May 10, 1827
Residence . . . . Minnesota
Date of appointment/age . . . . Mar 5, 1881, at age 53
Assumed office/age . . . . Mar 8, 1881, at age 53
Left office/age . . . . Nov 13, 1881, at age 54
President served . . . . Garfield
Cabinet service 8m 5d

Windom, William   Secretary of the Treasury 39

Date of appointment/age . . . . Mar 5, 1889, at age 61
Assumed office/age . . . . Mar 7, 1889, at age 61
Left office/age . . . . Jan 29, 1891, at age 63
President served . . . . Benjamin Harrison
Date of death/age . . . . Jan 29, 1891, at age 63
Cabinet service 1y 10m 22d
Total Cabinet service . . . . 2y 6m 27d (937 days)

Wirt, William   Attorney General 9

Date of birth . . . . Nov 8, 1772
Residence . . . . Virginia
Date of appointment/age . . . . Nov 13, 1817, at age 45
Assumed office/age . . . . Nov 15, 1817, at age 45
Left office/age . . . . Mar 3, 1825, at age 52
President served . . . . Monroe
Cabinet service 7y 3m 16d

Wirt, William   Attorney General 9

Date of appointment/age . . . . Mar 4, 1825, at age 52
Assumed office /age . . . . Mar 4, 1825, at age 52
Left office/age . . . . Mar 3, 1829, at age 56
President served . . . . John Q. Adams
Date of death/age . . . . Feb 18, 1834, at age 61
Cabinet service 4y
Total Cabinet service . . . . 11y 3m 16d (4,123 days)

Wirtz, W. Willard   Secretary of Labor 10

Date of birth . . . . Mar 14, 1912
Residence . . . . Illinois
Date of appointment/age . . . . Sep 25, 1962, at age 50
Assumed office/age . . . . Sep 25, 1962, at age 50
Left office/age . . . . Nov 22, 1963, at age 51
President served . . . . Kennedy
Cabinet service 1y 1m 28d

Wirtz, W. Willard — Secretary of Labor 10

Date of appointment/age . . . . Nov 22, 1963, at age 51
Assumed office/age . . . . Nov 22, 1963, at age 51
Left office/age . . . . Jan 20, 1969, at age 56
President served . . . . Lyndon B. Johnson
Date of death/age . . . . — — — —
Cabinet service 5y 1m 29d
Total Cabinet service . . . . 6y 3m 27d (2,308 days)

Wolcott, Oliver — Secretary of the Treasury 2

Date of birth . . . . Jan 11, 1760
Residence . . . . Connecticut
Date of appointment/age . . . . Feb 2, 1795, at age 35
Assumed office/age . . . . Feb 2, 1795, at age 35
Left office/age . . . . Mar 3, 1797, at age 37
President served . . . . Washington
Cabinet service 2y 1m 1d

Wolcott, Oliver — Secretary of the Treasury 2

Date of appointment/age . . . . Mar 4, 1797, at age 37
Assumed office/age . . . . Mar 4, 1797, at age 37
Left office/age . . . . Dec 30, 1800, at age 40
President served . . . . John Adams
Date of death/age . . . . Jun 1, 1833, at age 73
Cabinet service 3y 9m 26d
Total Cabinet service . . . . 5y 10m 27d (2,153 days)

Wood, Robert C. — Secretary of Housing and Urban Development 2

Date of birth . . . . Sep 16, 1923
Residence . . . . Massachusetts
Date of appointment/age . . . . Jan 3, 1969, at age 45
Assumed office/age . . . . Jan 8, 1969, at age 45
Left office/age . . . . Jan 21, 1969, at age 45
President served . . . . Lyndon B. Johnson
Date of death/age . . . . — — — —
Cabinet service . . . . 13d (13 days)

Woodbury, Levi — Secretary of the Navy 9

Date of birth . . . . Dec 22, 1789
Residence . . . . New Hampshire
Date of appointment/age . . . . May 23, 1831, at age 41
Assumed office/age . . . . May 23, 1831, at age 41
Left office/age . . . . Jun 29, 1834, at age 43
President served . . . . Jackson
Cabinet service 3y 1m 6d

Woodbury, Levi — Secretary of the Treasury 13

Date of appointment/age . . . . Jun 27, 1834, at age 44
Assumed office/age . . . . Jul 1, 1834, at age 44
Left office/age . . . . Mar 3, 1837, at age 47

President served .... Jackson
Cabinet service 2y 8m 2d

Woodbury, Levi — Secretary of the Treasury 13

Date of appointment/age .... Mar 4, 1837, at age 47
Assumed office/age .... Mar 4, 1837, at age 47
Left office/age .... Mar 3, 1841, at age 51
President served .... Van Buren
Date of death/age .... Sep 4, 1851, at age 61
Cabinet service 4y
Total Cabinet service .... 9y 9m 8d (3,565 days)
Other offices held AJ-27

Woodin, William H. — Secretary of the Treasury 51

Date of birth .... May 27, 1868
Residence .... New York
Date of appointment/age .... Mar 4, 1933, at age 64
Assumed office/age .... Mar 4, 1933, at age 64
Left office/age .... Dec 31, 1933, at age 65
President served .... Franklin D. Roosevelt
Date of death/age .... May 3, 1934, at age 65
Cabinet service .... 9m 27d (297 days)

Woodring, Harry H. — Secretary of War 55

Date of birth .... May 31, 1890
Residence .... Kansas
Date of appointment/age .... May 6, 1937, at age 46
Assumed office/age .... May 6, 1937, at age 46
Left office/age .... Jul 9, 1940, at age 50
President served .... Franklin D. Roosevelt
Date of death/age .... Sep 9, 1967, at age 77
Cabinet service .... 3y 2m 3d (1,158 days)

Work, Hubert — Postmaster General 47

Date of birth .... Jul 3, 1860
Residence .... Colorado
Date of appointment/age .... Mar 4, 1922, at age 61
Assumed office/age .... Mar 4, 1922, at age 61
Left office/age .... Feb 26, 1923, at age 62
President served .... Harding
Cabinet service 11m 22d

Work, Hubert — Secretary of the Interior 29

Date of appointment/age .... Feb 27, 1923, at age 62
Assumed office/age .... Mar 5, 1923, at age 62
Left office/age .... Aug 2, 1923, at age 63
President served .... Harding
Cabinet service 4m 28d

Work, Hubert — Secretary of the Interior 29

Date of appointment/age .... Aug 3, 1923, at age 63
Assumed office/age .... Aug 3, 1923, at age 63

Left office/age .... Jul 24, 1928, at age 68
President served .... Coolidge
Date of death/age .... Dec 14, 1942, at age 82
Cabinet service 4y 11m 21d
Total Cabinet service .... 6y 4m 11d (2,322 days)

Wright, Luke E.   Secretary of War 45

Date of birth .... Aug 29, 1846
Residence .... Tennessee
Date of appointment/age .... Jun 29, 1908, at age 61
Assumed office/age .... Jul 1, 1908, at age 61
Left office/age .... Mar 11, 1909, at age 62
President served .... Theodore Roosevelt
Date of death/age .... Nov 17, 1922, at age 76
Cabinet service .... 8m 10d (250 days)

Wynne, Robert John   Postmaster General 41

Date of birth .... Nov 18, 1851
Residence .... Pennsylvania
Date of appointment/age .... Oct 10, 1904, at age 52
Assumed office/age .... Oct 10, 1904, at age 52
Left office/age .... Mar 5, 1905, at age 53
President served .... Theodore Roosevelt
Date of death/age .... Mar 11, 1922, at age 70
Cabinet service .... 4m 23d (143 days)

Yeutter, Clayton Keith   Secretary of Agriculture 23

Date of birth .... Dec 10, 1930
Residence .... Nebraska
Confirmed/age .... Feb 8, 1989, at age 58
Left office/age .... Mar 1, 1991, at age 60
President served .... George Herbert Bush
Date of death/age .... ————
Cabinet service .... 2y 26d (756 days)

Supreme Court Appointees

CHIEF JUSTICES

John Jay 1789–1795
John Rutledge (acting/not confirmed) 1795
Oliver Ellsworth 1796–1800
John Marshall 1801–1835
Roger B. Taney 1836–1864
Salmon P. Chase 1864–1873
Morrison R. Waite 1874–1888
Melville W. Fuller 1888–1910

Edward D. White 1910–1921
William H. Taft 1921–1930
Charles E. Hughes 1930–1941
Harlan F. Stone 1941–1946
Fred M. Vinson 1946–1953
Earl Warren 1954–1969
Warren E. Burger 1969–1986
William H. Rehnquist 1986–

ASSOCIATE JUSTICES

John Rutledge 1789–1791
William Cushing 1789–1810
James Wilson 1789–1798
John Blair 1789–1796
James Iredell 1790–1799
Thomas Johnson 1791–1793
William Paterson 1793–1806
Samuel Chase 1796–1811
Bushrod Washington 1798–1829
Alfred Moore 1799–1804
William Johnson 1804–1834
Henry Brockholst Livingston 1806–1823
Thomas Todd 1807–1826
Joseph Story 1811–1845
Gabriel Duval 1811–1835
Smith Thompson 1823–1843
Robert Trimble 1826–1828
John McLean 1829–1861
Henry Baldwin 1830–1844

James M. Wayne 1835–1867
Philip P. Barbour 1836–1841
John Catron 1837–1865
John McKinley 1837–1852
Peter V. Daniel 1841–1860
Samuel Nelson 1845–1872
Levi Woodbury 1846–1851
Robert C. Grier 1846–1870
Benjamin R. Curtis 1851–1857
John A. Campbell 1853–1861
Nathan Clifford 1858–1881
Noah H. Swayne 1862–1881
Samuel F. Miller 1862–1890
David Davis 1862–1877
Stephen J. Field 1863–1897
Edwin M. Stanton 1869
William Strong 1870–1880
Joseph P. Bradley 1870–1892
Ward Hunt 1872–1882

John Marshall Harlan 1877–1911
William B. Woods 1880–1887
Stanley Matthews 1881–1889
Horace Gray 1881–1902
Samuel Blatchford 1882–1893
Lucius Q.C. Lamar 1888–1893
David J. Brewer 1889–1910
Henry B. Brown 1890–1906
George Shiras, Jr. 1892–1903
Howell E. Jackson 1893–1895
Edward D. White 1894–1910
Rufus W. Peckham 1895–1909
Joseph McKenna 1898–1925
Oliver W. Holmes, Jr. 1902–1932
William R. Day 1903–1922
William H. Moody 1906–1910
Horace H. Lurton 1909–1914
Charles E. Hughes 1910–1916
Willis Van Devanter 1910–1937
Joseph Rucker Lamar 1910–1916
Mahlon Pitney 1912–1922
James C. McReynolds 1914–1941
Louis D. Brandeis 1916–1939
John H. Clarke 1916–1922
George Sutherland 1922–1938
Pierce Butler 1922–1939
Edward T. Sanford 1923–1930
Harlan Fiske Stone 1925–1941
Owen J. Roberts 1930–1945
Benjamin Nathan Cardozo 1932–1938

Hugo L. Black 1937–1971
Stanley F. Reed 1938–1957
Felix Frankfurter 1939–1962
William O. Douglas 1939–1975
Frank Murphy 1940–1949
James F. Byrnes 1941–1942
Robert H. Jackson 1941–1954
Wiley B. Rutledge 1943–1949
Harold H. Burton 1945–1958
Tom C. Clark 1949–1967
Sherman Minton 1949–1956
John Marshall Harlan II 1955–1971
William J. Brennan, Jr. 1957–1990
Charles E. Whittaker 1957–1962
Potter Stewart 1959–1981
Byron R. White 1962–1993
Arthur J. Goldberg 1962–1965
Abe Fortas 1965–1969
Thurgood Marshall 1967–1991
Harry A. Blackmun 1970–1994
Lewis F. Powell, Jr. 1971–1987
William H. Rehnquist 1971–1986
John Paul Stevens 1975–
Sandra Day O'Connor 1981–
Antonin Scalia 1986–
Anthony M. Kennedy 1988–
David H. Souter 1990–
Clarence Thomas 1991–
Ruth Bader Ginsburg 1993–
Steven Breyer 1994–

Biographical Data — Supreme Court Justices

Baldwin, Henry — Associate Justice 19

Date of birth	Jan 14, 1780
Residence	Pennsylvania
Date of nomination/age	Jan 4, 1830, at age 49
Nominating president	Jackson
Confirmation/age	Jan 6, 1830, at age 49
Left office/age	Apr 21, 1844, at age 64
Reason for leaving office	Died in office
Date of death/age	Apr 21, 1844, at age 64
Term of service	14y 3m 15d (5,218 days)
Term of retirement	None

Barbour, Philip P. — Associate Justice 22

Date of birth	May 25, 1783
Residence	Virginia
Date of nomination/age	Dec 28, 1835, at age 52
Nominating president	Jackson
Confirmation/age	Mar 15, 1836, at age 52
Left office/age	Feb 25, 1841, at age 57
Reason for leaving office	Died in office
Date of death/age	Feb 25, 1841, at age 57
Term of service	4y 11m 10d (1,801 days)
Term of retirement	None

Black, Hugo Lafayette — Associate Justice 71

Date of birth	Feb 27, 1886
Residence	Alabama
Date of nomination/age	Aug 12, 1937, at age 51
Nominating president	Franklin D. Roosevelt
Confirmation/age	Aug 17, 1937, at age 51
Left office/age	Sep 18, 1971, at age 85
Reason for leaving office	Resigned
Date of death/age	Sep 25, 1971, at age 85

Term of service .... 34y 1m 1d (12,449 days)
Term of retirement .... 7d (7 days)

Blackmun, Harry Andrew   Associate Justice 90

Date of birth .... Nov 12, 1908
Residence .... Minnesota
Date of nomination/age .... Apr 14, 1970, at age 61
Nominating president .... Nixon
Confirmation/age .... May 12, 1970, at age 61
Left office/age .... Jun 30, 1994, at age 85
Reason for leaving office .... Resigned
Date of death/age .... Mar 4, 1999, at age 90
Term of service .... 24y 1m 18d (8,814 days)
Term of retirement .... 4y 8m 3d (1,704 days)

Blair, John, Jr.   Associate Justice 4

Date of birth 1732
Residence .... Virginia
Date of nomination/age .... Sep 24, 1789, at age 56
Nominating president .... Washington
Confirmation/age .... Sep 26, 1789, at age 56
Left office/age .... Jan 27, 1796, at age 63
Reason for leaving office .... Resigned
Date of death/age .... Aug 31, 1800, at age 67
Term of service .... 6y 4m 1d (2,315 days)
Term of retirement .... 4y 7m 4d (1,675 days)

Blatchford, Samuel M.   Associate Justice 44

Date of birth .... Mar 9, 1820
Residence .... New York
Date of nomination/age .... Mar 13, 1882, at age 62
Nominating president .... Arthur
Confirmation/age .... Mar 27, 1882, at age 62
Left office/age .... Jul 7, 1893, at age 72
Reason for leaving office .... Died in office
Date of death/age .... Jul 7, 1893, at age 72
Term of service .... 11y 3m 10d (4,117 days)
Term of retirement .... None

Bradley, Joseph P.   Associate Justice 38

Date of birth .... Mar 14, 1813
Residence .... New Jersey
Date of nomination/age .... Feb 7, 1870, at age 56
Nominating president .... Grant
Confirmation/age .... Mar 21, 1870, at age 57
Left office/age .... Jan 22, 1892, at age 78
Reason for leaving office .... Died in office
Date of death/age .... Jan 22, 1892, at age 78
Term of service .... 21y 10m 1d (7,971 days)
Term of retirement .... None

Brandeis, Louis D.   Associate Justice 63

Date of birth .... Nov 13, 1856
Residence .... Massachusetts
Date of nomination/age .... Jan 28, 1916, at age 59
Nominating president .... Wilson
Confirmation/age .... Jun 1, 1916, at age 59
Left office/age .... Feb 13, 1939, at age 82
Reason for leaving office .... Resigned
Date of death/age .... Oct 5, 1941, at age 84
Term of service .... 22y 8m 12d (8,287 days)
Term of retirement .... 2y 7m 22d (962 days)

Brennan, William Joseph, Jr.   Associate Justice 83

Date of birth .... Apr 25, 1906
Residence .... New Jersey
Date of nomination/age .... Oct 16, 1956, at age 50
Nominating president .... Eisenhower
Confirmation/age .... Mar 19, 1957, at age 50
Left office/age .... Jul 20, 1990, at age 84
Reason for leaving office .... Resigned
Date of death/age .... Jul 24, 1997, at age 91
Term of service .... 33y 4m 1d (12,174 days)
Term of retirement .... 7y 4d (2,560 days)

Brewer, David J.   Associate Justice 47

Date of birth .... Jan 20, 1837
Residence .... Kansas
Date of nomination/age .... Dec 4, 1889, at age 52
Nominating president .... Benjamin Harrison
Confirmation/age .... Dec 18, 1889, at age 52
Left office/age .... Mar 28, 1910, at age 73
Reason for leaving office .... Died in office
Date of death/age .... Mar 28, 1910, at age 73
Term of service .... 20y 3m 10d (7,405 days)
Term of retirement .... None

Breyer, Stephen Gerald   Associate Justice 100

Date of birth .... Aug 15, 1938
Residence .... Massachusetts
Date of nomination/age .... May 13, 1994, at age 55
Nominating president .... Clinton
Confirmation/age .... Jul 29, 1994, at age 55
Left office/age .... — — — — —
Reason for leaving office .... — — — — —
Date of death/age .... — — — — —
Term of service .... — — — — —
Term of retirement .... — — — — —

Brown, Henry B.   Associate Justice 48

Date of birth .... Mar 21, 1836
Residence .... Michigan

Date of nomination/age .... Dec 23, 1890, at age 54
Nominating president .... Grant
Confirmation/age .... Dec 29, 1890, at age 54
Left office/age .... May 28, 1906, at age 70
Reason for leaving office .... Resigned
Date of death/age .... Sep 4, 1913, at age 77
Term of service .... 15y 4m 29d (5,627 days)
Term of retirement .... 7y 3m 7d (2,652 days)

Burger, Warren Earl   Chief Justice 15

Date of birth .... Sep 17, 1907
Residence .... Virginia
Date of nomination/age .... May 21, 1969, at age 61
Nominating president .... Nixon
Confirmation/age .... Jun 9, 1969, at age 61
Left office/age .... Jun 17, 1986, at age 78
Reason for leaving office .... Resigned
Date of death/age .... Jun 25, 1995, at age 87
Term of service .... 25y 1m 1d (9,139 days)
Term of retirement .... 9y 1m 1d (3,295 days)

Burton, Harold H.   Associate Justice 79

Date of birth .... Jun 22, 1888
Residence .... Ohio
Date of nomination/age .... Sep 19, 1945, at age 57
Nominating president .... Truman
Confirmation/age .... Sep 19, 1945, at age 57
Left office/age .... Oct 13, 1958, at age 70
Reason for leaving office .... Resigned
Date of death/age .... Oct 28, 1964, at age 76
Term of service .... 13y 24d (4,772 days)
Term of retirement .... 6y 15d (2,206 days)

Butler, Pierce   Associate Justice 66

Date of birth .... Mar 17, 1866
Residence .... Minnesota
Date of nomination/age .... Nov 23, 1922, at age 56
Nominating president .... Harding
Confirmation/age .... Dec 21, 1922, at age 56
Left office/age .... Nov 16, 1939, at age 73
Reason for leaving office .... Died in office
Date of death/age .... Nov 16, 1939, at age 73
Term of service .... 16y 10m 26d (6,170 days)
Term of retirement .... None

Byrnes, James Francis   Associate Justice 76

Date of birth .... May 2, 1879
Residence .... South Carolina
Date of nomination/age .... Jun 12, 1941, at age 62
Nominating president .... Franklin D. Roosevelt
Confirmation/age .... Jun 12, 1941, at age 62
Left office/age .... Oct 3, 1942, at age 63

Reason for leaving office .... Resigned
Date of death/age .... Apr 9, 1972, at age 92
Term of service .... 1y 3m 21d (476 days)
Term of retirement .... 29y 6m 6d (10,778 days)
Other offices held ST-49

Campbell, John Archibald　　　　Associate Justice 30

Date of birth .... Jun 24, 1811
Residence .... Alabama
Date of nomination/age .... Mar 22, 1853, at age 41
Nominating president .... Pierce
Confirmation/age .... Mar 25, 1853, at age 41
Left office/age .... Apr 30, 1861, at age 49
Reason for leaving office .... Resigned
Date of death/age .... Mar 12, 1889, at age 77
Term of service .... 8y 1m 5d (2,957 days)
Term of retirement .... 27y 10m 12d (10,173 days)

Cardozo, Benjamin Nathan　　　　Associate Justice 70

Date of birth .... May 24, 1870
Residence .... New York
Date of nomination/age .... Feb 15, 1932, at age 61
Nominating president .... Hoover
Confirmation/age .... Feb 24, 1932, at age 61
Left office/age .... Jul 9, 1938, at age 68
Reason for leaving office .... Died in office
Date of death/age .... Jul 9, 1938, at age 68
Term of service .... 6y 4m 15d (2,326 days)
Term of retirement .... None

Catron, John　　　　Associate Justice 23

Date of birth 1786
Residence .... Tennessee
Date of nomination/age .... Mar 3, 1873, at age 51
Nominating president .... Jackson
Confirmation/age .... Mar 8, 1837, at age 51
Left office/age .... May 30, 1865, at age 79
Reason for leaving office .... Died in office
Date of death/age .... May 30, 1865, at age 79
Term of service .... 28y 2m 22d (10,309 days)
Term of retirement .... None

Chase, Salmon Portland　　　　Chief Justice 6

Date of birth .... Jan 13, 1808
Residence .... Ohio
Date of nomination/age .... Dec 6, 1864, at age 56
Nominating president .... Washington
Confirmation/age .... Dec 6, 1864, at age 56
Left office/age .... May 7, 1873, at age 65
Reason for leaving office .... Died in office
Date of death/age .... May 7, 1873, at age 65
Term of service .... 8y 5m 1d (3,073 days)

Term of retirement .... None
Other offices held TY-25

Chase, Samuel   Associate Justice 8

Date of birth .... Apr 17, 1741
Residence .... Maryland
Date of nomination/age .... Jan 26, 1796, at age 54
Nominating president .... Washington
Confirmation/age .... Jan 27, 1796, at age 54
Left office/age .... Jun 19, 1811, at age 70
Reason for leaving office .... Died in office
Date of death/age .... Jun 19, 1811, at age 70
Term of service .... 15y 4m 23d (5,621 days)
Term of retirement .... None

Clark, Thomas C.   Associate Justice 80

Date of birth .... Sep 23, 1899
Residence .... Texas
Date of nomination/age .... Aug 2, 1949, at age 49
Nominating president .... Truman
Confirmation/age .... Aug 19, 1949, at age 49
Left office/age .... Jun 12, 1967, at age 67
Reason for leaving office .... Resigned
Date of death/age .... Jun 13, 1977, at age 77
Term of service .... 17y 9m 24d (6,503 days)
Term of retirement .... 10y 1d (3,653 days)
Other offices held AT-59

Clarke, John Hessin   Associate Justice 64

Date of birth .... Sep 18, 1857
Residence .... Ohio
Date of nomination/age .... Jul 14, 1916, at age 58
Nominating president .... Wilson
Confirmation/age .... Jul 24, 1916, at age 58
Left office/age .... Sep 18, 1922, at age 65
Reason for leaving office .... Resigned
Date of death/age .... Mar 22, 1945, at age 87
Term of service .... 6y 1m 24d (2,245 days)
Term of retirement .... 22y 6m 4d (8,219 days)

Clifford, Nathan   Associate Justice 31

Date of birth .... Aug 18, 1803
Residence .... Maine
Date of nomination/age .... Dec 9, 1857, at age 54
Nominating president .... Buchanan
Confirmation/age .... Jan 12, 1858, at age 54
Left office/age .... Jul 25, 1881, at age 77
Reason for leaving office .... Died in office
Date of death/age .... Jul 25, 1881, at age 77
Term of service .... 23y 6m 13d (8,593 days)
Term of retirement .... None
Other offices held AT-19

Curtis, Benjamin Robbins   Associate Justice 29

Date of birth	Nov 4, 1809
Residence	Massachusetts
Date of nomination/age	Dec 11, 1851, at age 42
Nominating president	Fillmore
Confirmation/age	Dec 29, 1851, at age 42
Left office/age	Sep 1, 1857, at age 47
Reason for leaving office	Resigned
Date of death/age	Sep 15, 1874, at age 64
Term of service	5y 8m 3d (2,069 days)
Term of retirement	17y 14d (6,223 days)

Cushing, William   Associate Justice 2

Date of birth	Mar 1, 1732
Residence	Massachusetts
Date of nomination/age	Sep 24, 1789, at age 57
Nominating president	Washington
Confirmation/age	Sep 26, 1789, at age 57
Left office/age	Sep 13, 1810, at age 78
Reason for leaving office	Died in office
Date of death/age	Sep 13, 1810, at age 78
Term of service	20y 11m 18d (7,653 days)
Term of retirement	None

Daniel, Peter Vivian   Associate Justice 25

Date of birth	Apr 24, 1784
Residence	Virginia
Date of nomination/age	Feb 26, 1841, at age 56
Nominating president	Van Buren
Confirmation/age	Mar 2, 1841, at age 56
Left office/age	May 30, 1860 atage 76
Reason for leaving office	Died in office
Date of death/age	May 30, 1860, at age 76
Term of service	19y 2m 28d (7,027 days)
Term of retirement	None

Davis, David   Associate Justice 34

Date of birth	Mar 9, 1815
Residence	Illinois
Date of nomination/age	Dec 1, 1862, at age 47
Nominating president	Lincoln
Confirmation/age	Dec 8, 1862, at age 47
Left office/age	Mar 4, 1877, at age 61
Reason for leaving office	Resigned
Date of death/age	Jun 26, 1886, at age 70
Term of service	14y 2m 24d (5,197 days)
Term of retirement	9y 3m 22d (3,397 days)

Day, William Rufus   Associate Justice 55

Date of birth	Apr 17, 1849
Residence	Ohio

Date of nomination/age .... Feb 19, 1903, at age 53
Nominating president .... Theodore Roosevelt
Confirmation/age .... Feb 23, 1903, at age 53
Left office/age .... Nov 13, 1922, at age 73
Reason for leaving office .... Resigned
Date of death/age .... Jul 9, 1923, at age 74
Term of service .... 19y 8m 21d (7,200 days)
Term of retirement .... 7m 26d (236 days)
Other offices held ST-36

Douglas, William Orville   Associate Justice 74

Date of birth .... Oct 16, 1898
Residence .... Connecticut
Date of nomination/age .... Mar 20, 1939, at age 40
Nominating president .... Franklin D. Roosevelt
Confirmation/age .... Apr 4, 1939, at age 40
Left office/age .... Nov 12, 1975, at age 77
Reason for leaving office .... Resigned
Date of death/age .... Jan 19, 1980, at age 81
Term of service .... 36y 7m 8d (13,367 days)
Term of retirement .... 4y 2m 7d (1,528 days)

Duvall, Gabriel   Associate Justice 15

Date of birth .... Dec 6, 1752
Residence .... Maryland
Date of nomination/age .... Nov 15, 1811, at age 58
Nominating president .... Madison
Confirmation/age .... Nov 18, 1811, at age 58
Left office/age .... Jan 14, 1835, at age 82
Reason for leaving office .... Resigned
Date of death/age .... Mar 6, 1844, at age 91
Term of service .... 23y 1m 27d (8,457 days)
Term of retirement .... 9y 1m 21d (3,337 days)

Ellsworth, Oliver   Chief Justice 3

Date of birth .... Apr 29, 1745
Residence .... Connecticut
Date of nomination/age .... Mar 3, 1796, at age 50
Nominating president .... Washington
Confirmation/age .... Mar 4, 1796, at age 50
Left office/age .... Sep 30, 1800, at age 55
Reason for leaving office .... Resigned
Date of death/age .... Nov 26, 1807, at age 62
Term of service .... 4y 6m 24d (1,665 days)
Term of retirement .... 7y 1m 27d (2,613 days)

Field, Stephen J.   Associate Justice 35

Date of birth .... Nov 4, 1816
Residence .... California
Date of nomination/age .... Mar 6, 1863, at age 46
Nominating president .... Lincoln
Confirmation/age .... Mar 10, 1863, at age 46

Left office/age .... Dec 1, 1897, at age 81
Reason for leaving office .... Resigned
Date of death/age .... Apr 9, 1899, at age 82
Term of service .... 34y 8m 21d (12,679 days)
Term of retirement .... 1y 4m 8d (493 days)

Fortas, Abe   Associate Justice 88

Date of birth .... Jun 19, 1910
Residence .... Tennessee
Date of nomination/age .... Jul 28, 1965, at age 55
Nominating president .... Lyndon B. Johnson
Confirmation/age .... Aug 11, 1965, at age 55
Left office/age .... May 14, 1969, at age 58
Reason for leaving office .... Resigned
Date of death/age .... Apr 5, 1982, at age 71
Term of service .... 3y 9m 3d (1,368 days)
Term of retirement .... 12y 10m 22d (4,705 days)

Frankfurter, Felix   Associate Justice 73

Date of birth .... Nov 15, 1882
Residence .... Massachusetts
Date of nomination/age .... Jan 5, 1939, at age 56
Nominating president .... Franklin D. Roosevelt
Confirmation/age .... Jan 17, 1939, at age 56
Left office/age .... Aug 28, 1962, at age 79
Reason for leaving office .... Resigned
Date of death/age .... Feb 22, 1965, at age 82
Term of service .... 23y 7m 11d (8,621 days)
Term of retirement .... 2y 5m 25d (905 days)

Fuller, Melville Weston   Chief Justice 8

Date of birth .... Feb 11, 1833
Residence .... Illinois
Date of nomination/age .... May 2, 1888, at age 55
Nominating president .... Cleveland
Confirmation/age .... Jul 20, 1888, at age 55
Left office/age .... Jul 4, 1910, at age 77
Reason for leaving office .... Died in office
Date of death/age .... Jul 4, 1910, at age 77
Term of service .... 21y 11m 14d (8,014 days)
Term of retirement .... None

Ginsburg, Ruth Bader   Associate Justice 99

Date of birth .... Mar 15, 1933
Residence .... Washington, D.C.
Date of nomination/age .... Jun 14, 1993, at age 60
Nominating president .... Clinton
Confirmation/age .... Aug 3, 1993, at age 60
Left office/age .... — — — —
Reason for leaving office .... — — — —
Date of death/age .... — — — —

Term of service .... —————
Term of retirement .... —————

Goldberg, Arthur Joseph   Associate Justice 87

Date of birth .... Aug 8, 1908
Residence .... Illinois
Date of nomination/age .... Aug 31, 1962, at age 54
Nominating president .... Kennedy
Confirmation/age .... Sep 25, 1962, at age 54
Left office/age .... Jul 25, 1965, at age 56
Reason for leaving office .... Resigned
Date of death/age .... Jan 19, 1990, at age 81
Term of service .... 2y 10m (1,030 days)
Term of retirement .... 24y 5m 26d (8,942 days)
Other offices held LB-9

Gray, Horace   Associate Justice 43

Date of birth .... Mar 24, 1828
Residence .... Massachusetts
Date of nomination/age .... Dec 19, 1881, at age 53
Nominating president .... Arthur
Confirmation/age .... Dec 20, 1881, at age 53
Left office/age .... Jul 9, 1902, at age 74
Reason for leaving office .... Resigned
Date of death/age .... Sep 15, 1902, at age 74
Term of service .... 20y 6m 19d (7,504 days)
Term of retirement .... 2m 6d (66 days)

Grier, Robert Cooper   Associate Justice 28

Date of birth .... Mar 5, 1794
Residence .... Pennsylvania
Date of nomination/age .... Aug 4, 1846, at age 52
Nominating president .... James K. Polk
Confirmation/age .... Aug 4, 1846, at age 52
Left office/age .... Jan 31, 1870, at age 75
Reason for leaving office .... Resigned
Date of death/age .... Sep 26, 1870, at age 76
Term of service .... 23y 5m 27d (8,577 days)
Term of retirement .... 7m 26d (236 days)

Harlan, John Marshall   Associate Justice 40

Date of birth .... Jun 1, 1833
Residence .... Kentucky
Date of nomination/age .... Oct 17, 1877, at age 44
Nominating president .... Hayes
Confirmation/age .... Nov 29, 1877, at age 44
Left office/age .... Oct 14, 1911, at age 77
Reason for leaving office .... Died in office
Date of death/age .... Oct 14, 1911, at age 77
Term of service .... 33y 10m 15d (12,368 days)
Term of retirement .... None

Harlan, John Marshall II   Associate Justice 82

Date of birth .... May 20, 1899
Residence .... New York
Date of nomination/age .... Jan 10, 1955, at age 55
Nominating president .... Eisenhower
Confirmation/age .... Mar 16, 1955, at age 55
Left office/age .... Dec 29, 1971, at age 72
Reason for leaving office .... Died in office
Date of death/age .... Dec 29, 1971, at age 72
Term of service .... 16y 9m 13d (6,127 days)
Term of retirement .... None

Holmes, Oliver W., Jr.   Associate Justice 54

Date of birth .... Mar 8, 1841
Residence .... Massachusetts
Date of nomination/age .... Dec 2, 1902, at age 61
Nominating president .... Theodore Roosevelt
Confirmation/age .... Dec 4, 1902, at age 61
Left office/age .... Jan 12, 1932, at age 90
Reason for leaving office .... Resigned
Date of death/age .... Mar 6, 1935, at age 93
Term of service .... 29y 1m 8d (10,630 days)
Term of retirement .... 3y 1m 20d (1,145 days)

Hughes, Charles Evans   Associate Justice 58

Date of birth .... Apr 11, 1862
Residence .... New York
Date of nomination/age .... Apr 25, 1910, at age 48
Nominating president .... Taft
Confirmation/age .... May 2, 1910, at age 48
Left office/age .... Jun 10, 1916, at age 54
Reason for leaving office .... Resigned
Term of service .... 6y 1m 8d (2,229 days)
Time between appointments .... 13y 8m 3d (4,991 days)

Hughes, Charles Evans   Chief Justice 11

Date of nomination/age .... Feb 3, 1930, at age 67
Nominating president .... Wilson
Confirmation/age .... Feb 13, 1930, at age 67
Left office/age .... Jul 1, 1941, at age 79
Reason for leaving office .... Resigned
Date of death/age .... Aug 27, 1948, at age 86
Term of service .... 11y 4m 18d (4,155 days)
Total service .... 17y 5m 26d (6,384 days)
Term of retirement .... 7y 1m 26d (2,612 days)
Other offices held ST-44

Hunt, Ward   Associate Justice 39

Date of birth .... Jun 14, 1810
Residence .... New York
Date of nomination/age .... Dec 11, 1872, at age 62

Nominating president .... Grant
Confirmation/age .... Dec 11, 1872, at age 62
Left office/age .... Jan 7, 1882, at age 71
Reason for leaving office .... Resigned
Date of death/age .... Mar 24, 1886, at age 75
Term of service .... 9y 27d (3,313 days)
Term of retirement .... 4y 2m 17d (1,538 days)

Iredell, James   Associate Justice 5

Date of birth .... Oct 5, 1751
Residence .... North Carolina
Date of nomination/age .... Feb 9, 1790, at age 38
Nominating president .... Washington
Confirmation/age .... Feb 10, 1790, at age 38
Left office/age .... Oct 2, 1799, at age 47
Reason for leaving office .... Died in office
Date of death/age .... Oct 2, 1799, at age 47
Term of service .... 9y 7m 22d (3,519 days)
Term of retirement .... None

Jackson, Howell E.   Associate Justice 50

Date of birth .... Apr 8, 1832
Residence .... Tennessee
Date of nomination/age .... Feb 2, 1893, at age 60
Nominating president .... Benjamin Harrison
Confirmation/age .... Feb 18, 1893, at age 60
Left office/age .... Aug 8, 1895, at age 63
Reason for leaving office .... Died in office
Date of death/age .... Aug 8, 1895, at age 63
Term of service .... 2y 5m 21d (901 days)
Term of retirement .... None

Jackson, Robert H.   Associate Justice 77

Date of birth .... Feb 13, 1892
Residence .... New York
Date of nomination/age .... Jun 12, 1941, at age 49
Nominating president .... Franklin D. Roosevelt
Confirmation/age .... Jul 7, 1941, at age 49
Left office/age .... Oct 9, 1954, at age 62
Reason for leaving office .... Died in office
Date of death/age .... Oct 9, 1954, at age 62
Term of service .... 13y 3m 2d (4,840 days)
Term of retirement .... None
Other offices held AT-57

Jay, John   Chief Justice 1

Date of birth .... Dec 12, 1745
Residence .... New York
Date of nomination/age .... Sep 24, 1789, at age 43
Nominating president .... Washington
Confirmation/age .... Sep 26, 1789, at age 43
Left office/age .... Jun 25, 1795, at age 49

Reason for leaving office .... Resigned
Date of death/age .... May 17, 1829, at age 83
Term of service .... 5y 9m (2,096 days)
Term of retirement .... 33y 10m 22d (12,375 days)

Johnson, Thomas   Associate Justice 6

Date of birth .... Nov 4, 1732
Residence .... Maryland
Date of nomination/age .... Nov 1, 1791, at age 58
Nominating president .... Washington
Confirmation/age .... Nov 7, 1791, at age 59
Left office/age .... Mar 4, 1793, at age 60
Reason for leaving office .... Resigned
Date of death/age .... Oct 25, 1819, at age 86
Term of service .... 1y 3m 25d (480 days)
Term of retirement .... 26y 7m 21d (9,727 days)

Johnson, William   Associate Justice 11

Date of birth .... Dec 27, 1771
Residence .... South Carolina
Date of nomination/age .... Mar 22, 1804, at age 32
Nominating president .... Jefferson
Confirmation/age .... Mar 24, 1804, at age 32
Left office/age .... Aug 4, 1834, at age 62
Reason for leaving office .... Died in office
Date of death/age .... Aug 4, 1834, at age 62
Term of service .... 30y 4m 11d (11,088 days)
Term of retirement .... None

Kennedy, Anthony M.   Associate Justice 96

Date of birth .... Jul 23, 1936
Residence .... California
Date of nomination/age .... Nov 11, 1988, at age 52
Nominating president .... Reagan
Confirmation/age .... Feb 3, 1989, at age 52
Left office/age .... —————
Reason for leaving office .... —————
Date of death/age .... —————
Term of service .... —————
Term of retirement .... —————

Lamar, Joseph Rucker   Associate Justice 60

Date of birth .... Oct 14, 1857
Residence .... Georgia
Date of nomination/age .... Dec 12, 1910, at age 53
Nominating president .... Taft
Confirmation/age .... Dec 15, 1910, at age 53
Left office/age .... Jan 2, 1916, at age 58
Reason for leaving office .... Died in office
Date of death/age .... Jan 2, 1916, at age 58
Term of service .... 5y 18d (1,844 days)
Term of retirement .... None

Lamar, Lucius Q.C.   Associate Justice 45

Date of birth .... Sep 17, 1825
Residence .... Mississippi
Date of nomination/age .... Dec 6, 1887, at age 62
Nominating president .... Cleveland
Confirmation/age .... Jan 16, 1888, at age 62
Left office/age .... Jan 24, 1893, at age 67
Reason for leaving office .... Died in office
Date of death/age .... Jan 24, 1893, at age 67
Term of service .... 5y 8d (1,834 days)
Term of retirement .... None
Other offices held IN-16

Livingston, Henry Brockholst   Associate Justice 12

Date of birth .... Nov 26, 1757
Residence .... New York
Date of nomination/age .... Dec 13, 1806, at age 49
Nominating president .... Jefferson
Confirmation/age .... Dec 17, 1806, at age 49
Left office/age .... Mar 18, 1823, at age 65
Reason for leaving office .... Died in office
Date of death/age .... Mar 18, 1823, at age 65
Term of service .... 16y 3m 1d (5,935 days)
Term of retirement .... None

Lurton, Horace H.   Associate Justice 57

Date of birth .... Feb 26, 1844
Residence .... Tennessee
Date of nomination/age .... Dec 13, 1909, at age 65
Nominating president .... Taft
Confirmation/age .... Dec 20, 1909, at age 65
Left office/age .... Jul 12, 1914, at age 70
Reason for leaving office .... Died in office
Date of death/age .... Jul 12, 1914, at age 70
Term of service .... 4y 6m 22d (1,663 days)
Term of retirement .... None

McKenna, Joseph   Associate Justice 53

Date of birth .... Aug 10, 1843
Residence .... California
Date of nomination/age .... Dec 16, 1897, at age 54
Nominating president .... McKinley
Confirmation/age .... Jan 21, 1898, at age 54
Left office/age .... Jan 5, 1925, at age 81
Reason for leaving office .... Resigned
Date of death/age .... Nov 21, 1926, at age 83
Term of service .... 26y 11m 15d (9,841 days)
Term of retirement .... 1y 10m 16d (681 days)
Other offices held AT-42

McKinley, John   Associate Justice 24

Date of birth .... May 1, 1780
Residence .... Alabama

Date of nomination/age .... Sep 18, 1837, at age 57
Nominating president .... Van Buren
Confirmation/age .... Sep 25, 1837, at age 57
Left office/age .... Jul 19, 1852, at age 72
Reason for leaving office .... Died in office
Date of death/age .... Jul 19, 1852, at age 72
Term of service .... 14y 9m 24d (5,407 days)
Term of retirement .... None

McLean, John   Associate Justice 18

Date of birth .... Mar 11, 1785
Residence .... Ohio
Date of nomination/age .... Feb 16, 1829, at age 43
Nominating president .... Jackson
Confirmation/age .... Mar 7, 1829, at age 43
Left office/age .... Apr 4, 1861, at age 76
Reason for leaving office .... Died in office
Date of death/age .... Apr 4, 1861, at age 76
Term of service .... 32y 28d (11,716 days)
Term of retirement .... None
Other offices held PG-6

McReynolds, James Clark   Associate Justice 62

Date of birth .... Feb 3, 1862
Residence .... Tennessee
Date of nomination/age .... Aug 19, 1914, at age 52
Nominating president .... Wilson
Confirmation/age .... Aug 29, 1914, at age 52
Left office/age .... Jan 31, 1941, at age 78
Reason for leaving office .... Resigned
Date of death/age .... Aug 24, 1946, at age 84
Term of service .... 26y 5m 2d (9,648 days)
Term of retirement .... 5y 6m 24d (2,030 days)
Other offices held AT-48

Marshall, John   Chief Justice 4

Date of birth .... Sep 24, 1755
Residence .... Virginia
Date of nomination/age .... Jan 20, 1801, at age 45
Nominating president .... John Adams
Confirmation/age .... Jan 27, 1801, at age 45
Left office/age .... Jul 6, 1835, at age 79
Reason for leaving office .... Died in office
Date of death/age .... Jul 6, 1835, at age 79
Term of service .... 34y 5m 9d (12,577 days)
Term of retirement .... None
Other offices held ST-4

Marshall, Thurgood   Associate Justice 89

Date of birth .... Jul 2, 1908
Residence .... New York
Date of nomination/age .... Jun 13, 1967, at age 59

Nominating president .... Lyndon B. Johnson
Confirmation/age .... Aug 30, 1967, at age 59
Left office/age .... Jun 27, 1991, at age 82
Reason for leaving office .... Resigned
Date of death/age .... Jan 24, 1993, at age 84
Term of service .... 23y 9m 28d (8,698 days)
Term of retirement .... 1y 6m 28d (573 days)

Matthews, Stanley   Associate Justice 42

Date of birth .... Jul 21, 1824
Residence .... Ohio
Date of nomination/age .... May 21, 1881, at age 56
Nominating president .... Garfield
Confirmation/age .... May 21, 1881, at age 56
Left office/age .... Mar 22, 1889, at age 64
Reason for leaving office .... Died in office
Date of death/age .... Mar 22, 1889, at age 64
Term of service .... 7y 10m 1d (2,857 days)
Term of retirement .... None

Miller, Samuel F.   Associate Justice 33

Date of birth .... Apr 5, 1816
Residence .... Iowa
Date of nomination/age .... Jul 16, 1862, at age 46
Nominating president .... Lincoln
Confirmation/age .... Jul 16, 1862, at age 46
Left office/age .... Oct 14, 1890, at age 74
Reason for leaving office .... Died in office
Date of death/age .... Oct 14, 1890, at age 74
Term of service .... 28y 2m 28d (10,315 days)
Term of retirement .... None

Minton, Sherman   Associate Justice 81

Date of birth .... Oct 20. 1890
Residence .... Indiana
Date of nomination/age .... Sep 15, 1949, at age 58
Nominating president .... Truman
Confirmation/age .... Oct 4, 1949, at age 58
Left office/age .... Oct 15, 1956, at age 65
Reason for leaving office .... Resigned
Date of death/age .... Apr 9, 1965, at age 74
Term of service .... 7y 11m 8d (2,894 days)
Term of retirement .... 8y 5m 25d (3,097 days)

Moody, William H.   Associate Justice 56

Date of birth .... Dec 23, 1853
Residence .... Massachusetts
Date of nomination/age .... Dec 3, 1906, at age 52
Nominating president .... Theodore Roosevelt
Confirmation/age .... Dec 12, 1906, at age 52
Left office/age .... Nov 20, 1910, at age 56
Reason for leaving office .... Resigned

Date of death/age . . . . Jul 2, 1917, at age 63
Term of service . . . . 3y 11m 8d (1,433 days)
Term of retirement . . . . 6y 7m 12d (2,413 days)
Other offices held NV-35, AT-45

Moore, Alfred   Associate Justice 10

Date of birth . . . . May 21, 1755
Residence . . . . North Carolina
Date of nomination/age . . . . Dec 6, 1799, at age 44
Nominating president . . . . John Adams
Confirmation/age . . . . Dec 10, 1799, at age 44
Left office/age . . . . Jan 26, 1804, at age 48
Reason for leaving office . . . . Resigned
Date of death/age . . . . Oct 15, 1810, at age 55
Term of service . . . . 4y 3m 21d (1,572 days)
Term of retirement . . . . 6y 6m 15d (2,368 days)

Murphy, Frank W.   Associate Justice 75

Date of birth . . . . Apr 13, 1890
Residence . . . . Michigan
Date of nomination/age . . . . Jan 4, 1940, at age 49
Nominating president . . . . Franklin D. Roosevelt
Confirmation/age . . . . Jan 15, 1940, at age 49
Left office/age . . . . Jul 19, 1949, at age 59
Reason for leaving office . . . . Died in office
Date of death/age . . . . Jul 19, 1949, at age 59
Term of service . . . . 9y 6m 4d (3,471 days)
Term of retirement . . . . None
Other offices held AT-56

Nelson, Samuel   Associate Justice 26

Date of birth . . . . Nov 10, 1792
Residence . . . . New York
Date of nomination/age . . . . Feb 14, 1845, at age 52
Nominating president . . . . John Tyler
Confirmation/age . . . . Feb 14, 1845, at age 52
Left office/age . . . . Nov 28, 1872, at age 80
Reason for leaving office . . . . Resigned
Date of death/age . . . . Dec 13, 1873, at age 81
Term of service . . . . 27y 9m 14d (10,145 days)
Term of retirement . . . . 1y 15d (380 days)

O'Connor, Sandra Day   Associate Justice 94

Date of birth . . . . Mar 26, 1930
Residence . . . . Arizona
Date of nomination/age . . . . Jul 7, 1981, at age 51
Nominating president . . . . Reagan
Confirmation/age . . . . Sep 21, 1981, at age 51
Left office/age . . . . — — — — —
Reason for leaving office . . . . — — — — —
Date of death/age . . . . — — — — —
Term of service . . . . — — — — —
Term of retirement . . . . — — — — —

Paterson, William   Associate Justice 7

Date of birth .... Dec 24, 1745
Residence .... New Jersey
Date of nomination/age .... Mar 4, 1793, at age 47
Nominating president .... Washington
Confirmation/age .... Mar 4, 1793, at age 47
Left office/age .... Sep 9, 1806, at age 60
Reason for leaving office .... Died in office
Date of death/age .... Sep 9, 1806, at age 60
Term of service .... 13y 6m 5d (4,933 days)
Term of retirement .... None

Peckham, Rufus Wheeler   Associate Justice 52

Date of birth .... Nov 8, 1838
Residence .... New York
Date of nomination/age .... Dec 3, 1895, at age 57
Nominating president .... Cleveland
Confirmation/age .... Dec 9, 1895, at age 57
Left office/age .... Oct 24, 1909, at age 70
Reason for leaving office .... Died in office
Date of death/age .... Oct 24, 1909, at age 70
Term of service .... 13y 10m 15d (5,063 days)
Term of retirement .... None

Pitney, Mahlon   Associate Justice 61

Date of birth .... Feb 5, 1858
Residence .... New Jersey
Date of nomination/age .... Feb 19, 1912, at age 54
Nominating president .... Taft
Confirmation/age .... Mar 13, 1912, at age 54
Left office/age .... Dec 31, 1922, at age 64
Reason for leaving office .... Resigned
Date of death/age .... Dec 9, 1924, at age 66
Term of service .... 10y 9m 18d (3,940 days)
Term of retirement .... 1y 11m 9d (704 days)

Powell, Lewis Franklin, Jr.   Associate Justice 91

Date of birth .... Sep 19, 1907
Residence .... Virginia
Date of nomination/age .... Oct 21, 1971, at age 64
Nominating president .... Nixon
Confirmation/age .... Dec 6, 1971, at age 64
Left office/age .... Jun 26, 1987, at age 79
Reason for leaving office .... Resigned
Date of death/age .... Aug 25, 1998, at age 90
Term of service .... 15y 6m 20d (5,678 days)
Term of retirement .... 11y 2m (4,077 days)

Reed, Stanley F.   Associate Justice 72

Date of birth .... Dec 31, 1884
Residence .... Kentucky

Date of nomination/age .... Jan 15, 1938, at age 53
Nominating president .... Franklin D. Roosevelt
Confirmation/age .... Jan 25, 1938, at age 53
Left office/age .... Feb 25, 1957, at age 72
Reason for leaving office .... Resigned
Date of death/age .... Apr 3, 1980, at age 95
Term of service .... 19y 1m (6,969 days)
Term of retirement .... 13y 1m 9d (4,787 days)

Rehnquist, William H.　　　Associate Justice 92

Date of birth .... Oct 1, 1924
Residence .... Arizona
Date of nomination/age .... Oct 21, 1971, at age 47
Nominating president .... Nixon
Confirmation/age .... Dec 10, 1971, at age 47
Left office/age .... Sep 17, 1986, at age 61
Reason for leaving office .... Appointed chief justice
Term of service .... 14y 10m 27d (5,450 days)
Time between appointments .... None

Rehnquist, William H.　　　Chief Justice 16

Date of nomination/age .... Jun 17, 1986, at age 61
Nominating president .... Reagan
Confirmation/age .... Sep 17, 1986, at age 61
Left office/age .... — — — — —
Reason for leaving office .... — — — — —
Date of death/age .... — — — — —
Term of service .... — — — — —
Total term of service .... — — — — —
Term of retirement .... — — — — —

Roberts, Owen Josephus　　　Associate Justice 69

Date of birth .... May 2, 1875
Residence .... Pennsylvania
Date of nomination/age .... May 9, 1930, at age 55
Nominating president .... Hoover
Confirmation/age .... May 20, 1930, at age 55
Left office/age .... Jul 31, 1945, at age 70
Reason for leaving office .... Resigned
Date of death/age .... May 19, 1955, at age 80
Term of service .... 15y 2m 11d (5,549 days)
Term of retirement .... 9y 9m 19d (3,576 days)

Rutledge, John　　　Associate Justice 1

Date of birth .... Sep 1739
Residence .... South Carolina
Date of nomination/age .... Sep 24, 1789, at age 49
Nominating president .... Washington
Confirmation/age .... Sep 26, 1789, at age 49
Left office/age .... Mar 5, 1791, at age 51
Reason for leaving office .... Resigned
Term of service .... 1y 5m 7d (522 days)

Rutledge, John   Chief Justice 2

Date of nomination/age .... Aug 12, 1795, at age 55
Nominating president .... Washington
Time between appointments .... 4y 9m 10d (1,741 days)
Confirmation rejected/age .... Dec 15, 1795, at age 56
Date of death/age .... Jun 21, 1800, at age 60
Term of service .... 4m 3d (123 days)
Total term of service .... 1y 9m 10d (645 days)
Term of retirement .... 4y 6m 6d (1,647 days)

Rutledge, Wiley Blount   Associate Justice 78

Date of birth .... Jul 20, 1894
Residence .... Iowa
Date of nomination/age .... Jan 11, 1943, at age 48
Nominating president .... Franklin D. Roosevelt
Confirmation/age .... Feb 18, 1943, at age 48
Left office/age .... Sep 9, 1949, at age 55
Reason for leaving office .... Died in office
Date of death/age .... Sep 9, 1949, at age 55
Term of service .... 6y 7m 1d (2,402 days)
Term of retirement .... None

Sanford, Edward Terry   Associate Justice 67

Date of birth .... Jul 23, 1865
Residence .... Tennessee
Date of nomination/age .... Jan 24, 1923, at age 57
Nominating president .... Harding
Confirmation/age .... Jan 29, 1923, at age 57
Left office/age .... Mar 8, 1930, at age 64
Reason for leaving office .... Died in office
Date of death/age .... Mar 8, 1930, at age 64
Term of service .... 7y 1m 8d (2,594 days)
Term of retirement .... None

Scalia, Antonin   Associate Justice 95

Date of birth .... Mar 11, 1936
Residence .... Virginia
Date of nomination/age .... Jun 17, 1986, at age 50
Nominating president .... Reagan
Confirmation/age .... Sep 17, 1986, at age 50
Left office/age .... —————
Reason for leaving office .... —————
Date of death/age .... —————
Term of service .... —————
Term of retirement .... —————

Shiras, George, Jr.   Associate Justice 49

Date of birth .... Jan 26, 1832
Residence .... Pennsylvania
Date of nomination/age .... Jul 19, 1892, at age 60
Nominating president .... Benjamin Harrison
Confirmation/age .... Jul 26, 1892, at age 60

Left office/age . . . . Feb 23, 1903, at age 71
Reason for leaving office . . . . Resigned
Date of death/age . . . . Aug 21, 1924, at age 92
Term of service . . . . 10y 6m 28d (3,860 days)
Term of retirement . . . . 21y 5m 29d (7,849 days)

Souter, David Hackett   Associate Justice 97

Date of birth . . . . Sep 17, 1939
Residence . . . . New Hampshire
Date of nomination/age . . . . Jul 23, 1990, at age 50
Nominating president . . . . George Herbert Bush
Confirmation/age . . . . Oct 2, 1990, at age 51
Left office/age . . . . — — — — —
Reason for leaving office . . . . — — — — —
Date of death/age . . . . — — — — —
Term of service . . . . — — — — —
Term of retirement . . . . — — — — —

Stanton, Edwin M.   Associate Justice 36

Date of birth . . . . Dec 19, 1814
Residence . . . . Washington, D.C.
Date of nomination/age . . . . Dec 20, 1869, at age 55
Nominating president . . . . Grant
Confirmation/age . . . . Dec 20, 1869, at age 55
Left office/age . . . . Dec 24, 1869, at age 55
Reason for leaving office . . . . Died in office
Date of death/age . . . . Dec 24, 1869, at age 55
Term of service . . . . 4d (4 days)
Term of retirement . . . . None
Other offices held AT-25, WR-28

Stevens, John Paul   Associate Justice 93

Date of birth . . . . Apr 20, 1920
Residence . . . . Illinois
Date of nomination/age . . . . Nov 28, 1975, at age 55
Nominating president . . . . Ford
Confirmation/age . . . . Dec 17, 1975, at age 55
Left office/age . . . . — — — — —
Reason for leaving office . . . . — — — — —
Date of death/age . . . . — — — — —
Term of service . . . . — — — — —
Term of retirement . . . . — — — — —

Stewart, Potter   Associate Justice 85

Date of birth . . . . Jan 23, 1915
Residence . . . . Ohio
Date of nomination/age . . . . Jan 17, 1959, at age 43
Nominating president . . . . Eisenhower
Confirmation/age . . . . May 5, 1959, at age 44
Left office/age . . . . Jul 3, 1981, at age 66
Reason for leaving office . . . . Resigned
Date of death/age . . . . Dec 7, 1985, at age 70

Term of service .... 22y 1m 29d (8,094 days)
Term of retirement .... 4y 5m 4d (1,615 days)

Stone, Harlan Fiske   Associate Justice 68

Date of birth .... Oct 11, 1872
Residence .... New York
Date of nomination/age .... Jan 5, 1925, at age 52
Nominating president .... Coolidge
Confirmation/age .... Feb 5, 1925, at age 52
Left office/age .... Jun 27, 1941, at age 68
Reason for leaving office .... Appointed Chief Justice
Term of service .... 16y 4m 22d (5,986 days)
Time between appointments .... None

Stone, Harlan Fiske   Chief Justice 12

Date of nomination/age .... Jun 12, 1941, at age 68
Nominating president .... Franklin D. Roosevelt
Confirmation/age .... Jun 27, 1941, at age 68
Left office/age .... Apr 22, 1946, at age 73
Reason for leaving office .... Died in office
Date of death/age .... Apr 22, 1946, at age 73
Term of service .... 4y 8m 26d (1,727 days)
Total term of service .... 21y 2m 17d (7,747 days)
Term of retirement .... None
Other offices held AT-52

Story, Joseph   Associate Justice 14

Date of birth .... Sep 18, 1779
Residence .... Massachusetts
Date of nomination/age .... Nov 15, 1811, at age 32
Nominating president .... Madison
Confirmation/age .... Nov 18, 1811, at age 32
Left office/age .... Sep 10, 1845, at age 65
Reason for leaving office .... Died in office
Date of death/age .... Sep 10, 1845, at age 65
Term of service .... 33y 9m 23d (12,346 days)
Term of retirement .... None

Strong, William   Associate Justice 37

Date of birth .... Mar 6, 1806
Residence .... Pennsylvania
Date of nomination/age .... Feb 7, 1870, at age 63
Nominating president .... Grant
Confirmation/age .... Feb 18, 1870, at age 63
Left office/age .... Dec 14, 1880, at age 74
Reason for leaving office .... Died in office
Date of death/age .... Aug 19, 1895, at age 89
Term of service .... 10y 9m 26d (3,948 days)
Term of retirement .... 14y 8m 5d (5,358 days)

Sutherland, George   Associate Justice 65

Date of birth .... Mar 25, 1862
Residence .... Utah

Date of nomination/age .... Sep 5, 1922, at age 60
Nominating president .... Harding
Confirmation/age .... Sep 5, 1922, at age 60
Left office/age .... Jan 17, 1938, at age 75
Reason for leaving office .... Resigned
Date of death/age .... Jul 18, 1942, at age 80
Term of service .... 15y 4m 12d (5,610 days)
Term of retirement .... 4y 6m 1d (1,642 days)

Swayne, Noah Haynes   Associate Justice 32

Date of birth .... Dec 7, 1804
Residence .... Ohio
Date of nomination/age .... Jan 21, 1862, at age 57
Nominating president .... Lincoln
Confirmation/age .... Jan 24, 1862, at age 57
Left office/age .... Jan 21, 1881, at age 76
Reason for leaving office .... Resigned
Date of death/age .... Jun 8, 1884, at age 79
Term of service .... 18y 11m 27d (6,931 days)
Term of retirement .... 3y 4m 18d (1,233 days)

Taft, William Howard   Chief Justice 10

Date of birth .... Sep 15, 1857
Residence .... Connecticut
Date of nomination/age .... Jun 30, 1921, at age 63
Nominating president .... Harding
Confirmation/age .... Jun 30, 1921, at age 63
Left office/age .... Feb 3, 1930, at age 72
Reason for leaving office .... Resigned
Date of death/age .... Mar 8, 1930, at age 72
Term of service .... 8y 7m 4d (3,136 days)
Term of retirement .... 1m 5d (35 days)
Other offices held WR-44, PR-27

Taney, Roger Brooke   Chief Justice 5

Date of birth .... Mar 17, 1777
Residence .... Maryland
Date of nomination/age .... Dec 28, 1835, at age 58
Nominating president .... Andrew Jackson
Confirmation/age .... Mar 15, 1836, at age 58
Left office/age .... Oct 12, 1864, at age 87
Reason for leaving office .... Died in office
Date of death/age .... Oct 12, 1864, at age 87
Term of service .... 28y 6m 27d (10,434 days)
Term of retirement .... None
Other offices held AT-11, TY-12

Thomas, Clarence   Associate Justice 98

Date of birth .... Jun 23, 1948
Residence .... Virginia
Date of nomination/age .... Jul 1, 1991, at age 43
Nominating president .... George Herbert Bush

Confirmation/age . . . . Oct 15, 1991, at age 43
Left office/age . . . . — — — — —
Reason for leaving office . . . . — — — — —
Date of death/age . . . . — — — — —
Term of service . . . . — — — — —
Term of retirement . . . . — — — — —

Thompson, Smith
Associate Justice 16

Date of birth . . . . Jan 17, 1768
Residence . . . . New York
Date of nomination/age . . . . Sep 1, 1823, at age 55
Nominating president . . . . Monroe
Confirmation/age . . . . Dec 9, 1823, at age 55
Left office/age . . . . Dec 18, 1843, at age 75
Reason for leaving office . . . . Died in office
Date of death/age . . . . Dec 18, 1843, at age 75
Term of service . . . . 20y 9d (7,314 days)
Term of retirement . . . . None

Todd, Thomas
Associate Justice 13

Date of birth . . . . Jan 23, 1765
Residence . . . . Kentucky
Date of nomination/age . . . . Feb 28, 1807, at age 42
Nominating president . . . . Jefferson
Confirmation/age . . . . Mar 3, 1807, at age 42
Left office/age . . . . Feb 7, 1826, at age 61
Reason for leaving office . . . . Died in office
Date of death/age . . . . Feb 7, 1826, at age 61
Term of service . . . . 18y 11m 4d (6,908 days)
Term of retirement . . . . None

Trimble, Robert
Associate Justice 17

Date of birth . . . . Nov 17, 1776
Residence . . . . Kentucky
Date of nomination/age . . . . Apr 11, 1826, at age 49
Nominating president . . . . John Quincy Adams
Confirmation/age . . . . May 9, 1826, at age 49
Left office/age . . . . Aug 25, 1828, at age 51
Reason for leaving office . . . . Died in office
Date of death/age . . . . Aug 25, 1828, at age 51
Term of service . . . . 2y 3m 16d (836 days)
Term of retirement . . . . None

Van Devanter, Willis
Associate Justice 59

Date of birth . . . . Apr 17, 1859
Residence . . . . Wyoming
Date of nomination/age . . . . Dec 12, 1910, at age 51
Nominating president . . . . Taft
Confirmation/age . . . . Dec 15, 1910, at age 51
Left office/age . . . . Jun 2, 1937, at age 78
Reason for leaving office . . . . Resigned
Date of death/age . . . . Feb 8, 1951, at age 91

Term of service .... 26y 5m 18d (9,664 days)
Term of retirement .... 13y 8m 6d (4,994 days)

Vinson, Frederick Moore   Chief Justice 13

Date of birth .... Jan 22, 1890
Residence .... Kentucky
Date of nomination/age .... Jun 6, 1946, at age 56
Nominating president .... Truman
Confirmation/age .... Jun 20, 1946, at age 56
Left office/age .... Sep 8, 1953, at age 63
Reason for leaving office .... Died in office
Date of death/age .... Sep 8, 1953, at age 63
Term of service .... 7y 2m 19d (2,635 days)
Term of retirement .... None
Other offices held TY-53

Waite, Morrison Remick   Chief Justice 7

Date of birth .... Nov 29, 1816
Residence .... Ohio
Date of nomination/age .... Jan 19, 1874, at age 57
Nominating president .... Grant
Confirmation/age .... Jan 21, 1874, at age 57
Left office/age .... Mar 23, 1888, at age 71
Reason for leaving office .... Died in office
Date of death/age .... Mar 23, 1888, at age 71
Term of service .... 14y 2m 2d (5,175 days)
Term of retirement .... None

Warren, Earl   Chief Justice 14

Date of birth .... Mar 19, 1891
Residence .... California
Date of nomination/age .... Sep 30, 1953, at age 62
Nominating president .... Eisenhower
Confirmation/age .... Mar 1, 1954, at age 62
Left office/age .... Jun 24, 1969, at age 78
Reason for leaving office .... Resigned
Date of death/age .... Jul 9, 1974, at age 83
Term of service .... 15y 3m 23d (5,591 days)
Term of retirement .... 5y 15d (1,841 days)

Washington, Bushrod   Associate Justice 9

Date of birth .... Jun 5, 1762
Residence .... Virginia
Date of nomination/age .... Sep 29, 1798, at age 36
Nominating president .... John Adams
Confirmation/age .... Dec 20, 1798, at age 36
Left office/age .... Nov 26, 1829, at age 67
Reason for leaving office .... Died in office
Date of death/age .... Nov 26, 1829, at age 67
Term of service .... 30y 11m 6d (11,293 days)
Term of retirement .... None

Wayne, James M.   Associate Justice 20

Date of birth 1790
Residence .... Georgia
Date of nomination/age .... Jan 7, 1835, at age 44
Nominating president .... Jackson
Confirmation/age .... Jan 9, 1835, at age 44
Left office/age .... Jul 5, 1867, at age 77
Reason for leaving office .... Died in office
Date of death/age .... Jul 5, 1867, at age 77
Term of service .... 32y 5m 26d (11,864 days)
Term of retirement .... None

White, Byron R.   Associate Justice 86

Date of birth .... Jun 8, 1917
Residence .... Colorado
Date of nomination/age .... Apr 3, 1962, at age 44
Nominating president .... Kennedy
Confirmation/age .... Apr 11, 1962, at age 44
Left office/age .... Jun 28, 1993, at age 76
Reason for leaving office .... Resigned
Date of death/age .... Apr 15, 2002, at age 84
Term of service .... 31y 2m 17d (11,399 days)
Term of retirement .... 8y 9m 18d (3,210 days)

White, Edward Douglass   Associate Justice 51

Date of birth .... Nov 3, 1845
Residence .... Louisiana
Date of nomination/age .... Feb 19, 1894, at age 48
Nominating president .... Cleveland
Confirmation/age .... Feb 19, 1894, at age 48
Left office/age .... Dec 12, 1910, at age 65
Reason for leaving office .... Appointed Chief Justice
Term of service .... 16y 9m 23d (6,137 days)
Time between offices .... None

White, Edward Douglass   Chief Justice 9

Date of nomination/age .... Dec 12, 1910, at age 65
Nominating president .... Taft
Confirmation/age .... Dec 12, 1910, at age 65
Left office/age .... May 19, 1921, at age 75
Reason for leaving office .... Died in office
Date of death/age .... May 19, 1921, at age 75
Term of service .... 10y 5m 7d (3,809 days)
Total service .... 27y 3m (9,951 days)
Term of retirement .... None

Whittaker, Charles Evans   Associate Justice 84

Date of birth .... Feb 22, 1901
Residence .... Missouri
Date of nomination/age .... Mar 2, 1957, at age 56
Nominating president .... Eisenhower

Confirmation/age . . . . Mar 19, 1957, at age 56
Left office/age . . . . Apr 1, 1962, at age 61
Reason for leaving office . . . . Resigned
Date of death/age . . . . Nov 26, 1973
Term of service . . . . 5y 13d (1,839 days)
Term of retirement . . . . 11y 7m 25d (4,252 days)

Wilson, James   Associate Justice 3

Date of birth . . . . Sep 14, 1742
Residence . . . . Pennsylvania
Date of nomination/age . . . . Sep 24, 1789, at age 47
Nominating president . . . . Washington
Confirmation/age . . . . Sep 26, 1789, at age 47
Left office/age . . . . Aug 21, 1798, at age 55
Reason for leaving office . . . . Died in office
Date of death/age . . . . Aug 21, 1798, at age 55
Term of service . . . . 8y 10m 26d (3,248 days)
Term of retirement . . . . None

Woodbury, Levi   Associate Justice 27

Date of birth . . . . Dec 22, 1789
Residence . . . . New Hampshire
Date of nomination/age . . . . Dec 23, 1845, at age 56
Nominating president . . . . James K. Polk
Confirmation/age . . . . Jan 3, 1846, at age 56
Left office/age . . . . Sep 4, 1851, at age 61
Reason for leaving office . . . . Died in office
Date of death/age . . . . Sep 4, 1851, at age 61
Term of service . . . . 5y 8m 1d (2,067 days)
Term of retirement . . . . None
Other offices held NV-9, TY-13

Woods, William Burnham   Associate Justice 41

Date of birth . . . . Aug 3, 1824
Residence . . . . Georgia
Date of nomination/age . . . . Dec 15, 1880, at age 56
Nominating president . . . . Hayes
Confirmation/age . . . . Dec 21, 1880, at age 56
Left office/age . . . . May 14, 1887, at age 62
Reason for leaving office . . . . Died in office
Date of death/age . . . . May 14, 1887, at age 62
Term of service . . . . 6y 4m 23d (2,334 days)
Term of retirement . . . . None

Appendix A: Presidential and Vice Presidential Timelines

Presidential Timeline

The Presidential Timeline shows in chronological order, in separate entries, the birth, inauguration and death dates for the presidents. The bold type indicates how many former presidents were living at any given time. Each president's name is followed by a number in parentheses that indicates his ordinal rank in the series of presidents. The greatest number of former presidents living at the same time is five, and this has occurred at three points in American history: from Lincoln's inauguration in 1861 to the death of John Tyler 10 months and two weeks later; from Clinton's inauguration in 1993 to Nixon's death one year, three months and 18 days later; and from George Walker Bush's inauguration in 2001 to the time this book was finished (February 2003).

Feb 22, 1732	George Washington (1) born **0**
Oct 30, 1735	John Adams (2) born **0**
Apr 13, 1743	Thomas Jefferson (3) born **0**
Mar 16, 1751	James Madison (4) born **0**
Apr 28, 1758	James Monroe (5) born **0**
Mar 15, 1767	Andrew Jackson (7) born **0**
Jul 11, 1767	John Quincy Adams (6) born **0**
Feb 9, 1773	William Henry Harrison (9) born **0**
Dec 5, 1782	Martin Van Buren (8) born **0**

Nov 24, 1784	Zachary Taylor (12) born 0
Apr 30, 1789	George Washington (1) inaugurated 0
Mar 29, 1790	John Tyler (10 born 0
Apr 23, 1791	James Buchanan (15) born 0
Nov 2, 1795	James K. Polk (11) born 0
Mar 4, 1797	John Adams (2) inaugurated 1 — **Washington (1)**
Dec 14, 1799	George Washington (1) dies 0
Jan 7, 1800	Millard Fillmore (13) born 0
Mar 4, 1801	Thomas Jefferson (3) inaugurated 1 — **Adams (2)**
Nov 23, 1804	Franklin Pierce (14) born 1
Dec 29, 1808	Andrew Johnson (17) born 1
Feb 12, 1809	Abraham Lincoln (16) born 1
Mar 4, 1809	James Madison (4) inaugurated 2 — **Adams (2), Jefferson (3)**
Mar 4, 1817	James Monroe (5) inaugurated 3 — **Adams (2), Jefferson (3) , Madison (4)**
Apr 27, 1822	Ulysses S. Grant (18) born 3
Oct 2, 1822	Rutherford B. Hayes (19) born 3
Mar 4, 1825	John Quincy Adams (6) inaugurated 4 — **Adams (2), Jefferson (3), Madison (4), Monroe (5)**
Jul 4, 1826	John Adams (2) dies 3 — **Jefferson (3), Madison (4), Monroe (5)**
Jul 4, 1826	Thomas Jefferson (3) dies 2 — **Madison (4), Monroe (5)**
Mar 4, 1829	Andrew Jackson (7) inaugurated 3 — **Madison (4), Monroe (5), Adams (6)**
Oct 5, 1830	Chester A. Arthur (21) born 3
Jul 4, 1831	James Monroe (5) dies 2 — **Madison (4), Adams (6)**
Nov 19, 1831	James A. Garfield (20) born 2

Aug 20, 1833	Benjamin Harrison (23) born 2
Jun 28, 1836	James Madison (4) dies 1 — Adams (6)
Mar 4, 1837	Martin Van Buren (PR 8) inaugurated 2 — Adams (6), Jackson (7)
Mar 18, 1837	Grover Cleveland (22/24) born 2
Mar 4, 1841	William Henry Harrison (9) inaugurated 3 — Adams (6), Jackson (7), Van Buren (8)
Apr 4, 1841	William Henry Harrison (9) dies in office [natural causes] 3
Apr 6, 1841	John Tyler (10) inaugurated 3
Jan 29, 1843	William McKinley (25) born 3
Mar 4, 1845	James K. Polk (11) inaugurated 4 — Adams (6), Jackson (7), Van Buren (8), Tyler (10)
Jun 8, 1845	Andrew Jackson (7) dies 3 — Adams (6), Van Buren (8), Tyler (10)
Feb 23, 1848	John Quincy Adams (6) dies 2 — Van Buren (8), Tyler (10)
Mar 4, 1849	Zachary Taylor (PR 12) inaugurated 3 — Van Buren (8), Tyler (10), Polk (11)
Jun 15, 1849	James K. Polk (11) dies 2 — Van Buren (8), Tyler (10)
Jul 9, 1850	Zachary Taylor (12) dies in office [natural causes] 2
Jul 10, 1850	Millard Fillmore (13) inaugurated 2
Mar 4, 1853	Franklin Pierce (14) inaugurated 3 — Van Buren (8), Tyler (10), Fillmore (13)
Dec 28, 1856	Woodrow Wilson (28) born 3
Mar 4, 1857	James Buchanan (15) inaugurated 4 — Van Buren (8), Tyler (10), Fillmore (13), Pierce (14)
Sep 15, 1857	William H. Taft (27) born 4
Oct 27, 1858	Theodore Roosevelt (26) born 4
Mar 4, 1861	Abraham Lincoln (16) inaugurated 5 — Van Buren (8), Tyler (10), Fillmore (13), Pierce (14), Buchanan (15)
Jan 18, 1862	John Tyler (10) dies 4 — Van Buren (8), Fillmore (13), Pierce (14), Buchanan (15)
Jul 24, 1862	Martin Van Buren (8) dies 3 — Fillmore (13), Pierce (14), Buchanan (15)

Apr 15, 1865	Abraham Lincoln (16) dies in office [assassinated] 3
Apr 15, 1865	Andrew Johnson (17) inaugurated 3
Nov 2, 1865	Warren G. Harding (29) born 3
Jun 1, 1868	James Buchanan (15) dies 2 — **Fillmore (13), Pierce (14)**
Mar 4, 1869	Ulysses S. Grant (18) inaugurated 3 — **Fillmore (13), Pierce (14), Johnson (17)**
Oct 8, 1869	Franklin Pierce (14) dies 2 — **Fillmore (13), Johnson (17)**
Jul 4, 1872	Calvin Coolidge (30) born 2
Mar 8, 1874	Millard Fillmore (13) dies 1 — **Johnson (17)**
Aug 10, 1874	Herbert Hoover (31) born 1
Jul 31, 1875	Andrew Johnson (17) dies 0
Mar 4, 1877	Rutherford B. Hayes (19) inaugurated 1 — **Grant (18)**
Mar 4, 1881	James A. Garfield (20) inaugurated 2 — **Hayes (19), Grant (18)**
Sep 19, 1881	James A. Garfield (20) dies in office [assassinated] 2
Sep 20, 1881	Chester A. Arthur (21) inaugurated 2
Jan 30, 1882	Franklin D. Roosevelt (32) born 2
May 8, 1884	Harry S Truman (33) born 2
Mar 4, 1885	Grover Cleveland (PR — 22) inaugurated 3 — **Hayes (19), Arthur (21), Grant (18)**
Jul 23, 1885	Ulysses S. Grant (18) dies 2 — **Hayes (19), Arthur (21)**
Nov 18, 1886	Chester A. Arthur (21) dies 1 — **Hayes (19)**
Mar 4, 1889	Benjamin Harrison (23) inaugurated 2 — **Hayes (19), Cleveland (22)**
Oct 14, 1890	Dwight D. Eisenhower (34) born 2
Jan 17, 1893	Rutherford B. Hayes (19) dies 1 — **Cleveland (22)**
Mar 4, 1893	Grover Cleveland (24) inaugurated 1 — **Harrison (23)**

Mar 4, 1897	William McKinley (25) inaugurated **2 — Cleveland (22/24), Harrison (23)**
Mar 13, 1901	Benjamin Harrison (23) dies **1 — Cleveland (22/24)**
Sep 14, 1901	William McKinley (25) dies in office [assassinated] **1**
Sep 14, 1901	Theodore Roosevelt (26) inaugurated **1**
Jun 24, 1908	Grover Cleveland (22/24) dies **0**
Aug 27, 1908	Lyndon B. Johnson (36) born **0**
Mar 4, 1909	William H. Taft (27) inaugurated **1 — Roosevelt (26)**
Feb 6, 1911	Ronald Reagan (40) born **1**
Jan 9, 1913	Richard M. Nixon (37) born **1**
Mar 4, 1913	Woodrow Wilson (28) inaugurated **2 — Roosevelt (26), Taft (27)**
Jul 14, 1913	Gerald R. Ford (38) born **2**
May 29, 1917	John F. Kennedy (35) born **2**
Jan 6, 1919	Theodore Roosevelt (26) dies **1 — Taft (27)**
Mar 4, 1921	Warren G. Harding (29) inaugurated **2 — Taft (27), Wilson (28)**
Aug 2, 1923	Warren G. Harding (29) dies in office [natural causes] **2**
Aug 3, 1923	Calvin Coolidge (30) inaugurated **2**
Feb 3, 1924	Woodrow Wilson (28) dies **1 — Taft (27)**
Jun 12, 1924	George Herbert Walker Bush (41) born **1**
Oct 1, 1924	Jimmy Carter (39) born **1**
Mar 4, 1929	Herbert Hoover (31) inaugurated **2 — Taft (27), Coolidge (30)**
Mar 8, 1930	William H. Taft (27) dies **1 — Coolidge (30)**
Jan 5, 1933	Calvin Coolidge (30) dies **0**
Mar 4, 1933	Franklin D. Roosevelt (32) inaugurated **1 — Hoover (31)**

Apr 12, 1945	Franklin D. Roosevelt (32) dies in office [natural causes] 1
Apr 12, 1945	Harry S Truman (33) inaugurated 1
Jul 6, 1946	George Walker Bush (43) born 1
Aug 19, 1946	Bill Clinton (42) born 1
Jan 20, 1953	Dwight D. Eisenhower (34) inaugurated 2 — Hoover (31), Truman (33)
Jan 20, 1961	John F. Kennedy (35) inaugurated 3 — Hoover (31), Truman (33), Eisenhower (34)
Nov 22, 1963	John F. Kennedy (35) dies in office [assassinated] 3
Nov 22, 1963	Lyndon B. Johnson (36) inaugurated 3
Oct 20, 1964	Herbert Hoover (31) dies 2 — Truman (33), Eisenhower (34)
Jan 20, 1969	Richard M. Nixon (37) inaugurated 3 — Truman (33), Eisenhower (34), Johnson (36)
Mar 28, 1969	Dwight D. Eisenhower (34) dies 2 — Truman (33), Johnson (36)
Dec 26, 1972	Harry S Truman (33) dies 1 — Johnson (36)
Jan 22, 1973	Lyndon B. Johnson (36) dies 0
Aug 9, 1974	Gerald R. Ford (38) inaugurated 1 — Nixon (37)
Jan 20, 1977	Jimmy Carter (39) inaugurated 2 — Nixon (37), Ford (38)
Jan 20, 1981	Ronald Reagan (40) inaugurated 3 — Nixon (37), Ford (38), Carter (39)
Jan 20, 1989	George Herbert Walker Bush (41) inaugurated 4 — Nixon (37), Ford (38), Carter (39), Reagan (40)
Jan 20, 1993	Bill Clinton (42) inaugurated 5 — Nixon (37), Ford (38), Carter (39), Reagan (40), Bush (41)
Apr 22, 1994	Richard M. Nixon (37) dies 4 — Ford (38), Carter (39), Reagan (40), Bush (41)
Jan 20, 2001	George Walker Bush (43) inaugurated 5 — Ford (38), Carter (39), Reagan (40), Bush (41), Clinton (42)

VICE PRESIDENTIAL TIMELINE

The vice president often is said to be "one heartbeat away from the presidency," but there have been 17 periods in which there was no vice president to take up the reins of government. The first vice presidential vacancy occurred on April 20, 1812, when Vice President George Clinton died of natural causes; the 17th such occasion occurred during the period between Vice President Spiro T. Agnew's resignation from office on October 10, 1973, and Gerald R. Ford's inauguration as the 40th vice president on December 6, 1973. Between 1812 and 1973, the U.S. was without a vice president for a total of 39 years, two months and 16 days, or 14,320 days. Though the 17 periods without a vice president ranged in duration from 1m 26d to 3y 10m 27d, they averaged 842 days each, or 2y 3m 22d. The situation is unlikely to arise again, as constitutional provisions now allow the appointment of a new vice president if the president is killed or incapacitated and the vice president is inaugurated as president.

This vice presidential timeline shows how many former vice presidents were living at any one time. In that respect, the information here is very similar to that provided by the presidential timeline, with again the ordinal rank in parentheses, but also included are the exact periods of time the U.S. was without a vice president. The greatest number of former vice presidents living at one time was six, a situation which occurred on January 20, 1993, when Al Gore was inaugurated, and lasted for about 15 months, until April 22, 1994, when former president and former vice president Richard M. Nixon died.

Oct 30, 1735	Adams (1) born 0
Jul 26, 1739	Clinton (4) born 0
Apr 13, 1743	Jefferson (2) born 0
Jul 17, 1744	Gerry (5) born 0
Feb 6, 1756	Burr (3) born 0
Jun 21, 1774	Tompkins (6) born 0
Oct 17, 1780	Johnson (9) born 0
Mar 18, 1782	Calhoun (7) born 0
Dec 5, 1782	Van Buren (8) born 0
Apr 7, 1786	King (13) born 0
Apr 21, 1789	Adams (1) inaugurated 0
Mar 29, 1790	Tyler (10) born 0

Jul 10, 1792	Dallas (11) born **0**
Mar 4, 1797	Jefferson (2) inaugurated **1 — Adams (1)**
Jan 7, 1800	Fillmore (12) born 1
Mar 4, 1801	Burr (3) inaugurated **2 — Adams (1), Jefferson (2)**
Mar 4, 1805	Clinton (4) inaugurated (1st term) **3 — Adams (1), Jefferson (2), Burr (3)**
Dec 29, 1808	Johnson (16) born 3
Mar 4, 1809	Clinton (4) inaugurated (2nd term) 3
Aug 27, 180	Hamlin (15) born 3
Feb 16, 1812	Wilson (18) born 3
Apr 20, 1812	Clinton (4) dies in office *[When Clinton (4) died in office, the U.S. was left without a vice president for the first time.]* 3
Mar 4, 1813	Gerry (5) inaugurated *[When Gerry (5) was inaugurated, the U.S. had been without a vice president for 10 m 12d.]* 3
Nov 23, 1814	Gerry (5) dies in office *[When Gerry (5) died in office, the U.S. was left without a vice president for the second time.]* 3
Mar 4, 1817	Tompkins (6) inaugurated *[When Tompkins (6) was inaugurated, the U.S. had been without a vice president for 2y 3m 9d.]* 3
Jun 30, 1819	Wheeler (19) born 3
Sep 7, 1819	Hendricks (21) born 3
Jan 21, 1821	Breckinridge (14) born 3
Mar 23, 1823	Colfax (17) born 3
May 16, 1824	Morton (22) born 3
Mar 4, 1825	Calhoun (7) inaugurated (1st term — served Adams PR-6) **4 — Adams (1), Jefferson (2), Burr (3), Tompkins (6)**
Jun 11, 1825	Tompkins (6) dies **3 — Adams (1), Jefferson (2), Burr (3)**
Jul 4, 1826	Adams (1) dies 1

Jul 4, 1826	Jefferson (2) dies 1 — **Burr (3)**
Mar 4, 1829	Calhoun (7) inaugurated (2nd term — served Jackson PR-7) 1
Oct 5, 1830	Arthur (20) born 1
Dec 28, 1832	Calhoun (7) resigns *[When Calhoun (7) resigned, the U.S. was left without a vice president for the third time.]* 2 — **Burr (3), Calhoun (7)**
Mar 4, 1833	Van Buren (8) inaugurated *[When Van Buren (8) was inaugurated, the U.S. had been without a vice president for 2m 4d.]* 2
Oct 23, 1835	Stevenson (23) born 2
Sep 14, 1836	Burr (3) dies 1 — **Calhoun (7)**
Mar 4, 1837	Johnson (9) inaugurated 2 — **Calhoun (7), Van Buren (8)**
Mar 4, 1841	Tyler (10) inaugurated 3 — **Calhoun (7), Van Buren (8), Johnson (9)**
Apr 4, 1841	Harrison (9) dies in office 3
Apr 6, 1841	Tyler (10) inaugurated as 10th president *[When William Henry Harrison died in office, Tyler was inaugurated as the 10th president, leaving the U.S. without a vice president for the fourth time.]* 4 — **Calhoun (7), Van Buren (8), Johnson (9),Tyler (10)**
Jun 3, 1844	Hobart (24) born 4
Mar 4, 1845	Dallas (11) inaugurated *[When Dallas (11) was inaugurated, the U.S. had been without a vice president for 3y 10m 27d.]* 4
Mar 4, 1849	Fillmore (12) inaugurated 5 — **Calhoun (7), Van Buren (8), Johnson (9), Tyler (10), Dallas (11)**
Mar 31, 1850	Calhoun (7) dies 4 — **Van Buren (8), Johnson (9), Tyler (10), Dallas (11)**
Jul 9, 1850	Taylor (12) dies in office 4
Jul 10, 1850	Fillmore (12) inaugurated as 13th president *[Zachary Taylor's death and Fillmore's in auguration eft the U.S. without a vice president for the fifth time.]* 5 — **Van Buren (8), Johnson (9), Tyler (10), Dallas (11), Fillmore (12)**
Nov 19, 1850	Johnson (9) dies 4 — **Van Buren (8), Tyler (10), Dallas (11), Fillmore (12)**
May 11, 1852	Fairbanks (26) born 4
Mar 4, 1853	King (13) inaugurated *[When King (13) was inaugurated, the U.S. had been without a vice president for 2y 7m 22d.]* 4

Apr 18, 1853	King (13) dies in office *[King's death left U.S. with no vice president for the sixth time.]* 4
Mar 14, 1854	Marshall (28) born 4
Oct 24, 1855	Sherman (27) born 4
Mar 4, 1857	Breckinridge (14) inaugurated *[When Breckinridge was inaugurated, the U.S. had been without a vice president for 3y 10m 14d.]* 4
Oct 27, 1858	Roosevelt (25) born 4
Jan 25, 1860	Curtis (31) born 4
Mar 4, 1861	Hamlin (15) inaugurated 5 — Van Buren (8), Tyler (10), Dallas (11), Fillmore (12), Breckinridge (14)
Jan 18, 1862	Tyler (10/PR-10) dies 4 — Van Buren (8), Dallas (11), Fillmore (12), Breckinridge (14)
Jul 24, 1862	Van Buren (8) dies 3 — Dallas (11), Fillmore (12), Breckinridge (14)
Dec 31, 1864	Dallas (11) dies 2 — Fillmore (12), Breckinridge (14)
Mar 4, 1865	Johnson (16) inaugurated 3 — Fillmore (12), Breckinridge (14), Hamlin (15)
Apr 15, 1865	Lincoln (PR-16) assassinated 3
Apr 15, 1865	Johnson (16) inaugurated as 17th president *[When Johnson was inaugurated as 17th president, the U.S. was left without a a vice president for the seventh time.]* 4 — Fillmore (12), Breckinridge (14), Hamlin (15), Johnson (16)
Aug 27, 1865	Dawes (30) born 4
Nov 22, 1868	Garner (32) born 4
Mar 4, 1869	Colfax (17) inaugurated *[When Colfax was inaugurated, the U.S. had been without a vice president 3y 7m 17d.]* 4
Jul 4, 1872	Coolidge (29) born 4
Mar 4, 1873	Wilson (18) inaugurated 5 — Fillmore (12), Breckinridge (14), Hamlin (15), Johnson (16), Colfax (17)
Mar 8, 1874	Fillmore (12) dies 4 — Breckinridge (14), Hamlin (15), Johnson (16), Colfax (17)
May 17, 1875	Breckinridge (14) dies 3 — Hamlin (15), Johnson (16), Colfax (17)
Jul 31, 1875	Johnson (16/PR-17) dies 2 — Hamlin (15), Colfax (17)

Nov 22, 1875	Wilson (18) dies in office *[When Wilson died in office, the U.S. was left with no vice president for the eighth time.]* 2
Mar 4, 1877	Wheeler (19) inaugurated *[When Wheeler was inaugurated, the U.S. had been without a vice president for 1y 3m 10d.]* 2
Nov 24, 1877	Barkley (35) born 2
Mar 4, 1881	Arthur (20) inaugurated 3 — Hamlin (15), Colfax (17), Wheeler (19)
Sep 19, 1881	Garfield (PR-20) dies in office 3
Sep 20, 1881	Arthur (20) inaugurated as 21st president *[When Garfield died in office and Arthur was inaugurated 21st president, the U.S. was left with no vice president for the ninth time.]* 4 — Hamlin (15), Colfax (17), Wheeler (19), Arthur (20)
May 8, 1884	Truman (34) born 4
Jan 13, 1885	Colfax (17) dies 3 — Hamlin (15), Wheeler (19), Arthur (20)
Mar 4, 1885	Hendricks (21) inaugurated *[When Hendricks was inaugurated, the U.S. had been without a vice president for 3y 5m 12d.]* 3
Nov 25, 1885	Hendricks (21) dies in office *[When Hendricks died in office, the U.S. was left with no vice president for the 10th time.]* 3
Nov 18, 1886	Arthur (20) dies 2 — Hamlin (15), Wheeler ((19)
Jun 4, 1887	Wheeler (19) dies 1 — Hamlin (15)
Oct 7, 1888	Wallace (33) born 1
Mar 4, 1889	Morton (22) inaugurated *[When Morton was inaugurated, the U.S. had been without a vice president for 3y 3m 7d.]* 1
Jul 4, 1891	Hamlin (15) dies 0
Mar 4, 1893	Stevenson (23) inaugurated 1 — Morton (22)
Mar 4, 1897	Hobart (24) inaugurated 2 — Morton (22), Stevenson (23)
Nov 21, 1899	Hobart (24) dies in office *[When Hobart died in office, the U.S. was left without a vice president for the 11th time.]* 2
Mar 4, 1901	Roosevelt (25) inaugurated *[When Roosevelt was inaugurated, the U.S. had been without a vice president for 1y 3m 11d.]* 2

Sep 14, 1901	McKinley (PR-25) assassinated 2
Sep 14, 1901	Roosevelt (41) inaugurated as 26th president *[When McKinley was assassinated and Roosevelt inaugurated, the U.S. was left without a president for the 12th time.]* **3 — Morton (22), Stevenson (23), Roosevelt (25)**
Mar 4, 1905	Fairbanks (26) inaugurated *[When Fairbanks was inaugurated, the U.S. had been without a vice president for 3y 5m 18d.]* 3
Jul 8, 1908	Rockefeller (41) born 3
Aug 27, 1908	Johnson (37) born 3
Mar 4, 1909	Sherman (27) inaugurated **4 — Morton (22), Stevenson (23), Roosevelt (25), Fairbanks (26)**
May 27, 1911	Humphrey (38) born 4
Oct 30, 1912	Sherman (27) dies in office *[When Sherman died in office, the U.S. was left with no vice president for the 13th time.]* 4
Jan 9, 191	Nixon (36) born 4
Mar 4, 1913	Marshall (28) inaugurated *[When Marshall was inaugurated, the U.S. had been without a vice president for 4m 2d.]* 4
Jul 14, 1913	Ford (40) born 4
Jun 14, 1914	Stevenson (23) dies **3 — Morton (22), Roosevelt (25), Fairbanks (26)**
Jun 4, 1918	Fairbanks (26) dies **2 — Morton (22), Roosevelt (25)**
Nov 9, 1918	Agnew (39) born 2
Jan 6, 1919	Roosevelt (25/PR-26) dies **1 — Morton (22)**
May 16, 1920	Morton (22) dies 0
Mar 4, 1921	Coolidge (29) inaugurated **1 — Marshall (28)**
Aug 2, 1923	Harding (PR-29) dies in office 1
Aug 3, 1923	Coolidge (29) inaugurated as 30th president *[After Harding's death and Coolidge's inauguration, the U.S. was left with no vice president for the 14th time.]* **2 — Marshall (28), Coolidge (29)**
Jun 12, 1924	Bush (43) born 2

Mar 4, 1925	Dawes (30) inaugurated *[When Dawes was inaugurated, the U.S. had been without a vice president 1y 7m 1d.]* 2
Jun 1, 1925	Marshall (28) dies 1 — **Coolidge (29)**
Jan 5, 1928	Mondale (42) born 1
Mar 4, 1929	Curtis (31) inaugurated 2 — **Coolidge (29), Dawes (30)**
Jan 5, 1933	Coolidge (29/PR-30) dies 1 — **Dawes (30)**
Mar 4, 1933	Garner (32) inaugurated 2 — **Dawes (30), Curtis (31)**
Feb 8, 1936	Curtis (31) dies 1 — **Dawes (30)**
Jan 20, 1941	Wallace (33) inaugurated 2 — **Dawes (30), Garner (32)**
Jan 30, 1941	Cheney (46) born 2
Jan 20, 1945	Truman (34) inaugurated 3 — **Dawes (30), Garner (32), Wallace (33)**
Apr 12, 1945	Roosevelt (PR-32) dies in office *[When Roosevelt died in office and Truman was inaugurated, the U.S. was left with no vice president for the 15th time.]* 3
Apr 12, 1945	Truman (34) inaugurated as 33rd president 4 — **Dawes (30), Garner (32), Wallace (33), Truman (34)**
Feb 4, 1947	Quayle (44) born 4
Mar 31, 1948	Gore (45) born 4
Jan 20, 1949	Barkley (35) inaugurated *[When Barkley was inaugurated, the U.S. had been without a vice president 3y 9m 8d.]* 4
Apr 23, 1951	Dawes (30) dies 3 — **Garner (32), Wallace (33), Truman (34)**
Jan 20, 1953	Nixon (36) inaugurated 4 — **Garner (32), Wallace (33), Truman (34), Barkley (35)**
Apr 30, 1956	Barkley (35) dies 3 — **Garner (32), Wallace (33), Truman (34)**
Jan 20, 1961	Johnson (37) inaugurated 4 — **Garner (32), Wallace (33), Truman (34), Nixon (36)**
Nov 22, 1963	Kennedy (PR-35) assassinated 4
Nov 22, 1963	Johnson (37) inaugurated as 36th president *[When Kennedy was assassinated and Johnson inaugurated, the U.S. was left without a vice president for the 16th time.]* 5 — **Garner (32), Wallace (33), Truman (34), Nixon (36), Johnson (37)**

Jan 20, 1965	Humphrey (38) inaugurated *[When Humphrey was inaugurated, the U.S. had been without a vice president 1y 3m 26d.]* 5
Nov 18, 1965	Wallace (33) dies 4 — Garner (32), Truman (34), Nixon (36), Johnson (37)
Nov 7, 1967	Garner (32) dies 3 — Truman (34), Nixon (36), Johnson (37)
Jan 20, 1969	Agnew (39) inaugurated 4 — Truman (34), Nixon (36), Johnson (37), Humphrey (38)
Dec 26, 1972	Truman (34) dies 3 — Nixon (36), Johnson (37), Humphrey (38)
Jan 22, 1973	Johnson (37/PR-36) dies 2 — Nixon (36), Humphrey (38)
Oct 10, 1973	Agnew (39) resigns from office *[When Agnew resigned from office, the U.S. was without a vice president for the 17th time]* 3 — Nixon (36), Humphrey (38), Agnew (39)
Dec 6, 1973	Ford (40) inaugurated *[When Ford was inaugurated, the U.S. had been without a vice president 1m 26d.]* 3
Aug 9, 1974	Nixon (PR-37) resigns from presidency 3
Aug 9, 1974	Ford (40) inaugurated as 38th president 4 — Nixon (36), Humphrey (38), Agnew (39), Ford (VP40)
Dec 19, 1974	Rockefeller (41) inaugurated *[When Rockefeller was inaugurated, the U.S. had been without a vice president 4m 10d.]* 4
Jan 20, 1977	Mondale (42) inaugurated 5 — Nixon (36), Humphrey (38), Agnew (39), Ford (40), Rockefeller (41)
Jan 13, 1978	Humphrey (38) dies 4 — Nixon (36), Agnew (39), Ford (40), Rockefeller (41)
Jan 26, 1979	Rockefeller (41) dies 3 — Nixon (36), Agnew (39), Ford (40)
Jan 20, 1981	Bush (43) inaugurated 4 — Nixon (36), Agnew (39), Ford (40), Mondale (42)
Jan 20, 1989	Quayle (44) inaugurated 5 — Nixon (36), Agnew (39), Ford (40), Mondale (42), Bush (43)
Jan 20, 1993	Gore (45) inaugurated 6 — Nixon (36), Agnew (39), Ford (40), Mondale (42), Bush (43), Quayle (44)
Apr 22, 1994	Nixon (36) dies 5 — Agnew (39), Ford (40), Mondale (42), Bush (43), Quayle (44)
Sep 17, 1996	Agnew (39) dies 4 — Ford (40), Mondale (42), Bush (43), Quayle (44)
Jan 21, 2001	Cheney (46) inaugurated 5 — Ford (40), Mondale (42), Bush (43), Quayle (44)

Appendix B:
Facts About the Offices

PRESIDENTS

Nine U.S. presidents failed to complete their terms of office because of resignation, assassination or death by natural causes. Richard M. Nixon resigned; Zachary Taylor, Warren G. Harding, William Henry Harrison and Franklin D. Roosevelt died in office; and James A. Garfield, John F. Kennedy, Abraham Lincoln and William McKinley were assassinated.

The only president ever to serve two nonconsecutive terms was Grover Cleveland, who was president 1885–1889 and 1893–1897.

The president whose administration was served by more vice presidents than any other was Franklin D. Roosevelt: the three vice presidents who served him were John N. Garner 1933–1941, Henry A. Wallace 1941–1945 and Harry S Truman 1945.

The only U.S. president ever inaugurated who was not elected either president or vice president first was Gerald R. Ford. When Nixon's vice president, Spiro Agnew, resigned, Ford was appointed vice president under a new constitutional provision. Then, when Nixon resigned, Ford became president without ever being elected either to the presidency or the vice presidency.

The president who served the shortest term was William Henry Harrison, who died one month after taking office; the president who served longest was Franklin D. Roosevelt, who was elected to an unprecedented fourth term and was serving that term when he died in office. (See complete list of time served in the presidency and other offices in Appendix C.)

The greatest number of former U.S. presidents living at one time was five, and this has occurred three times: March 4, 1861, to January 18, 1862; January 20, 1993, to April 22, 1994; and January 20, 2001, to the time at which this book was finished, February 2003. (See complete list of presidents living at these times in the Presidential Timeline in Appendix A.)

It is a popular misconception that John F. Kennedy was the youngest man ever to serve as the President of the U.S., but at the age of 42, Theodore Roosevelt was the elected vice president when President William McKinley was assassinated. Roosevelt was then sworn in as president, and was the youngest man to serve in that capacity to date. John F. Kennedy was 43 years old when he was inaugurated.

Ronald Reagan, at the age of 69, was the oldest man to be inaugurated president.

Seven presidents served in the Cabinet before being elected president: John Quincy Adams, James Buchanan, Thomas Jefferson, James Madison and Martin Van Buren all served in the Cabinet as Secretary of State; James Monroe served as Secretary of State and Secretary of War (interim); and Herbert Hoover served as Secretary of Commerce.

William Howard Taft was the only president ever to be appointed to the Supreme Court.

233

VICE PRESIDENTS

Nine U.S. vice presidents became president upon the death or resignation of the president. Those who were sworn in as president upon the death of the president by natural causes were Millard Fillmore, sworn in after the death of Zachary Taylor; Harry S Truman, sworn in after the death of Franklin D. Roosevelt; John Tyler, sworn in after the death of William Henry Harrison; and Calvin Coolidge, sworn in after the death of Warren G. Harding.

The vice presidents who were sworn in after the assassination of a president were Andrew Johnson, sworn in after the death of Abraham Lincoln; Chester A. Arthur, sworn in after the death of James A. Garfield; Theodore Roosevelt, sworn in after the death of William McKinley; and Lyndon B. Johnson, sworn in after the death of John F. Kennedy. Gerald R. Ford became president upon the resignation of Richard M. Nixon.

Only two vice presidents resigned from office: John C. Calhoun (1832) and Spiro T. Agnew (1973).

Seven vice presidents died in office, all of natural causes: George Clinton, Elbridge Gerry, Thomas A. Hendricks, Garrett Hobart, William R. King, James S. Sherman and Henry Wilson.

The youngest man to serve as vice president, to date, was John C. Breckinridge, who took the oath of office at the age of 36.

The oldest man to be sworn in as vice president was Alben W. Barkley, who was 71 at the time of his inauguration. (See complete list of the ages of president, vice presidents, Supreme Court justices and Cabinet officers at the time of their inauguration or confirmation in Appendix E.)

John C. Calhoun was the only man ever to be elected vice president to serve in the administrations of two different presidents. He served as vice president for John Quincy Adams from 1825 to 1829, and Andrew Jackson from 1829 to 1832.

The greatest number of former vice president living at one time was six, a circumstance which has occurred only once, from January 20, 1993, to April 22, 1994.

Because of deaths and resignations, the U.S. has been without a vice president on 17 occasions. The longest of these was nearly four years and the shortest was two months. The total of all 17 periods of time without a vice president is just over 39 years. (See complete list of vice presidents living at any given time period, and the dates of the periods when there was no vice president, the Vice Presidential Timeline in Appendix A.)

CABINET MEMBERS

Elliott Lee Richardson served in four Cabinet offices, more than any other secretary in a president's Cabinet. The Cabinet posts he held included Secretary of the Department of Health, Education and Welfare, the Department of Defense and the office of the Attorney General, all for President Nixon, and Secretary of the Department of Commerce for President Ford.

Six Cabinet members served in three different Cabinet posts: George B. Cortelyou (Commerce and Labor, Postmaster General, Secretary of the Treasury); Walter Q. Gresham (Postmaster General, Secretary of the Treasury, Secretary of State); Patricia Roberts Harris (Housing and Urban Development, Health Education and Welfare, and Health and Human Services); Philander C. Knox (Secretary of War, Attorney General, Secretary of State); Timothy Pickering (Postmaster General, Secretary of War, Secretary of State); and George P. Shultz (Secretary of Labor, Secretary of the Treasury, Secretary of State).

There have been 35 Cabinet officers who have served as secretary in two departments.

The Cabinet member who served the greatest number of presidents was Philander Chase Knox, who served as the Attorney General for presidents William McKinley and Theodore Roosevelt, and as the Secretary of State for presidents William Howard Taft and Woodrow Wilson.

There have been seven members of the

Cabinet who served one term in a Cabinet office, and then after at least one other Secretary served in that office, were reappointed to second terms in the same office. In descending order, ranked by the length of time between the two terms served in the office, they are: Henry L. Stimson, Secretary of War 47 and 56, was appointed to the office after a hiatus of 27y 4m 7d; Donald H. Rumsfeld, Secretary of Defense 13 and 21, was reappointed to the office by President George Walker Bush 24y after serving in that post just over a year for President Ford; Hugh McCulloch, Secretary of the Treasury 27 and 36, left the post in 1869 and was reappointed 15y 7m 27d later; William Windom, Secretary of the Treasury 33 and 39, was appointed to the office a second time after 7y 3m 22d had elapsed; James G. Blaine, Secretary of State 28 and 31, served twice, with the two terms of service separated by 7y 2m 16d; Daniel Webster, Secretary of State 14 and 19, returned to the State Department for a second time 7y 2m 13d after his first term of service there ended; and John Y. Mason, Secretary of the Navy 16 and 18, served two terms in that Cabinet post separated by 6m.

SUPREME COURT JUSTICES

All Supreme Court justices were male for the first 192 years of the court's existence, and in recent years there have been only two female justices appointed, both still serving — Sandra Day O'Connor, confirmed in 1981, and Ruth Bader Ginsburg, confirmed in 1993.

Only five justices served as Associate Justice before appointment as Chief Justice: Edward D. White, Harlan F. Stone, Charles Evans Hughes, John Rutlege and William Rehnquist.

Sixteen of the justices were appointed Chief Justice and served in the Supreme Court only in that capacity; 98 served only as associate justices.

Supreme Court Justices are appointed for life, so death in office is much more common for this office than for others. Fifty justices have died in office, and 51 resigned and lived for varying lengths of time in retirement.

Charles Evans Hughes was the only justice ever to resign twice from the Supreme Court. He was confirmed to the court as an associate justice in 1910, served until 1916, and resigned the first time; 14 years later, in 1930, he was nominated and confirmed to the office of chief justice, where he served for more than 11 years until his second resignation in 1941.

Four justices served in two Cabinet offices before appointment to the Supreme Court: William Moody served as secretary of the Department of the Navy and as Attorney General; Edwin M. Stanton served as Attorney General and as secretary of the War Department; Roger B. Taney served as Attorney General and as secretary of the Department of the Treasury; and Levi Woodbury served as secretary of the Department of the Navy and the Department of the Treasury.

Fifteen justices served in one Cabinet position before appointment to the Supreme Court: Salmon P. Chase, Thomas C. Clark, Nathan Clifford, William R. Day, Arthur Goldberg, Charles Hughes, Lucius Q.C. Lamar, Joseph McKenna, John McLean, James McReynolds, John Marshall, Frank W. Murphy, Harlan F. Stone, William H. Taft and Frederick M. Vinson.

Appendix C: Listings of Total Length of Service by Separate Office; by All Officeholders in All Cabinet Offices; and by Officeholders in Each Office

These listings provide rankings for the amount of time each officeholder spent in a particular office. The totals are given both as a years-months-days total and, in parentheses, as a "total days in office" ranking. There are two Cabinet listings; the first provides a total amount of time each officeholder spent in all offices (some Cabinet officers served in multiple Cabinet offices) and the second is a separate listing for each office, giving the amount of time each person served in that particular office. In the Supreme Court section, for justices who served only as associate or chief justice, there is only one entry. For justices who have served both as an associate justice and a chief justice, there are three entries—time served as an associate justice, time served as a chief justice, and total time served in the Supreme Court.

PRESIDENTS

Franklin D. Roosevelt (32) .... 12y 1m 8d. .... (4,421 days)
Grover Cleveland (22/24) .... 8y .... (2,922 days)
Bill [William Jefferson] Clinton (42) .... 8y .... (2,922 days)
Dwight D. Eisenhower (34) .... 8y .... (2,922 days)
Ulysses S. Grant (18) .... 8y .... (2,922 days)
Andrew Jackson (7) .... 8y .... (2,922 days)
Thomas Jefferson (3) .... 8y .... (2,922 days)

James Madison (4). . . . . 8y . . . . (2,922 days)
James Monroe (5) . . . . 8y . . . . (2,922 days)
Ronald Reagan (40). . . . . 8y . . . . (2,922 days)
Woodrow Wilson (28). . . . . 8y . . . . (2,922 days)
George Washington (1). . . . . 7y 10m 3d. . . . . (2,859 days)
Harry S Truman (33) . . . . 7y 9m 8d . . . . (2,834 days)
Theodore Roosevelt (26). . . . . 7y 5m 17d. . . . . (2,723 days)
Calvin Coolidge (30). . . . . 5y 7m . . . . (2,036 days)
Richard M. Nixon (37) . . . . 5y 6m 20d. . . . . (2,026 days)
Lyndon B. Johnson (36) . . . . 5y 1m 29d. . . . . (1,885 days)
John Tyler (10) . . . . 4y 10m 25d. . . . . (1,786 days)
Abraham Lincoln (16). . . . . 4y 1m 11d. . . . . (1,502 days)
John Adams (2). . . . . 4y . . . . (1,461 days)
John Quincy Adams (6) . . . . 4y . . . . (1,461 days)
James Buchanan (15). . . . . 4y . . . . (1,461 days)
George Herbert Walker Bush (41) . . . . 4y . . . . (1,461 days)
Jimmy [James Earl] Carter (39) . . . . 4y . . . . (1,461 days)
Benjamin Harrison (23) . . . . 4y . . . . (1,461 days)
Rutherford B. Hayes (19) . . . . 4y . . . . (1,461 days)
Herbert Hoover (31). . . . . 4y . . . . (1,461 days)
Franklin Pierce (14). . . . . 4y . . . . (1,461 days)
James K. Polk (11). . . . . 4y . . . . (1,461 days)
William H. Taft (27). . . . . 4y . . . . (1,461 days)
Martin Van Buren (8) . . . . 4y . . . . (1,461 days)
Andrew Johnson (7) . . . . 3y 10m 16d. . . . . (1,411 days)
William McKinley (25). . . . . 3y 6m 10d. . . . . (1,285 days)
Chester A. Arthur (21) . . . . 3y 5m 11d. . . . . (1,256 days)
John F. Kennedy (35) . . . . 2y 10m 2d. . . . . (1,032 days)
Millard Fillmore (13) . . . . 2y 7m 21d . . . . (961 days)
Gerald R. Ford (38). . . . . 2y 5m 11d . . . . (891 days)
Warren G. Harding (29) . . . . 2y 4m. . . . . (850 days)
Zachary Taylor (12). . . . . 1y 4m 5d . . . . (490 days)
James A. Garfield (20). . . . . 6m 15d . . . . (195 days)
William Henry Harrison (9). . . . . 1m. (30 days)
George Walker Bush (43) . . . . — — —

VICE PRESIDENTS

George Herbert Bush (43). . . . . 8y . . . . (2,922 days)
Al Gore (45). . . . . 8y . . . . (2,922 days)
Thomas R. Marshall (28) . . . . 8y . . . . (2,922 days)
Richard M. Nixon (36) . . . . 8y . . . . (2,922 days)
Daniel D. Tompkins (6) . . . . 8y . . . . (2,922 days)
John N. Garner (32) . . . . 7y 10m 15d. . . . . (2,871 days)
John Adams (1). . . . . 7y 10m 10d. . . . . (2,866 days)
John C. Calhoun (7) . . . . 7y 9m 24d. . . . . (2,850 days)
George Clinton (4) . . . . 7y 1m 16d. . . . . (2,602 days)
Spiro Theodore Agnew (39) . . . . 4y 8m 20d. . . . . (1,721 days)
Alben W. Barkley (35). . . . . 4y . . . . (1,461 days)

John C. Breckinridge (14)........................ 4y .... (1,461 days)
Aaron Burr (3)................................. 4y .... (1,461 days)
Schuyler Colfax (17)............................ 4y .... (1,461 days)
Charles Curtis (31) .... 4y .... (1,461 days)
George M. Dallas (11)........................... 4y .... (1,461 days)
Charles G. Dawes (30)........................... 4y .... (1,461 days)
Charles W. Fairbanks (26)........................ 4y .... (1,461 days)
Hannibal Hamlin (15)............................ 4y .... (1,461 days)
Hubert A. Humphrey (38) .... 4y .... (1,461 days)
Thomas Jefferson (2)........................... 4y .... (1,461 days)
Richard M. Johnson (9).......................... 4y .... (1,461 days)
Walter Frederick Mondale (42).................... 4y .... (1,461 days)
Levi P. Morton (22)............................. 4y .... (1,461 days)
Dan Quayle (44) .... 4y .... (1,461 days)
Adlai E. Stevenson (23).......................... 4y .... (1,461 days)
Martin Van Buren (8) .... 4y .... (1,461 days)
Henry A. Wallace (33)........................... 4y .... (1,461 days)
William A. Wheeler (19).......................... 4y .... (1,461 days)
James S. Sherman (27) .... 3y 7m 26d .... (1,331 days)
Lyndon B. Johnson (37) .... 2y 10m 2d .... (1,032 days)
Garrett A. Hobart (24) .... 2y 8m 17d............ (987 days)
Calvin Coolidge (29)............................ 2y 5m .... (880 days)
Henry Wilson (18) .... 2y 3m 18d .... (838 days)
Nelson A. Rockefeller (41) .... 2y 1m 1d .... (761 days)
Elbridge Gerry (5).............................. 1y 8m 19d .... (624 days)
Millard Fillmore (12) .... 1y 4m 5d .... (490 days)
Thomas A. Hendricks (21) .... 8m 21d .... (261 days)
Gerald R. Ford (40)............................. 8m 3d .... (243 days)
Chester A. Arthur (20) .... 6m 15d .... (195 days)
Theodore Roosevelt (25)......................... 6m 10d .... (190 days)
Harry S Truman (34) .... 2m 23d .... (83 days)
William R. King (13)............................ 1m 14d .... (44 days)
Andrew Johnson (16) .... 1m 11d .... (41 days)
John Tyler (10) .... 1m 2d .... (32 days)
Dick Cheney (46) .... ———

CABINET—COMBINED SERVICE IN ALL OFFICES

James Wilson.................................. 15y 11m 26d.............. (5,834 days)
Harold L. Ickes .... 12y 11m 11d............. (4,724 days)
Albert Gallatin................................ 12y 8m 21d.............. (4,644 days)
Gideon Granger................................ 12y 4m 10d.............. (4,513 days)
Frances Perkins .... 12y 3m 26d.............. (4,499 days)
Cordell Hull.................................. 11y 8m 26d.............. (4,283 days)
Henry Morgenthau, Jr. .... 11y 6m 14d.............. (4,211 days)
William Wirt.................................. 11y 3m 16d.............. (4,123 days)
Andrew W. Mellon .... 10y 11m 8d.............. (3,990 days)
William Harris Crawford .... 10y 10m 28d............. (3,980 days)
Henry Lewis Stimson .... 10y 5m 15d.............. (3,817 days)

George Pratt Shultz	9y 10m 6d	(3,593 days)
Levi Woodbury	9y 9m 8d	(3,565 days)
James J. Davis	9y 9m 4d	(3,561 days)
Robert Smith	9y 8m 8d	(3,535 days)
Caspar Willard Weinberger	9y 4m	(3,407 days)
Return Jonathan Meigs, Jr.	9y 2m 17d	(3,364 days)
Henry A. Wallace	9y 25d	(3,312 days)
Lewis Cass	8y 11m 4d	(3,256 days)
Franklin K. Lane	8y 2m 13d	(2,995 days)
John Caldwell Calhoun	8y 1m 20d	(2,967 days)
Timothy Pickering	8y 1m 5d	(2,952 days)
Elihu Root	8y 7d	(2,929 days)
Bruce Babbitt	8y	(2,922 days)
Albert Sidney Burleson	8y	(2,922 days)
Josephus Daniels	8y	(2,922 days)
Orville Lothrop Freeman	8y	(2,922 days)
Richard Wilson Riley	8y	(2,922 days)
Dean Rusk	8y	(2,922 days)
Arthur Ellsworth Summerfield	8y	(2,922 days)
William B. Wilson	8y	(2,922 days)
Donna Edna Shalala	8y	(2,922 days)
Stewart Lee Udall	7y 11m 29d	(2,915 days)
Samuel Riley Pierce, Jr.	7y 11m 28d	(2,914 days)
David F. Houston	7y 11m 27d	(2,913 days)
William Learned Marcy	7y 11m 27d	(2,913 days)
William H. Seward	7y 11m 27d	(2,913 days)
Gideon Welles	7y 11m 24d	(2,910 days)
Hamilton Fish	7y 11m 21d	(2,907 days)
Henry Dearborn	7y 11m 11d	(2,897 days)
Janet Reno	7y 10m 8d	(2,865 days)
James Madison	7y 10m 1d	(2,857 days)
George M. Robeson	7y 8m 14d	(2,810 days)
William Pierce Rogers	7y 7m 6d	(2,772 days)
Ezra Taft Benson	7y 7m	(2,766 days)
James A. Farley	7y 6m 5d	(2,741 days)
Herbert C. Hoover	7y 5m 16d	(2,722 days)
John Q. Adams	7y 5m 9d	(2,715 days)
Richard Rush	7y 3m 18d	(2,664 days)
James P. Mitchell	7y 3m 11d	(2,657 days)
Philander Chase Knox	7y 2m 22d	(2,638 days)
James Addison Baker, III	7y 1m 18d	(2,604 days)
Robert Strange McNamara	7y 1m 8d	(2,594 days)
William C. Redfield	6y 9m 10d	(2,471 days)
Joseph Habersham	6y 9m 2d	(2,463 days)
John Hay	6y 9m 1d	(2,462 days)
John Forsyth	6y 8m 4d	(2,435 days)
Elizabeth Hanford Dole	6y 7m 24d	(2,425 days)
John Wesley Snyder	6y 6m 26d	(2,397 days)
Howard Malcolm Baldridge	6y 6m 3d	(2,374 days)
Hubert Work	6y 4m 11d	(2,322 days)
Claude A. Swanson	6y 4m 3d	(2,314 days)

William W. Belknap . . . . 6y 4m . . . . (2,311 days)
W. Willard Wirtz. . . . . 6y 3m 27d. . . . . (2,308 days)
John Foster Dulles. . . . . 6y 3m . . . . (2,281 days)
Donald Paul Hodel . . . . 6y 1m 13d. . . . . (2,234 days)
William T. Barry . . . . 6y 24d. . . . . (2,215 days)
George von L. Meyer. . . . . 6y . . . . (2,191 days)
James Monroe . . . . 6y . . . . (2,191 days)
Harry Stewart New . . . . 5y 11m 29d. . . . . (2,185 days)
Oliver Wolcott. . . . . 5y 10m 27d. . . . . (2,153 days)
Homer S. Cummings . . . . 5y 9m 28d. . . . . (2,124 days)
Daniel C. Roper. . . . . 5y 9m 19d. . . . . (2,115 days)
William G. McAdoo . . . . 5y 9m 9d. . . . . (2,105 days)
Edwin McMasters Stanton . . . . 5y 9m 3d. . . . . (2,099 days)
John McLean. . . . . 5y 8m 3d. . . . . (2,069 days)
Edmund Randolph . . . . 5y 7m 14d. . . . . (2,050 days)
Samuel L. Southard. . . . . 5y 5m 15d. . . . . (1,991 days)
Daniel Webster . . . . 5y 5m 7d. . . . . (1,983 days)
Alexander Hamilton . . . . 5y 4m 21d. . . . . (1,967 days)
George B. Cortelyou . . . . 5y 4m 14d. . . . . (1,960 days)
John W. Weeks . . . . 5y 4m 8d. . . . . (1,954 days)
John A.J. Creswell . . . . 5y 4m 1d. . . . . (1,947 days)
Henry Knox. . . . . 5y 3m 20d. . . . . (1,936 days)
Charles Lee . . . . 5y 2m 21d. . . . . (1,907 days)
John D. Long. . . . . 5y 1m 25d. . . . . (1,881 days)
Frederico F. Pena. . . . . 5y 1m 19d. . . . . (1,875 days)
John Sherman . . . . 5y 1m 15d. . . . . (1,871 days)
Jesse Monroe Donaldson. 5y 1m 4d. . . . . (1,860 days)
Leslie M. Shaw. . . . . 5y 1m 2d. . . . . (1,858 days)
John Rusling Block, III . . . . 5y 25d. . . . . (1,851 days)
Amos Kendall . . . . 5y 23d. . . . . (1,849 days)
Newton D. Baker. . . . . 4y 11m 26d. . . . . (1,817 days)
Curtis D. Wilbur. . . . . 4y 11m 14d. . . . . (1,805 days)
Jesse Brown . . . . 4y 11m 11d. . . . . (1,802 days)
John Y. Mason. . . . . 4y 11m 6d. . . . . (1,797 days)
Lyman J. Gage . . . . 4y 11m 5d. . . . . (1,796 days)
Columbus O. Delano . . . . 4y 10m 29d. . . . . (1,790 days)
Rogers C.B. Morton . . . . 4y 10m 13d. . . . . (1,774 days)
George Wilcken Romney . . . . 4y 10m 7d. . . . . (1,768 days)
James V. Forrestal . . . . 4y 10m 5d. . . . . (1,766 days)
Earl Laver Butz . . . . 4y 10m 3d. . . . . (1,764 days)
Claude R. Wickard . . . . 4y 9m 24d. . . . . (1,755 days)
Benjamin Franklin Butler. . . . . 4y 9y 23d . . . . (1,754 days)
Sinclair Weeks. . . . . 4y 9m 22d. . . . . (1,753 days)
Daniel Robert Glickman. 4y 9m 20d. . . . . (1,751 days)
Caesar Augustus Rodney . . . . 4y 9m 15d. . . . . (1,746 days)
Frank Comerford Walker . . . . 4y 8m 21d. . . . . (1,722 days)
Charles Sawyer . . . . 4y 8m 14d. . . . . (1,715 days)
Charles E. Wilson . . . . 4y 8m 10d. . . . . (1,711 days)
Isaac Toucey . . . . 4y 8m 3d. . . . . (1,704 days)
Robert Lansing . . . . 4y 7m 21d. . . . . (1,692 days)
Charles Franklin Brannan. . . . . 4y 7m 18d. . . . . (1,689 days)

Fred A. Seaton.............................4y 7m 12d...............(1,683 days)
William M. Evarts..........................4y 7m 7d................(1,678 days)
Smith Thompson ....4y 7m..................(1,671 days)
George M. Humphrey.......................4y 6m 7d................(1,648 days)
Thomas W. Gregory ....4y 6m 1d................(1,642 days)
Robert E. Rubin ....4y 5m 22d...............(1,633 days)
William H. Moody ....4y 5m 15d...............(1,626 days)
Jesse Jones ....4y 5m 10d...............(1,621 days)
Maurice J. Tobin...........................4y 5m 7d................(1,618 days)
Nicholas Frederick Brady ....4y 5m 2d................(1,613 days)
William H. Taft............................4y 4m 29d...............(1,610 days)
Victor H. Metcalf ....4y 4m 28d...............(1,609 days)
Elliot Lee Richardson ....4y 4m 11d...............(1,592 days)
Hugh McCulloch..........................4y 4m 1d................(1,582 days)
James McHenry...........................4y 3m 23d...............(1,574 days)
Robert B. Reich...........................4y 3m 18d...............(1,569 days)
James Rodney Schlesinger...................4y 3m ....(1,551 days)
James G. Blaine ....4y 2m 29d...............(1,550 days)
Raymond James Donovan...................4y 2m 26d...............(1,547 days)
Clarence Douglas Dillon....................4y 2m 10d...............(1,531 days)
Thomas C. Clark...........................4y 1m 22d...............(1,513 days)
Hazel Rollins O'Leary......................4y 1m 18d...............(1,509 days)
William French Smith.......................4y 1m..................(1,491 days)
Frank Billings Kellog.......................4y 23d.................(1,484 days)
Robert F. Kennedy.........................4y 22d.................(1,483 days)
Terrel Howard Bell ....4y 15d.................(1,476 days)
Ethan A. Hitchcock........................4y 12d.................(1,473 days)
Henry Gabriel Cisneros ....4y 8d..................(1,469 days)
Donald Thomas Regan ....4y 7d..................(1,468 days)
George S. Boutwell ....4y 5d..................(1,466 days)
Warren Minor Christopher..................4y 3d..................(1,464 days)
Caleb Cushing.............................4y 3d..................(1,464 days)
Robert McClelland ....4y 2d..................(1,463 days)
Dean G. Acheson..........................4y ....(1,461 days)
Cecil D. Andrus...........................4y ....(1,461 days)
Robert S. Berglund ....4y ....(1,461 days)
Harold Brown ....4y ....(1,461 days)
Patricia Roberts Harris ....4y ....(1,461 days)
Frank Harris Hitchcock ....4y ....(1,461 days)
Charles Evans Hughes.......................4y ....(1,461 days)
William M. Jardine ....4y ....(1,461 days)
Cave Johnson ....4y ....(1,461 days)
William H.H. Miller ....4y ....(1,461 days)
Charles Nagel ....4y ....(1,461 days)
Benjamin F. Tracy.........................4y ....(1,461 days)
John Anthony Volpe ....4y ....(1,461 days)
James Campbell............................3y 11m 29d.............(1,454 days)
Charles Francis Adams ....3y 11m 28d.............(1,453 days)
John G. Carlisle............................3y 11m 28d.............(1,453 days)
James C. Dobbin ....3y 11m 28d.............(1,453 days)
William C. Endicott ....3y 11m 28d.............(1,453 days)

James Guthrie . . . . 3y 11m 28d . . . . (1,453 days)
Hilary A. Herbert . . . . 3y 11m 28d . . . . (1,453 days)
Daniel S. Lamont . . . . 3y 11m 28d . . . . (1,453 days)
William C. Whitney . . . . 3y 11m 28d . . . . (1,453 days)
Ray Lyman Wilbur . . . . 3y 11m 28d . . . . (1,453 days)
Madeleine K. Albright. . . . . 3y 11m 27d . . . . (1,452 days)
Thomas Francis Bayard. . . . . 3y 11m 27d . . . . (1,452 days)
Walter Folger Brown. . . . . 3y 11m 27d . . . . (1,452 days)
Herbert Brownell, Jr.. . . . . 3y 11m 27d . . . . (1,452 days)
William Sebastian Cohen . . . . 3y 11m 27d . . . . (1,452 days)
Luther H. Hodges . . . . 3y 11m 27d . . . . (1,452 days)
Franklin MacVeagh. . . . . 3y 11m 27d . . . . (1,452 days)
William D. Mitchell . . . . 3y 11m 27d . . . . (1,452 days)
William F. Vilas. . . . . 3y 11m 27d . . . . (1,452 days)
Robert J. Walker . . . . 3y 11m 27d . . . . (1,452 days)
John Wanamaker. . . . . 3y 11m 27d . . . . (1,452 days)
George Woodward Wickersham. . . . . 3y 11m 27d . . . . (1,452 days)
Augustus H. Garland . . . . 3y 11m 26d . . . . (1,451 days)
Melvin B. Laird. . . . . 3y 11y 26d . . . . (1,451 days)
J. Sterling Morton . . . . 3y 11m 26d . . . . (1,451 days)
Richard Olney. . . . . 3y 11m 26d . . . . (1,451 days)
Jeremiah M. Rusk . . . . 3y 11m 26d . . . . (1,451 days)
Jefferson Davis. . . . . 3y 11m 25d . . . . (1,450 days)
John W. Noble. . . . . 3y 11m 25d . . . . (1,450 days)
Henry Clay . . . . 3y 11m 24d . . . . (1,449 days)
Charles Devens . . . . 3y 11m 24d . . . . (1,449 days)
Freddie Ray Marshall . . . . 3y 11m 24d . . . . (1,449 days)
James Buchanan . . . . 3y 11m 23d . . . . (1,448 days)
Carl Schurz . . . . 3y 11m 23d . . . . (1,448 days)
Andrew M. Cuomo . . . . 3y 11m 22d . . . . (1,447 days)
Robert T. Lincoln . . . . 3y 11m 22d . . . . (1,447 days)
Jeremiah S. Black. . . . . 3y 11m 21d . . . . (1,446 days)
Joel R. Poinsett . . . . 3y 11m 20d . . . . (1,445 days)
John G.Sargent . . . . 3y 11m 18d . . . . (1,443 days)
Manuel Lujan . . . . 3y 11m 17d . . . . (1,442 days)
Jack F. Kemp . . . . 3y 11m 14d . . . . (1,439 days)
John Stewart Herrington . . . . 3y 11m 13d . . . . (1,438 days)
Arthur M. Hyde . . . . 3y 11m 11d . . . . (1,436 days)
Rodney E. Slater . . . . 3y 11m 6d . . . . (1,431 days)
Louis Wade Sullivan . . . . 3y 10m 19d . . . . (1,414 days)
James David Watkins . . . . 3y 10m 19d . . . . (1,414 days)
John B. Floyd. . . . . 3y 10m 11d . . . . (1,406 days)
Richard B. (Dick) Cheney. . . . . 3y 10m 3d . . . . (1,398 days)
Mahlon Dickerson . . . . 3y 10m . . . . (1,395 days)
Jacob Thompson . . . . 3y 10m . . . . (1,395 days)
Levi Lincoln . . . . 3y 9m 26d . . . . (1,391 days)
Francis Biddle . . . . 3y 9m 25d . . . . (1,390 days)
William Franklin Knox. . . . . 3y 9m 18d . . . . (1,383 days)
Thomas Jefferson. . . . . 3y 9m 11d . . . . (1,376 days)
Walter Q. Gresham . . . . 3y 9m 8d . . . . (1,373 days)
Richard W. Thompson . . . . 3y 9m 7d . . . . (1,372 days)

Howell Cobb	3y 9m 3d	(1,368 days)
Edward Bates	3y 8m 29d	(1,364 days)
William Eustis	3y 8m 23d	(1,358 days)
Henry Hamill Fowler	3y 8m 19d	(1,354 days)
Charles Emory Smith	3y 8m 19d	(1,354 days)
Julius A. Krug	3y 8m 12d	(1,347 days)
Benjamin W. Crowninshield	3y 8m 11d	(1,346 days)
Charles J. Bonaparte	3y 8m	(1,335 days)
Henry Cantwell Wallace	3y 7m 21d	(1,326 days)
Paul Hamilton	3y 7m 16d	(1,321 days)
William John Bennett	3y 7m 14d	(1,319 days)
Edward J. Derwinski	3y 7m 11d	(1,316 days)
Montgomery Blair	3y 6m 21d	(1,296 days)
Hoke Smith	3y 5m 25d	(1,270 days)
George H. Dern	3y 5m 23d	(1,268 days)
Robert B. Anderson	3y 5m 22d	(1,267 days)
Edwin L. Meese, III	3y 5m 17d	(1,262 days)
David McKendree Key	3y 5m 12d	(1,257 days)
Robert P. Lamont	3y 5m 2d	(1,247 days)
Frederick T. Frelinghuysen	3y 5m	(1,245 days)
J. Howard McGrath	3y 4m 27d	(1,242 days)
Charles Anderson Wickliffe	3y 4m 20d	(1,235 days)
Dwight F. Davis	3y 4m 19d	(1,234 days)
McKay, Douglas McKay	3y 4m 17d	(1,232 days)
William M. Daley	3y 4m 16d	(1,231 days)
George H. Williams	3y 4m 4d	(1,219 days)
Henry A. Kissinger	3y 4m 1d	(1,216 days)
Richard Thornburgh	3y 3m 18d	(1,203 days)
Neil H. McElroy	3y 3m 11d	(1,196 days)
Cyrus Roberts Vance	3y 3m 9d	(1,194 days)
Salmon P. Chase	3y 2m 27d	(1,182 days)
Patrick J. Hurley	3y 2m 22d	(1,177 days)
James Barbour	3y 2m 18d	(1,173 days)
Ronald Harmon Brown	3y 2m 12d	(1,167 days)
Benjamin H. Brewster	3y 2m 5d	(1,160 days)
Harry H. Woodring	3y 2m 3d	(1,158 days)
John W. Griggs	3y 2m	(1,155 days)
Otis Ray Bowen	3y 1m 18d	(1,143 days)
Harry M. Daugherty	3y 1m 4d	(1,129 days)
Maurice Hubert Stans	3y 28d	(1,123 days)
John J. Crittenden	3y 27d	(1,122 days)
John Newton Mitchell	3y 25d	(1,120 days)
Togo Dennis West, Jr.	3y 18d	(1,113 days)
Anthony J. Celebrezze	3y 17d	(1,112 days)
Edwin Denby	3y 13d	(1,108 days)
Oscar L. Chapman	3y 2d	(1,097 days)
Robert Clifton Weaver	3y 2d	(1,097 days)
Marion B. Folsom	3y	(1,095 days)
George C. Marshall, Jr.	2y 11m 25d	(1,085 days)
Samuel Knox Skinner	2y 11m 21d	(1,081 days)
William James Perry	2y 11m 17d	(1,077 days)

Robert Adam Mosbacher . . . . 2y 11m 14d . . . . (1,074 days)
Lewis B. Schwellenbach . . . . 2y 11m 9d . . . . (1,069 days)
Lindley M. Garrison . . . . 2y 11m 6d . . . . (1,066 days)
Roger B. Taney . . . . 2y 11m 4d . . . . (1,064 days)
Clinton P. Anderson . . . . 2y 11m 1d . . . . (1,061 days)
Louis McLane . . . . 2y 10m 24d . . . . (1,054 days)
William E. Chandler . . . . 2y 10m 16d . . . . (1,046 days)
Henry M. Teller . . . . 2y 10m 14d . . . . (1,044 days)
Richard Edmund Lyng . . . . 2y 10m 13d . . . . (1,043 days)
Lucius Q.C. Lamar . . . . 2y 10m 4d . . . . (1,034 days)
James Gaius Watt . . . . 2y 10m . . . . (1,030 days)
Charles J. Folger . . . . 2y 9m 21d . . . . (1,021 days)
Clifford Hardin . . . . 2y 9m 19d . . . . (1,019 days)
Benjamin Stoddert . . . . 2y 9m 11d . . . . (1,011 days)
Juanita M. Kreps . . . . 2y 9m 10d . . . . (1,010 days)
Margaret Mary Heckler . . . . 2y 9m 8d . . . . (1,008 days)
Henry C. Payne . . . . 2y 9m . . . . (1,000 days)
Redfield Proctor . . . . 2y 9m . . . . (1,000 days)
George W. McCrary . . . . 2y 8m 29d . . . . (999 days)
William E. Simon . . . . 2y 8m 19d . . . . (989 days)
Alexis M. Herman . . . . 2y 8m 11d . . . . (981 days)
James Edward Day . . . . 2y 8m 8d . . . . (978 days)
James K. Paulding . . . . 2y 8m 3d . . . . (973 days)
William Emerson (Bill) Brock, III . . . . 2y 7m 18d . . . . (958 days)
Alexander Williams Randall . . . . 2y 7m 14d . . . . (954 days)
Thomas Corwin . . . . 2y 7m 11d . . . . (951 days)
James Day Hodgson . . . . 2y 6m 29d . . . . (939 days)
William Windom . . . . 2y 6m 27d . . . . (937 days)
Charles M. Conrad . . . . 2y 6m 19d . . . . (929 days)
John C. Spencer . . . . 2y 6m 17d . . . . (927 days)
John W. Gardner . . . . 2y 6m 11d . . . . (921 days)
Joseph A. Califano, Jr. . . . . 2y 6m 10d . . . . (920 days)
Orville H. Browning . . . . 2y 6m 2d . . . . (912 days)
Brockman Adams . . . . 2y 6m . . . . (910 days)
Werner Michael Blumenthal . . . . 2y 5m 29d . . . . (909 days)
Griffin Boyette Bell . . . . 2y 5m 24d . . . . (904 days)
Lauro Fred Cavazos, Jr. . . . . 2y 5m 22d . . . . (902 days)
Arthur Sherwood Flemming . . . . 2y 5m 19d . . . . (899 days)
Alex H.H. Stuart . . . . 2y 5m 18d . . . . (898 days)
Robert Emmet Hannegan . . . . 2y 5m 14d . . . . (894 days)
Lawrence F. O'Brien . . . . 2y 5m 7d . . . . (887 days)
William Blaine (Bill) Richardson . . . . 2y 5m 2d . . . . (882 days)
Russell A. Alger . . . . 2y 4m 26d . . . . (876 days)
Abel P. Upshur . . . . 2y 4m 16d . . . . (866 days)
John P. Usher . . . . 2y 4m 6d . . . . (856 days)
John T. Connor . . . . 2y 4m 4d . . . . (854 days)
Oveta Culp Hobby . . . . 2y 3m 20d . . . . (840 days)
Samuel D. Ingham . . . . 2y 3m 14d . . . . (834 days)
John M. Berrien . . . . 2y 3m 13d . . . . (833 days)
John H. Eaton . . . . 2y 3m 10d . . . . (830 days)
William J. Bryan . . . . 2y 3m 3d . . . . (823 days)

William N. Doak	2y 2m 22d	(812 days)
Frederick Bailey Dent	2y 2m 19d	(809 days)
Oscar S. Straus	2y 2m 13d	(803 days)
Jacob M. Dickinson	2y 2m 9d	(799 days)
John Branch	2y 2m 2d	(792 days)
Martin Van Buren	2y 1m 25d	(785 days)
Nathan Kelsey Hall	2y 1m 21d	(781 days)
William Pinkney	2y 1m 4d	(764 days)
John Austin Gronouski	2y 1m 3d	(763 days)
Peter J. Brennan	2y 29d	(759 days)
Wilson Shannon Bissell	2y 28d	(758 days)
Clayton Keith Yeutter	2y 26d	(756 days)
Daniel Manning	2y 23d	(753 days)
Claude Stout Brinegar	2y 14d	(744 days)
David M. Kennedy	2y 10d	(740 days)
Charles Foster	2y 9d	(739 days)
Andrew Lindsay Lewis, Jr.	2y 9d	(739 days)
Paul Henry O'Neill	2y 9d	(739 days)
Alexander J. Dallas	2y 7d	(737 days)
Alan S. Boyd	2y 4d	(734 days)
Edward Livingston	2y 4d	(734 days)
Aaron V. Brown	2y 2d	(732 days)
James R. Garfield	2y 1d	(731 days)
Albert B. Fall	2y	(730 days)
Alexander Mitchell Palmer	2y	(730 days)
Walter L. Fisher	1y 11m 25d	(720 days)
William A. Graham	1y 11m 23d	(718 days)
Richard Schultz Schweiker	1y 11m 21d	(716 days)
Benjamin H. Bristow	1y 11m 17d	(712 days)
Cornelius N. Bliss	1y 11m 14d	(709 days)
Edward Hirsh Levi	1y 11m 14d	(709 days)
Lynn Martin	1y 10m 29d	(708 days)
Mike Espy	1y 11m 10d	(705 days)
Charles S. Fairchild	1y 11m 5d	(700 days)
Lloyd Millard Bentsen, Jr.	1y 11m 2d	(697 days)
James Thomas Lynn	1y 11m 2d	(697 days)
William Lyne Wilson	1y 11m 1d	(696 days)
Samuel Osgood	1y 10m 23d	(688 days)
William Thaddeus Coleman, Jr.	1y 10m 16d	(681 days)
Carla Anderson Hills	1y 10m 14d	(679 days)
Edward Madigan	1y 10m 13d	(678 days)
William Jones	1y 10m 12d	(677 days)
Marshall Jewell	1y 10m 10d	(675 days)
Lamar Alexander	1y 10m 6d	(671 days)
William Ramsey Clark	1y 10m 2d	(667 days)
Walter Joseph Hickel	1y 10m 1d	(666 days)
Robert P. Patterson	1y 9m 27d	(662 days)
Caleb B. Smith	1y 9m 26d	(661 days)
Joseph Holt	1y 9m 17d	(652 days)
William Dennison	1y 9m 15d	(650 days)
James Burrows Edwards	1y 9m 13d	(648 days)

Hugh S. Legare . . . . 1y 9m. . . . . (635 days)
Christian A. Herter. . . . . 1y 8m 29d . . . . (634 days)
Judson Harmon. . . . . 1y 8m 23d . . . . (628 days)
John Nelson. . . . . 1y 8m 9d . . . . (614 days)
Arthur Joseph Goldberg . . . . 1y 8m 3d . . . . (608 days)
Harry L. Hopkins . . . . 1y 7m 26d . . . . (601 days)
Jacob D. Cox . . . . 1y 7m 22d . . . . (597 days)
Nicholas de Belleville Katzenbach . . . . 1y 7m 19d . . . . (594 days)
Robert H. Jackson . . . . 1y 7m 17d . . . . (592 days)
James Speed. . . . . 1y 7m 11d . . . . (586 days)
Thomas Ewing. . . . . 1y 6m 27d . . . . (572 days)
William Bradford . . . . 1y 6m 25d . . . . (570 days)
John Armstrong . . . . 1y 6m 24d . . . . (569 days)
Lawrence H. Summers . . . . 1y 6m 18d . . . . (563 days)
James F. Byrnes . . . . 1y 6m 17d . . . . (562 days)
Abraham Alexander Ribicoff . . . . 1y 6m 9d . . . . (554 days)
Amos T. Akerman . . . . 1y 6m 1d . . . . (546 days)
Richard A. Ballinger . . . . 1y 5m 29d . . . . (544 days)
George Bancroft . . . . 1y 5m 29d . . . . (544 days)
Forrest D. Mathews. . . . . 1y 5m 28m. . . . . (543 days)
James C. McReynolds . . . . 1y 5m 27d . . . . (542 days)
Louis A. Johnson. . . . . 1y 5m 23d . . . . (538 days)
Charles William Duncan, Jr.. . . . . 1y 5m 20d . . . . (535 days)
Benjamin R. Civiletti . . . . 1y 5m 18d . . . . (533 days)
George William Miller . . . . 1y 5m 17d . . . . (532 days)
Walter Forward . . . . 1y 5m 15d . . . . (530 days)
Frederick H. Mueller. . . . . 1y 5m 10d . . . . (525 days)
Winton Malcolm Blount. . . . . 1y 5m 9d . . . . (524 days)
Alexander Meigs Haig, Jr.. . . . . 1y 5m 4d . . . . (519 days)
Nathan Clifford . . . . 1y 5m 1d . . . . (516 days)
Zachariah Chandler . . . . 1y 4m 20d . . . . (505 days)
John Middleton Clayton. 1y 4m 15d . . . . (500 days)
Robert Hutchinson Finch. . . . . 1y 4m 15d . . . . (500 days)
Jacob Collamer . . . . 1y 4m 14d . . . . (499 days)
Reverdy Johnson. . . . . 1y 4m 14d . . . . (499 days)
William M. Meredith . . . . 1y 4m 14d . . . . (499 days)
William B. Preston . . . . 1y 4m 14d . . . . (499 days)
Robert Abercrombie Lovett . . . . 1y 4m 10d . . . . (495 days)
Felix Grundy. . . . . 1y 4m 9d . . . . (494 days)
George W. Crawford . . . . 1y 4m 8d . . . . (493 days)
John Breckinridge. . . . . 1y 4m 7d . . . . (492 days)
Neil E. Goldschmidt . . . . 1y 3m 28d . . . . (483 days)
Ebenezer Hoar. . . . . 1y 3m 26d . . . . (481 days)
Maurice Edwin (Moon) Landrieu . . . . 1y 3m 26d . . . . (481 days)
James Harlan. . . . . 1y 3m 16d . . . . (471 days)
Thomas Savig Kleppe . . . . 1y 3m 10d . . . . (465 days)
William Averell Harriman . . . . 1y 3m 7d . . . . (462 days)
John Bowden Connally, Jr.. . . . . 1y 3m 5d . . . . (460 days)
Calvin William Verity, Jr.. . . . . 1y 3m 1d . . . . (456 days)
Alexander Ramsey. . . . . 1y 2m 26d . . . . (451 days)
Timothy Otis Howe . . . . 1y 2m 20d . . . . (445 days)

William Patrick Clark	1y 2m 17d	(442 days)
William A. Richardson	1y 2m 17d	(442 days)
Joshua W. Alexander	1y 2m 16d	(441 days)
Stephen B. Elkins	1y 2m 9d	(434 days)
William P. Barr	1y 2m	(425 days)
Frank Charles Carlucci, III	1y 2m	(425 days)
Henry D. Gilpin	1y 1m 20d	(415 days)
Shirley Mount Hufstedler	1y 1m 19d	(414 days)
Thomas Sovereign Gates, Jr.	1y 1m 18d	(413 days)
James Horace Burnley IV	1y 1m 17d	(412 days)
Donald M. Dickinson	1y 1m 16d	(411 days)
Carter Glass	1y 1m 16d	(411 days)
James Albert Gary	1y 1m 15d	(410 days)
William H. Hunt	1y 1m 9d	(404 days)
Samuel J. Kirkwood	1y 1m 8d	(403 days)
Ann Dore McLaughlin	1y 1m 3d	(398 days)
Edwin T. Meredith	1y 1m 2d	(397 days)
Philip M. Klutznik	1y 1m	(395 days)
Ogden L. Mills	1y 20d	(385 days)
Edwards Pierrepont	1y 16d	(381 days)
William Wilkins	1y 15d	(380 days)
Leslie Aspin, Jr.	1y 12d	(377 days)
Alphonso Taft	1y 3d	(368 days)
Paul Morton	1y	(365 days)
Frank Murphy	1y	(365 days)
Andrew H. Card, Jr.	11m 29d	(359 days)
William Harrison Hays	11m 28d	(358 days)
Bainbridge Colby	11m 20d	(350 days)
John B. Payne	11m 19d	(349 days)
William Julian (Willie) Usery, Jr.	11m 15d	(345 days)
James M. Porter	11m 11d	(341 days)
William B. Saxbe	11m 10d	(340 days)
Frederick M. Vinson	11m 1d	(331 days)
Peter George Peterson	10m 27d	(327 days)
Samuel Dexter	10m 24d	(324 days)
Barbara Hackman Franklin	10m 24d	(324 days)
Harlan F. Stone	10m 22d	(322 days)
Clark McAdams Clifford	10m 19d	(319 days)
Richard Gordon Kleindienst	10m 18d	(318 days)
Joseph McKenna	10m 18d	(318 days)
Cyrus R. Smith	10m 18d	(318 days)
John Thomas Dunlop	10m 13d	(313 days)
Simon Cameron	10m 8d	(308 days)
Wilbur Joseph Cohen	9m 28d	(298 days)
Thomas Lemuel James	9m 27d	(297 days)
William H. Woodin	9m 27d	(297 days)
Michael (Mickey) Kantor	9m 17d	(287 days)
James D. Cameron	9m 10d	(280 days)
John M. Schofield	9m 9d	(279 days)
John Milton Niles	9m 7d	(277 days)
Lewis L. Strauss	8m 27d	(267 days)

William Marvin Watson . . . . 8m 23d . . . . (263 days)
Alex Buel Trowbridge, Jr. . . . . 8m 20d . . . . (260 days)
Martin P. Durkin . . . . 8m 17d . . . . (257 days)
Edmund Sixtus Muskie . . . . 8m 12d . . . . (252 days)
Peter B. Porter . . . . 8m 11d . . . . (251 days)
Luke E. Wright . . . . 8m 10d . . . . (250 days)
Isaac Wayne McVeagh . . . . 8m 7d . . . . (247 days)
George W. Campbell . . . . 8m 4d . . . . (244 days)
George M. Bibb . . . . 8m 3d . . . . (243 days)
James W. Good . . . . 8m 3d . . . . (243 days)
Lot M. Morrill . . . . 8m 2d . . . . (242 days)
John Marshall . . . . 7m 29d . . . . (239 days)
James Noble Tyner . . . . 7m 29d . . . . (239 days)
William P. Fessenden . . . . 7m 26d . . . . (236 days)
John W. Foster . . . . 7m 24d . . . . (234 days)
Edward Reilly Stettinius, Jr. . . . . 7m 11d . . . . (221 days)
John P. Kennedy . . . . 7m 8d . . . . (218 days)
David Henshaw . . . . 6m 25d . . . . (205 days)
Horace Maynard . . . . 6m 10d . . . . (190 days)
George E. Badger . . . . 6m 6d . . . . (186 days)
John Bell . . . . 6m 6d . . . . (186 days)
Francis Granger . . . . 6m 5d . . . . (185 days)
David R. Francis . . . . 6m . . . . (180 days)
Charles Edison . . . . 5m 28d . . . . (178 days)
Hershel W. Gober . . . . 4m 26d . . . . (176 days)
John A. Rawlins . . . . 5m 25d . . . . (175 days)
Frank Hatton . . . . 5m 23d . . . . (173 days)
Samuel Dickinson Hubbard . . . . 5m 20d . . . . (170 days)
Lawrence Sidney Eagleburger . . . . 4m 26d . . . . (146 days)
Robert John Wynne . . . . 4m 23d . . . . (143 days)
William R. Day . . . . 4m 19d . . . . (139 days)
Henry Stanbery . . . . 4m 8d . . . . (128 days)
Edward Everett . . . . 3m 25d . . . . (115 days)
William J. Duane . . . . 3m 21d . . . . (111 days)
John A. Knebel . . . . 3m 19d . . . . (109 days)
Adolph E. Borie . . . . 3m 15d . . . . (105 days)
Howard M. Gore . . . . 3m 10d . . . . (100 days)
Truman H. Newberry . . . . 3m 3d . . . . (93 days)
William F. Whiting . . . . 2m 21d . . . . (81 days)
Roy D. Chapin . . . . 2m 17d . . . . (77 days)
Nathan Goff, Jr. . . . . 2m . . . . (60 days)
Kenneth C. Royall . . . . 1m 23d . . . . (53 days)
William T. Sherman . . . . 1m 20d . . . . (50 days)
John A. Dix . . . . 1m 17d . . . . (47 days)
James William Marshall . . . . 1m 17d . . . . (47 days)
Stanley Knapp Hathaway . . . . 1m 13d . . . . (43 days)
Roy Owen West . . . . 1m 10d . . . . (40 days)
Robert Bacon . . . . 1m 6d . . . . (36 days)
Phillip F. Thomas . . . . 1m 2d . . . . (32 days)
Joseph W. Barr . . . . 26d . . . . (26 days)
Horatio King . . . . 24d . . . . (24 days)

Norman J. Colman . . . . 21d . . . . (21 days)
Robert C. Wood . . . . 13d . . . . (13 days)
Thomas M.T. McKennan . . . . 11d . . . . (11 days)
Elihu B. Washburne . . . . 11d . . . . (11 days)
Thomas W. Gilmer . . . . 9d . . . . (9 days)
Spencer Abraham . . . . —— ——
John Ashcroft . . . . —— ——
Elaine Lan Chao . . . . —— ——
Donald Louis Evans . . . . —— ——
Melquiades Rafael Martinez . . . . —— ——
Norman Yoshio Mineta . . . . —— ——
Gale Ann Norton . . . . —— ——
Paul Henry O'Neill . . . . —— ——
Roderick R. Paige . . . . —— ——
Colin Luther Powell . . . . —— ——
Anthony Joseph Principi . . . . —— ——
Thomas Ridge . . . . —— ——
Donald H. Rumsfeld . . . . —— ——
John William Snow . . . . —— ——
Tommy G. Thompson . . . . —— ——
Ann Margaret Veneman . . . . —— ——

CABINET—SERVICE IN EACH SEPARATE OFFICE

Secretary of State

Cordell Hull (47) . . . . 11y 8m 26d . . . . (4,283 days)
Dean Rusk (54) . . . . 8y . . . . (2,922 days)
William H. Seward (24) . . . . 7y 11m 27d . . . . (2,913 days)
Hamilton Fish (26) . . . . 7y 11m 21d . . . . (2,907 days)
James Madison (5) . . . . 7y 10m 1d . . . . (2,857 days)
John Q. Adams (8) . . . . 7y 5m 9d . . . . (2,715 days)
Philander Chase Knox (40) . . . . 7y 2m 22d . . . . (2,638 days)
John Hay (37) . . . . 6y 9m 1d . . . . (2,462 days)
John Forsyth (13) . . . . 6y 8m 4d . . . . (2,435 days)
George Pratt Shultz (60) . . . . 6y 6m 5d . . . . (2,376 days)
John Foster Dulles (52) . . . . 6y 3m . . . . (2,281 days)
James Monroe (7) . . . . 5y 10m 26d . . . . (2,152 days)
Robert Lansing (42) . . . . 4y 7m 21d . . . . (1,692 days)
William Pierce Rogers (55) . . . . 4y 7m 13d . . . . (1,684 days)
Daniel Webster (14/19) . . . . 4y 5m 7d . . . . (1,618 days)
Lewis Cass (22) . . . . 3y 9m 8d . . . . (1,582 days)
Frank Billings Kellog (45) . . . . 4y 23d . . . . (1,484 days)
James G. Blaine (28/31) . . . . 4y 7d . . . . (1,468 days)
Warren Minor Christopher (63) . . . . 4y 3d . . . . (1,464 days)
Dean G. Acheson (51) . . . . 4y . . . . (1,461 days)
William Learned Marcy (21) . . . . 4y . . . . (1,461 days)
Charles Evans Hughes (44) . . . . 4y . . . . (1,461 days)
Madeleine K. Albright (64) . . . . 3y 11m 27d . . . . (1,452 days)
Thomas Francis Bayard (30) . . . . 3y 11m 27d . . . . (1,452 days)

Henry Lewis Stimson (46) .... 3y 11m 26d .... (1,451 days)
William M. Evarts (27) .... 3y 11m 25d .... (1,450 days)
Henry Clay (9) .... 3y 11m 24d .... (1,449 days)
James Buchanan (17) .... 3y 11m 23d .... (1,448 days)
Thomas Jefferson (1) .... 3y 9m 11d .... (1,376 days)
James Addison Baker III (61) .... 3y 6m 29d .... (1,304 days)
Elihu Root (38) .... 3y 6m 7d .... (1,282 days)
Timothy Pickering (3) .... 3y 5m 28d .... (1,273 days)
Frederick T. Frelinghuysen (29) .... 3y 5m .... (1,245 days)
Henry A. Kissinger (56) .... 3y 4m 1d .... (1,216 days)
Cyrus Roberts Vance (57) .... 3y 3m 9d .... (1,194 days)
William J. Bryan (41) .... 2y 3m 3d .... (823 days)
Walter Q. Gresham (33) .... 2y 2m 22d .... (812 days)
Martin Van Buren (10) .... 2y 1m 25d .... (785 days)
Robert Smith (6) .... 2y 1m .... (760 days)
Edward Livingston (11) .... 2y 4d .... (734 days)
George C. Marshall, Jr. (50) .... 2y .... (730 days)
Christian A. Herter (53) .... 1y 8m 29d .... (634 days)
Richard Olney (34) .... 1y 8m 22d .... (627 days)
Edmund Randolph (2) .... 1y 7m 18d .... (593 days)
James F. Byrnes (49) .... 1y 6m 17d .... (562 days)
Alexander Meigs Haig, Jr. (59) .... 1y 5m 4d .... (519 days)
John Middleton Clayton (18) .... 1y 4m 15d .... (500 days)
John Sherman (35) .... 1y 1m 22d .... (417 days)
Louis McLane (12) .... 1y 1m 1d .... (396 days)
Bainbridge Colby (43) .... 11m 20d .... (350 days)
John Caldwell Calhoun (16) .... 11m 3d .... (333 days)
Edmund Sixtus Muskie (58) .... 8m 12d .... (252 days)
John Marshall (4) .... 7m 29d .... (239 days)
John W. Foster (32) .... 7m 24d .... (234 days)
Edward Reilly Stettinius, Jr. (48) .... 7m 11d .... (221 days)
Abel P. Upshur (15) .... 7m 4d .... (214 days)
Lawrence Sidney Eagleburger (62) .... 4m 26d .... (146 days)
William R. Day (36) .... 4m 19d .... (139 days)
Edward Everett (20) .... 3m 25d .... (115 days)
Jeremiah S. Black (23) .... 2m 11d .... (71 days)
Robert Bacon (39) .... 1m 6d .... (36 days)
Elihu B. Washburne (25) .... 11d .... (11 days)
Colin Luther Powell (65) .... ———

Secretary of War

Henry Dearborn (5) .... 7y 11m 11d .... (2,897 days)
John Caldwell Calhoun (10) .... 7y 2m 17d .... (2,633 days)
William W. Belknap (32) .... 6y 4m .... (2,311 days)
Henry Lewis Stimson (47/56) .... 6y 6m 11d .... (2,202 days)
Edwin McMasters Stanton (28) .... 5y 6m 22d .... (2,028 days)
John W. Weeks (50) .... 5y 4m 8d .... (1,954 days)
Henry Knox (1) .... 5y 3m 20d .... (1,936 days)
Lewis Lewis (14) .... 5y 1m 26d .... (1,882 days)
Newton D. Baker (49) .... 4y 11m 26d .... (1,817 days)
Elihu Root (43) .... 4y 6m .... (1,641 days)

William H. Taft (44) .... 4y 4m 29d .... (1,610 days)
James McHenry (3) .... 4y 3m 23d .... (1,574 days)
William C. Endicott (38) .... 3y 11m 28d .... (1,453 days)
Daniel S. Lamont (41) .... 3y 11m 28d .... (1,453 days)
Jefferson Davis (24) .... 3y 11m 25d .... (1,450 days)
Robert T. Lincoln (37) .... 3y 11m 22d .... (1,447 days)
Joel R. Poinsett (16) .... 3y 11m 20d .... (1,445 days)
William Learned Marcy (21) .... 3y 11m 29d .... (1,434 days)
John B. Floyd (25) .... 3y 10m 11d .... (1,406 days)
William Eustis (6) .... 3y 8m 23d .... (1,358 days)
George H. Dern (54) .... 3y 5m 23d .... (1,268 days)
Dwight F. Davis (51) .... 3y 4m 19d .... (1,234 days)
Patrick J. Hurley (53) .... 3y 2m 22d .... (1,177 days)
James Barbour (11)........................... 3y 2m 18d .... (1,173 days)
Harry H. Woodring (55) .... 3y 2m 3d .... (1,158 days)
Lindley M. Garrison (48).................... 2y 11m 6d .... (1,066 days)
Redfield Proctor (39) .... 2y 9m .... (1,000 days)
George W. McCrary (35) .... 2y 8m 29d .... (999 days)
Charles M. Conrad (23) .... 2y 6m 19d .... (929 days)
Russell A. Alger (42)......................... 2y 4m 26d .... (876 days)
John H. Eaton (13).......................... 2y 3m 10d .... (830 days)
Jacob M. Dickinson (46) .... 2y 2m 9d .... (799 days)
Robert P. Patterson (57) .... 1y 9m 27d .... (662 days)
John Armstrong (7) .... 1y 6m 24d .... (569 days)
John C. Spencer (18) .... 1y 4m 23d .... (508 days)
George W. Crawford (22)..................... 1y 4m 8d .... (493 days)
Alexander Ramsey (36) .... 1y 2m 26d .... (451 days)
William Harris Crawford (9) .... 1y 2m 13d .... (438 days)
Stephen B. Elkins (40) .... 1y 2m 9d .... (434 days)
Timothy Pickering (2) .... 1y 1m 3d .... (398 days)
William Wilkins (20)......................... 1y 15d................ (380 days)
James M. Porter (19) .... 11m 11d................ (341 days)
Simon Cameron (27) .... 10m 8d................. (308 days)
James D. Cameron (34) .... 9m 10d................. (280 days)
John M. Schofield (29)....................... 9m 9d................. (279 days)
Peter B. Porter (12)........................... 8m 11d................. (251 days)
Luke E. Wright (45) .... 8m 10d................. (250 days)
James W. Good (52) .... 8m 3d................. (243 days)
Samuel Dexter (4) .... 6m 19d................. (199 days)
John Bell (17) .... 6m 6d................. (186 days)
John A. Rawlins (30) .... 5m 25d................. (175 days)
Alphonso Taft (33)........................... 2m 23d................. (83 days)
Kenneth C. Royall (58)....................... 1m 23d................. (53 days)
William T. Sherman (31) .... 1m 20d................. (50 days)
Joseph Holt (26)............................. 1m 13d................. (43 days)
James Monroe (8)............................ 1m 4d................. (34 days)
Benjamin Franklin Butler (15)................ 11d...................... (11 days)

Secretary of the Treasury

Albert Gallatin (4) .... 12y 8m 21d .... (4,644 days)
Henry Morgenthau, Jr. (52)................... 11y 6m 14d .... (4,211 days)

Andrew W. Mellon (49) . . . . 10y 11m 8d . . . . (3,982 days)
William Harris Crawford (7) . . . . 8y 4m 7d . . . . (3,049 days)
Levi Woodbury (13) . . . . 6y 8m 2d . . . . (2,433 days)
John Wesley Snyder (54) . . . . 6y 6m 26d . . . . (2,397 days)
Oliver Wolcott (2) . . . . 5y 10m 27d . . . . (2,153 days)
William G. McAdoo (46) . . . . 5y 9m 9d . . . . (2,105 days)
Alexander Hamilton (1) . . . . 5y 4m 21d . . . . (1,967 days)
Leslie M. Shaw (43) . . . . 5y 1m 2d . . . . (1,858 days)
Lyman J. Gage (42) . . . . 4y 11m 5d . . . . (1,796 days)
George M. Humphrey (55) . . . . 4y 6m 7d . . . . (1,648 days)
Robert E. Rubin (70) . . . . 4y 5m 22d . . . . (1,633 days)
Nicholas Frederick Brady (68) . . . . 4y 5m 2d . . . . (1,613 days)
Hugh McCulloch (27/36) . . . . 4y 4m 1d . . . . (1,582 days)
Clarence Douglas Dillon (57) . . . . 4y 2m 10d . . . . (1,531 days)
Donald Thomas Regan (66) . . . . 4y 7d . . . . (1,468 days)
George S. Boutwell (28) . . . . 4y 5d . . . . (1,466 days)
John G. Carlisle (41) . . . . 3y 11m 28d . . . . (1,453 days)
James Guthrie (21) . . . . 3y 11m 28d . . . . (1,453 days)
Franklin MacVeagh (45) . . . . 3y 11m 27d . . . . (1,452 days)
Robert J. Walker (18) . . . . 3y 11m 27d . . . . (1,452 days)
John Sherman (32) . . . . 3y 11m 23d . . . . (1,448 days)
Howell Cobb (22) . . . . 3y 9m 3d . . . . (1,368 days)
Henry Hamill Fowler (58) . . . . 3y 8m 19d . . . . (1,354 days)
Richard Rush (8) . . . . 3y 7m 2d . . . . (1,307 days)
James Addison Baker, III (67) . . . . 3y 6m 19d . . . . (1,294 days)
Robert B. Anderson (56) . . . . 3y 5m 22d . . . . (1,267 days)
Salmon P. Chase (25) . . . . 3y 2m 27d . . . . (1,182 days)
Charles J. Folger (34) . . . . 2y 9m 21d . . . . (1,021 days)
William E. Simon (63) . . . . 2y 8m 19d . . . . (989 days)
Thomas Corwin (20) . . . . 2y 7m 11d . . . . (951 days)
William Windom (33/39) . . . . 2y 6m 27d . . . . (937 days)
Werner Michael Blumenthal (64) . . . . 2y 5m 29d . . . . (909 days)
Samuel D. Ingham (9) . . . . 2y 3m 14d . . . . (834 days)
Daniel Manning (37) . . . . 2y 23d . . . . (753 days)
David M. Kennedy (60) . . . . 2y 10d . . . . (740 days)
Charles Foster (40) . . . . 2y 9d . . . . (739 days)
Paul Henry O'Neill (72) . . . . 26 9d . . . . (739 days)
Alexander J. Dallas (6) . . . . 2y 7d . . . . (737 days)
George B. Cortelyou (44) . . . . 2y 3d . . . . (733 days)
Benjamin H. Bristow (30) . . . . 1y 11m 17d . . . . (712 days)
Charles S. Fairchild (38) . . . . 1y 11m 5d . . . . (700 days)
Lloyd Millard Bentsen, Jr. (69) . . . . 1y 11m 2d . . . . (697 days)
George Pratt Shultz (62) . . . . 1y 10m 22d . . . . (687 days)
Louis McLane (10) . . . . 1y 9m 23d . . . . (658 days)
Lawrence H.Summers (71) . . . . 1y 6m 18d . . . . (563 days)
George William Miller (65) . . . . 1y 5m 17d . . . . (532 days)
Walter Forward (15) . . . . 1y 5m 15d . . . . (530 days)
William M. Meredith (19) . . . . 1y 4m 14d . . . . (499 days)
John Bowden Connally, Jr. (61) . . . . 1y 3m 5d . . . . (460 days)
William A. Richardson (29) . . . . 1y 2m 17d . . . . (442 days)
John C. Spencer (16) . . . . 1y 1m 24d . . . . (419 days)

Carter Glass (47) .... 1y 1m 16d .... (411 days)
David F. Houston (48) .... 1y 1m 1d .... (396 days)
Ogden L. Mills (50) .... 1y 20d.................. (385 days)
Frederick M. Vinson (53)..................... 11m 1d.................. (331 days)
William H. Woodin (51) .... 9m 27d.................. (297 days)
Roger B. Taney (12) .... 9m 1d.................. (271 days)
George W. Campbell (5)....................... 8m 4d.................. (244 days)
George M. Bibb (17)......................... 8m 3d.................. (243 days)
Lot M. Morrill (31)........................... 8m 2d.................. (242 days)
William P. Fessenden (26) .... 7m 26d.................. (236 days)
Samuel Dexter (3) .... 4m 5d.................. (125 days)
William J. Duane (11) .... 3m 21d.................. (111 days)
Thomas Ewing (14) .... 2m 13d................. (73 days)
John A. Dix (24)............................ 1m 17d................. (47 days)
Walter Q. Gresham (35)....................... 1m 3d................. (33 days)
Phillip F. Thomas (23) .... 1m 2d................. (32 days)
Joseph W. Barr (59) .... 26d..................... (26 days)
John William Snow (73)...................... — — —

Postmaster General

Gideon Granger (4) .... 12y 4m 10d .... (4,513 days)
Return Jonathan Meigs, Jr. (5)................. 9y 2m 17d .... (3,364 days)
Albert Sidney Burleson (45) .... 8y..................... (2,922 days)
Arthur Ellsworth Summerfield (54) .... 8y..................... (2,922 days)
James A. Farley (50)......................... 7y 6m 5d............... (2,741 days)
Joseph Habersham (3) .... 6y 9m 2d .... (2,463 days)
William T. Barry (7) .... 6y 24d .... (2,215 days)
Harry Stewart New (48) .... 5y 11m 29d .... (2,185 days)
John McLean (6) .... 5y 8m 3d .... (2,069 days)
John A.J. Creswell (23) .... 5y 4m 1d .... (1,947 days)
Jesse Monroe Donaldson (53) .... 5y 1m 4d .... (1,860 days)
Amos Kendall (8)............................ 5y 23d .... (1,849 days)
Frank Comerford Walker (51).................. 4y 8m 21d .... (1,722 days)
Cave Johnson (12).......................... 4y..................... (1,461 days)
Frank Harris Hitchcock (44)................... 4y..................... (1,461 days)
James Campbell (16) .... 3y 11m 29d .... (1,454 days)
Walter Folger Brown (49) .... 3y 11m 27d .... (1,452 days)
John Wanamaker (35) .... 3y 11m 27d .... (1,452 days)
Charles Emory Smith (39).................... 3y 8m 19d .... (1,354 days)
Montgomery Blair (20) .... 3y 6m 21d .... (1,296 days)
Timothy Pickering (2)....................... 3y 6m 3d .... (1,278 days)
David McKendree Key (27).................... 3y 5m 12d .... (1,257 days)
Charles Anderson Wickliffe (11)............... 3y 4m 20d .... (1,235 days)
William F. Vilas (33) .... 2y 10m 9d .... (1,039 days)
Henry C. Payne (40) .... 2y 9m................. (1,000 days)
James Edward Day (55)....................... 2y 8m 8d............... (978 days)
Alexander Williams Randall (22) .... 2y 7m 14d............. (954 days)
Robert Emmet Hannegan (52) .... 2y 5m 14d............. (894 days)
Lawrence F. O'Brien (57)...................... 2y 5m 7d.............. (887 days)
Nathan Kelsey Hall (14)...................... 2y 1m 21d............. (781 days)
John Austin Gronouski (56) .... 2y 1m 3d.............. (763 days)

Wilson Shannon Bissell (36) . . . . 2y 28d . . . . (758 days)
Aaron V. Brown (17) . . . . 2y 2d . . . . (732 days)
George von L. Meyer (43) . . . . 2y . . . . (730 days)
George B. Cortelyou (42) . . . . 1y 11m 27d . . . . (722 days)
William Lyne Wilson (37) . . . . 1y 11m 1d . . . . (696 days)
Samuel Osgood (1) . . . . 1y 10m 23d . . . . (688 days)
Marshall Jewell (25) . . . . 1y 10m 10d . . . . (675 days)
Joseph Holt (18) . . . . 1y 9m 17d . . . . (652 days)
William Dennison (21) . . . . 1y 9m 15d . . . . (650 days)
Walter Q. Gresham (31) . . . . 1y 5m 13d . . . . (528 days)
Winton Malcolm Blount (59) . . . . 1y 5m 9d . . . . (524 days)
Jacob Collamer (13) . . . . 1y 4m 14d . . . . (499 days)
Timothy Otis Howe (30) . . . . 1y 2m 20d . . . . (445 days)
Donald M. Dickinson (34) . . . . 1y 1m 16d . . . . (411 days)
James Albert Gary (38) . . . . 1y 1m 15d . . . . (410 days)
William Harrison Hays (46) . . . . 11m 28d . . . . (358 days)
Hubert Work (47) . . . . 11m 22d . . . . (352 days)
Thomas Lemuel James (29) . . . . 9m 27d . . . . (297 days)
John Milton Niles (9) . . . . 9m 7d . . . . (277 days)
William Marvin Watson (58) . . . . 8m 23d . . . . (263 days)
James Noble Tyner (26) . . . . 7m 29d . . . . (239 days)
Horace Maynard (28) . . . . 6m 10d . . . . (190 days)
Francis Granger (10) . . . . 6m 5d . . . . (185 days)
Frank Hatton (32) . . . . 5m 23d . . . . (173 days)
Samuel Dickinson Hubbard (15) . . . . 5m 20d . . . . (170 days)
Robert John Wynne (41) . . . . 4m 23d . . . . (143 days)
James William Marshall (24) . . . . 1m 17d . . . . (47 days)
Horatio King (19) . . . . 24d . . . . (24 days)

Attorney General

William Wirt (9) . . . . 11y 3m 16d . . . . (4,123 days)
Janet Reno (78) . . . . 7y 10m 8d . . . . (2,865 days)
Homer S. Cummings (55) . . . . 5y 9m 28d . . . . (2,124 days)
Charles Lee (3) . . . . 5y 2m 21d . . . . (1,907 days)
John Y. Mason (18) . . . . 4y 11m 6d . . . . (1,797 days)
Caesar Augustus Rodney (6) . . . . 4y 9m 15d . . . . (1,746 days)
Benjamin Franklin Butler (12) . . . . 4y 9m 12d . . . . (1,743 days)
Thomas W. Gregory (49) . . . . 4y 6m 1d . . . . (1,642 days)
Thomas C. Clark (59) . . . . 4y 1m 22d . . . . (1,513 days)
William French Smith (74) . . . . 4y 1m . . . . (1,491 days)
Robert F. Kennedy (64) . . . . 4y 22d . . . . (1,483 days)
Caleb Cushing (23) . . . . 4y 3d . . . . (1,464 days)
William H.H. Miller (39) . . . . 4y . . . . (1,461 days)
William D. Mitchell (54) . . . . 3y 11m 27d . . . . (1,452 days)
Herbert Brownell, Jr. (62) . . . . 3y 11m 27d . . . . (1,452 days)
George Woodward Wickersham (47) . . . . 3y 11m 27d . . . . (1,452 days)
Augustus H. Garland (38) . . . . 3y 11m 26d . . . . (1,451 days)
Edmund Randolph (1) . . . . 3y 11m 26d . . . . (1,451 days)
Charles Devens (35) . . . . 3y 11m 24d . . . . (1,449 days)
John G. Sargent (53) . . . . 3y 11m 18d . . . . (1,443 days)
Levi Lincoln (4) . . . . 3y 9m 26d . . . . (1,391 days)

Francis Biddle (58)	3y 9m 25d	(1,390 days)
Jeremiah S. Black (24)	3y 9m 10d	(1,375 days)
Edward Bates (26)	3y 8m 29d	(1,364 days)
Richard Rush (8)	3y 8m 16d	(1,351 days)
Edwin L. Meese III (75)	3y 5m 17d	(1,262 days)
George H. Williams (32)	3y 4m 4d	(1,219 days)
Richard Thornburgh (76)	3y 3m 18d	(1,203 days)
Philander Chase Knox (44)	3y 2m 21d	(1,176 days)
Benjamin H. Brewster (37)	3y 2m 5d	(1,160 days)
John W. Griggs (43)	3y 2m	(1,155 days)
Harry M. Daugherty (51)	3y 1m 4d	(1,129 days)
John J. Crittenden (15/22)	3y 27d	(1,122 days)
John Newton Mitchell (67)	3y 25d	(1,120 days)
William Pierce Rogers (63)	2y 11m 23d	(1,083 days)
J. Howard McGrath (60)	2y 9m 7d	(1,007 days)
Griffin Boyette Bell (72)	2y 5m 24d	(904 days)
William H. Moody (45)	2y 5m 15d	(895 days)
John M. Berrien (10)	2y 3m 13d	(833 days)
Richard Olney (40)	2y 3m 4d	(824 days)
Charles J. Bonaparte (46)	2y 2m 15d	(805 days)
Roger B. Taney (11)	2y 2m 3d	(793 days)
William Pinkney (7)	2y 1m 4d	(764 days)
Alexander Mitchell Palmer (50)	2y	(730 days)
Edward Hirsh Levi (71)	1y 11m 14d	(709 days)
William Ramsey Clark (66)	1y 10m 2d	(667 days)
Hugh S. Legare (16)	1y 9m	(635 days)
Judson Harmon (41)	1y 8m 23d	(628 days)
John Nelson (17)	1y 8m 9d	(614 days)
Nicholas de Belleville Katzenbach(65)	1y 7m 19d	(594 days)
Robert H. Jackson (57)	1y 7m 17d	(592 days)
James Speed (27)	1y 7m 11d	(586 days)
William Bradford (2)	1y 6m 25d	(570 days)
Amos T. Akerman (31)	1y 6m 1d	(546 days)
James C. McReynolds (48)	1y 5m 27d	(542 days)
Benjamin R. Civiletti (73)	1y 5m 18d	(533 days)
Nathan Clifford (19)	1y 5m 1d	(516 days)
Reverdy Johnson (21)	1y 4m 14d	(499 days)
Felix Grundy (13)	1y 4m 9d	(494 days)
John Breckenridge (5)	1y 4m 7d	(492 days)
Ebenezer Hoar (30)	1y 3m 26d	(481 days)
William P. Barr (77)	1y 2m	(425 days)
Henry D. Gilpin (14)	1y 1m 20d	(415 days)
Edwards Pierrepont (33)	1y 16d	(381 days)
Frank Murphy (56)	1y	(365 days)
William B. Saxbe (70)	11m 10d	(340 days)
Harlan F. Stone (52)	10m 22d	(322 days)
Richard Gordon Kleindienst (68)	10m 18d	(318 days)
Joseph McKenna (42)	10m 18d	(318 days)
Alphonso Taft (34)	9m 10d	(280 days)
Isaac Wayne McVeagh (36)	8m 7d	(247 days)
Isaac Toucey (20)	8m 7d	(247 days)

James Patrick McGranery (61) .... 7m 24d .... (234 days)
William M. Evarts (29) .... 7m 12d .... (222 days)
Elliot Lee Richardson (69)...................... 4m 27d .... (147 days)
Henry Stanbery (28) .... 4m 8d .... (128 days)
Edwin McMasters Stanton (25)................. 2m 11d .... (71 days)
John Ashcroft (79)............................. — — —

Secretary of the Navy

Josephus Daniels (41) .... 8y .... (2,922 days)
Gideon Welles (24) .... 7y 11m 24d .... (2,910 days)
George M. Robeson (26) .... 7y 8m 14d .... (2,810 days)
Robert Smith (2) .... 7y 7m 8d .... (2,774 days)
Claude A. Swanson (45)......................... 6y 4m 3d .... (2,314 days)
John Young Mason (16/18) .... 5y 10m 19d .... (2,145 days)
Samuel L. Southard (7) .... 5y 5m 15d .... (1,991 days)
John D. Long (34) .... 5y 1m 25d .... (1,881 days)
Curtis D. Wilbur (43) .... 4y 11m 14d .... (1,805 days)
Smith Thompson (6)............................ 4y 7m................... (1,671 days)
George von L. Meyer (40) .... 4y .... (1,461 days)
Benjamin F. Tracy (32) .... 4y .... (1,461 days)
Charles Francis Adams (44)..................... 3y 11m 28d .... (1,453 days)
James C. Dobbin (22) .... 3y 11m 28d .... (1,453 days)
Hilary A. Herbert (33)......................... 3y 11m 28d .... (1,453 days)
William C. Whitney (31)........................ 3y 11m 28d .... (1,453 days)
Isaac Toucey (23)............................. 3y 11m 25d .... (1,450 days)
Mahlon Dickerson (10) .... 3y 10m .... (1,395 days)
William Franklin Knox (47) .... 3y 9m 18d .... (1,383 days)
Richard W. Thompson (27)...................... 3y 9m 7d .... (1,372 days)
Benjamin W. Crowninshield (5).................. 3y 8m 11d .... (1,346 days)
Paul Hamilton (3) .... 3y 7m 16d .... (1,321 days)
James V. Forrestal (48)........................ 3y 4m .... (1,215 days)
Levi Woodbury (9) .... 3y 1m 6d .... (1,131 days)
Edwin Denby (42) .... 3y 13d .... (1,108 days)
William E. Chandler (30) .... 2y 10m 16d .... (1,046 days)
Benjamin Stoddert (1).......................... 2y 9m 11d .... (1,011 days)
James K. Paulding (11) .... 2y 8m 3d................ (973 days)
John Branch (8)............................... 2y 2m 2d................ (792 days)
William H. Moody (35)......................... 2y .... (730 days)
William A. Graham (20) .... 1y 11m 23d.............. (718 days)
Victor H. Metcalf (38)......................... 1y 11m 13d.............. (708 days)
William Jones (4).............................. 1y 10m 12d.............. (677 days)
Abel P. Upshur (13) .... 1y 9m 12d............... (647 days)
George Bancroft (17).......................... 1y 5m 29d............... (544 days)
Charles J. Bonaparte (37)...................... 1y 5m 15d .... (530 days)
William B. Preston (19)........................ 1y 4m 14d.............. (499 days)
William H. Hunt (29) .... 1y 1m 9d............... (404 days)
Paul Morton (36).............................. 1y .... (365 days)
John P. Kennedy (21).......................... 7m 8d.................. (218 days)
David Henshaw (14) .... 6m 25d .... (205 days)
George E. Badger (12) .... 6m 6d .... (186 days)
Charles Edison (46)........................... 5m 28d .... (178 days)

Adolph E. Borie (25) .... 3m 15d .... (105 days)
Truman H. Newberry (39)................... 3m 3d .... (93 days)
Nathan Goff, Jr. (28) .... 2m .... (60 days)
Thomas W. Gilmer (15) .... 9d .... (9 days)

Secretary of the Interior

Harold L. Ickes (32) .... 12y 11m 11d .... (4,724 days)
Franklin K. Lane (26)....................... 8y 2m 13d .... (2,995 days)
Bruce Babbitt (47) .... 8y...................... (2,922 days)
Stewart Lee Udall (37) .... 7y 11m 29d .... (2,915 days)
Columbus O. Delano (11) .... 4y 10m 29d .... (1,790 days)
Fred A. Seaton (36) .... 4y 7m 12d .... (1,683 days)
Rogers C.B. Morton (39) .... 4y 2m 28d .... (1,548 days)
Ethan A. Hitchcock (22) .... 4y 12d .... (1,473 days)
Cecil D. Andrus (42) .... 4y...................... (1,461 days)
Ray Lyman Wilbur (31)..................... 3y 11m 28d .... (1,453 days)
Robert McClelland (4) .... 3y 11m 25d .... (1,450 days)
John W. Noble (18) .... 3y 11m 25d .... (1,450 days)
Hubert Work (29) .... 3y 11m 23d .... (1,448 days)
Carl Schurz (13)........................... 3y 11m 22d .... (1,447 days)
Manuel Lujan (46) .... 3y 11m 17d .... (1,442 days)
Donald P. Hodel (45) .... 3y 11m 13d .... (1,438 days)
Jacob Thompson (5)........................ 3y 10m................... (1,395 days)
Julius A. Krug (33)......................... 3y 8m 12d .... (1,347 days)
Hoke Smith (19)........................... 3y 5m 25d .... (1,270 days)
Douglas McKay (35) .... 3y 4m 17d .... (1,232 days)
Oscar L. Chapman (34) .... 3y 2d .... (1,097 days)
Henry M. Teller (15) .... 2y 10m 14d .... (1,044 days)
Lucius Q.C. Lamar (16)..................... 2y 10m 4d .... (1,034 days)
James Gaius Watt (43) .... 2y 10m................... (1,030 days)
Orville H. Browning (9)..................... 2y 6m 2d................... (912 days)
Alex H.H. Stuart (3)........................ 2y 5m 18d................. (898 days)
John P. Usher (7) .... 2y 4m 6d................... (856 days)
James R. Garfield (23) .... 2y 1d..................... (731 days)
Albert B. Fall (28).......................... 2y .... (730 days)
Walter L. Fisher (25) .... 1y 11m 25d................. (720 days)
Cornelius N. Bliss (21)...................... 1y 11m 14d................. (709 days)
Walter Joseph Hickel (38) .... 1y 10m 1d.................. (666 days)
Caleb B. Smith (6) .... 1y 9m 26d................. (661 days)
Jacob D. Cox (10).......................... 1y 7m 22d................. (597 days)
Richard A. Ballinger (24).................... 1y 5m 29d................. (544 days)
Zachariah Chandler (12) .... 1y 4m 20d................. (505 days)
Thomas Ewing (1) .... 1y 4m 14d................. (499 days)
James Harlan (8) .... 1y 3m 16d................. (471 days)
Thomas Savig Kleppe (41)................... 1y 3m 10d................. (465 days)
William Patrick Clark (44)................... 1y 2m 17d................. (442 days)
William F. Vilas (17) .... 1y 1m 18d................. (413 days)
Samuel J. Kirkwood (14) .... 1y 1m 8d.................. (403 days)
John B. Payne (27) .... 11m 19d .... (349 days)
David R. Francis (20)....................... 6m .... (180 days)

Stanley Knapp Hathaway (40) .... 1m 13d .... (43 days)
Roy Owen West (30) .... 1m 10d .... (40 days)
Thomas M.T. McKennan (2) .... 11d .... (11 days)
Gale Ann Norton (48) .... — — —

Secretary of Agriculture

James Wilson (4) .... 15y 11m 26d .... (5,834 days)
Orville Lothrop Freeman (16) .... 8y .... (2,922 days)
Ezra Taft Benson (15) .... 7y 7m .... (2,766 days)
Henry A. Wallace (11) .... 7y 6m .... (2,736 days)
David F. Houston (5) .... 6y 10m 26d .... (2,517 days)
John Rusling Block III (21) .... 5y 25d .... (1,851 days)
Earl Laver Butz (18) .... 4y 10m 3d .... (1,764 days)
Claude R. Wickard (12) .... 4y 9m 24d .... (1,755 days)
Daniel Robert Glickman (26) .... 4y 9m 20d .... (1,751 days)
Charles Franklin Brannan (14) .... 4y 7m 18d .... (1,689 days)
William M. Jardine (9) .... 4y .... (1,461 days)
Robert S. (Bob) Berglund (20) .... 4y .... (1,461 days)
J. Sterling Morton (3) .... 3y 11m 26d .... (1,451 days)
Jeremiah M. Rusk (2) .... 3y 11m 26d .... (1,451 days)
Arthur M. Hyde (10) .... 3y 11m 11d .... (1,436 days)
Henry Cantwell Wallace (7) .... 3y 7m 21d .... (1,326 days)
Clinton P. Anderson (13) .... 2y 11m 1d .... (1,061 days)
Richard Edmund Lyng (22) .... 2y 10m 13d .... (1,043 days)
Clifford Hardin (17) .... 2y 9m 19d .... (1,019 days)
Clayton Keith Yeutter (23) .... 2y 26d .... (756 days)
Mike Espy (25) .... 1y 11m 10d .... (705 days)
Edward Madigan (24) .... 1y 10m 13d .... (678 days)
Edwin T. Meredith (6) .... 1y 1m 2d .... (397 days)
John A. Knebel (19) .... 3m 19d .... (109 days)
Howard M. Gore (8) .... 3m 10d .... (100 days)
Norman J. Colman (1) .... 21d .... (21 days)
Ann Margaret Veneman (27) .... — — —

Secretary of Commerce and Labor

Charles Nagel (4) .... 4y .... (1,461 days)
Victor H. Metcalf (2) .... 2y 5m 15d .... (895 days)
Oscar S. Straus (3) .... 2y 2m 13d .... (803 days)
George B. Cortelyou (1) .... 1y 4m 14d .... (499 days)

Secretary of Labor

Frances Perkins (4) .... 12y 3m 26d .... (4,499 days)
James J. Davis (2) .... 9y 9m 4d .... (3,561 days)
William B. Wilson (1) .... 8y .... (2,922 days)
James P. Mitchell (8) .... 7y 3m 11d .... (2,657 days)
W. Willard Wirtz (10) .... 6y 3m 27d .... (2,308 days)
Maurice J. Tobin (6) .... 4y 5m 7d .... (1,618 days)
Robert B. Reich (22) .... 4y 3m 18d .... (1,569 days)
Raymond James Donovan (17) .... 4y 2m 26d .... (1,547 days)
Freddie Ray Marshall (16) .... 3y 11m 24d .... (1,449 days)

Lewis B. Schwellenbach (5) .... 2y 11m 9d .... (1,069 days)
Alexis M. Herman (23) .... 2y 8m 11d .... (981 days)
William Emerson (Bill) Brock III (18) .... 2y 7m 18d .... (958 days)
James Day Hodgson (12) .... 2y 6m 29d .... (939 days)
William N. Doak (3) .... 2y 2m 22d .... (812 days)
Peter J. Brennan (13) .... 2y 29d .... (759 days)
Lynn Martin (21) .... 1y 11m 13d .... (708 days)
Elizabeth Hanford Dole (20) .... 1y 9m 28d .... (663 days)
Arthur Joseph Goldberg (9) .... 1y 8m 3d .... (608 days)
George Pratt Shultz (11) .... 1y 5m 9d .... (524 days)
Ann Dore McLaughlin (19) .... 1y 1m 3d .... (398 days)
William Julian (Willie) Usery, Jr. (15) ....11m 15d .... (345 days)
John Thomas Dunlop (14) ....10m 13d .... (313 days)
Martin P. Durkin (7) .... 8m 17d .... (257 days)
Elaine Lan Chao (24) .... — — —

Secretary of Commerce

Herbert C. Hoover (3) .... 7y 5m 16d .... (2,722 days)
William C. Redfield (1) .... 6y 9m 10d .... (2,471 days)
Howard Malcolm Baldridge (27) .... 6y 6m 3d .... (2,374 days)
Daniel C. Roper (7) .... 5y 9m 19d .... (2,115 days)
Sinclair Weeks (13) .... 4y 9m 22d .... (1,753 days)
Charles Sawyer (12) .... 4y 8m 14d .... (1,715 days)
Jesse Jones (9) .... 4y 5m 10d .... (1,621 days)
Luther H. Hodges (16) .... 3y 11m 27d .... (1,452 days)
Robert P. Lamont (5) .... 3y 5m 2d .... (1,247 days)
William M. Daley (33) .... 3y 4m 16d .... (1,231 days)
Ronald Harmon Brown (31) .... 3y 2m 12d .... (1,167 days)
Maurice Hubert Stans (20) .... 3y 28d .... (1,123 days)
Robert Adam Mosbacher (29) .... 2y 11m 14d .... (1,074days)
Juanita M. Kreps (25) .... 2y 9m 10d .... (1,010 days)
John T. Connor (17) .... 2y 4m 4d .... (854 days)
Frederick Bailey Dent (22) .... 2y 1m 24d .... (784 days)
Harry L. Hopkins (8) .... 1y 7m 26d .... (601 days)
Henry A. Wallace (10) .... 1y 6m 25d .... (570 days)
Frederick H. Mueller (15) .... 1y 5m 10d .... (525 days)
William Averell Harriman (11) .... 1y 3m 7d .... (462 days)
Calvin William Verity, Jr. (28) .... 1y 3m 1d .... (456 days)
Joshua W. Alexander (2) .... 1y 2m 16d .... (441 days)
Elliot Lee Richardson (24) .... 1y 1m 9d .... (404 days)
Philip M. Klutznik (26) .... 1y 1m .... (395 days)
Peter George Peterson (21) ....10m 27d .... (327 days)
Barbara Hackman Franklin (30) ....10m 24d .... (324 days)
Cyrus R. Smith (19) ....10m 18d .... (318 days)
Michael (Mickey) Kantor (32) .... 9m 17d .... (287 days)
Lewis L. Strauss (14) .... 8m 27d .... (267 days)
Alex Buel Trowbridge , Jr. (18) .... 8m 20d .... (260 days)
Rogers C.B. Morton (23) .... 7m 15d .... (225 days)
Norman Yoshio Mineta (34) .... 6m. .... (180 days)
William F. Whiting (4) .... 2m 21d .... (81 days)

Roy D. Chapin (6) .... 2m 17d .... (77 days)
Donald Louis Evans (354) .... — — —

Secretary of Defense

Robert Strange McNamara (8) .... 7y 1m 8d .... (2,594 days)
Caspar Willard Weinberger (15) .... 6y 10m 2d .... (2,493 days)
Charles E. Wilson (5) .... 4y 8m 10d .... (1,711 days)
William Sebastian Cohen (20) .... 3y 11m 27d .... (1,452 days)
Harold Brown (14) .... 4y .... (1,461 days)
Melvin B. Laird (10) .... 3y 11y 26d .... (1,451 days)
Richard B. (Dick) Cheney (17) .... 3y 10m 3d .... (1,398 days)
Neil H. McElroy (6) .... 3y 3m 11d .... (1,196 days)
William James Perry (19) .... 2y 11m 17d .... (1,077 days)
James Rodney Schlesinger (12) .... 2y 4m 6d .... (856 days)
James V. Forrestal (1) .... 1y 6m 5d .... (550 days)
Louis A. Johnson (2) .... 1y 5m 23d .... (538 days)
Robert Abercrombie Lovett (4) .... 1y 4m 10d .... (495 days)
Frank Charles Carlucci III (16) .... 1y 2m .... (425 days)
Donald H. Rumsfeld (13) .... 1y 2m .... (425 days)
Thomas Sovereign Gates, Jr. (7) .... 1y 1m 18d .... (413 days)
Leslie Aspin, Jr. (18) .... 1y 12d .... (377 days)
George C. Marshall, Jr. (3) .... 11m 25d .... (355 days)
Clark McAdams Clifford (9) ....10m 19d .... (319 days)
Elliot Lee Richardson (11) .... 3m 1d .... (91 days)
Donald H. Rumsfeld (21) .... — — —

Secretary of Health, Education and Welfare

Anthony J. Celebrezze (5) .... 3y 17d .... (1,112 days)
Marion B. Folsom (2) .... 3y .... (1,095 days)
Elliot Lee Richardson (9) .... 2y 7m 4d .... (944 days)
John W. Gardner (6) .... 2y 6m 11d .... (921 days)
Joseph A. Califano, Jr. (12) .... 2y 6m 10d .... (920 days)
Caspar Willard Weinberger (10) .... 2y 5m 28d .... (908 days)
Arthur Sherwood Flemming (3) .... 2y 5m 19d .... (899 days)
Oveta Culp Hobby (1) .... 2y 3m 20d .... (840 days)
Abraham Alexander Ribicoff (4) .... 1y 6m 9d .... (554 days)
Forrest D. Mathews (11) .... 1y 5m 28m .... (543 days)
Robert Hutchinson Finch (8) .... 1y 4m 15d .... (500 days)
Wilbur Joseph Cohen (7) .... 9m 28d .... (298 days)
Patricia Roberts Harris (13) .... 2m 14d .... (74 days)

Secretary of Housing and Urban Development

Samuel Riley Pierce, Jr. (8) .... 7y 11m 28d .... (2,914 days)
George Wilcken Romney (3) .... 4y 10m 7d .... (1,768 days)
Henry Gabriel Cisneros (10) .... 4y 8d .... (1,469 days)
Andrew M. Cuomo (11) .... 3y 11m 22d .... (1,447 days)
Jack F. Kemp (9) .... 3y 11m 14d .... (1,439 days)
Robert Clifton Weaver (1) .... 3y 2d .... (1,097 days)
Patricia Roberts Harris (6) .... 2y 6m 14d .... (924 days)
James Thomas Lynn (4) .... 1y 11m 2d .... (697 days)
Carla Anderson Hills (5) .... 1y 10m 14d .... (679 days)

Maurice Edwin (Moon) Landrieu (7) .... 1y 3m 26d............. (481 days)
Robert C. Wood (2) ....13d .... (13 days)
Melquiades Rafael Martinez (12) .... — — —

Secretary of Transportation

Elizabeth Hanford Dole (8)..................... 4y 9m 26d .... (1,757 days)
Frederico F. Pena (12) .... 4y 24d .... (1,485 days)
John Anthony Volpe (2) .... 4y.................... (1,461 days)
Rodney E. Slater (13)......................... 3y 11m 6d .... (1,431 days)
Samuel Knox Skinner (10) .... 2y 11m 21d .... (1,081 days)
Brockman Adams (5).......................... 2y 6m .... (910 days)
Claude Stout Brinegar (3) .... 2y 14d................. (744 days)
Andrew Lindsay Lewis, Jr. (7).................. 2y 9d.................. (739 days)
Alan S. Boyd (1)............................. 2y 4d.................. (734 days)
William Thaddeus Coleman, Jr. (4) .... 1y 10m 16d .... (681 days)
Neil E. Goldschmidt (6) .... 1y 3m 28d............. (483 days)
James Horace Burnley, IV (9) .... 1y 1m 17d............. (412 days)
Andrew H. Card, Jr. (11)...................... 11m 29d .... (359 days)
Norman Yoshio Mineta (14).................... — — —

Secretary of Energy

Hazel Rollins O'Leary (7) .... 4y 1m 18d .... (1,509 days)
John Stewart Herrington (5).................... 3y 11m 13d .... (1,438 days)
James David Watkins (6)....................... 3y 10m 19d .... (1,414 days)
William Blaine (Bill) Richardson (9) .... 2y 5m 2d............. (882 days)
Donald Paul Hodel (4)......................... 2y 2m .... (790 days)
James Rodney Schlesinger (1) .... 1y 10m 24d............ (689 days)
James Burrows Edwards (3)..................... 1y 9m 13d............. (648 days)
Charles William Duncan, Jr. (2) .... 1y 5m 20d............. (535 days)
Frederico F. Pena (8) .... 1y 25d.................. (390 days)
Spencer Abraham (10)......................... — — —

Secretary of Health and Human Services

Donna Edna Shalala (6)....................... 8y.................... (2,922 days)
Louis Wade Sullivan (5)....................... 3y 10m 19d .... (1,414 days)
Otis Ray Bowen (4) .... 3y 1m 18d .... (1,143 days)
Margaret Mary Heckler (3)..................... 2y 9m 8d .... (1,008 days)
Richard Schultz Schweiker (2) .... 1y 11m 21d............ (716 days)
Patricia Roberts Harris (1) .... 1y 3m 2d............. (457 days)
Tommy G. Thompson (7)....................... — — —

Secretary of Education

Richard Wilson Riley (6)....................... 8y.................... (2,922 days)
Terrel Howard Bell (2)......................... 4y 15d .... (1,476 days)
William John Bennett (3) .... 3y 7m 14d .... (1,319 days)
Lauro Fred Cavazos, Jr. (4) .... 2y 5m 22d............. (902 days)
Lamar Alexander (5) .... 1y 10m 6d............. (671 days)
Shirley Mount Hufstedler (1) .... 1y 1m 19d.............. (414 days)
Roderick R. Paige (7).......................... — — —

Secretary of Veterans' Affairs

Jesse Brown (2)	4y 11m 11d	(1,802 days)
Edward J. Derwinski (1)	3y 7m 11d	(1,316 days)
Togo D. West, Jr. (3)	3y 18d	(1,113 days)
Hershel W. Gober (acting)	5m 26d................	(176 days)
Anthony Joseph Principi (4)....................	———	

Secretary of Homeland Security

Thomas Ridge (1)	———	

SUPREME COURT JUSTICES

William Orville Douglas (AJ)....................	36y 7m 8d	(13,367)
Stephen J. Field (AJ)...........................	34y 8m 21d	(12,679)
John Marhall (CJ).............................	34y 5m 9d	(12,577)
Hugo Lafayette Black (AJ)	34y 1m 1d	(12,449)
John Marshall Harlan (AJ).....................	33y 10m 15d	(12,368)
Joseph Story (AJ)	33y 9m 23d	(12,346)
William Joseph Brennan, Jr. (AJ)................	33y 4m 1d	(12,174)
James M. Wayne (AJ)	32y 5m 26d	(11,864)
John McLean (AJ).............................	32y 28d	(11,716)
Byron R. White (AJ)...........................	31y 2m 17d	(11,399)
Bushrod Washington (AJ)	30y 11m 6d	(11,293)
William Johnson (AJ)..........................	30y 4m 11d	(11,088)
Oliver W. Holmes, Jr. (AJ)	29y 1m 8d	(10,630)
Roger Brooke Taney (CJ)	28y 6m 27d	(10,434)
Samuel F. Miller (AJ)	28y 2m 28d	(10,315)
John Catron (AJ)..............................	28y 2m 22d	(10,309)
Samuel Nelson (AJ)............................	27y 9m 14d	(10,145)
Edward Douglass White (AJ/CJ)	27y 3m	(9,951)
Joseph McKenna (AJ)..........................	26y 11m 15d	(9,841)
Willis Van Devanter (AJ)	26y 5m 18d	(9,664)
James Clark McReynolds (AJ)	26y 5m 2d	(9,648)
Warren Earl Burger (CJ)........................	25y 1m 1d	(9,139)
Harry Andrew Blackmun (AJ)	24y 1m 18d	(8,814)
Thurgood Marshall (AJ)........................	23y 9m 28d	(8,698)
Felix Frankfurter (AJ)..........................	23y 7m 11d	(8,621)
Nathan Clifford (AJ)...........................	23y 6m 13d	(8,593)
Robert Cooper Grier (AJ).......................	23y 5m 27d	(8,577)
Gabriel Duvall (AJ)............................	23y 1m 27d	(8,457)
Louis D. Brandeis (AJ)	22y 8m 12d	(8,287)
Potter Stewart (AJ)	22y 1m 29d	(8,094)
Melville Weston Fuller (CJ)	21y 11m 14d	(8,014)
Joseph P. Bradley (AJ).........................	21y 10m 1d	(7,971)
Harlan Fiske Stone (AJ/CJ)......................	21y 2m 17d	(7,747)
William Cushing (AJ)..........................	20y 11m 18d	(7,653)
Horace Gray (AJ)	20y 6m 19d	(7,504)
David J. Brewer (AJ)...........................	20y 3m 10d	(7,405)

Smith Thompson (AJ) .... 20y 9d .... (7,314)
William Rufus Day (AJ) .... 19y 8m 21d .... (7,200)
Peter Vivian Daniel (AJ)...................... 19y 2m 28d .... (7,027)
Stanley F. Reed (AJ) .... 19y 1m .... (6,969)
Noah Haynes Swayne (AJ) .... 18y 11m 27d .... (6,931)
Thomas Todd (AJ) .... 18y 11m 4d .... (6,908)
Tom C. Clark (AJ) .... 17y 9m 24d .... (6,503)
Charles Evans Hughes (AJ/CJ) .... 17y 5m 26d .... (6,384)
Pierce Butler (AJ) .... 16y 10m 26d .... (6,170)
Edward Douglass White (AJ) .... 16y 9m 23d .... (6,137)
John Marshall Harlan II (AJ) .... 16y 9m 13d .... (6,127)
Harlan Fiske Stone (AJ) .... 16y 4m 22d .... (5,986)
Henry Brockholst Livingston (AJ) .... 16y 3m 1d .... (5,935)
Lewis Franklin Powell, Jr. (AJ)................ 15y 6m 20d .... (5,678)
Henry B. Brown (AJ) .... 15y 4m 29d .... (5,627)
Samuel Chase (AJ) .... 15y 4m 23d .... (5,621)
George Sutherland (AJ) .... 15y 4m 12d .... (5,610)
Earl Warren (CJ)........................... 15y 3m 23d .... (5,591)
Owen Josephus Roberts (AJ) .... 15y 2m 11d .... (5,549)
William H. Rehnquist (AJ)................... 14y 10m 27d .... (5,450)
John McKinley (AJ) .... 14y 9m 24d .... (5,407)
Henry Baldwin (AJ) .... 14y 3m 15d .... (5,218)
David Davis (AJ) .... 14y 2m 24d .... (5,197)
Morrison Remick Waite (CJ) .... 14y 2m 2d .... (5,175)
Rufus Wheeler Peckham (AJ)................. 13y 10m 15d .... (5,063)
William Paterson (AJ) .... 13y 6m 5d .... (4,933)
Robert H. Jackson (AJ)...................... 13y 3m 2d .... (4,840)
Harold H. Burton (AJ) .... 13y 24d .... (4,772)
Charles Evans Hughes (CJ).................... 11y 4m 18d .... (4,155)
Samuel M. Blatchford (AJ).................... 11y 3m 10d .... (4,117)
William Strong (AJ) .... 10y 9m 26d .... (3,948)
Mahlon Pitney (AJ).......................... 10y 9m 18d .... (3,940)
George Shiras, Jr. (AJ) .... 10y 6m 28d .... (3,860)
Edward Douglass White (CJ) .... 10y 5m 7d .... (3,809)
James Iredell (AJ) .... 9y 7m 22d .... (3,519)
Frank W. Murphy (AJ) .... 9y 6m 4d .... (3,471)
Ward Hunt (AJ) .... 9y 27d .... (3,313)
James Wilson (AJ).......................... 8y 10m 26d .... (3,248)
William Howard Taft (CJ) .... 8y 7m 4d .... (3,136)
Salmon Portland Chase (CJ).................. 8y 5m 1d .... (3,073)
John Archibald Campbell (AJ)................. 8y 1m 5d .... (2,957)
Sherman Minton (AJ)........................ 7y 11m 8d .... (2,894)
Stanley Matthews (AJ) .... 7y 10m 1d .... (2,857)
Frederick Moore Vinson (CJ).................. 7y 2m 19d .... (2,635)
Edward Terry Sanford (AJ).................... 7y 1m 8d .... (2,594)
Wiley Blount Rutledge (AJ) .... 6y 7m 1d .... (2,402)
William Burnham Woods (AJ)................. 6y 4m 23d .... (2,334)
Benjamin Nathan Cardozo (AJ)................ 6y 4m 15d .... (2,326)
John Blair, Jr. (AJ) .... 6y 4m 1d .... (2,315)
John Hessin Clarke (AJ)...................... 6y 1m 24d .... (2,245)
Charles Evans Hughes (AJ)................... 6y 1m 8d .... (2,229)

John Jay (CJ)................................. 5y 9m .... (2,096)
Benjamin Robbins Curtis (AJ)................... 5y 8m 3d.................. (2,069)
Levi Woodbury (AJ)........................... 5y 8m 1d.................. (2,067)
Joseph Rucker Lamar (AJ) .... 5y 18d.................... (1,844)
Charles Evans Whittaker (AJ) .... 5y 13d.................... (1,839)
Lucius Q.C. Lamar (AJ) .... 5y 8d .... (1,834)
Philip P. Barbour (AJ)......................... 4y 11m 10d............... (1,801)
Harlan Fiske Stone (CJ) .... 4y 8m 26d............... (1,727)
Oliver Ellsworth (CJ) .... 4y 6m 24d............... (1,665)
Horace H. Lurton (AJ) .... 4y 6m 22d............... (1,663)
Alfred Moore (AJ)............................ 4y 3m 21d............... (1,572)
William H. Moody (AJ) .... 3y 11m 8d............... (1,433)
Abe Fortas (AJ)............................... 3y 9m 3d............... (1,368)
Arthur Joseph Goldberg (AJ) .... 2y 10m .... (1,030)
Howell E. Jackson (AJ) .... 2y 5m 21d .... (901)
Robert Trimble (AJ).......................... 2y 3m 16d .... (836)
John Rutledge (AJ/CJ) .... 1y 9m 10d .... (645)
John Rutledge (AJ) .... 1y 5m 7d .... (522)
Thomas Johnson (AJ).......................... 1y 3m 25d .... (480)
James F. Byrnes (AJ).......................... 1y 3m 21d .... (476)
John Rutledge (CJ) .... 4m 3d........................ (123)
Edwin M. Stanton (AJ)........................ 4d........................... (4)
Stephen Gerald Breyer (AJ) .... ———
Ruth Bader Ginsburg (AJ) .... ———
Anthony M. Kennedy (AJ) .... ———
Sandra Day O'Connor (AJ) .... ———
William H. Rehnquist (CJ)...................... ———
William H. Rehnquist (AJ/CJ) .... ———
Antonin Scalia (AJ)............................ ———
David Hackett Souter (AJ) .... ———
John Paul Stevens (AJ) .... ———
Clarence Thomas (AJ) .... ———

Appendix D:
Listings of Longest and Shortest Time in Office; Oldest and Youngest to Be Elected or Appointed to Office

President

Youngest at inauguration . . . . Theodore Roosevelt 42y 10m 18d (15,658 days)
Oldest at inauguration. . . . . Ronald Reagan 69y 11m 14d (25,546 days)
Avg. age at inauguration . . . . 55y 3m 13d (20,191 days)
Longest term of service . . . . Franklin D. Roosevelt 12y 1m 8d (4,421 days)
Shortest term of service . . . . William Henry Harrison 1m (30 days)
Average term of service . . . . 5y 1m 29d (1,884 days)

Vice President

Youngest at inauguration . . . . John C. Breckinridge 36y 1m 11d (13,190 days)
Oldest at inauguration . . . . Alben W. Barkley 71y 1m 26d (25,988 days)
Avg. age at inauguration . . . . 54y 8m 6d (19,969 days)
Longest term of service . . . . George Herbert Bush, Al Gore,
. . . . Thomas R.Marshall, Richard M. Nixon,
. . . . Daniel D. Tompkins 8y (2,922 days)
Shortest term of service . . . . John Tyler 1m 2d (32 days)
Average term of service . . . . 3y 10m 12d (1,407 days)

Cabinet at Large

Youngest appointee/age . . . . Alexander Hamilton 32y 8m (11,928 days)
Oldest appointee/age . . . . Lewis Cass 74y 4m 25d (27,173 days)
Avg. age of appointees . . . . 52y 11m 3d (19,326 days)
Longest term of service . . . . James Wilson 15y 11m 26d (5,834 days)
Shortest term of service . . . . Thomas W. Gilmer 9d (9 days)
Average term of service . . . . 3y 4d (1,099 days)

Separate Cabinet Posts

Secretary of State

Youngest appointee .... Edmund Randolph 40y 4m 23d (14,753 days)
Oldest appointee .... Lewis Cass 74y 4m 25d (27,173 days)
Avg. age of appointees .... 57y 10d (20,829 days)
Longest term of service .... Cordell Hull 11y 8m 26d (4,283 days)
Shortest term of service .... Elihu B. Washburne 11d (11 days)
Average term of service .... 3y 5m (1,245 days)

Secretary of War

Youngest appointee .... John C. Calhoun 35y 8m 22d (13,045 days)
Oldest appointee .... Henry L. Stimson (2nd term) 72y 9m 19d (26,587 days)
Avg. age of appointees .... 50y 1m 9d (18,301 days)
Longest term of service .... Henry Dearborn 7y 11m 11d (2,897 days)
Shortest term of service .... Benjamin Franklin Butler 11d (11 days)
Average term of service .... 2y 8m 2d (972 days)

Secretary of the Treasury

Youngest appointee .... Alexander Hamilton 32y 8m (11,928 days)
Oldest appointee .... Lloyd M. Bentsen, Jr. 71y 11m 9d (26,271 days)
Avg. age of appointees .... 53y 5m 9d (19,517 days)
Longest term of service .... Albert Gallatin 12y 8m 21d (4,644 days)
Shortest term of service .... Joseph W. Barr 26d (26 days)
Average term of service .... 3y 11d (1,106 days)

Postmaster General

Youngest appointee .... Gideon Granger 34y 4m 9d (12,547 days)
Oldest appointee .... Horace Maynard 65y 11m 26d (24,097 days)
Avg. age of appointees .... 49y 8m 23d (18,160 days)
Longest term of service .... Gideon Granger 12y 4m 10d (4,513 days)
Shortest term of service .... Horatio King 24d (24 days)
Average term of service .... 3y 17d (1,112 days)

Attorney General

Youngest appointee/age .... Richard Rush 33y 5m 13d (12,216 days)
Oldest appointee/age .... Edward Bates 67y 6m 1d (24,652 days)
Avg. age of appointees .... 51y 2d (18,629 days)
Longest term of service .... William Wirt 11y 3m 16d (4,123 days)
Shortest term of service .... Edwin M. Stanton 2m 11d (71 days)
Average term of service .... 2y 8m 13d (983 days)

Secretary of the Navy

Youngest appointee/age .... Samuel L. Southard 36y 3m 7d (13,246 days)
Oldest appointee/age .... Claude A. Swanson 70y 11m 1d (25,898 days)
Avg. age of appointees .... 51y 6m 1d (18,808 days)
Longest term of service .... Josephus Daniels 8y (2,922 days)
Shortest term of service .... Thomas W. Gilmer 9d (9 days)
Average term of service .... 3y 2m 2d (1,157 days)

Secretary of the Interior

Youngest appointee/age .... Hoke Smith 37y 6m 4d (13,698 days)
Oldest appointee/age .... Samuel J. Kirkwood 67y 2m 16d (24,547 days)

Avg. age of appointees . . . . 52y (18,987 days)
Longest term of service . . . . Harold L. Ickes 12y 11m 11d (4,724 days)
Shortest term of service . . . . Thomas M.T. McKennan 11d (11 days)
Average term of service . . . . 3y 1m 1d (1,126 days)

Secretary of Agriculture

Youngest appointee/age . . . . Howard M. Gore 37y 1m 10d (13,554 days)
Oldest appointee/age . . . . Richard E. Lyng 67y 8m 6d (24,717 days)
Avg. age of appointees . . . . 50y 11m 27d (18,619 days)
Longest term of service . . . . James Wilson 15y 11m 26d (5,834 days)
Shortest term of service . . . . Norman J. Colman 21d (21 days)
Average term of service . . . . 4y 2m 21d (1,541 days)

Secretary of Commerce and Labor

Youngest appointee/age . . . . George B. Cortelyou 40y 6m 21d (14,811 days)
Oldest appointee/age . . . . Charles Nagel 59y 6m 24d (21,753 days)
Avg. age of appointees . . . . 51y 8m 15d (18,882 days)
Longest term of service . . . . Charles Nagel 4y (1,461 days)
Shortest term of service . . . . George B. Cortelyou 1y 4m 14d (499 days)
Average term of service . . . . 2y 6m 5d (915 days)

Secretary of Labor

Youngest appointee/age . . . . Ann D. McLaughlin 46y 1m 1d (16,832 days)
Oldest appointee/age . . . . John T. Dunlop 60y 8m 13d (22,168 days)
Avg. age of appointees . . . . 51y 3m 20d (18,737 days)
Longest term of service . . . . Frances Perkins 12y 3m 26de (4,499 days)
Shortest term of service . . . . Martin P. Durkin 8m 17d (257 days)
Average term of service . . . . 3y 9m 2d (1,367 days)

Secretary of Commerce

Youngest appointee/age . . . . Alex B. Trowbridge, Jr. 37y 5m 28d (13,692 days)
Oldest appointee/age . . . . Philip M. Klutznik 72y 5m 12d (26,460 days)
Avg. age of appointees . . . . 58y 12d (21,196 days)
Longest term of service . . . . Herbert C. Hoover 7y 5m 16d (2,722 days)
Shortest term of service . . . . Roy D. Chapin 2m 17d (77 days)
Average term of service . . . . 2y 5m 29d (909 days)

Secretary of Defense

Youngest appointee/age . . . . Donald H. Rumsfeld 43y 4m 11d (15,836 days)
Oldest appointee/age . . . . George C. Marshall, Jr. 69y 8m 21d (25,463 days)
Avg. age of appointees . . . . 55y 11m 23d (20,441 days)
Longest term of service . . . . Robert S. McNamara 7y 1m 8d (2,594 days)
Shortest term of service . . . . Elliot Lee Richardson 3m 1d (91 days)
Average term of service . . . . 2y 8m 14d (984 days)

Secretary of Health, Education and Welfare

Youngest appointee/age . . . . Forrest D. Mathews 39y 7m 17d (14,471 days)
Oldest appointee/age . . . . Marion B. Folsom 61y 8m 9d (22,529 days)
Avg. age of appointees . . . . 51y 1m 19d (18,676 days)
Longest term of service . . . . Anthony Celebrezze 3y 17d (1,112 days)
Shortest term of service . . . . Patricia Roberts Harris 74d (74 days)
Average term of service . . . . 2y 9d (739 days)

Secretary of Housing and Urban Development

Youngest appointee/age .... Andrew M. Cuomo 39y 1m 23d (14,297 days)
Oldest appointee/age .... George W. Romney 61y 6m 13d (22,473 days)
Avg. age of appointees .... 50y 4m 23d (18,405 days)
Longest term of service .... Samuel R. Pierce, Jr. 7y 11m 28d (2,914 days)
Shortest term of service .... Robert C. Wood 13d (13 days)
Average term of service .... 3y 2m 20d (1,175 days)

Secretary of Transportation

Youngest appointee/age .... Neil E. Goldschmidt 39y 3m 6d (14,340 days)
Oldest appointee/age .... Norman Y. Mineta 69y 2m 12d (25,274 days)
Avg. age of appointees .... 49y 40d (17,937 days)
Longest term of service .... Elizabeth H. Dole 4y 9m 26d (1,757 days)
Shortest term of service .... Andrew H. Card, Jr. 11m 29d (359 days)
Average term of service .... 2y 7m 4d (944 days)

Secretary of Energy

Youngest appointee/age .... John S. Herrington 45y 8m 7d (16,683 days)
Oldest appointee/age .... James D. Watkins 61y 11m 22d (22,632 days)
Avg. age of appointees .... 51y 6m 18d (18,813 days)
Longest term of service .... Hazel Rollins O'Leary 4y 1m 18d (1,509 days)
Shortest term of service .... Frederico F. Pena 1y 25d (390 days)
Average term of service .... 2y 6m 12d (922 days)

Secretary of Health and Human Services

Youngest appointee/age .... Margaret M. Heckler 51y 8m 11d (18,878 days)
Oldest appointee/age .... Otis R. Bowen 67y 9m 16d (24,757 days)
Avg. age of appointees .... 56y 6m 29d (20,662 days)
Longest term of service .... Donna E. Shalala 7y 11m 29d (2,915 days)
Shortest term of service .... Patricia Roberts Harris 1y 3m 2d (457 days)
Average term of service .... 3y 6m 1d (1,276 days)

Secretary of Education

Youngest appointee/age .... William John Bennett 41y 7m 7d (15,192 days)
Oldest appointee/age .... Roderick R. Paige 67y 6m 12d (24,663 days)
Avg. age of appointees .... 56y 5m 8d (20,611 days)
Longest term of service .... Richard W. Riley 8y (2,922 days)
Shortest term of service .... Shirley M. Hufstedler 1y 1m 19d (414 days)
Average term of service .... 3y 6d (1,101 days)

Secretary of Veterans' Affairs

Youngest appointee/age .... Jesse Brown 48y 9m 25d (17,827 days)
Oldest appointee/age .... Hershel W. Gober (acting) 63y 7m 4d (23,224 days)
Avg. age of appointees .... 57y 5m 8d (20,977 days)
Longest term of service .... Jesse Brown 4y 11m 11d (1,802 days)
Shortest term of service .... Hershel W. Gober (acting) 5m 26d (176 days)
Average term of service .... 3y 7d (1,102 days)

Supreme Court Justices-Chief Justices

Youngest appointee/age .... John Jay 43y 9m 14d (15,989 days)
Oldest appointee/age .... Harlan F. Stone 68y 8m 16d (25,093 days)
Avg. age of appointees .... 58y 3m 24d (21,298 days)

Longest term of service .... John Marshall 34y 5m 9d (12,577 days)
Shortest term of service .... John Rutledge 4m 3d (123 days)
Average term of service .... 13y 4m 22d (4,890 days)

Supreme Court Justices-Associate Justices

Youngest appointee/age.............................. Joseph Story 32y 1m (11,718 days)
Oldest appointee/age .... Horace H. Lurton 65y 9m 24d (24,035 days)
Avg. age of appointees .... 47y 11m 1d (17,497 days)
Longest term of service .... William O. Douglas 36y 7m 8d (13,367 days)
Shortest term of service .... Edwin M. Stanton 4d (4 days)
Average term of service .... 16y 4d (5,849 days)

Appendix E: Listings of Age at Inauguration or Confirmation for Presidents, Vice Presidents, Cabinet Members and Supreme Court Justices

PRESIDENTS

Ronald Reagan	69y 11m 14d	(25,546 days)
William Henry Harrison	68y 23d	(24,860 days)
James Buchanan	65y 10m 9d	(24,050 days)
George Herbert Bush	64y 7m 8d	(23,594 days)
Zachary Taylor	64y 3m 8d	(23,474 days)
Dwight D. Eisenhower	62y 3m 6d	(22,741 days)
Andrew Jackson	61y 11m 17d	(22,627 days)
John Adams	61y 7m 26d	(22,516 days)
Gerald R. Ford	61y 26d	(22,306 days)
Harry S Truman	60y 11m 4d	(22,249 days)
James Monroe	58y 10m 4d	(21,488 days)
James Madison	57y 11m 16d	(21,165 days)
Thomas Jefferson	57y 10m 19d	(21,138 days)
George Washington	57y 2m 8d	(20,887 days)
John Quincy Adams	57y 4m 7d	(20,946 days)
Andrew Johnson	56y 3m 17d	(20,561 days)
Woodrow Wilson	56y 2m 4d	(20,518 days)
Richard M. Nixon	56y 11d	(20,465 days)
Grover Cleveland	55y 11m 4d	(20,422 days)
Benjamin Harrison	55y 6m 12d	(20,280 days)
Warren G. Harding	55y 4m 2d	(20,210 days)
Lyndon B. Johnson	55y 2m 26d	(20,174 days)
Herbert Hoover	54y 6m 22d	(19,925 days)
George Walker Bush	54y 6m 14d	(19,917 days)

Rutherford B. Hayes .... 54y 5m 2d .... (19,875 days)
Martin Van Buren .... 54y 2m 27d .... (19,810 days)
William McKinley .... 54y 1m 3d .... (19,756 days)
Jimmy Carter........................... 52y 3m 19d .... (19,102 days)
Abraham Lincoln........................ 52y 20d.................... (19,013 days)
William H. Taft........................ 51y 5m 17d .... (18,794 days)
Franklin D. Roosevelt .... 51y 1m 2d .... (18,659 days)
Calvin Coolidge......................... 51y 1m.................... (18,657 days)
John Tyler .... 51y 8d..................... (18,635 days)
Chester A. Arthur .... 50y 11m 15d .... (18,607 days)
Millard Fillmore....................... 50y 6m 3d .... (18,445 days)
James K. Polk.......................... 49y 4m 2d .... (18,019 days)
James A. Garfield...................... 49y 3m 13d .... (18,000 days)
Franklin Pierce........................ 48y 3m 9d.................. (17,631 days)
Grover Cleveland....................... 47y 11m 14d................ (17,510 days)
Ulysses S. Grant....................... 46y 10m 5d................. (17,106 days)
Bill Clinton .... 46y 5m 1d .... (16,952 days)
John F. Kennedy........................ 43y 7m 22d .... (15,937 days)
Theodore Roosevelt..................... 42y 10m 18d .... (15,658 days)

VICE PRESIDENTS

Alben W. Barkley........................ 71y 1m 26d .... (25,988 days)
George Clinton (2nd term)............... 69y 7m 6d .... (25,418 days)
Charles Curtis .... 69y 1m 7d .... (25,239 days)
Elbridge Gerry......................... 68y 7m 15d .... (25,062 days)
William R. King........................ 66y 10m 25d .... (24,431 days)
Nelson A. Rockefeller.................... 66y 5m 11d .... (24,267 days)
George Clinton (1st term) .... 65y 7m 6d .... (23,957 days)
Thomas A. Hendricks .... 65y 5m 25d .... (23,916 days)
Levi P. Morton......................... 64y 9m 16d .... (23,662 days)
John N. Garner .... 64y 8m 18d .... (23,634 days)
Henry Wilson .... 61y 16d.................... (22,296 days)
Harry S Truman .... 60y 8m 12d .... (22,167 days)
Gerald R. Ford......................... 60y 4m 22d .... (22,057 days)
Richard B. [Dick] Cheney .... 59y 11m 22d .... (21,901 days)
Charles G. Dawes....................... 59y 6m 5d .... (21,734 days)
Thomas R. Marshall .... 58y 11m 18d .... (21,532 days)
William A. Wheeler..................... 57y 8m 2d .... (21,061 days)
Adlai E. Stevenson .... 57y 4m 9d .... (20,948 days)
George Herbert Bush.................... 56y 7m 8d .... (20,672 days)
Richard M. Johnson..................... 56y 4m 5d .... (20,579 days)
Andrew Johnson .... 56y 2m 2d .... (20,516 days)
Thomas Jefferson....................... 53y 10m 19d .... (19,677 days)
Hubert H. Humphrey .... 53y 9m 21d .... (19,649 days)
John Adams .... 53y 5m 22d .... (19,530 days)
James S. Sherman....................... 53y 4m 8d .... (19,486 days)
Charles W. Fairbanks................... 52y 9m 21d .... (19,284 days)
Garrett A. Hobart .... 52y 9m 1d .... (19,264 days)

George M. Dallas . . . . 52y 7m 22d . . . . (19,225 days)
Lyndon B. Johnson . . . . 52y 6m 21d . . . . (19,194 days)
Henry A. Wallace . . . . 52y 3m 13d . . . . (19,096 days)
Hannibal Hamlin . . . . 51y 6m 5d . . . . (18,812 days)
John Tyler . . . . 50y 11m 3d . . . . (18,595 days)
Chester A. Arthur . . . . 50y 4m 27d . . . . (18,409 days)
Martin Van Buren . . . . 50y 2m 27d . . . . (18,349 days)
Spiro T. Agnew . . . . 50y 2m 11d . . . . (18,333 days)
Millard Fillmore . . . . 49y 1m 5d . . . . (17,932 days)
Walter F. Mondale . . . . 49y 15d . . . . (17,912 days)
Calvin Coolidge . . . . 48y 8m . . . . (17,772 days)
John C. Calhoun (2nd term) . . . . 46y 11m 14d . . . . (17,145 days)
Schuyler Colfax . . . . 45y 11m 9d . . . . (16,775 days)
Aaron Burr . . . . 45y 26d . . . . (16,462 days)
Al Gore . . . . 44y 9m 20d . . . . (16,361 days)
John C. Calhoun (1st term) . . . . 42y 11m 14d . . . . (15,684 days)
Daniel D. Tompkins . . . . 42y 8m 12d . . . . (15,592 days)
Theodore Roosevelt . . . . 42y 4m 5d . . . . (15,465 days)
Dan Quayle . . . . 41y 11m 16d . . . . (15,321 days)
Richard M. Nixon . . . . 40y 11d . . . . (14,940 days)
John C. Breckenridge . . . . 36y 1m 11d . . . . (13,190 days)

Secretary of State

Lewis Cass . . . . 74y 4m 25d . . . . (27,173 days)
John Sherman . . . . 73y 9m 23d . . . . (26,956 days)
Daniel Webster (2nd term) . . . . 68y 6m 4d . . . . (25,021 days)
Frank Billings Kellogg . . . . 68y 2m 13d . . . . (24,910 days)
Warren Minor Christopher . . . . 67y 2m 24d . . . . (24,555 days)
Edward Livingston . . . . 66y 11m 26d . . . . (24,462 days)
William Learned Marcy . . . . 66y 2m 23d . . . . (24,189 days)
James F. Byrnes . . . . 66y 2m 1d . . . . (24,167 days)
Edmund Sixtus Muskie . . . . 66y 1m 10d . . . . (24,146 days)
George C. Marshall, Jr. 66y 21d . . . . (24,127 days)
John Foster Dulles . . . . 64y 10m 27d . . . . (23,703 days)
Frederick T. Frelinghuysen . . . . 64y 4m 15d . . . . (23,511 days)
Christian A. Herter . . . . 64y 25d . . . . (23,401 days)
Colin Luther Powell . . . . 63y 9m 15d . . . . (23,295 days)
Lawrence Sidney Eagleburger . . . . 62y 22d . . . . (22,667 days)
John Caldwell Calhoun . . . . 62y 14d . . . . (22,659 days)
George Pratt Shultz . . . . 61y 7m 3d . . . . (22,493 days)
Henry Lewis Stimson . . . . 61y 6m 8d . . . . (22,468 days)
Cordell Hull . . . . 61y 5m 2d . . . . (22,432 days)
Walter Q. Gresham . . . . 60y 11m 17d . . . . (22,262 days)
Hamilton Fish . . . . 60y 7m 14d . . . . (22,139 days)
Elihu Root . . . . 60y 5m 4d . . . . (22,069 days)
John Hay . . . . 59y 11m 22d . . . . (21,901 days)
Cyrus Roberts Vance . . . . 59y 9m 25d . . . . (21,844 days)
William H. Seward . . . . 59y 9m 17d . . . . (21,836 days)

Madeleine K. Albright . . . . 59y 8m 8d . . . . (21,797 days)
Daniel Webster (1st term) . . . . 59y 1m 15d . . . . (21,594 days)
James G. Blaine (2nd term) . . . . 59y 1m 7d . . . . (21,586 days)
William M. Evarts . . . . 59y 1m 6d . . . . (21,585 days)
Charles Evans Hughes . . . . 58y 10m 22d . . . . (21,506 days)
Edward Everett . . . . 58y 6m 26d . . . . (21,390 days)
Richard Olney . . . . 57y 5m 19d . . . . (20,988 days)
Thomas Francis Bayard . . . . 56y 4m 5d . . . . (20,579 days)
John W. Foster . . . . 56y 3m 27d . . . . (20,571 days)
Alexander Meigs Haig, Jr. . . . . 56y 1m 20d . . . . (20,504 days)
Dean G. Acheson . . . . 55y 9m 8d . . . . (20,366 days)
Philander Chase Knox . . . . 55y 8m 27d . . . . (20,355 days)
William Pierce Rogers . . . . 55y 6m 29d . . . . (20,297 days)
James Addison Baker III . . . . 54y 9m 1d . . . . (19,994 days)
James Buchanan . . . . 53y 10m 17d . . . . (19,675 days)
John Forsyth . . . . 53y 9m 9d . . . . (19,637 days)
William J. Bryan . . . . 52y 11m 15d . . . . (19,338 days)
James Monroe . . . . 52y 11m 9d . . . . (19,332 days)
John Middleton Clayton . . . . 52y 7m 11d . . . . (19,214 days)
Elihu B. Washburne . . . . 52y 5m 10d . . . . (19,153 days)
Abel P. Upshur . . . . 52y 1m 7d . . . . (19,030 days)
Dean Rusk . . . . 51y 11m 12d . . . . (18,969 days)
Robert Smith . . . . 51y 4m 3d . . . . (18,750 days)
James G. Blaine (1st term) . . . . 51y 1m 7d . . . . (18,664 days)
Jeremiah S. Black . . . . 50y 11m 11d . . . . (18,603 days)
Robert Lansing . . . . 50y 8m 6d . . . . (18,508 days)
Henry A. Kissinger . . . . 50y 3m 25d . . . . (18,377 days)
Bainbridge Colby . . . . 50y 3m 1d . . . . (18,353 days)
John Q. Adams . . . . 50y 2m 11d . . . . (18,333 days)
James Madison . . . . 50y 1m 16d . . . . (18,296 days)
Timothy Pickering . . . . 50y 1m 3d . . . . (18,295 days)
William R. Day . . . . 49y 11d . . . . (18,227 days)
Robert Bacon . . . . 48y 6m 22d . . . . (17,734 days)
Henry Clay . . . . 47y 10m 23d . . . . (17,489 days)
Louis McLane . . . . 47y 1d . . . . (17,167 days)
Thomas Jefferson . . . . 46y 11m 9d . . . . (17,140 days)
Martin Van Buren . . . . 46y 3m 23d . . . . (16,914 days)
John Marshall . . . . 44y 8m 13d . . . . (16,324 days)
Edward Reilly Stettinius, Jr. . . . . 44y 1m 9d . . . . (16,110 days)
Edmund Randolph . . . . 40y 4m 23d . . . . (14,753 days)

Secretary of War

Henry Lewis Stimson (2nd term) . . . . 72y 9m 19d . . . . (26,587 days)
Alphonso Taft . . . . 65y 4m 3d . . . . (23,864 days)
Alexander Ramsey . . . . 64y 3m 4d . . . . (23,470 days)
James W. Good . . . . 62y 5m 10d . . . . (22,805 days)
Simon Cameron . . . . 62y 3d . . . . (22,648 days)

Luke E. Wright . . . . 61y 10m 2d . . . . (22,582 days)
Russell A. Alger . . . . 61y 6d . . . . (22,286 days)
John W. Weeks . . . . 60y 10m 22d . . . . (22,237 days)
George H. Dern . . . . 60y 5m 24d . . . . (22,089 days)
William C. Endicott . . . . 58y 3m 15d . . . . (21,289 days)
William Learned Marcy . . . . 58y 2m 24d . . . . (21,268 days)
Jacob M. Dickinson . . . . 58y 1m 4d . . . . (21,218 days)
Joel R. Poinsett . . . . 58y 12d . . . . (21,196 days)
Redfield Proctor . . . . 57y 9m 4d . . . . (20,913 days)
William Eustis . . . . 55y 9m 29d . . . . (20,387 days)
Peter B. Porter . . . . 54y 10m 7d . . . . (20,030 days)
James Monroe (interim) . . . . 54y 8m 4d . . . . (19,967 days)
Robert P. Patterson . . . . 54y 7m 15d . . . . (19,948 days)
Elihu Root . . . . 54y 5m 17d . . . . (19,890 days)
John Armstrong . . . . 54y 2m 11d . . . . (19,794 days)
Joseph Holt (interim) . . . . 54y 12d . . . . (19,735 days)
William Wilkins . . . . 53y 10m 20d . . . . (19,678 days)
John C. Spencer . . . . 53y 9m 4d . . . . (19,632 days)
Kenneth C. Royall . . . . 53y 1d . . . . (19,359 days)
John B. Floyd . . . . 50y 9m 5d . . . . (18,537 days)
Stephen B. Elkins . . . . 50y 2m 28d . . . . (18,350 days)
George W. Crawford . . . . 50y 2m 20d . . . . (18,342 days)
James M. Porter . . . . 50y 2m 2d . . . . (18,324 days)
Henry Dearborn . . . . 50y 10d . . . . (18,272 days)
James Barbour . . . . 49y 8m 25d . . . . (18,162 days)
William T. Sherman . . . . 49y 7m 3d . . . . (18,110 days)
Timothy Pickering . . . . 49y 5m 16d . . . . (18,063 days)
Lewis Cass . . . . 48y 10m . . . . (17,832 days)
Lindley M. Garrison . . . . 48y 3m 5d . . . . (17,627 days)
Edwin McMasters Stanton . . . . 47y 1m 1d . . . . (17,197 days)
Harry H. Woodring . . . . 46y 11m 5d . . . . (17,136 days)
Patrick J. Hurley . . . . 46y 11m 1d . . . . (17,132 days)
William H. Taft . . . . 46y 4m 17d . . . . (16,938 days)
Dwight F. Davis . . . . 46y 3m 9d . . . . (16,900 days)
Charles M. Conrad . . . . 45y 7m 22d . . . . (16,668 days)
Jefferson Davis . . . . 44y 9m 4d . . . . (16,345 days)
Newton D. Baker . . . . 44y 3m 6d . . . . (16,167 days)
John Bell . . . . 44y 18d . . . . (16,089 days)
Henry Lewis Stimson (1st term) . . . . 43y 8m 1d . . . . (15,946 days)
William Harris Crawford . . . . 43y 5m 15d . . . . (15,870 days)
James D. Cameron . . . . 43y 18d . . . . (15,723 days)
James McHenry . . . . 42y 2m 21d . . . . (15,421 days)
Daniel S. Lamont . . . . 42y 25d . . . . (15,365 days)
George W. McCrary . . . . 41y 6m 11d . . . . (15,166 days)
Benjamin Franklin Butler (interim) . . . . 41y 2m 17d . . . . (15,052 days)
William W. Belknap . . . . 40y 1m 9d . . . . (14,649 days)
Henry Knox . . . . 39y 1m 18d . . . . (14,292 days)
Samuel Dexter . . . . 39y 28d . . . . (14,272 days)
John H. Eaton . . . . 38y 8m 19d . . . . (14,138 days)
Robert T. Lincoln . . . . 37y 7m 10d . . . . (13,734 days)
John A. Rawlins . . . . 38y 26d . . . . (13,905 days)

John M. Schofield . . . . 36y 8m 3d . . . . (13,392 days)
John Caldwell Calhoun . . . . 35y 8m 22d . . . . (13,045 days)

Secretary of the Treasury

Hugh McCulloch (2nd term) . . . . 75y 10m 24d. . . . . (27,717 days)
Lloyd Millard Bentsen, Jr. . . . . 71y 11m 9d . . . . (26,271 days)
Franklin MacVeagh . . . . 71y 3m 14d . . . . (26,036 days)
George M. Bibb . . . . 67y 8m 4d . . . . (24,715 days)
Andrew W. Mellon. . . . . 65y 11m 9d . . . . (24,080 days)
Paul Henry O'Neill . . . . 65y 1m 16d . . . . (23,787 days)
William H. Woodin. . . . . 64y 9m 5d . . . . (23,651 days)
Lot M. Morrill . . . . 64y 2m 4d . . . . (23,440 days)
Charles J. Folger. . . . . 63y 6m 29d . . . . (23,219 days)
David M. Kennedy. . . . . 63y 6m 1d . . . . (23,191 days)
John William Snow . . . . 63y 5m 28d . . . . (23,188 days)
Salmon P. Chase. . . . . 63y 1m 22d . . . . (23,062 days)
George M. Humphrey . . . . 62y 10m 13d . . . . (22,958 days)
Charles Foster . . . . 62y 10m 12d . . . . (22,957 days)
John A. Dix . . . . 62y 7m 19d . . . . (22,874 days)
Donald Thomas Regan . . . . 62y 1m 1d . . . . (22,676 days)
William Windom (2nd term) . . . . 61y 9m 25d . . . . (22,575 days)
Carter Glass. . . . . 60y 11m 12d . . . . (22,257 days)
Lyman J. Gage . . . . 60y 8m 5d . . . . (22,160 days)
James Guthrie . . . . 60y 3m 2d . . . . (22,007 days)
Nicholas Frederick Brady . . . . 58y 4m 7d . . . . (21,311 days)
William P. Fessenden. 57y 8m 19d . . . . (21,078 days)
John G. Carlisle . . . . 57y 6m 1d . . . . (21,000 days)
Henry Hamill Fowler. 56y 5m 24d . . . . (20,628 days)
Robert E. Rubin. . . . . 56y 4m 12d . . . . (20,586 days)
Hugh McCulloch (1st term) . . . . 56y 3m 2d . . . . (20,546 days)
Thomas Corwin. . . . . 55y 11m 24d . . . . (20,442 days)
Walter Forward . . . . 55y 7m 21d . . . . (20,319 days)
Frederick M. Vinson . . . . 55y 6m 1d . . . . (20,269 days)
Alexander J. Dallas. . . . . 55y 3m 23d . . . . (20,201 days)
John C. Spencer . . . . 55y 2m . . . . (20,135 days)
James Addison Baker III . . . . 54y 9m 1d . . . . (19,994 days)
George William Miller. . . . . 54y 4m 25d . . . . (19,868 days)
Roger B. Taney. . . . . 54y 4m 3d . . . . (19,846 days)
David F. Houston. . . . . 53y 11m 16d . . . . (19,704 days)
John Bowden Connally, Jr. . . . . 53y 11m 14d . . . . (19,702 days)
John Sherman . . . . 53y 10m . . . . (19,658 days)
William Windom (1st term). . . . . 53y 9m 26d . . . . (19,654 days)
Daniel Manning. . . . . 53y 9m 20d . . . . (19,648 days)
Leslie M. Shaw . . . . 53y 3m . . . . (19,448 days)
William J. Duane . . . . 53y 23d. . . . . (19,381 days)
Walter Q. Gresham . . . . 52y 7m 11d . . . . (19,214 days)
George Pratt Shultz . . . . 51y 6m . . . . (18,807 days)
Clarence Douglas Dillon . . . . 51y 5m . . . . (18,777 days)

William A. Richardson .... 51y 4m 15d .... (18,762 days)
Thomas Ewing.......................... 51y 2m 5d .... (18,692 days)
George S. Boutwell .... 51y 1m 11d .... (18,668 days)
Werner Michael Blumenthal .... 51y 18d................... (18,645 days)
John Wesley Snyder..................... 51y 4d.................... (18,631 days)
Joseph W. Barr......................... 50y 11m 7d .... (18,599 days)
Phillip F. Thomas....................... 50y 3m .... (18,352 days)
William M. Meredith.................... 49y 9m .... (18,167 days)
Samuel D. Ingham .... 49y 5m 18d .... (18,065 days)
William G. McAdoo..................... 49y 4m 3d .... (18,020 days)
Ogden L. Mills........................ 47y 5m 21d.................. (17,337 days)
Robert B. Anderson .... 47y 1m 25d.................. (17,221 days)
William E. Simon....................... 46y 5m 4d .... (16,955 days)
Louis McLane.......................... 45y 2m 11d .... (16,507 days)
George W. Campbell .... 45y 1d.................... (16,437 days)
Richard Rush .... 44y 11m 3d .... (16,404 days)
Charles S. Fairchild .... 44y 11m 2d .... (16,403 days)
George B. Cortelyou .... 44y 7m 5d .... (16,286 days)
Levi Woodbury .... 44y 6m 9d .... (16,260 days)
Lawrence H. Summers................... 44y 6m 2d .... (16,253 days)
Robert J. Walker....................... 43y 7m 17d .... (15,932 days)
William Harris Crawford................. 43y 5m 15d .... (15,870 days)
Henry Morgenthau, Jr. .... 42y 9m 25d .... (15,635 days)
Benjamin H. Bristow.................... 42y 13d.................... (15,353 days)
Howell Cobb .... 41y 5m 27d .... (15,152 days)
Samuel Dexter .... 39y 7m 18d .... (14,472 days)
Albert Gallatin........................ 40y 3m 17d .... (14,717 days)
Oliver Wolcott........................ 35y 22d.................... (12,805 days)
Alexander Hamilton .... 32y 8m .... (11,928 days)

POSTMASTER GENERAL

Horace Maynard .... 65y 11m 26d .... (24,097 days)
Timothy Otis Howe...................... 65y 10m 12d .... (24,053 days)
Harry Stewart New .... 64y 2m 2d .... (23,438 days)
James Albert Gary .... 63y 4m 11d .... (23,141 days)
Jesse Monroe Donaldson .... 62y 3m 29d .... (22,764 days)
Cave Johnson.......................... 62y 1m 23d .... (22,698 days)
Hubert Work .... 61y 8m 1d .... (22,521 days)
Aaron V. Brown .... 61y 6m 19d .... (22,479 days)
Walter Folger Brown .... 59y 9m 3d .... (21,822 days)
Jacob Collamer......................... 58y 2m .... (21,244 days)
Henry C. Payne .... 58y 1m 17d .... (21,231 days)
Charles Emory Smith.................... 56y 2m 3d .... (20,517 days)
Frank Comerford Walker................. 54y 3m 11d .... (19,824 days)
Arthur Ellsworth Summerfield .... 53y 10m 4d .... (19,662 days)
Charles Anderson Wickliffe.............. 53y 4m 5d .... (19,483 days)
David McKendree Key................... 53y 1m 13d .... (19,401 days)
Samuel Dickinson Hubbard .... 53y 1m 4d .... (19,392 days)

Robert John Wynne . . . . 52y 10m 22d . . . . (19,315 days)
John Milton Niles . . . . 52y 8m 29d . . . . (19,262 days)
Joseph Holt . . . . 52y 2m 8d . . . . (19,061 days)
William Lyne Wilson . . . . 51y 11m 1d . . . . (18,958 days)
James William Marshall . . . . 51y 10m 23d . . . . (18,950 days)
Walter Q. Gresham . . . . 51y 25d . . . . (18,652 days)
John Wanamaker . . . . 50y 7m 22d . . . . (18,494 days)
James Noble Tyner . . . . 50y 5m 25d . . . . (18,437 days)
Thomas Lemuel James . . . . 49y 11m 7d . . . . (18,234 days)
Albert Sidney Burleson . . . . 49y 8m 26d . . . . (18,163 days)
Horatio King . . . . 49y 7m 22d . . . . (18,129 days)
Return Jonathan Meigs, Jr. . . . . 49y 4m 26d . . . . (18,043 days)
William Dennison . . . . 48y 10m 8d . . . . (17,840 days)
Marshall Jewell . . . . 48y 10m 4d . . . . (17,836 days)
George von L. Meyer . . . . 48y 8m 8d . . . . (17,780 days)
Lawrence F. O'Brien . . . . 48y 3m 27d . . . . (17,649 days)
Francis Granger . . . . 48y 3m 7d . . . . (17,629 days)
Winton Malcolm Blount . . . . 47y 11m 20d . . . . (17,516 days)
Montgomery Blair . . . . 47y 9m 27d . . . . (17,463 days)
Alexander Williams Randall . . . . 46y 8m 17d . . . . (17,058 days)
James Edward Day . . . . 46y 3m 10d . . . . (16,901 days)
Timothy Pickering . . . . 46y 1m 2d . . . . (16,833 days)
Amos Kendall . . . . 45y 8m 15d . . . . (16,691 days)
Wilson Shannon Bissell . . . . 45y 2m 3d . . . . (16,469 days)
James A. Farley . . . . 44y 9m 2d . . . . (16,343 days)
William F. Vilas . . . . 44y 7m 25d . . . . (16,306 days)
William T. Barry . . . . 44y 2m 1d . . . . (16,132 days)
John Austin Gronouski . . . . 43y 11m 4d . . . . (16,039 days)
William Marvin Watson . . . . 43y 10m 20d . . . . (16,025 days)
Joseph Habersham . . . . 43y 6m 28d . . . . (15,913 days)
Samuel Osgood . . . . 42y 7m 23d . . . . (15,573 days)
George B. Cortelyou . . . . 42y 7m 8d . . . . (15,558 days)
Robert Emmet Hannegan . . . . 42y 1d . . . . (15,341 days)
Donald M. Dickinson . . . . 42y . . . . (15,340 days)
William Harrison Hays . . . . 41y 4m . . . . (15,095 days)
James Campbell . . . . 40y 6m 6d . . . . (14,796 days)
Nathan Kelsey Hall . . . . 40y 3m 25d . . . . (14,725 days)
John A.J. Creswell . . . . 40y 3m 15d . . . . (14,715 days)
Frank Harris Hitchcock . . . . 39y 5m . . . . (14,394 days)
John McLean . . . . 38y 3m 20d . . . . (13,989 days)
Frank Hatton . . . . 36y 10m 26d . . . . (13,475 days)
Gideon Granger . . . . 34y 4m 9d . . . . (12,547 days)

ATTORNEY GENERAL

Edward Bates . . . . 67y 6m 1d . . . . (24,652 days)
Alphonso Taft . . . . 65y 6m 27d . . . . (23,948 days)
Benjamin H. Brewster . . . . 65y 2m 21d . . . . (23,822 days)
Henry Stanbery . . . . 65y 20d . . . . (23,761 days)

John G. Sargent . . . . 64y 5m 5d . . . . (23,531 days)
Edward Hirsh Levi. . . . . 63y 7m 11d . . . . (23,231 days)
Harry M. Daugherty . . . . 63y 7m 7d . . . . (23,227 days)
William French Smith . . . . 63y 4m 28d . . . . (23,158 days)
John J. Crittenden (2nd term). . . . . 62y 11m 4d . . . . (22,979 days)
Homer S. Cummings. 62y 10m 2d . . . . (22,947 days)
Felix Grundy . . . . 60y 11m 21d . . . . (22,266 days)
John Ashcroft. . . . . 58y 8m 23d . . . . (21,447 days)
Griffin Boyette Bell . . . . 58y 2m 26d . . . . (21,270 days)
Edwards Pierrepont. . . . . 58y 2m 11d . . . . (21,255 days)
William B. Saxbe . . . . 57y 8m 8d . . . . (21,067 days)
Richard Olney . . . . 57y 5m 19d . . . . (20,988 days)
Charles Devens . . . . 56y 11m 8d . . . . (20,792 days)
James Patrick McGranery . . . . 56y 10m 19d . . . . (20,773 days)
Richard Thornburgh . . . . 56y 27d. (20,481 days)
Isaac Toucey. . . . . 55y 7m 14d . . . . (20,312 days)
John Newton Mitchell . . . . 55y 4m 7d . . . . (20,215 days)
Francis Biddle . . . . 55y 3m 27d . . . . (20,195 days)
Janet Reno . . . . 54y 7m 19d . . . . (19,952 days)
William D. Mitchell. 54y 5m 25d . . . . (19,898 days)
Roger B. Taney. . . . . 54y 4m 3d . . . . (19,846 days)
Edwin L. Meese III . . . . 54y 2m 23d . . . . (19,806 days)
Charles J. Bonaparte . . . . 54y 22d. (19,745 days)
Joseph McKenna . . . . 53y 6m 25d . . . . (19,563 days)
John J. Crittenden (1st term) . . . . 53y 5m 23d . . . . (19,531 days)
Caleb Cushing . . . . 53y 1m 18d . . . . (19,406 days)
Ebenezer Hoar . . . . 53y 19d. (19,377 days)
Elliot Lee Richardson. . . . . 52y 10m 3d . . . . (19,296 days)
Thomas W. Gregory. 52y 9m 28d . . . . (19,291 days)
Reverdy Johnson . . . . 52y 9m 15d . . . . (19,278 days)
Augustus H. Garland. . . . . 52y 8m 26d . . . . (19,259 days)
James Speed . . . . 52y 8m 24d . . . . (19,257 days)
Levi Lincoln. . . . . 51y 9m 19d . . . . (18,916 days)
George H. Williams. 51y 9m 15d . . . . (18,912 days)
Harlan F. Stone . . . . 51y 5m 29d . . . . (18,806 days)
Judson Harmon . . . . 51y 1m 3d . . . . (18,660 days)
James C. McReynolds . . . . 51y 1m 3d . . . . (18,660 days)
William H. Moody. . . . . 50y 6m 8d . . . . (18,450 days)
George Woodward Wickersham . . . . 50y 5m 14d . . . . (18,427 days)
William M. Evarts . . . . 50y 5m 14d . . . . (18,426 days)
Amos T. Akerman . . . . 49y 4m 15d . . . . (18,032 days)
John Nelson . . . . 49y 1m . . . . (17,927 days)
Herbert Brownell, Jr. 48y 11m 1d. . . . . (17,863 days)
Richard Gordon Kleindienst . . . . 48y 10m 7d. . . . . (17,839 days)
Frank Murphy. . . . . 48y 9m 4d. . . . . (17,806 days)
John W. Griggs. . . . . 48y 6m 22d. . . . . (17,734 days)
William H.H. Miller . . . . 48y 5m 27d. . . . . (17,709 days)
Robert H. Jackson . . . . 47y 11m 5d. . . . . (17,501 days)
Philander Chase Knox. . . . . 47y 11m 3d. . . . . (17,499 days)
Isaac Wayne McVeagh . . . . 47y 10m 16d. . . . . (17,482 days)
William Pinkney . . . . 47y 9m 20d. . . . . (17,456 days)

John M. Berrien . . . . 47y 6m 14d . . . . (17,360 days)
Jeremiah S. Black . . . . 47y 2m 1d . . . . (17,227 days)
Alexander Mitchell Palmer . . . . 46y 10m 1d . . . . (17,102 days)
Edwin McMasters Stanton . . . . 46y 3d . . . . (16,804 days)
John Y. Mason . . . . 45y 10m 21d . . . . (16,757 days)
Thomas C. Clark . . . . 45y 9m 8d . . . . (16,714 days)
J. Howard McGrath . . . . 45y 8m 22d . . . . (16,698 days)
William Wirt . . . . 45y 7d . . . . (16,443 days)
Hugh S. Legare . . . . 44y 8m 18d . . . . (16,329 days)
John Breckenridge . . . . 44y 8m 5d . . . . (16,316 days)
William Pierce Rogers . . . . 44y 7m 4d . . . . (16,285 days)
Benjamin R. Civiletti . . . . 44y 16d . . . . (16,087 days)
Nathan Clifford . . . . 43y 1m 29d . . . . (15,764 days)
Nicholas de Belleville Katzenbach . . . . 43y 27d . . . . (15,732 days)
William P. Barr . . . . 41y 5m 28d . . . . (15,153 days)
William Ramsey Clark . . . . 39y 2m 12d . . . . (14,316 days)
Henry D. Gilpin . . . . 38y 8m 28d . . . . (14,147 days)
William Bradford . . . . 38y 4m 15d . . . . (14,014 days)
Benjamin Franklin Butler . . . . 37y 11m 4d . . . . (13,848 days)
Charles Lee . . . . 36y 11m 9d . . . . (13,488 days)
Edmund Randolph . . . . 36y 5m 23d . . . . (13,322 days)
Robert F. Kennedy . . . . 35y 2m 1d . . . . (12,844 days)
Caesar Augustus Rodney . . . . 35y 16d . . . . (12,799 days)
Richard Rush . . . . 33y 5m 13d . . . . (12,216 days)

SECRETARY OF THE NAVY

Claude A. Swanson . . . . 70y 11m 1d . . . . (25,898 days)
Isaac Toucey . . . . 68y 3m 17d . . . . (24,944 days)
Smith Thompson . . . . 67y 9m 3d . . . . (24,744 days)
Richard W. Thompson . . . . 67y 9m 3d . . . . (24,744 days)
William Franklin Knox . . . . 66y 6m 9d . . . . (24,295 days)
Mahlon Dickerson . . . . 64y 2m 13d . . . . (23,449 days)
Charles Francis Adams . . . . 62y 7m 3d . . . . (22,858 days)
James K. Paulding . . . . 59y 10m 9d . . . . (21,858 days)
Adolph E. Borie . . . . 59y 3m 12d . . . . (21,651 days)
Hilary A. Herbert . . . . 58y 11m 22d . . . . (21,536 days)
Benjamin F. Tracy . . . . 58y 10m 7d . . . . (21,491 days)
Gideon Welles . . . . 58y 8m 6d . . . . (21,430 days)
John D. Long . . . . 58y 4m 6d . . . . (21,310 days)
William H. Hunt . . . . 57y 8m 23d . . . . (21,082 days)
John P. Kennedy . . . . 57y 4m 9d . . . . (20,948 days)
Curtis D. Wilbur . . . . 56y 10m 8d . . . . (20,762 days)
Charles J. Bonaparte . . . . 54y 22d . . . . (19,745 days)
Victor H. Metcalf . . . . 53y 2m 7d . . . . (19,425 days)
David Henshaw . . . . 52y 3m 22d . . . . (19,105 days)
James V. Forrestal . . . . 52y 3m 3d . . . . (19,086 days)
William Jones . . . . 52y 19d . . . . (19,012 days)
Edwin Denby . . . . 51y 15d . . . . (18,642 days)

Josephus Daniels . . . . 50y 9m 15d . . . . (18,547 days)
George von L. Meyer . . . . 50y 8m 9d . . . . (18,511 days)
Abel P. Upshur . . . . 50y 3m 24d . . . . (18,376 days)
Charles Edison . . . . 49y 5m 8d . . . . (18,055 days)
William H. Moody . . . . 48y 4m 8d . . . . (17,660 days)
Paul Morton . . . . 47y 1m 9d . . . . (17,205 days)
Paul Hamilton . . . . 46y 6m 29d . . . . (17,010 days)
Benjamin Stoddert . . . . 46y 6m 13d . . . . (16,994 days)
John Branch . . . . 46y 4m 5d . . . . (16,926 days)
William E. Chandler . . . . 46y 3m 20d . . . . (16,911 days)
William A. Graham . . . . 45y 10m 28d . . . . (16,764 days)
John Young Mason (2nd term) . . . . 45y 10m 23d . . . . (16,759 days)
George E. Badger . . . . 45y 10m 16d . . . . (16,752 days)
John Young Mason (1st term) . . . . 44y 11m 8d . . . . (16,409 days)
George Bancroft . . . . 44y 5m 7d . . . . (16,228 days)
Truman H. Newberry . . . . 44y 26d . . . . (16,097 days)
Robert Smith . . . . 43y 8m 24d . . . . (15,969 days)
William C. Whitney . . . . 43y 8m 1d . . . . (15,946 days)
William B. Preston . . . . 43y 3m 7d . . . . (15,802 days)
Benjamin W. Crowninshield . . . . 42y 20d . . . . (15,360 days)
Thomas W. Gilmer . . . . 41y 10m 13d . . . . (15,288 days)
Levi Woodbury . . . . 41y 5m 1d . . . . (15,126 days)
George M. Robeson . . . . 40y 3m 9d . . . . (14,709 days)
James C. Dobbin . . . . 39y 1m 18d . . . . (14,292 days)
Nathan Goff, Jr. . . . . 37y 10m 28d . . . . (13,842 days)
Samuel L. Southard . . . . 36y 3m 7d . . . . (13,246 days)

SECRETARY OF THE INTERIOR

Samuel J. Kirkwood . . . . 67y 2m 16d . . . . (24,547 days)
John B. Payne . . . . 65y 1m 15d . . . . (23,786 days)
Cornelius N. Bliss . . . . 64y 1m 7d . . . . (23,413 days)
Ethan A. Hitchcock . . . . 63y 5m 1d . . . . (23,161 days)
Hubert Work . . . . 62y 8m 2d . . . . (22,887 days)
Columbus O. Delano . . . . 61y 4m 27d . . . . (22,427 days)
Manuel Lujan . . . . 60y 8m 22d . . . . (22,177 days)
Orville H. Browning . . . . 60y 6m 22d . . . . (22,117 days)
Roy Owen West . . . . 60y 2m 25d . . . . (22,000 days)
Douglas McKay . . . . 59y 6m 28d . . . . (21,757 days)
Lucius Q.C. Lamar . . . . 59y 5m 17d . . . . (21,716 days)
Albert B. Fall . . . . 59y 3m 7d . . . . (21,646 days)
Thomas Ewing . . . . 59y 2m 8d . . . . (21,617 days)
Harold L. Ickes . . . . 58y 11m 17d . . . . (21,531 days)
John W. Noble . . . . 57y 4m 9d . . . . (20,948 days)
Thomas M.T. McKennan . . . . 56y 4m 15d . . . . (20,589 days)
Rogers C.B. Morton . . . . 56y 4m 10d . . . . (20,584 days)
Thomas Savig Kleppe . . . . 56y 3m 9d . . . . (20,553 days)
Bruce Babbitt . . . . 54y 6m 24d . . . . (19,927 days)
Ray Lyman Wilbur . . . . 53y 10m 20d . . . . (19,678 days)

Oscar L. Chapman . . . . 53y 1m 9d . . . . (19,397 days)
Caleb B. Smith . . . . 52y 10m 7d . . . . (19,300 days)
William Patrick Clark . . . . 52y 29d. . . . . (19,022 days)
Henry M. Teller . . . . 51y 10m 25d . . . . (18,952 days)
Stanley Knapp Hathaway . . . . 50y 10m 24d . . . . (18,586 days)
Richard A. Ballinger. . . . . 50y 7m 24d . . . . (18,496 days)
Walter Joseph Hickel . . . . 49y 5m 6d . . . . (18,053 days)
Walter L. Fisher . . . . 48y 8m 3d. . . . . (17,775 days)
Franklin K. Lane . . . . 48y 7m 18d. . . . . (17,760 days)
Carl Schurz . . . . 48y 10d. . . . . (17,542 days)
Donald P. Hodel. . . . . 47y 6m 15d. . . . . (17,361 days)
John P. Usher . . . . 47y . . . . (17,166 days)
Gale Ann Norton . . . . 46y 10m 19d. . . . . (17,120 days)
Jacob Thompson . . . . 46y 9m 23d. . . . . (17,094 days)
Fred A. Seaton . . . . 46y 5m 28d . . . . (16,979 days)
Zachariah Chandler . . . . 46y 3m 20d . . . . (16,911 days)
David R. Francis . . . . 45y 11m 3d . . . . (16,769 days)
Robert McClelland. 45y 7m 6d . . . . (16,652 days)
Cecil D. Andrus. . . . . 45y 4m 27d . . . . (16,583 days)
James Harlan . . . . 44y 8m 29d . . . . (16,340 days)
William F. Vilas . . . . 44y 7m 25d . . . . (16,306 days)
Alex H.H. Stuart . . . . 43y 5m 14d . . . . (15,869 days)
James Gaius Watt. . . . . 42y 11m 21d . . . . (15,691 days)
James R. Garfield. . . . . 41y 4m 15d . . . . (15,110 days)
Stewart Lee Udall. . . . . 40y 11m 22d . . . . (14,962 days)
Jacob D. Cox . . . . 40y 7m 18d . . . . (14,838 days)
Julius A. Krug . . . . 38y 3m 23d . . . . (13,992 days)
Hoke Smith . . . . 37y 6m 4d . . . . (13,698 days)

Secretary of Agriculture

Richard Edmund Lyng. . . . . 67y 8m 6d . . . . (24,717 days)
Earl Laver Butz . . . . 62y 4m 29d . . . . (22,794 days)
Norman J. Colman. 61y 8m 28d . . . . (22,548 days)
J. Sterling Morton . . . . 60y 10m 12d . . . . (22,227 days)
James Wilson . . . . 60y 6m 17d . . . . (22,112 days)
Jeremiah M. Rusk . . . . 58y 8m 18d . . . . (21,442 days)
Clayton Keith Yeutter . . . . 58d 1m 29d . . . . (21,243 days)
Edward Madigan . . . . 55y 1m 22d . . . . (20,140 days)
Henry Cantwell Wallace . . . . 54y 9m 22d . . . . (20,015 days)
Ezra Taft Benson . . . . 53y 10m 17d . . . . (19,675 days)
Clifford Hardin . . . . 53y 3m 13d . . . . (19,461 days)
Arthur M. Hyde. . . . . 51y 7m 22d . . . . (18,859 days)
Ann Margaret Veneman . . . . 51y 6m 22d . . . . (18,829 days)
Daniel Robert Glickman . . . . 50y 4m 7d . . . . (18,269 days)
Clinton P. Anderson. . . . . 49y 8m 7d . . . . (18,144 days)
Robert S. (Bob) Berglund. . . . . 48y 6m . . . . (17,712 days)
Claude R. Wickard . . . . 47y 6m 8d . . . . (17,354 days)
David F. Houston. . . . . 47y 17d. . . . . (17,183 days)

William M. Jardine .... 46y 2m .... (16,861 days)
John Rusling Block III .... 45y 11m 5d .... (16,771 days)
Charles Franklin Brannan .... 44y 9m 10d .... (16,351 days)
Henry A. Wallace .... 44y 4m 25d .... (16,216 days)
Edwin T. Meredith .... 43y 1m 10d .... (15,745 days)
Orville Lothrop Freeman .... 42y 8m 13d .... (15,593 days)
John A. Knebel .... 40y 1d .... (14,611 days)
Mike Espy .... 39y 1m 22d .... (14,296 days)
Howard M. Gore .... 37y 1m 10d .... (13,554 days)

SECRETARY OF COMMERCE AND LABOR

Charles Nagel .... 59y 6m 24d .... (21,753 days)
Oscar S. Straus .... 55y 11m 24d .... (20,442 days)
Victor H. Metcalf .... 50y 8m 21d .... (18,523 days)
George B. Cortelyou .... 40y 6m 21d .... (14,811 days)

SECRETARY OF COMMERCE

Philip M. Klutznik .... 72y 5m 12d .... (26,460 days)
Calvin William Verity, Jr. .... 70y 8m 23d .... (25,830 days)
Norman Yoshio Mineta .... 68y 8m 8d .... (25,085 days)
Cyrus R. Smith .... 68y 5m 21d .... (25,008 days)
Joshua W. Alexander .... 67y 10m 24d .... (24,795 days)
Jesse Jones .... 66y 5m 14d .... (24,270 days)
Daniel C. Roper .... 65y 11m 3d .... (24,074 days)
Frederick H. Mueller .... 65y 8m 19d .... (24,000 days)
William F. Whiting .... 64y 4m 21d .... (23,517 days)
Lewis L. Strauss .... 62y 9m 12d .... (22,927 days)
Luther H. Hodges .... 62y 1m 16d .... (22,691 days)
Robert Adam Mosbacher .... 61y 10m 21d .... (22,601 days)
Robert P. Lamont .... 61y 3m 4d .... (22,374 days)
Charles Sawyer .... 61y 2m 26d .... (22,366 days)
Maurice Hubert Stans .... 60y 8m 20d .... (22,175 days)
Rogers C.B. Morton .... 60y 7m 7d .... (22,132 days)
Sinclair Weeks .... 59y 7m 6d .... (21,765 days)
Howard Malcolm Baldridge .... 58y 3m 18d .... (21,292 days)
Michael (Mickey) Kantor .... 56y 8m 5d .... (20,699 days)
Henry A. Wallace .... 56y 4m 23d .... (20,597 days)
Juanita M. Kreps .... 56y 10d .... (20,464 days)
Elliot Lee Richardson .... 55y 4m 21d .... (20,229 days)
William Averell Harriman .... 55y 2m 13d .... (20,161 days)
William C. Redfield .... 54y 8m 15d .... (19,978 days)
Donald Louis Evans .... 54y 5m 24d .... (19,897 days)
Roy D. Chapin .... 52y 9m 21d .... (19,284 days)
Barbara Hackman Franklin .... 51y 11m 8d .... (18,965 days)
Ronald Harmon Brown .... 51y 5m 20d .... (18,797 days)

Frederick Bailey Dent . . . . 50y 5m 16d . . . . (18,428 days)
John T. Connor . . . . 50y 2m 15d . . . . (18,337 days)
William M. Daley . . . . 48y 5m 21d. . . . . (17,703 days)
Harry L. Hopkins . . . . 48y 5m 6d. . . . . (17,688 days)
Herbert C. Hoover. . . . . 46y 6m 23d. . . . . (17,004 days)
Peter George Peterson . . . . 45y 4m 11d . . . . (16,567 days)
Alex Buel Trowbridge, Jr. . . . . 37y 5m 28d . . . . (13,692 days)

SECRETARY OF LABOR

John Thomas Dunlop . . . . 60y 8m 13d . . . . (22,168 days)
Martin P. Durkin . . . . 58y 10m 3d . . . . (21,487 days)
James Day Hodgson. . . . . 56y 6m 29d . . . . (20,663 days)
Peter J. Brennan. . . . . 54y 8m 7d . . . . (19,970 days)
William Emerson (Bill) Brock III. . . . . 54y 5m 6d . . . . (19,879 days)
James P. Mitchell . . . . 52y 10m 27d . . . . (19,320 days)
Frances Perkins . . . . 52y 10m 22d . . . . (19,315 days)
Elizabeth Hanford Dole. . . . . 52y 5m 27d . . . . (19,170 days)
Arthur Joseph Goldberg . . . . 52y 5m 13d . . . . (19,156 days)
William Julian (Willie) Usery, Jr.. . . . . 52y 1m 15d . . . . (19,038 days)
Lynn Martin. . . . . 51y 1m 12d . . . . (18,669 days)
William B. Wilson . . . . 50y 11m 3d . . . . (18,595 days)
Lewis B. Schwellenbach. . . . . 50y 9m 11d . . . . (18,543 days)
W. Willard Wirtz . . . . 50y 6m 11d . . . . (18,453 days)
Raymond James Donovan . . . . 50y 5m 3d . . . . (18,415 days)
Alexis M. Herman . . . . 49y 9m 23d . . . . (18,190 days)
Freddie Ray Marshall. 48y 5m 5d. . . . . (17,687 days)
George Pratt Shultz . . . . 48y 1m 9d. . . . . (17,571 days)
William N. Doak . . . . 47y 11m 27d . . . . (17,523 days)
Elaine Lan Chao. . . . . 47y 10m 3d. . . . . (17,469 days)
James J. Davis Davis . . . . 47y 4m 6d. . . . . (17,292 days)
Maurice J. Tobin . . . . 47y 2m 22d. . . . . (17,248 days)
Ann Dore McLaughlin. . . . . 46y 1m 1d . . . . (16,832 days)
Robert B. Reich . . . . 46y 6m 28d. . . . . (17,009 days)

SECRETARY OF DEFENSE

George C. Marshall, Jr. . . . . 69y 8m 21d . . . . (25,463 days)
Donald H. Rumsfeld (2nd term) . . . . 68y 6m 11d . . . . (25,028 days)
William James Perry . . . . 66y 3m 23d . . . . (24,219 days)
Caspar Willard Weinberger. . . . . 63y 5m 3d . . . . (23,163 days)
Charles E. Wilson . . . . 62y 6m 10d . . . . (22,835 days)
Clark McAdams Clifford . . . . 61y 2m 4d . . . . (22,344 days)
Richard B. (Dick) Cheney . . . . 58y 10m 13d . . . . (21,497 days)
Louis A. Johnson . . . . 58y 2m 18d . . . . (21,262 days)
Frank Charles Carlucci III. . . . . 57y 1m 3d . . . . (20,852 days)
William Sebastian Cohen . . . . 56y 4m 27d . . . . (20,600 days)

Robert Abercrombie Lovett . . . . 56y 3d. . . . . (20,457 days)
James V. Forrestal. . . . . 55y 7m 2d . . . . (20,300 days)
Leslie Aspin, Jr. . . . . 54y 6m 1d . . . . (19,904 days)
Thomas Sovereign Gates, Jr. . . . . 53y 7m 22d . . . . (19,590 days)
Neil H. McElroy. . . . . 52y 11m 9d . . . . (19,332 days)
Elliot Lee Richardson. 52y 6m 9d . . . . (19,182 days)
Harold Brown . . . . 49y 4m 2d . . . . (18,019 days)
Melvin B. Laird . . . . 46y 4m 21d . . . . (16,942 days)
Robert Strange McNamara . . . . 44y 5m 12d . . . . (16,233 days)
James Rodney Schlesinger . . . . 44y 4m 14d . . . . (16,205 days)
Donald H. Rumsfeld (1st term) . . . . 43y 4m 11d . . . . (15,836 days)

Secretary of Health, Education & Welfare

Marion B. Folsom . . . . 61y 8m 9d . . . . (22,529 days)
Caspar Willard Weinberger. . . . . 56y 11m 22d . . . . (20,806 days)
Wilbur Joseph Cohen . . . . 55y 7m 10d . . . . (20,308 days)
Patricia Roberts Harris . . . . 55y 2m 4d . . . . (20,152 days)
Arthur Sherwood Flemming. . . . . 53y 10m 11d . . . . (19,669 days)
John W. Gardner . . . . 52y 10m 10d . . . . (19,303 days)
Anthony J. Celebrezze . . . . 51y 1m 4d . . . . (18,661 days)
Abraham Alexander Ribicoff. . . . . 50y 9m 12d . . . . (18,544 days)
Elliot Lee Richardson. 49y 10m 26d . . . . (18,223 days)
Oveta Culp Hobby. . . . . 48y 2m 23d. . . . . (17,615 days)
Joseph A. Califano, Jr. 45y 8m 10d . . . . (16,686 days)
Robert Hutchinson Finch . . . . 43y 3m 20d . . . . (15,815 days)
Forrest D. Mathews . . . . 39y 7m 17d . . . . (14,471 days)

Secretary of Housing & Urban Development

Robert Clifton Weaver. . . . . 58y 20d. (21,204 days)
Robert C. Wood. . . . . 45y 3m 22d . . . . (16,548 days)
George Wilcken Romney. . . . . 61y 6m 13d . . . . (22,473 days)
James Thomas Lynn. . . . . 45y 11m 4d . . . . (16,770 days)
Carla Anderson Hills . . . . 41y 2m 3d . . . . (15,038 days)
Patricia Roberts Harris . . . . 52y 7m 21d . . . . (19,224 days)
Maurice Edwin (Moon) Landrieu . . . . 49y 2m 2d. . . . . (17,959 days)
Samuel Riley Pierce, Jr. . . . . 58y 4m 14d . . . . (21,318 days)
Jack F. Kemp . . . . 53y 6m 24d . . . . (19,562 days)
Henry Gabriel Cisneros. . . . . 45y 7m 10d . . . . (16,656 days)
Andrew M. Cuomo . . . . 39y 1m 23d . . . . (14,297 days)
Melquiades Rafael Martinez . . . . 54y 3m . . . . (19,813 days)

Secretary of Transportation

Norman Yoshio Mineta . . . . 69y 2m 12d . . . . (25,274 days)
John Anthony Volpe . . . . 60y 1m 13d . . . . (21,958 days)

William Thaddeus Coleman, Jr. . . . . 54y 8m . . . . (19,963 days)
Samuel Knox Skinner . . . . 53y 7m 12d . . . . (19,580 days)
Brockman Adams . . . . 50y 8d. . . . . (18,270 days)
Andrew Lindsay Lewis, Jr. . . . . 49y 9m 10d . . . . (18,177 days)
Elizabeth Hanford Dole . . . . 46y 6m 9d . . . . (16,990 days)
Alan S. Boyd. . . . . 46y 5m 27d . . . . (16,978 days)
Claude Stout Brinegar . . . . 46y 1m 3d . . . . (16,834 days)
Frederico F. Pena . . . . 45y 10m 6d . . . . (16,742 days)
Andrew H. Card, Jr. . . . . 44y 8m 12d . . . . (16,323 days)
James Horace Burnley IV. . . . . 39y 4m 3d . . . . (14,367 days)
Neil E. Goldschmidt . . . . 39y 3m 6d . . . . (14,340 days)
Rodney E. Slater. . . . . 41y 11m 22d . . . . (15,327 days)

SECRETARY OF ENERGY

James David Watkins. 61y 11m 22d . . . . (22,632 days)
Hazel Rollins O'Leary . . . . 55y 8m 4d . . . . (20,332 days)
James Burrows Edwards . . . . 53y 6m 28d . . . . (19,566 days)
Charles William Duncan, Jr. . . . . 52y 10m 23d . . . . (19,316 days)
William Blaine (Bill) Richardson . . . . 50y 9m 3d . . . . (18,535 days)
Frederico F. Pena . . . . 49y 11m 28d . . . . (18,255 days)
Spencer Abraham. . . . . 48y 7m 8d. . . . . (17,750 days)
James Rodney Schlesinger . . . . 48y 5m 21d. . . . . (17,703 days)
Donald Paul Hodel. . . . . 47y 6m 15d. . . . . (17,361 days)
John Stewart Herrington . . . . 45y 8m 7d . . . . (16,683 days)

SECRETARY OF HEALTH & HUMAN SERVICES

Otis Ray Bowen . . . . 67y 9m 16d . . . . (24,757 days)
Tommy G. Thompson. . . . . 59y 2m 4d . . . . (21,613 days)
Patricia Roberts Harris . . . . 55y 4m 17d . . . . (20,225 days)
Louis Wade Sullivan. . . . . 55y 3m 26d . . . . (20,204 days)
Richard Schultz Schweiker . . . . 54y 7m 21d . . . . (19,994 days)
Donna Edna Shalala. . . . . 51y 11m 8d . . . . (18,965 days)
Margaret Mary Heckler. . . . . 51y 8m 11d . . . . (18,878 days)

SECRETARY OF EDUCATION

Roderick R. Paige. . . . . 67y 6m 12d . . . . (24,663 days)
Cavazos, Lauro Fred Cavazos, Jr. . . . . 61y 8m 16d . . . . (22,536 days)
Richard Wilson Riley. 60y 19d. . . . . (21,934 days)
Terrel Howard Bell . . . . 59y 2m 12d . . . . (21,621 days)
Shirley Mount Hufstedler . . . . 54y 3m 7d . . . . (19,820 days)
Lamar Alexander . . . . 50y 8m 11d . . . . (18,513 days)
William John Bennett . . . . 41y 7m 7d . . . . (15,192 days)

SECRETARY OF VETERANS AFFAIRS

Hershel W. Gober* . . . . 63y 7m 4d . . . . (23,224 days)
Edward J. Derwinski . . . . 62y 6m . . . . (22,825 days)
Anthony Joseph Principi . . . . 56y 9m 7d . . . . (20,731 days)
Togo D. West, Jr. . . . . 55y 6m 12d . . . . (20,280 days)
Jesse Brown . . . . 48y 9m 25d . . . . (17,827 days)

Nominated and was acting Secretary of Veterans Affairs but not confirmed by the Senate. The date used is that of his nomination.

SECRETARY OF HOMELAND SECURITY

Thomas Ridge . . . . 57y 4m 27d . . . . (20,966 days)

SUPREME COURT—CHIEF JUSTICES

Harlan F. Stone . . . . 68y 8m 16d . . . . (25,093 days)
Charles E. Hughes . . . . 67y 10m 2d . . . . (24,772 days)
Edward D. White . . . . 65y 1m 9d . . . . (23,780 days)
William H. Taft . . . . 63y 9m 15d . . . . (23,295 days
Earl Warren . . . . 62y 11m 10d . . . . (22,985 days)
William H. Rehnquist . . . . 61y 11m 16d . . . . (22,626 days)
Warren E. Burger . . . . 61y 8m 22d . . . . (22,542 days)
Roger B. Taney . . . . 58y 11m 27d . . . . (21,541 days)
Morrison R. Waite . . . . 57y 1m 23d . . . . (20,872 days)
Salmon P. Chase . . . . 56y 10m 19d . . . . (20,773 days)
Fred M. Vinson . . . . 56y 4m 28d . . . . (20,602 days)
John Rutledge* . . . . 56y 2m 15d . . . . (20,529 days)
Melville W. Fuller . . . . 55y 5m 9d . . . . (20,247 days)
Oliver Ellsworth . . . . 50y 10m 3d . . . . (18,565 days)
John Marshall . . . . 45y 4m 3d . . . . (16,559 days)
John Jay . . . . 43y 9m 14d . . . . (15,989 days)

Nominated and was acting Chief Justice but not confirmed by the Senate. The date used is that of his nomination.

SUPREME COURT—ASSOCIATE JUSTICES

Horace H. Lurton . . . . 65y 9m 24d . . . . (24,035 days)
Lewis F. Powell, Jr. . . . . 64y 2m 17d . . . . (23,453 days)
William Strong . . . . 63y 11m 12d . . . . (23,352 days)
Ward Hunt . . . . 62y 5m 27d . . . . (22,822 days)
Lucius Q.C. Lamar . . . . 62y 4m . . . . (22,765 days)
James F. Byrnes . . . . 62y 1m 10d . . . . (22,685 days)
Samuel Blatchford . . . . 62y 18d . . . . (22,663 days)

Benjamin Nathan Cardozo . . . . 61y 9m . . . . (22,550 days)
Oliver W. Holmes, Jr. 61y 8m 26d . . . . (22,546 days)
Harry A. Blackmun . . . . 61y 6m . . . . (22,460 days)
Howell E. Jackson . . . . 60y 10m 10d . . . . (22,225 days)
George Shiras, Jr. . . . . 60y 6m . . . . (22,095 days)
George Sutherland . . . . 60y 5m 11d . . . . (22,076 days)
Ruth Bader Ginsburg . . . . 60y 4m 19d . . . . (22,054 days)
Louis D. Brandeis . . . . 59y 6m 19d . . . . (21,748 days)
Thurgood Marshall . . . . 59y 1m 28d . . . . (21,607 days)
Thomas Johnson . . . . 59y 3d . . . . (21,552 days)
Sherman Minton . . . . 58y 11m 14d . . . . (21,528 days)
Gabriel Duvall . . . . 58y 11m 12d . . . . (21,526 days)
John H. Clarke . . . . 58y 10m 6d . . . . (21,490 days)
William Cushing . . . . 57y 6m 25d . . . . (21,024 days)
Edward T. Sanford . . . . 57y 5m 24d . . . . (20,993 days)
John McKinley . . . . 57y 4m 24d . . . . (20,963 days)
Noah H. Swayne . . . . 57y 1m 17d . . . . (20,866 days)
Rufus W. Peckham . . . . 57y 1m 1d . . . . (20,850 days)
Harold H. Burton . . . . 57y 27d . . . . (20,846 days)
Joseph P. Bradley . . . . 57y 7d . . . . (20,826 days)
Peter V. Daniel . . . . 56y 10m 6d . . . . (20,760 days)
Stanley Matthews . . . . 56y 10m . . . . (20,754 days)
Pierce Butler . . . . 56y 9m 4d . . . . (20,728 days)
John Blair . . . . 56y 8m 26d . . . . (20,720 days)
William B. Woods . . . . 56y 4m 18d . . . . (20,592 days)
Felix Frankfurter . . . . 56y 2m 2d . . . . (20,516 days)
Charles E. Whittaker . . . . 56y 27d . . . . (20,481 days)
Levi Woodbury . . . . 56y 12d . . . . (20,466 days)
Steven Breyer . . . . 55y 11m 14d . . . . (20,432 days)
Smith Thompson . . . . 55y 10m 22d . . . . (20,410 days)
John Marshall Harlan II. . . . . 55y 9m 24d . . . . (20,382 days)
John Paul Stevens . . . . 55y 7m 27d . . . . (20,325 days)
Abe Fortas . . . . 55y 1m 23d . . . . (20,141 days)
Owen J. Roberts . . . . 55y 18d . . . . (20,106 days)
Edwin M. Stanton . . . . 55y 1d . . . . (20,089 days)
Samuel Chase . . . . 54y 9m 10d . . . . (20,003 days)
Henry B. Brown . . . . 54y 9m 8d . . . . (20,001 days)
Joseph McKenna . . . . 54y 5m 11d . . . . (19,884 days)
Nathan Clifford . . . . 54y 4m 25d . . . . (19,855 days)
Arthur J. Goldberg . . . . 54y 1m 17d . . . . (19,770 days)
Mahlon Pitney . . . . 54y 22d . . . . (19,745 days)
William R. Day . . . . 53y 10m 6d . . . . (19,664 days)
Horace Gray . . . . 53y 8m 26d . . . . (19,624 days)
Joseph Rucker Lamar . . . . 53y 2m 1d . . . . (19,419 days)
Stanley F. Reed . . . . 53y 25d . . . . (19,383 days)
William H. Moody . . . . 52y 11m 10d . . . . (19,333 days)
David J. Brewer . . . . 52y 10m 14d . . . . (19,307 days)
Samuel Nelson . . . . 52y 3m 4d . . . . (19,297 days)
Philip P. Barbour . . . . 52y 9m 18d . . . . (19,281 days)
James C. McReynolds . . . . 52y 6m 26d . . . . (19,199 days)
Anthony M. Kennedy . . . . 52y 6m 10d . . . . (19,183 days)

Robert C. Grier .... 52y 5m .... (19,143 days)
Harlan Fiske Stone........................ 52y 3m 25d .... (19,108 days)
Willis Van Devanter....................... 51y 7m 28d .... (18,865 days)
Sandra Day O'Connor..................... 51y 5m 26d .... (18,803 days)
Hugo L. Black .... 51y 5m 21d .... (18,798 days)
John Catron.............................. 51y 2m 8d .... (18,695 days)
David H. Souter........................... 51y 15d..................... (18,642 days)
Antonin Scalia .... 50y 6m 6d .... (18,448 days)
William J. Brennan, Jr. .... 50y 5m 21d .... (18,433 days)
John Rutledge .... 49y 11m 25d .... (18,252 days)
Henry Baldwin............................ 49y 11m 23d .... (18,250 days)
Tom C. Clark............................. 49y 10m 27d .... (18,224 days)
Frank Murphy .... 49y 9m 2d .... (18,169 days)
Robert Trimble .... 49y 5m 22d .... (18,069 days)
Robert H. Jackson .... 49y 4m 24d .... (18,041 days)
Henry Brockholst Livingston .... 49y 21d..................... (17,918 days)
Wiley B. Rutledge .... 48y 5m 2d................... (17,684 days)
Edward D. White.......................... 48y 3m 16d................. (17,638 days)
Charles E. Hughes .... 48y 21d..................... (17,553 days)
David Davis............................... 47y 8m 29d................. (17,435 days)
William H. Rehnquist .... 47y 2m 9d.................. (17,235 days)
William Paterson.......................... 47y 2m 8d.................. (17,234 days)
James Wilson............................. 47y 12d..................... (17,178 days)
Stephen J. Field .... 46y 4m 6d .... (16,927 days)
Samuel F. Miller.......................... 46y 3m 11d .... (16,902 days)
Byron R. White .... 44y 10m 3d .... (16,374 days)
Alfred Moore............................. 44y 6m 19d .... (16,270 days)
John Marshall Harlan .... 44y 5m 28d .... (16,249 days)
Potter Stewart .... 44y 3m 12d .... (16,173 days)
James M. Wayne .... 44y 9d..................... (16,080 days)
John McLean .... 43y 11m 24d .... (16,059 days)
Clarence Thomas.......................... 43y 3m 22d .... (15,807 days)
Benjamin R. Curtis .... 42y 1m 25d .... (15,395 days)
Thomas Todd............................. 42y 1m 8d .... (15,378 days)
John A. Campbell.......................... 41y 9m 1d .... (15,246 days)
William O. Douglas........................ 40y 5m 4d .... (14,764 days)
James Iredell............................. 38y 4m 5d .... (14,004 days)
Bushrod Washington...................... 36y 6m 15d .... (13,344 days)
William Johnson .... 32y 2m 25d .... (11,773 days)
Joseph Story.............................. 32y 1m .... (11,718 days)

Appendix F:
Women in the Cabinet

The presidential Cabinet was staffed entirely by men for its first 144 years. Franklin D. Roosevelt was the first U.S. president to challenge the unspoken and unwritten rule against appointing women to Cabinet posts. Frances Perkins was the first woman appointed to the Cabinet. Named to the office of Secretary of Labor, she served in that post for over 12 years.

It would be just over 20 years— eight days over —from Perkins' appointment until a president would appoint the second female Cabinet member. In 1953, President Dwight D. Eisenhower appointed Oveta Culp Hobby to the secretaryship of the Department of Health, Education and Welfare. She served for just over two years, and from the date of her confirmation to the confirmation of a third woman to a Cabinet post was another 22 years. But after President Gerald Ford appointed Carla Anderson Hills to the office of Secretary of Housing and Urban Development, the time between the appointment of female Cabinet members would decrease rapidly.

There are 19 women who have been appointed to Cabinet positions, although that number represents only 3.5 percent of all those who have served in the Cabinet. The greatest number of female appointments to Cabinet positions by one president occurred in the Bill Clinton administration. President Clinton appointed five women to Cabinet positions. Women served in five different Cabinet positions in the Jimmy Carter administration, although one woman served in three different Cabinet posts during the period of time when the new Health and Human Services office was being created. President Ronald Reagan appointed three women; President George Herbert Bush appointed three; President George Walker now has three women in his Cabinet; and presidents Ford, Eisenhower and Roosevelt each appointed one woman to a Cabinet post.

Three women have served as the first Cabinet secretary for newly-created departments: Oveta Culp Hobby, Secretary of Health, Education and Welfare; Patricia Roberts Harris, Secretary of Health and Human Services; and Shirley Hufstedler, Secretary of Education.

LISTING BY DATE OF CONFIRMATION

Frances Perkins (LB-4) .... Mar 4, 1933
Oveta Culp Hobby (HW-1) .... Apr 11, 1953
Carla Anderson Hills (HD-5) .... Mar 6, 1975
Patricia Roberts Harris (HD-6) .... Jan 21, 1977
Juanita M. Kreps (CM-25) .... Jan 21, 1977
Patricia Roberts Harris (HW-13) .... Aug 4, 1979

Patricia Roberts Harris (HH-1) .... Oct 18, 1979
Shirley Mount Hufstedler (ED-1) .... Dec 1, 1979
Elizabeth Hanford Dole (TR-8) .... Feb 7, 1983
Margaret Mary Heckler (HH-3) .... Mar 4, 1983
Ann Dore McLaughlin (LB-19) .... Dec 17, 1987
Elizabeth Hanford Dole (LB-20) .... Jan 25, 1989
Lynn M. Martin (LB-21) .... Feb 7, 1991
Barbara Hackman Franklin (CM-30) .... Feb 27, 1992
Hazel Rollins O'Leary (EN-7) .... Jan 21, 1993
Donna Edna Shalala (HH-6) .... Jan 21, 1993
Janet Reno (AT-78) .... Mar 11, 1993
Madeleine K. Albright (ST-64) .... Jan 23, 1997
Alexis M. Herman (LB-23) .... May 9, 1997
Ann Margaret Veneman (AG-27) .... Jan 20, 2001
Elaine Lan Chao (LB-24) .... Jan 29, 2001
Gale Ann Norton (IN-38) .... Jan 30, 2001

LISTING BY TOTAL TIME SERVED IN CABINET

Frances Perkins .... 12y 3m 26d .... (4,499 days)
Donna Edna Shalala...................... 8y .... (2,922 days)
Janet Reno .... 7y 10m 9d .... (2,865 days)
Elizabeth Hanford Dole.................. 6y 7m 24d .... (2,425 days)
Hazel Rollins O'Leary .... 4y 1m 18d .... (1,509 days)
Patricia Roberts Harris .... 4y .... (1,461 days)
Madeleine K. Albright.................... 3y 11m 27d .... (1,452 days)
Juanita M. Kreps .... 2y 9m 10d .... (1,010 days)
Margaret Mary Heckler................... 2y 9m 8d .... (1,008 days)
Alexis M. Herman .... 2y 8m 11d .... (981 days)
Oveta Culp Hobby....................... 2y 3m 20d .... (840 days)
Lynn M. Martin......................... 1y 10m 29d .... (708 days)
Carla Anderson Hills.................... 1y 10m 14d .... (679 days)
Shirley Mount Hufstedler .... 1y 1m 19d .... (414 days)
Ann Dore McLaughlin.................... 1y 1m 3d .... (398 days)
Ann Margaret Veneman .... ———
Elaine Lan Chao........................ ———
Gale Ann Norton....................... ———

LISTING BY AGE AT CONFIRMATION

Madeleine K. Albright.................... 59y 8m 8d .... (21,797 days)
Juanita M. Kreps .... 56y 10d..................... (20,464 days)
Hazel Rollins O'Leary .... 55y 8m 4d .... (20,332 days)
Patricia Roberts Harris .... 55y 4m 17d .... (20,225 days)
Patricia Roberts Harris .... 55y 2m 4d .... (20,152 days)
Janet Reno .... 54y 6m 18d .... (19,921 days)
Shirley Mount Hufstedler .... 54y 3m 7d .... (19,820 days)

Frances Perkins . . . . 52y 10m 22d . . . . (19,315 days)
Patricia Roberts Harris . . . . 52y 7m 21d . . . . (19,224 days)
Elizabeth Hanford Dole . . . . 52y 5m 27d . . . . (19,170 days)
Barbara Hackman Franklin . . . . 51y 11m 8d . . . . (18,965 days)
Donna Edna Shalala . . . . 51y 11m 7d . . . . (18,964 days)
Lynn M. Martin . . . . 51y 1m 12d . . . . (18,669 days)
Margaret Mary Heckler . . . . 51y 8m 11d . . . . (18,878 days)
Ann Margaret Veneman . . . . 51y 6m 22d . . . . (18,829 days)
Alexis M. Herman . . . . 49y 9m 23d . . . . (18,190 days)
Oveta Culp Hobby . . . . 48y 2m 23d . . . . (17,615 days)
Elaine Lan Chao . . . . 47y 10m 3d . . . . (17,469 days)
Gale Ann Norton . . . . 46y 10m 19d . . . . (17,120 days)
Elizabeth Hanford Dole . . . . 46y 6m 9d . . . . (16,990 days)
Ann Dore McLaughlin . . . . 46y 1m 1d . . . . (16,832 days)
Carla Anderson Hills . . . . 41y 2m 3d . . . . (15,038 days)

RECORDS & AVERAGES

Youngest at confirmation . . . . Carla Anderson Hills 41y 2m 3d (15,038 days)
Oldest at confirmation . . . . Madeleine K. Albright 59y 8m 8d (21,797 days)
Avg. age at confirmation . . . . 51y 6m 10d (18,817 days)
Longest term of service . . . . Frances Perkins 12y 3m 26d (4,499 days)
Shortest term of service . . . . Barbara Hackman Franklin 10m 24d (324 days)
Average term of service . . . . 4y 7d (1,468 days)

Index